A PURE SOLAR WORLD

Discovering
AMERICA

Mark Crispin Miller, Series Editor

This series begins with a startling premise—that even now, more than two hundred years since its founding, America remains a largely undiscovered country with much of its amazing story yet to be told. In these books, some of America's foremost historians and cultural critics bring to light episodes in our nation's history that have never been explored. They offer fresh takes on events and people we thought we knew well and draw unexpected connections that deepen our understanding of our national character.

A PURE SOLAR WORLD

SUN RA

— AND THE BIRTH OF —

AFROFUTURISM

—

PAUL YOUNGQUIST

UNIVERSITY OF TEXAS PRESS

AUSTIN

Requests for permission to reproduce material
from this work should be sent to:
Permissions
University of Texas Press
P.O. Box 7819
Austin, TX 78713-7819
http://utpress.utexas.edu/index.php/rp-form

The paper used in this book meets the minimum requirements
of ANSI/NISO Z39.48-1992 (R1997) (Permanence of Paper).

Library of Congress Cataloging-in-Publication Data

Names: Youngquist, Paul, author.
Title: A pure solar world : Sun Ra and the birth of Afrofuturism / Paul Youngquist.
Other titles: Discovering America series.
Description: Austin : University of Texas Press, 2016. Series:
Discovering America | Includes bibliographical references and index.
Identifiers: LCCN 2016005943
ISBN 978-0-292-72636-9 (cloth : alk. paper)
ISBN 978-1-4773-1117-2 (library e-book)
ISBN 978-1-4773-1118-9 (non-library e-book)
Subjects: LCSH: Sun Ra. | Jazz musicians—Biography. |
Jazz—History and criticism.
Classification: LCC ML410.S978 Y68 2016 | DDC 781.65092—dc23
LC record available at http://lccn.loc.gov/2016005943

doi:10.7560/726369

For Joanne, my mother,
and
Thelma, my other mother

The impossible is the watchword of the greater space age. The space age cannot be avoided and the space music is the key to understanding the meaning of the impossible and every other enigma.

SUN RA

———

The Weirdness, Outness, Way Outness, Otherness was immediate. Some space metaphysical philosophical surrealistic bop funk. Some blue pyramid home nigger southern different color meaning hip shit. Ra. Sun Ra.

AMIRI BARAKA

———

CONTENTS

CONTENTS

A PURE SOLAR WORLD

PRELUDE TO INFINITY

A book on Sun Ra should begin in cacophony. That's how he opened many, many shows: with a chaos of sounds that cleared the air for the music to come. Horns squeal, drums thump, the bass growls, and the piano piles chord on chord; a space opens for exploration, and music becomes a means of traveling to other worlds. Most Sun Ra fans come to love him and his formidable ensembles through the audacity of his music. It exhilarates, shocks, and complicates, making life feel better than it was before. Music, apparently, can change the world. This inscrutable possibility provided the driving force behind Sun Ra's creativity. It's the premise of this book, too. What makes Sun Ra important as a composer and an artist is his unwavering belief that music can take its players and listeners to better worlds—better, at least, by the measure of joyous sounds.

Music isn't just music. It's also a social event in a couple of senses. Music occurs as entertainment (a night out, a special occasion) but also as politics (a demonstration, an insurgence). This book approaches

Sun Ra's music as a social event in the latter sense. For all its pursuit of better worlds, his art arose in response to this one, in particular, the brutally segregated world of mid-twentieth-century America. Like most of his black contemporaries, Sun Ra experienced the brutalities of segregation, but his response to injustice was unusual—and unusually inspiring. Instead of pursuing a solution through traditional political means, he turned to culture—music and related forms of expression—to imagine and advance an alternative to an oppressive reality. He practiced a cultural politics of sound and, with the support of a loyal cadre of friends, used every available means of musical production and distribution to promote his message of a better life for black Americans and anyone else who had ears to hear.

This book's emphasis falls, then, as much on the social conditions that inspired Sun Ra's music as on the music itself. While the best possible result of reading these pages would be voraciously listening to the vast array of his available recordings, they sound better—more purposeful and canny—to ears tuned to social frequencies. Two such frequencies in particular throw Sun Ra's music into bold political relief: the segregation of metropolitan Chicago and the popular culture of the Space Age. Brilliantly and with abandon, Sun Ra crossed the inner city with outer space to create music as progressive socially as it was aesthetically. As a response to a world preoccupied with the space race and oblivious to racial injustice, Sun Ra's music announces not merely a demand for a better world but a program for building one. That's what its cacophony is all about.

The chapters that follow examine influences often missing from assessments of Sun Ra's music: occult wisdom, business strategy, the space race, Chicago's black metropolis, and the popular culture of the Space Age. Sun Ra himself occasionally drifts pretty far back in the mix—a situation necessary to give the political dimension of his work a full hearing. His significant—and overlooked—achievement as a poet receives special attention. Sun Ra viewed his poems (he wrote many over the course of a long career) as a verbal equivalent to his music. Read in that light, they become a kind of user's guide to infinity, offering instructions about listening to music meant to change the world. The poems may resemble little else in contemporary literature, but that's what makes them original, important, and even beautiful. Sun Ra believed that beauty is necessary for survival and that creating and communicating it makes life better. However strange, his remarkable poetry contributes to that aim, enhancing the beauty of his music by translating its aspirations into words.

One measure of Sun Ra's success in envisioning a better, more beautiful tomorrow lies in the number and talent of the musicians his work continues to inspire, a rich variety of creative heirs. Their kaleidoscopic musical adventures keep Sun Ra's visionary purpose alive. His standing as the great forefather of Afrofuturism, a movement devoted to imagining new black futures, guarantees the longevity of his renown. Sun Ra took it upon himself and his music not to demand freedom and equality in this world but to create even greater possibilities, even better worlds to come. His fellow Afrofuturists adapt his example to new opportunities and terrains. They and the many other artists and activists he inspires embrace culture rather than the ballot or the church as the most effective means of improving the world. Together they travel the spaceways, from planet to imagined planet.

Readers interested in accompanying him should have some sense of what lies ahead. This book does not provide a full introduction to Sun Ra's life. John Szwed's biography, *Space Is the Place: The Lives and Times of Sun Ra*, fulfills that task magisterially. It's an indispensable guide to an incomparable life. Although biography provides a loose narrative arc to the chapters that follow, they are thematically focused and can productively be read in any order or disorder. A book on Sun Ra and his explosive music should eschew too tidy a linearity. This one shares with most others, even Szwed's, a preoccupation with Sun Ra's formative years in Chicago. Work needs to be done on the later years in Philadelphia, but that will have to wait for future hands—let's hope not for long. Perhaps it's clear that love and admiration for Sun Ra's joyous music inform everything that follows. The greatest compliment we can pay that art is simply to listen and live with happiness.

WONDER INN

"Play it. Play it, Sun Ra!"

1960. The Arkestra is gigging at the Wonder Inn, swinging hard on one of Sun Ra's compositions, "Space Aura," sixteen hammering bars of harmonized saxophone jabs punctuated by a slithering trumpet reveille.[1] John Gilmore then takes off on tenor for two tone-pounding choruses, attacking notes from below, garroting them from behind, making them wail. George Hudson follows on trumpet, quavering and snarling over those harmonies until the head returns and the Arkestra churns to a cacophonous finish, resolving on a darkly beautiful chord, Gilmore's tenor two octaves below Hudson's trumpet—but a quarter tone above the pitch.

Play it, Sun Ra!

The Wonder Inn. Say it fast and it's "wonderin'," a place of possibility and speculation: the Arkestra's steady gig for more than a year, sometimes seven nights a week (after six hours of rehearsal). Just south of Seventy-Fifth at Cottage Grove, the Wonder Inn occupied a red brick building, with frosted glass blocks in front flanked by two doors and capped with a crenellated parapet. The door on the left opened directly into the club, a single long room with a bar along one wall and tables along the other. At the far end, a small stage stood under a gazebo-like dome decorated with an ivy motif hung from the ceiling.

The space barely contained the Arkestra. Crammed behind Sun Ra's piano, the band played intrepid sets that could last for hours, making the room reverberate with expansive, often experimental sounds. As patrons drank and hustled and talked, occasionally urging the music on, the Arkestra played with audacity and imagination, one of the best working bands in Chicago—or anywhere else. Its members took their music seriously but made it entertaining, too, eschewing the austerities of the beboppers, with their aloof virtuosity and windowpane shades. Their attire was sharp but relaxed, even playful; they sported bow ties and jackets with skinny lapels, their heads topped sometimes with a fez and sometimes with a space hat blinking red and green in the smoky light.

They followed Sun Ra's music down pathways to unknown worlds. They were space explorers, six to ten players in close solar orbit. They pursued musical perihelion, aspiring beyond worldly music to skirt the sun—often as the tape rolled, as it did on that night in 1960 at the Wonder Inn. Released as *Music from Tomorrow's World* in 2002, long after the passing of both club and composer, the recording provides a high-altitude transmission from the Arkestra in flight. Joy echoes in the air. The crowd comes alive with booze and chatter. The spacious set list includes standards, show tunes, originals, and a hip instance of exotica.

The Arkestra could play anything—and on this recording it does so with discipline, energy, and wit. By turns tender and raucous, the music soars and swings sideways. Something funny begins to happen. There is a joker in the pack of charts. Sun Ra calls "It Ain't Necessarily So," the old Gershwin number, and the Arkestra serves up a staid cover as straight as anything Fletch ever played, until it breaks into song with a wink and a nudge: "The stories you're liable / To read in the Bible / They ain't necessarily so!"[2] Really? They ain't? A soft voice follows whisper-lisping something barely audible over the Inn's din, something a bit weird and a little lyrical. A poem maybe?

Imagination is a magic carpet
Upon which we may soar
To distant lands and climes
And even go beyond the moon to any planet in the sky.

It's Sun Ra's voice, in recitation mode. A wry preacher, he calls a question that ends in a shout: "If we are here / *Why can't we be there?*" The Arkestra laughs, sputters, and launches full throttle into "How High the Moon," the standard beloved of the bebop set now turned propulsion device for space travel to another world. And why not?

Why can't we be *there*?

1

ALIEN

He came from Saturn. Arrival date: May 22, 1914. Place: the Magic City, Birmingham, Alabama. Terrestrial identity: Herman Poole Blount, the apparent son of Cary and Ida, who had moved to Birmingham from Demopolis, a one-time French utopian community.[1] They started a family, adding a girl and two boys to Cary's son from an earlier marriage, but their hopes for happiness together flagged, and before long, Cary and Ida separated. Ida and the children moved in with her mother and an aunt. Their house was spacious and only a block from Birmingham's Terminal Station, the biggest depot in the South, where Ida and her aunt both worked in the adjacent restaurant. With the two of them gone much of the time, the day-to-day task of raising Herman fell to Ida's mother. He grew up with mothers all around him, or so the women thought. But the boy felt otherwise. "I never called anybody 'mother,'" he once confessed. "The woman who's supposed to be my mother I call 'other momma.' I never call anybody 'mother.' I never called anybody 'father.' I never felt that way."[2]

The musician and poet who dubbed himself Sun Ra likewise never called planet Earth his home. "I'm not human," he said. "I've never been part of the planet. I've been isolated from a child away from it."[3] In the world but not of it: Sonny Blount (as he was known in his early years) lived at a distance from others and the common concerns that ruled their lives—getting and spending, winning and losing, courting and marrying, even living and dying. He would reject his family. He would leave Birmingham. He felt he was not human. He liked to say he belonged to another race altogether, the angel race, which graced him with an awareness of worlds far superior to planet Earth. "It was as if I was somewhere else that imprinted this purity on my mind, another kind of world. That is my music playing the kind of world I know about. It's like someone else from another planet trying to find out what to do [. . .] a pure solar world."[4]

Have you ever felt like an alien? Homeless in a deep cosmic sense? How would you live on a strange planet? The answer for Sonny Blount was his music. The words he uses to describe it sound strange, however: "my music playing the kind of world I know about." His music plays a world, a "pure solar world." A world beyond this one, better than this one. This book listens to Sonny's music as it plays that solar world in all its extraterrestrial strangeness, space music that nevertheless arose in response to life on planet Earth in a country called America and a city called Chicago. However alien Sonny may have felt, he composed music peculiarly suited to the hopes and needs of living people, black city people inhabiting an inhospitable white world. He was the original brother from another planet, dedicated to inventing a future for fellow aliens consigned to dark streets and dead-end dreams.[5]

An astonishing body of work testifies to the vitality of his vision and ranks Sonny Blount among the planet's most important artists: over two hundred recordings, myriad poems, and countless performances, interviews, videos, and visual images.[6] But he was equally important as a social activist, using his art to awaken a world on the brink of upheaval. His creative development coincided with the restless decades of the fifties and sixties. As the movement for civil rights gave way to black power, as passive resistance crackled into open defiance, Sonny envisioned another way to change society. "Politics, religion, philosophy have all been tried," he said, "but music has not been given a chance."[7] His activism drew its inspiration not from a moral or political imperative but, more simply and beautifully, from sound: music to change the planet, space music heralding other, happier worlds. Making it became the purpose of his sojourn on planet Earth: "I would hate to pass through a planet," he said, "and not leave it a better place."[8] Through numerous compositions and recordings, he labored tirelessly to improve life on planet Earth, challenging listeners everywhere to heed a simple call to joy. He became the prophet of a better tomorrow, and music was his message.

Sonny was fond of telling a story that explains how he acquired this vocation. "These space men contacted me. They wanted me to go to outer space with them. They were looking for somebody who had that type of mind."[9] Through a process of "transmolecularization," he lost his human form and found himself transported to the planet Saturn, where the spacemen, little antennas over each ear, taught him "things" that would save planet Earth: "When it looked like the world was going into complete chaos, when there was no hope for nothing, then I could speak, but not until then. I would speak, and the world would listen."[10] In this narrative, spacemen abduct Sonny and prepare him to communicate a message of salvation to a doomed planet.

In a curious way, this story retells the whole harrowing history of African slavery. Africans were abductees, after all, and the slave ships of the Middle Passage were the first alien motherships. This account of alien abduction assimilates a three-hundred-year history of subjugation to futuristic images of flying saucers and spacemen. It looks backward and forward. It retrofits a history of terror to the Space Age, transforming both to make the world a better place. Sonny Blount was a brilliant and innovative musician. But he was more than that; he was also a poet, a mythmaker, an activist, and a movie star. In everything he did, he worked to beat chains and manacles into dreams, turn history into myth, and transform cries of terror into sounds of joy. "The outer space beings are my brothers," he said. "They *sent* me here. They *already* know my music."[11] Sonny's music reaches other worlds. Maybe it takes an alien to change planet Earth.

2

MARIENVILLE

Before migrating to Chicago in his early thirties, Sonny had an experience, among his most formative, that prepared him for life in that segregated city even more completely than growing up in Birmingham had done. By 1941 the United States government was seeking able-bodied men for the war effort, harvesting them like summer wheat. Sonny would not be the only African American musician to fall afoul of the draft (others who did included Charlie Parker, Charles Mingus, and, most notoriously, Lester Young), but the pale touch of the Selective Service System would leave an indelible mark on his life and music.

Work in Birmingham was steady for a musician of Sonny's caliber. Sonny led his own highly acclaimed band, the Sonny Blount Orchestra, playing throughout Alabama and the neighboring territory. As war drained away his most experienced players, he turned to high-school students for replacements, often training them himself. Then his own induction notices came in the mail, first one and then another, addressed to "Herman P. Blount (colored)."[1] He ignored the letters. What use had he for this white man's war? Clearly it had a use for him: catching bullets or shrapnel on some desolate battlefield. He didn't have time for mortality. He lacked interest in death and the portentous words like "heroism" and "honor" that made it appealing to so many young men. His life was music.

He had recently happened upon another word—one full of whispers—that promised happier prospects: "pacifism." Perhaps he was a pacifist. He wanted to find out, and so he attended a meeting of the Fellowship of Reconciliation, an organization committed to peace, justice, and nonviolence that had been founded by an English Quaker and a German Lutheran just after the start of World War I. Some years later, it would sponsor the first Freedom Ride across the southern United States. Now it offered support and assistance to men who, as Herman Poole Blount did, found the project of killing other men intolerable.[2] The people in attendance welcomed him warmly. They understood the prompting of his heart. Address the draft board directly, they said. Take your case downtown in person. Become a conscientious objector.

Sonny arranged an appointment with the draft board. On October 10, 1941, wearing the dark suit he reserved for society bookings, he walked purposefully toward the Brown-Marx Building at First Avenue North and Twentieth Street, with sixteen stories once the tallest building in Birmingham but now just another high-rise. "The heaviest corner on Earth"—that's what they used to call First and Twentieth. Four skyscrapers in the Chicago style buttressed the sun, their glass-eyed façades crowning steel pylons sunk deep. Looking up from the corner, he felt small, creeped out by all those staring windows. He pushed through the brass-trimmed door and entered a mausoleum-like lobby, all marble, hush, and echo. His shoes double-slapped the shiny floor with every step. A woman stood in a pool of light, her face shrouded by a veil. When he reached the elevator, Sonny touched the "up" button and waited. He felt a low rumble in his gut as the car descended and heard a faint keening four octaves higher. Comforting somehow, the sound of machinery in motion.

The draft board—three white men in dark suits—awaited his arrival in a small room on the fourth floor. Sonny entered, introduced himself, and took a seat at the polished oak table. They asked if he had received his induction papers. He admitted he had. They asked why he had not responded. He said he could not believe the papers could possibly refer to him. And why not? Because he was twenty-eight and the papers listed him as twenty-five. One member of the board noted that they did not grant exceptions to military service for clerical errors. Sonny informed them that he was the main source of income and support for his seventy-five-year-old great-aunt. Another member remarked that many men with responsibilities had left home and family to fight Nazi Germany. Sonny replied with a list of personal qualities that, to his mind, rendered him ineligible for military service. He was not like other men. He suffered a debilitating physical complaint (a congenital hernia resulting from a maldeveloped testicle). He opposed violence, especially killing, and while not a member of any particular congregation, he was enough of a Christian to know that murder is a spiritual crime. The draft board said they had no further questions and thanked him for his testimony.

To Sonny's surprise and momentary relief, he was later informed that the board had granted him a 4-E classification as a conscientious objector opposed to military service of all kinds, on or off the battlefield.[3] But Selective Service Regulations section 652.11 required a person so designated to be issued an Order to Report for Work: "It shall be his duty to comply therewith, to report to the camp at the time and place designated therein, and thereafter to perform work of national importance under civilian direction for the period, at the place, and in the manner provided by law."[4] Sonny's readiness to comply appears clearly on the questionnaire he completed for the National Service Board for Religious Objectors (NSBRO), where he listed his skills as writing poetry, playing piano, and composing music.[5] The only options available to conscientious objectors with a 4-E classification, however, were prison or a more benign confinement at the inmate's expense in one of the Civilian Public Service camps, which were run by a consortium of pacifist churches. That both were anathema to Sonny Blount appears clearly on the questionnaire:

Music to me is the only worthwhile thing in the world, and [. . .] I am sure no one could begrudge me this one happiness. [. . .] To separate me from music would be more cruel than standing me by a wall and shooting me. I think I would prefer the latter. I hope you can understand why I am so staunchly against being in any kind of camp where one must live according to certain rules and regulations and requirements.[6]

For Sonny, life was not possible without music. Confinement would mean spiritual death.

The NSBRO remanded Sonny to Civilian Public Service Camp 48, in Marienville, Pennsylvania, ordering him to appear there on December 8. He didn't. Technically in contempt of Selective Service regulations, Sonny went about his daily business, playing his piano and rehearsing his band. Authorities apprehended him at home, took him into custody, and confined him to a space in an old post office reserved, in John Szwed's words, "for malingerers and subversives."[7] A formal hearing of his case could not be scheduled until after Christmas.

When Sonny appeared before the judge, he brought his Bible, prepared to counter legal precept with a higher authority.[8]

"This is a court of law, son, not a Sunday School. Your Bible doesn't get the last word here. You may be a conscientious objector, but you broke the law when you didn't report for national service."

"The first thing that happens when a man is brought before a court of law, your Honor, is he swears on the Bible to tell the whole truth."

"That may indeed be so. And I expect you to tell the truth. Here you will abide by the rule of law."

"'He who loves his neighbor has fulfilled the law,' your Honor. That's Romans 13. I'm a pacifist. I love my neighbor. How can I do that and kill him at the same time? Fighting in this war would make me a criminal. By the law of Jesus Christ."

"I know my Bible too, boy. Here's your loving Jesus: 'Do not think that I have come to bring peace on earth; I have not come to bring peace, but a sword.' Matthew 10:34. And do you know why? Because men are evil and bloody minded. Isaiah 26:21, 'For behold, the Lord is coming forth out of his place to punish the inhabitants of the earth

for their iniquity, and the earth will disclose the blood shed upon her.'
Do you not believe these Nazis are men of iniquity?"

"It is not for me to judge human beings, your Honor. Vengeance
is not my business or any man's. It belongs to the Lord, you see. Isaiah also says that the Lord shall judge between nations, that 'nation
shall not lift sword against nation, neither shall they learn war any
more.' Why does the United States lift its sword against Germany and
Japan?"

"I'll tell you why. Because of what Exodus 21:33 says, is why: 'If any
harm follows, then you shall give life for life, tooth for tooth, hand
for hand, foot for foot, burn for burn, wound for wound, stripe for
stripe.'"

The judge leaned forward in his chair, the collar of his black robe
cinching the skin around his bull neck. He lowered his voice to a low
hiss: "I'd say a little harm followed the Japanese visit to Pearl Harbor.
And what about those bombers over London? I sense a little harm
there too."

"Ain't no concern of mine, your Honor. Once you start killing, killing never ends. This war will cover the planet with corpses. You worship a god of death, you see. But it's not too late to change. 'Put your
sword back into its place; for all who take the sword will perish by the
sword.' That's Matthew. So is this: 'Love your enemies and pray for
those who persecute you.' I will pray for you, your Honor."

"I don't need your prayers, Mr. Blount. I need your service to this
country, if not with a rifle in your hands then in a camp where you and
your high and mighty notions can do the war effort no harm."

"You put a rifle in my hands, your Honor, and you teach me how to
shoot it, force me to shoot it, I swear on this Bible I'll shoot my commanding officers. I think they already dead."

"Your so-called 'pacifism' is beginning to worry me, boy. Aren't you
grateful for your freedom? You have some strange notions. I've never
seen a nigger like you before."

"And you never will again."

The judge ordered that Sonny be confined to the Walker County
Jail in Jasper, Alabama, while his case was investigated further.[9] For
thirty-nine days he inhabited a crowded cell with no clear sense of

what awaited him. He appealed to the warden, the FBI, and even a US marshal for help in securing his release to camp 48, a fate now preferable to imprisonment. The language of his pleas is heart wrenching: "I am so unhappy and bewildered that I am almost crazed. [. . .] This morning I took a razor and started to slash my wrists or mutilate the one testicle I have, but I thought of the wrong of murder in any form. [. . .] It would probably be more merciful to be killed than to be as I am."[10] Thirty-nine days of confinement. No playing, no composing, no music. It was a kind of death in life. Then, on February 6 (whether a grand jury ever convened to hear his case remains unclear), Sonny was freed from prison and placed directly on a train, first to Washington, DC, and then to Kane, Pennsylvania, where he got off and waited for the truck that would take him to Marienville and camp 48.

It looked as if this southern, city-born musician would sit out the war under gun-barrel skies in rural Pennsylvania. He trimmed scrub and raked underbrush in the forest during the day, discussing spiritual matters with fellow inmates and reading what books he could find in the evening. He was ill-suited to labor and confinement, as a growing file of his correspondence with various officials would attest, letters that described his physical symptoms and mental distress in painful detail. When the file found its way to camp 48's administration, the director recommended a full medical and psychiatric exam. The results were exculpatory, if not flattering. The psychiatric evaluation concluded that Sonny was "a well-educated colored intellectual" who possessed "a psychopathic personality" that tended, in Szwed's words, toward "neurotic depression and sexual perversion."[11] The psychiatrist concurred, however, with the examining physician that confinement in a Civilian Public Service camp would produce no benefit to either Sonny or the war effort. Both recommended discharge on the grounds of physical disability. In the meantime, Sonny would be allowed to practice piano by day and play for his fellow inmates after dinner. On March 22 he was released from camp 48 and driven back to the train station in Kane. After nearly six weeks of incarceration in the name of national service as a conscientious objector, Sonny was free to return home to Birmingham and resume his life of playing and composing music.

Free. Free from what? A social reality consumed by death and eager to tag a black pacifist with the stigma of psychosis? Hardly. His experience as a conscientious objector—his confinement, distress, and humiliation—would stay with Sonny the rest of his life and permanently mark his music. It inspired him to approach music as a means of social as much as artistic expression. It brought a political edge to his composition and performance, an activist agenda that aimed at transforming the world, using sound as an agent of change. When Herman Poole Blount left Marienville, he nursed a fierce indignation toward a society devoted to war and the incarceration of its most creative members. But he cherished a vision, too. He would pursue a higher calling. He would promote a better world. He would produce a happier future through music, celebrating, in his words, "a universal existence . . . common to all the living."[12] He would leave Birmingham and, with many southern blacks seeking greater opportunity after the war, board a northbound train to Chicago, where he might discover circumstances equal to his dreams.

3

BRONZEVILLE

Sonny landed in a city alive with possibility. Workers who had come to Chicago to drive wartime production stayed there. More joined them, pursuing dreams of postwar prosperity. The majority of those new workers were black. While Chicago's white population remained fairly steady during the forties and fifties, its black population burgeoned, rising from 8.2 percent of the total in 1940 to 22.9 percent by 1960.[1] All that growth produced opportunities in every sector of black life, including entertainment and the arts. For Sonny, it meant the prospect of steady work in the company of top musicians who might share his interest in large ensembles at a time when smaller combos—thanks to first bebop and then rock and roll—were becoming the preferred format. The city seemed hungry for new sounds. Sonny could create them. So he found a small apartment in the heart of the Black Belt on Chicago's South Side, where, as an African American, he was all but sentenced to live.

Blacks didn't call this part of the city the Black Belt. Those were white words, used to mark a difference also deemed a deficiency. Blacks called it Bronzeville and had done so since 1934, when James J. Gentry, a writer for the *Chicago Defender*, inaugurated with the newspaper's blessing an annual "Mayor of Bronzeville" election.[2] Bronzeville became a place where African Americans could feel a lift, find some pride. However segregated the area was, it developed into an extraordinarily vibrant community, driven by powerful hopes and schemes of its own. To the west lived working-class whites, guarding their ethnic purity, and to the east resided affluent WASPs and Jews, protecting their lakefront property values. Room for black expansion lay in areas whites would abandon for the allure of suburbia.

Within this confined but expanding space, Chicago's blacks created a world as rich and complex as the one that segregated them. Rural migrants moved in, amusing seasoned city dwellers with their country ways. People with a little money moved up, leaving mean streets and old tenements to the poor. Bronzeville had social distinctions and political intrigues of its own to complicate those imposed by the surrounding white city. Segregation had its uses, understood well by black political bosses such as William Dawson, who was elected to the US House of Representatives in 1942. He knew the power of "policy"—a word used to describe the gambling racket.[3] Dawson opposed all efforts to shut it down, believing that money earned in Bronzeville, in however dubious a manner, should stay there. Gaming garnered millions for its sponsors, and to those who played the numbers, it offered some excitement and even hope. Dawson's twenty-seven years as a congressman attest to his deep regard for Bronzeville's way of life and the respect his legislative patronage won from his constituents.

"Segregated as it was," writes Thomas Dyja, "Bronzeville shared White Chicago's gargantuan energy for making money, and had used its segregation to consolidate capital and power."[4] Black Chicago created black institutions to sustain its thriving life apart. The black real estate magnate Jesse Binga founded the Binga State Bank and built a nearby row of shops that he called the Binga Arcade.[5] The *Chicago Defender* had been appearing weekly since 1905, but new media outlets suddenly multiplied: the *Associated Negro Press*, *Negro Digest*, and, to even greater renown, *Ebony* and *Jet*. *Ebony* cannily represented the social aspirations of mainstream Bronzeville in its glossy spreads of fashionably attired women and its smiling endorsements of consumer culture. John H. Johnson, one of its founding editors, put its mission memorably: "In a world that said Blacks could do a few things, we wanted to say they could do everything."[6]

Across a broad range of activities, from playing the policy wheel to purchasing the latest appliance, that spirit of possibility suffused everyday life and sustained hopes for a better future, doing so nowhere more powerfully than in the wildly profitable insurance industry. Headquartered in black Chicago, Supreme Liberty Life was the world's largest black-owned insurance company, accruing 18 million dollars in assets by the 1950s.[7] Insurance in Bronzeville was a medium for dreams, a symbolic investment transforming hard times in the present into future rewards. It secularized old-time salvation and made life after death imaginable in material terms. The fiscal gift of such a future gave social aspiration weight and heft. The right insurance policy could help build a better world for coming generations—at a tidy profit to the underwriter. Such prospects encouraged an entrepreneurial spirit in postwar Bronzeville. As Dempsey Travis put it, "Business was the pillar of optimism," especially for blacks with middle-class aspirations.[8]

This sense of material possibility was more than matched by cultural achievements of black artists in Bronzeville. The thirties and early forties witnessed a magnificent flowering of artistic energies, a second renaissance of black culture in America (the first had occurred in Harlem during the twenties).[9] A list of the era's black artists puts Chicago—but more particularly Bronzeville—on any map of American cultural achievement. Richard Wright began his career there, publishing his disturbing novel *Native Son* (1940) to great acclaim and the promise of lasting literary achievement.[10] Gwendolyn Brooks rose from the South Side's squalid streets to become one of America's most heralded African American poets. Katherine Dunham, who founded the first black ballet company—the Ballet Nègre—received a degree in anthropology from the University of Chicago and proceeded to reinvent modern choreography. Gordon Parks came to Chicago in 1940 and used his photography to chronicle life among poor blacks in Bronzeville. Then there were the musicians: Thomas A. Dorsey, "the father of gospel music," who took the blues to church; his spiritual daughter, Mahalia Jackson, whose harrowing, sweet voice proved how close hell stands to heaven; the bluesman Muddy Waters, up from the Delta, playing a guitar so raw it conjured up a whole new kind of blues, the Chicago blues; and Muddy Waters's cronies, too, including Jimmy Rogers, Little Walter, and Willie Dixon. Bronzevillle channeled the urban spirit of American black vernacular art.

As for jazz, Chicago was without peer. "By the end of the 1940s," says Szwed, "Chicago was possibly the best city in America for jazz musicians."[11] Like industry and commerce, music was thriving. A player with decent chops and a union card could make a living. An abundance of clubs opened doors nightly to crowds eager for diversion—as many as seventy-five clubs in Bronzeville alone. They came in all sizes and catered to all tastes: Roberts Show Lounge (later called Roberts Show Club), a dance hall with a thousand seats; the Savoy Ballroom, capacity six thousand dancers; the Pershing Hotel, with its famous ballroom upstairs and the lounge called Birdland (later Budland) in the basement; the Grand Terrace; Casino Moderne; and many smaller venues, such as Duke Slater's Vincennes Lounge, 5th Jack Show Lounge, Queen's Mansion, Flame Lounge, and the Wonder Inn.[12] In the coming years, these and many other spots made Chicago an inevitable stop for gigging musicians in either big bands hawking fare to suit the fading taste for swing or small units pitching bebop, hard bop, and even avant-garde. Everybody passed through: Duke Ellington, Count Basie, Jimmie Lunceford, and Benny Goodman; Coleman Hawkins, Miles Davis, John Coltrane, Sonny Stitt, and Charles Mingus; and a host of other musicians, some well known, some less so. Chicago raised its own talent too—Gene Ammons, Johnny Griffin, and Von Freeman, all great tenor saxophonists, among others.[13] It was a mecca of improvised music, an urban space peculiarly conducive to the sly alchemy of tradition and innovation, sustained by an avid audience of dancers, drinkers, hipsters, and hangers-on.

Racial uplift took a downturn, however, just as Sonny reached Chicago, particularly among creative and working-class blacks. Some of the artists associated with the Black Chicago Renaissance, weary of the city's overt racism, departed for more hospitable climes: Wright, for New York; Parks, for Washington, DC; Dunham, for a career that would take her around the world. McCarthyism dampened the enthusiasm of those who remained, and not merely because of alleged connections with the Communist Party or the WPA. Civil rights organizations, the NAACP most prominent among them, openly endorsed Cold War policies limiting civil liberties.[14] Between the aspirations of the black bourgeoisie and a general politics of conformity, Bronzeville politicians seemed more interested in tailoring democracy to the marketplace than in transforming a segregated society.

For poor blacks, that meant almost complete disfranchisement from the American dream and confinement to Bronzeville's hardest neighborhoods. These were the people Gwendolyn Brooks wrote about when she turned her poetic attention to the places she lived and worked, buildings such as the Mecca, at the intersection of Thirty-Fourth and State Streets, where she spent her early days peddling tracts for a spiritualist named E. N. French.[15] To accommodate increasing numbers of blacks, once-spacious apartments in such buildings were carved into "kitchenettes," single rooms with a small kitchen—minus a sink—along one wall. Whole families inhabited them, sharing toilets with neighbors living behind thin pressboard dividers. Trash piled up in the hallways, adding a pungent odor to buildings meant for many fewer tenants than they contained. Between 1940 and 1950, the number of kitchenettes in Bronzeville increased by over 36,000 units.[16] Brooks asks an implacable question about such spaces in a poem entitled "kitchenette building," from her early collection *A Street in Bronzeville* (1944):

> But could a dream send up through onion fumes
> Its white and violet, fight with fried potatoes
> And yesterday's garbage ripening in the hall,
> Flutter, or sing an aria down these rooms

Even if we were willing to let it in,
Had time to warm it, keep it very clean,
Anticipate a message, let it begin?[17]

The inevitable, unbearable answer is no. Such spaces throttle dreams. Confined to kitchenettes and cracked streets, Bronzeville's poorest residents lived a life without song.

Or so it seemed to Sonny Blount. Sonny lived twenty blocks south of the Mecca in a building at 5414 South Prairie Avenue (now an empty parcel). His apartment was just a block from a train stop—Chicago's famous "L"—and two from Washington Park, a wide, green space that would become important to his intellectual and creative development. It was cramped, not quite a kitchenette, but close quarters even for just one person, with cupboards above the stove, a bed tucked into a small second room, and, in the middle of the living room, a spinet piano with a small electronic keyboard (a Hammond Solovox) attached beneath the piano's keys and used for creating organ sounds.

Something feels strange about the space,[18] as if it contains more stuff than the laws of physics should allow: stacks of hand-scrawled staff paper, several music stands, a recording machine (using paper tape), a stuffed chair piled with sheet music, torn-open envelopes and densely typed papers and inky drafts of what look like poems on an old battered table under the window, empty glasses on the counter, shoes in a corner, books, books, books, a record player next to a leaning pile of 78s, several brown-paper and red-print sleeves scattered on the floor. A chaos of stuff, but orderly, too, as if the apartment warps to accommodate it. The piano vibrates softly as if just played, the player stepping away to make a phone call or order takeout. A vibration more felt than heard hangs in the air, a background radiation that sustains this particular arrangement of things in such a small space.

Sonny slept in his apartment between gigs. He began hearing and tentatively playing music he hoped would open new horizons in Chicago. The union placed him in good jobs with notable musicians: Wynonie Harris, whose randy rhythm and blues took Sonny to Nashville for three months, where he made his first recordings in March 1946;

Lil Green, a country belter from Mississippi who would introduce Sonny to a drummer he would work with frequently over the years, Tommy "Bugs" Hunter; and Sir Oliver Bibb, whose unabashedly commercial band dressed like Revolutionary War–era fops, sporting tricorns, wigs, and ruffs.[19] Sonny didn't care. He was a seasoned sideman and performed the music he got paid to play with skill and precision. His heart, however, belonged to big bands, with their harmonically dense sound palette, vast canvas, and huge spectrum of sonic colors. When he wasn't on a gig, he could usually be found at Club DeLisa, where five nights a week showgirls shimmied and dancers swayed to the elegant arrangements of the Fletcher Henderson Orchestra. The DeLisa was just a few blocks from Sonny's place, and to him Henderson was the living god of the large ensemble.

Or something close. "Fletcher was part of an angelic thing," Sonny once said. "I would say he wasn't a man. [. . .] A lot of things that some men do . . . come from somewhere else, or they're inspired by something's that not of this planet."[20] Henderson could take eleven musicians, all with their own distinct powers, problems, and presumptions, and—by the force of imagination, discipline, and Don Redman's arrangements—forge them into an ensemble capable of communicating beauty with harmonious precision. Some felt Henderson and the swing sound he favored were both past their prime. Not Sonny. He heard there a commitment to possibilities higher than mere entertainment. He quickly made Henderson's acquaintance, swapped ideas about tempos and voicings, and earnestly described his approach to composing.

Henderson no longer played piano with the band much. His regular pianist, Marl Young, himself a seasoned leader trying to mix music with law school, had suddenly left the band to start a recording label.[21] Sonny could play like a veteran and read like a professor. Henderson asked him to fill in and eventually offered him a spot in his orchestra for the remainder of its contract with Club DeLisa. Sonny would rehearse the band and play nightly for the stage revues, which included costumes, choreography, and song—the whole range of club theatrics that would shape his sense of showmanship. The work was not without its challenges. Henderson's musicians often ridiculed the strange harmonies of Sonny's arrangements, a situation he once addressed by placing a straight razor on top of his piano.[22] Henderson stood by his piano player, however, and his musicians backed down. When his contract with the DeLisa ran out in May 1947, Henderson left for California. Red Saunders and his orchestra took over the job. Sonny stayed on for five years as rehearsal pianist and copyist, tweaking otherwise staid arrangements into music that was always a little richer and stranger for his touch.

There was nothing rich and strange about the music Sonny played in the sweaty bars in Calumet City, south of Chicago—"Sin City," as it was called, packed with sleazy clubs and strip joints run mostly by the mob. The money was good, but the hours were grueling, eight to twelve at a stretch, with strippers coming and going behind a flimsy partition hiding white bodies from black eyes. Bugs Hunter formed a trio with Sonny and Red Holloway on saxophone to comp the sex and sin that simmered in clubs such as the Capital Bar, Sid's Oasis, and the Peacock Club.[23] Their music was the usual dive-bar bump and grind. Sonny played it straight, honking and tonking while the dancers bobbed. But Hunter and Holloway both noted his tendency to play outside the changes when the chance arose.[24] Calumet City put his spirit to the test, but Sonny was a master of any idiom—or maybe a medicine man. Late one hot night, the strippers hard at it, he leaned over to Bugs and said, "Watch this," pointing to a drunk passed out at the bar. Staring fiercely, Sonny played a series of angular, weird chords. The drunk twitched, lifted his head slowly, swung his feet under him, and wobbled toward the door.[25] Sonny smiled at the effect. His own music could do so much more than paint the walls behind jiggling women. Even confined to dank spaces playing the rhythms of sin, he dispensed medicine for nightmares that might awaken the soul.

4

THMEI

In the late forties and early fifties, Sonny lived a life confined to the South Side and the few other places where blacks could move with relative ease. It wasn't a *bad* life, exactly. He was making his way as a journeyman musician, arranging and copying charts for several successful bands and individuals: the Red Saunders Orchestra, now the house band at Club DeLisa and recording regularly for Columbia and OKeh; the Dukes of Swing and their vocalists, the Dozier Boys, playing steadily at the Pershing Hotel; and LaVerne Baker, a rhythm and blues singer also known as "Little Miss Sharecropper" and appearing frequently in a variety of South Side venues.[1] Sonny once played with Coleman Hawkins at an after-hours club on the North Side and wrote an arrangement of "I'll Remember April" whose chord changes the giant of the tenor saxophone, by his own admission, couldn't play. Sonny would also record with Hawkins in 1953, six tracks that the Savoy label later released on an LP entitled *The Hawk Returns*.[2] In general, money was tight and the hours were uneven. Sonny kept working the Calumet City strip clubs to make money for rent and expenses, arranging, copying, comping, and sleeping a little here and there. It was a living. But was it a life?

Perhaps it was. But only if you were willing to accept its limits. For a black pianist and composer, they were pretty constraining. Just two blocks from Washington Park and with easy access to the "L," his little apartment was home, the place where he conducted the everyday activities that sustained him. He slept and ate there, read his books, wrote his poetry, and played his piano, often in the company of other musicians. He liked to record what he played, alone or in small groups of talented players, such as Jesse Miller, Stuff Smith, and Wilbur Ware. He used the latest available devices: at first, a machine called the Sound Mirror, which recorded on tape made of paper, and then other devices employing the more durable iron oxide tape.[3] The 5414 South Prairie apartment provided a safe haven for his imagination. He could experiment musically in peace, sharing his ideas with players open to new possibilities. His various jobs, whether harmonizing pop melodies or orchestrating swing standards, demanded a strict temper. He was a professional, arriving promptly and arranging inventively, but he was an artist, too, taking harmonies in fresh directions whenever he could.

The circle of his activity was fairly small. Club DeLisa, where he worked almost daily for five years rehearsing and arranging material for Red Saunders, was at 5521 South Street, just a few blocks west of his apartment. The Pershing Hotel, located ten blocks farther south, at Sixty-Fourth and Cottage Grove, was still an easy walk. Studio work (as an arranger, Sonny would be in the room for last-minute changes) required a crosstown train ride. The famous Universal Recording studios were on the North Side, not far from United Broadcasting. It took a car to work Sin City, but Bugs Hunter had one for the long drive along Lake Calumet and the river of the same name. The gigs were regular and so was the money, paid in cool mobster cash. Such was the circuit of Sonny's mobility as a black musician in Chicago during the late forties and early fifties, mapping an existence confined to the places blacks could move independently if not exactly freely. The Black Belt set life's limits, with an occasional excursion north or south.

It was an invisible cage. Bronzeville may have offered opportunity for uplift to blacks of middling means and bourgeois aspirations, but for the working poor (and a musician of even Sonny's caliber was usually just a step ahead of public relief), the world was an inner-city keep called the South Side. As postwar urban renewal razed old tenements to raise vertical ghettos, and as postwar industry relocated to Chicago's suburbs and white outmigration followed, the South Side got bigger, blacker, and inevitably poorer, much to the consternation of a thoughtful man such as Sonny Blount. The heady days of the Chicago Black Renaissance were done. Its heirs inherited a segregated city without much prospect for improvement. Life on the South Side could be a death sentence. Richard Wright described it in morbid detail in *Native Son*, his harrowing novel about a boy named Bigger Thomas growing up black and poor on the South Side. Wright left for New York in 1937. Published in 1940, his novel advanced a searing critique of segregation in Chicago.

Wright's angry indictment of racism so pervasive that it physically partitioned urban space remains pertinent to the Chicago that Sonny would inhabit a few years later. The mass migration of blacks after World War II only worsened social conditions that, in Wright's novel, drive young Bigger Thomas to commit unspeakable but somehow inevitable crimes: the murders of two young women, one white and one black. Bigger doesn't willfully plot these murders. He commits them at the dictate of motives more social than private. Wright blames the very space of the segregated metropolis for producing the forces that could drive someone like Bigger to kill, ending not only the lives of two apparently innocent victims but also his own. *Native Son* provides a test case for the social effects of American apartheid, summing up with grisly clarity the terminal logic of life on the South Side.

The exposition of that logic is disarmingly simple: live in a cage, die in a prison. The physical space of the South Side sentences poor blacks to a life of confinement, which judicial incarceration only literalizes. In Wright's book, Bigger lives out what most urban blacks of the time only intuited: the lethal force of segregation. The novel opens in the small, single room that Bigger shares with his mother, sister, and brother in a tenement at 3721 Indiana Avenue. The family awakens beset by an intruder: "There he is again, Bigger!"[4] It's a huge rat. The ensuing chase ends in violence as Bigger smashes the rat with a skillet and crushes its head beneath his heel. The scene plays as an overture to the tragedy to come: Bigger's trespass into an inimical space, with all the resulting violence. At the behest of his betters (an offer of employment), Bigger crosses the line that divides his black world from the surrounding white one. That line defines him as a young black man. That line confines him to the South Side. "Bigger could not live in a building across the 'line.'"[5] He can work there, perhaps, but not live: Bigger inhabits a contradiction between the physical conditions of his life and the aspirations (as simple as working) that bring him into contact with people who draw the line, enforce constraint.

And they mean business:

> As long as he and his black folks did not go beyond certain limits, there was no need to fear that white force. But whether they feared it or not, each and every day of their lives they lived with it; even when words did not sound its name, they acknowledged its reality. As long as they lived here in this prescribed corner of the city, they paid mute tribute to it.[6]

Life on the South Side wasn't simple confinement. It was a form of bondage that required acknowledging the superiority of white force with the words and deeds of everyday life, living on the condition that you walk only these particular streets, talk only these sanctioned words, feel only these permissible feelings. That's what it meant to be poor and black on Chicago's South Side in the forties and fifties. Bigger sums it all up in conversation with his friend Gus: "Goddammit look! We live here and they live there. We black and they white. They got things and we ain't. They do things and we can't. It's just like living in jail. [. . .] I reckon we the only things in this city that can't go where we want to go and do what we want to do."[7] Bigger feels his way to a terrible truth: the South Side is a jail. Being black and poor in Chicago is somehow a crime that justifies a life sentence to the South Side, where identity arises by negation ("we ain't," "we can't") and desire occurs to no avail. Such is the cunning of white force: blacks sustain it simply by living.

When the killing comes, it seems more like something that *happens* to Bigger than like something he does. Circumstances conspire to put him on the wrong side of the line separating black from white. He finds himself in the bedroom of his rich white employer's daughter at a delicate moment when silencing her and killing her take the same touch: "he pushed downward upon the pillow with all of his weight, determined that she must not move or make any sound that would betray him." A poor black youth in the bedroom of a rich white heiress is a formula for disaster, which is exactly Wright's point: forces beyond Bigger's control maneuver him into the position of murdering a white girl. Space itself is culpable, the urban space of American apartheid that turns black agency into transgression. An abyss separates the single room of Bigger's family from the bedroom of an heiress, and death connects them: "As he took his hands from the pillow he heard a long slow sigh go up from the bed into the air of the darkened room, a sigh which afterwards, when he remembered it, seemed final, irrevocable."[8] Securing his safety is the same as killing. Bigger confronts a horrible truth: survival is a crime when you live in confinement.

Rather than resist the baleful circumstances that determine his fate, Bigger accepts them, even glories in them. If to live is to kill, then so be it. His second murder simply follows from the first, collateral damage of his will to live. That this time it's a black woman makes no difference: Bigger kills again to stay—and to feel—alive. That's the hard fact of inhabiting a cage. The act of living exceeds it, even unto death: "'What I killed for must've been good!' Bigger's voice was full of frenzied anguish. 'It must have been good! When a man kills, it's for something. . . . I didn't know I was really alive in this world until I felt things hard enough to kill for 'em.'"[9] The South Side criminalizes life to the point that killing offers its richest satisfaction, not as a voluntary act, but as the imperative of social circumstances.

Bigger affirms the fate that ultimately destroys him, celebrating murder as his only real means of moving beyond the color line that confines him. At his trial, a ritual application of white force, Bigger's lawyer at least defends the feeling of life and possibility that come with killing: "It was the first full act of his life; it was the most meaningful, exciting and stirring thing that had ever happened to him. He accepted it because it made him free, gave him the possibility of choice, of action, the opportunity to act and to feel that his actions carried weight." But something is wrong when freedom coincides with killing. The South Side turns black agency against itself. And yet Bigger takes the destiny he has been handed and creates life in his own image, however fatal the results. As his lawyer says: "He was *living*, only as he knew how, and as we have forced him to live. The actions that resulted in the death of those two women were as instinctive and inevitable as breathing or blinking one's eyes. It was an act of *creation*!"[10] Bigger's lawyer gets him slightly wrong; not instinct alone but also Bigger's astonishing capacity to affirm it are what transform killing another into an act of self-creation. Feeling alive, Bigger looms above the segregated world that confined him.

Native Son offers a scathing diagnosis of segregation in Chicago and its effects on blacks and whites alike. For all its intensity, however, Bigger's story offers little in the way of compensation for social contradictions. Bigger dies alone as the South Side lives on, a space of perpetual apartheid in a racist democracy. Blacks haunt that "complex civilization like wailing ghosts." They wander "like fiery planets lost from their orbits." If they love, it's with the diffuse passion of "disembodied spirits."[11] Wright's vision for the revitalization of Chicago's segregated space fades into a pallid dream of the hapless leftist who may understand Bigger but can't do much to help him. Confined in a prison cell, however, Bigger discovers for himself a bolder, more visionary prospect, one that chimes strangely with developments to come:

> Another impulse rose in him, born of desperate need, and his mind clothed it in an image of a strong blinding sun sending hot rays down and he was standing in the midst of a vast crowd of men, white men and black men and all men, and the sun's rays melted away the many differences, the colors, the clothes, and drew what was common and good upward toward the sun. . . .[12]

Solicit the sun. Perhaps there is a force counter to the white one, a vitalizing power from above that might blind blank eyes and burn away difference. One whose rays might raise people above race. A force to transform the space of segregation. A new dawn for the South Side.

Sonny would pursue that impossibility. Where *Native Son* diagnoses black suffering as a morbid effect of segregation, he would seek a healing treatment—but not alone. Solo insurgency ends in death: that is one lesson of Bigger's ordeal. And Sonny's feelings of intense solitude living a musician's life on the South Side are the message of several early compositions, recorded in his apartment, with such telling titles as "I've Got Some New Blues," "The Darkness Within," "All Alone," and "If They Only Knew," a brooding poem that reveals a glimpse of the suffering he kept mostly to himself.[13] He would later say of this period that he "wasn't even really here," that he "was busy with spirit things."[14] He was figuring out how to respond to a world inimical to blacks: "You look out at the world and you say 'Something's wrong with this stuff.' [. . .] If you're not mad at the world you don't have what it takes. [. . .] This planet is like a prison."[15] Such a planet is doomed.

To his good fortune and ours, in 1951 Sonny fell into the company of Alton Abraham, a man with similar feelings who would become his close friend, business partner, and fellow architect of better worlds. Together they would build what Bigger never has, a black activist collective to create and sustain a dream of better living. For all his extraordinary importance to the history of jazz and black activism, though, Abraham remains a misty figure. He was born in Chicago during the late twenties and, as did some of the musicians Sonny would soon be recruiting, graduated from DuSable High School. Perhaps they came to know each other through such mutual acquaintances. Unlike Sonny, Abraham volunteered for military service, shipping out with the army to the Philippines soon after World War II ended. He eventually came to share something of his friend's disdain for the military, joining several others in signing a letter sent to the *Chicago Defender* comparing the army's racial policies with those of "the old sunny South."[16] Abraham served as a regimental clerk in Manila and upon his return enrolled at Wilson Junior College to study electrical engineering and radiology, fields that would sustain his professional and musical pursuits. He eventually found employment as a radiology technician at Mount Sinai Hospital.

A passion for music inspired him to join a serious vocal ensemble called the Knights of Music in 1951. Before long, he was serving as its treasurer. E. Virgil Abner directed the group then, with Elnora Carter accompanying on piano. A printed statement describes the ensemble's aims: "The title 'The Knights of Music' is indicative of the groups [sic] desire to champion the advent of good music as well as to achieve technical and interpretive skills in the translation of various types of compositions."[17] The Knights performed a wide range of songs, from Bach, Handel, and Wagner to Rodgers and Hammerstein to spirituals and pop tunes. One program lists as "guest accompanist" a young Ramsey E. Lewis Jr., soon to rise to distinction on the Chicago scene. The first page of another bears a testimonial under the heading "I am Music" that sets an agenda surprisingly compatible with what lay ahead for Sonny and Alton: "Through me spirits immortal speak the message that makes the world weep and laugh, and wonder and worship."[18] Abraham's involvement with the Knights of Music prepared him well for his association with Sonny.

Shared intellectual interests drew them together most strongly. Both were inveterate readers, tenacious researchers, and deep scholars of occult wisdom. Sonny lined his little apartment with books, and Abraham hunted them ravenously, compiling by some accounts a collection of 15,000 volumes at 4115 South Drexel, his mother's three-story walk-up. The drummer Robert Barry recalls it with awe: "In the basement, it was like going into a library, lots and lots of books, but dusty and dank. Maybe more like a catacomb. These books were old, you wondered who read them."[19] They weren't just old; they were arcane—counterculture tomes for conjuring an alternative destiny. An undated mailer from "The Saturn Research Foundation" and bearing the South Drexel address offers 427 used books for sale beneath a spirited admonition: "What you don't know . . . Hurts! Be well informed . . . It Pays!"[20] Their titles bear pondering: *The Negro in Our History*, by C. G. Woodson; *Manual of Historical Literature*, by Charles

Kendall Adams; *Asiatic Elements of Greek Civilization*, by William M. Ramsay; *The Racial Myth*, by P. Radin; *The Legacy of Egypt*, by S. R. K. Granville; *The Wealth of Nations*, by Adam Smith; *Ceremonies of Judaism*, by Abrahamz Idelsohn; *Thelyphthora; or, A Treatise on Female Ruin*, by Martin Madan; *Kropotkin's Revolutionary Pamphlets*, by P. A. Kropotkin; *The Political Future of India*, by L. Lajpat Rai; *Cavalcade of the American Negro*, produced by the WPA; *Judas*, by J. Sturge Moore; *Fingerprints Can Be Forged*, by Albert Wehde and John Nicholas Beffel; *Histopathology of the Teeth and Their Surrounding Structures*, by R. Kronfeld; and *Democratic Education in Practice*, by R. Schneideman.

Unlikely to appear on many college syllabi even in the fifties (and certainly not today), titles such as these map a territory beyond the pale of majority culture and its secular pieties. From them, Sonny and Abraham would cobble together an intellectual countertradition for the South Side, a forgotten legacy of wisdom to invigorate a people caged without a key. In seeking release, Bigger Thomas could appeal only to a bankrupt Christianity. Sonny and Abraham would invent an alternative tradition of greater force and promise gleaned from the combined mystical traditions of Egyptology, theosophy, numerology, and others among the occult. They would forge weapons for political resistance from a slagheap of beliefs deemed irrational, obsolete, or just plain crackpot by Western religion, philosophy, and science. They would create an intellectual heritage for the thing that Bigger lives and dies without: a community of support for blacks aspiring to transcend the social confines of Chicago's South Side. Deep, continuing research would be required, and a scholar's devotion to study and reflection—but not in solitude. An activist collective would do this work, a band of like-minded street intellectuals devoted to changing the world from the bottom up, a secret society of black radicals armed with the obscure wisdom of things occult.[21]

The society would have a suitably mysterious name: "Thmei." The two men probably found it in one of Abraham's old books, possibly J. G. Wilkinson's five-volume *Manners and Customs of the Ancient Egyptians* (3rd ed., 1847). Thmei fit the character and agenda of the collective perfectly. The Egyptian goddess of truth and justice, she was a double deity, often represented by two female figures standing side by side or by one figure wearing two matched ostrich feathers on her head. As goddess of the "two truths," Thmei combines the inner perception of what is (truth) with its outer manifestation (justice).[22] Pharaohs held her image in their hands, and judges wore it while hearing cases. Breastplates depicted her with Ra, god of the sun, and in a development that surely interested Sonny, similar images came to adorn the breastplate of the high priest of Israel. "Thmei" also survives in the Hebrew word "thummim," a plural form for "truth." The Egyptian goddess lived on surreptitiously among the Israelites. Wilkinson claims Thmei to possess a special status, that of "the great cardinal virtue," for "the Ancients considered that [. . .] Truth or Justice influenced men's conduct toward their neighbours, and tended to maintain that harmony and good will which were most essential for the welfare of society."[23] Such would become the function of the secret society called Thmei Research: to advance the welfare of society through promoting harmony and goodwill.

The group's membership remains murky, and its reach is hard to measure, but Thmei clearly aspired to improving the lot of blacks living on the South Side. Abraham was a prime mover, but other members included his brother Artis; a friend from the Knights of Music named Lawrence M. Allen; another friend from his army days, Luis T. Clarin; and James Bryant, who would remain a close associate for many years.[24] Abraham took the group seriously enough to print letterhead and cover sheets for a journal to disseminate scholarly research. Along the journal's left margin, in red ink, appear words that define the work of its editors: "RESEARCHERS IN SUBJECTS COSMIC, SPIRITUAL, PHILOSOPHICAL, RELIGIOUS, HISTORICAL, SCIENTIFIC, ECONOMICAL, ETC." Immediately below and in quotation marks runs the hieratic imperative "SEEK YE WISDOM, KNOWLEDGE, AND UNDERSTANDING." A double-ruled border sets off a brief description of the journal—"INFORMATIVE FACTUAL SERIES ISSUED BI-MONTHLY"—which is followed by the recommendation that "SUBSCRIBERS SEND MONTHLY DONATION" to a post office box in Chicago.[25] One such cover sheet contains a lengthy typed description of the "religion of Sokagakkai," a Japanese variant of Buddhism capable of securing happiness during (not after) life for "all color and races of people in this world."[26] The Thmei collective dedicated much of its energy to producing and distributing research to promote countercultural spirituality.

Theirs was a black radicalism from beyond, wisdom politics for a segregated people. In this, it resembles similar initiatives undertaken to better the lives of blacks in Chicago and elsewhere. Thmei's agenda chimes with that of an emerging black nationalism, the activism on behalf of all African Americans that Wright describes in *Native Son*: "Taken collectively, they are not simply twelve million people; in reality they constitute a separate nation, stunted, stripped, and held captive *within* this nation, devoid of political, social, economic, and property rights."[27] These are the people Thmei Research served, most immediately those living on Chicago's South Side. Its activism aligns with the Pan-Africanism of the writer and physician Martin R. Delany (1812–1885) and Marcus Garvey (1887–1940), whose Universal Negro Improvement Association and Black Star Line steamships pursued a black nationalist dream of African repatriation. By the twenties, as William Sites observes, "nationalist conceptions [. . . had] attracted a newly growing constituency in Chicago's black community."[28] Black activist groups would appear with increasing frequency and vigor, the most notable among them being two rival organizations founded in Detroit: the Moorish Science Temple, led by Noble Drew Ali (1886–1929), and the Nation of Islam, founded by the obscure Wallace Fard Muhammad (1893–1934?) and nurtured by his close disciple Elijah Muhammad (1897–1975).

Both orders flourished on the South Side of Chicago, preaching black self-determination and uplift, the former drawing together traditions as diverse as Islam, Freemasonry, Buddhism, and Christianity, and the latter relying largely on teachings derived from Islam. Both fought social degradation with spiritual weaponry, beating sectarian plowshares into swords. Wallace Fard Muhammad began as a member of the Moorish Science Temple but left to found the Nation of Islam, disappearing soon thereafter.[29] Elijah Muhammad, a conscientious objector, like Sonny, but imprisoned for it for four years, came to

Chicago after World War II and built the Nation of Islam into the most visible black nationalist organization on the South Side and perhaps in all of America. The existence of such orders shows Thmei to have been a little less eccentric than it might otherwise seem. Szwed draws an interesting contrast between its tenets and those of the Nation of Islam.[30] Both reject history as *white* history and challenge blacks to live according to another kind of wisdom. They part company, however, on the question of race. The Nation of Islam asserts an irremediable difference between blacks and whites. Thmei takes a more meliorist position, answering racial difference and its urban horrors with the prospect, however abstract, of universal truth and justice.

Hence Thmei's interest in occult wisdom. Orders appealing to Islam for an alternative to Western rationality nevertheless accept Abrahamic scriptural tradition (the Torah, New Testament, or Qur'an) as the trunk on which to graft a new branch of black wisdom. Thmei sought something more radical: a deeper antiquity, older and more authoritative than Islam, Christianity, or Judaism. It rejected those later, paler pieties for the solemn wisdom of Egypt—the blank gaze of the sacred sun, the soul's posthumous passage to immortality. The People of the Book (Muslims, Christians, and Jews) all take scripture for the word of God, *the* source of truth in a tinsel world. But what if their scripture were inspired not by the Creator but by a lesser god? What if the Good Book were a bad translation? What if it were written in a secret code? Thmei's turn to Egypt for an alternative source of wisdom achieves two important rhetorical effects: it recovers a tradition whose sheer antiquity makes Western culture look jejune, and it repositions scripture as text that, however sacred, might profitably be reexamined in that ancient light. Thmei would make bold use of both effects, countering conventional religiosity with Egyptian wisdom and subjecting scripture to radical critique.

Thmei aimed less to revive that wisdom per se than to direct it toward the social end of black uplift on the South Side. Nor was Thmei a particularly scrupulous interpreter of Egyptian tradition. It slid easily into other esoteric systems of thought, especially those associated with theosophy and oriented toward direct knowledge of the divine.

Whether understood as a broad esoteric tradition running back to Jakob Boehme and (the possibly fictional) Christian Rosenkreuz or more specifically as the occult science of Helena Blavatsky and the Theosophical Society, theosophy presented Western thought with a correlative to the wisdom of ancient Egypt. Abraham and Sonny immersed themselves in its works, and Thmei absorbed them, too: works by Emanuel Swedenborg, Mary Baker Eddy, Rudolf Steiner, George Gurdjieff, and P. D. Ouspensky—the whole legacy of counter-rational writing current in the West.[31] Thmei conjured from such sources a spiritual imperative for radical social critique that bypassed both Christian quietism and Muslim militancy. Its unique contribution to black nationalism could be called "political theosophy," a radicalism combining the spiritual imperative of esoteric wisdom with a social agenda of black advancement.[32] Not Jesus, not Muhammad, neither Marx nor Mao, but Ra: Thmei practiced political activism inspired by a wisdom as inhuman as the sun.

Thmei responded to crass consumerism and oppressive poverty alike with a message of spiritual awakening, aesthetic transcendence, and social transformation designed specifically for blacks. Political theosophy arose as a race-based response to racial oppression, open perhaps to everyone at the eschatological level but tailored to the social needs of blacks in a particular place at a particular time—namely, the South Side in the fifties. Sonny would later explain why: "Because of segregation I have only a vague knowledge of the white world, and that knowledge is superficial."[33] Political theosophy answered black segregation with black wisdom, a deeper knowledge for darker aspirations. A touching handwritten note addressed to "Brother Thmei Research" from one "Sister Jones" nicely illustrates the group's racial agenda: "Because Some of our Leaders is Wrong an I want to [know] the tru fact I Diden [know] that the New testament Was the White Race Book So You Know I am interest in Learn[ing] the true Salvation."[34]

Thmei fought political ignorance with occult wisdom deriving from esoteric traditions and inspiring unorthodox biblical critique, always with an eye on real-world social uplift and black advancement. Witness in this regard a prayer James Bryant recorded sometime in the midsixties on a large, loose page of yellow paper. He prays for things worldly and divine:

> Better money and business for research and all necessity of better living. For a better self and a better galaxy and universe. We will be on forever progressing and building. May God grant to me to speak properly and to have thoughts worthy of what and all he has given, for it is you that guides wisdom and directs the wise.[35]

Bryant's prayer nicely encapsulates the Thmei agenda: better living on Earth and throughout the universe through wisdom guided by the Creator. This is no Christian petition. It beseeches an abstract, impersonal deity for practical advantage and spiritual growth. Thmei Research interrogates the world to create a better life that leads beyond it. Bryant (who often signed his names backward, "Semaj Tnayrb") prays to align himself with the larger and interminable task of "forever progressing and building."

That Alton Abraham himself nurtured such sentiments is the lesson of a prayer of his own dated July 20, 1958, and recorded in a large, store-bought record book:

> I, Alton Abraham, petition that the Better Spirits and Vibrations, that have been, still are and that may, in my part of the future come near me, be commanded to bring more Wisdom, knowledge and understanding and to bring better happiness, to work with the live better vibrations in my favor instead of against me.
> Alton Abraham.[36]

In a manner resembling Bryant's invocation, Abraham petitions "Better Spirits" for the kind of wisdom that might foster happiness *now*, "better vibrations" to work practically in *this* world on his behalf. Thmei's radical social vision arises from this devotion to better living here and now. Its racial register comes in part from a revisionist reading of Christian scripture, as Abraham indicates in a strange but revealing document typed on Mount Sinai Hospital letterhead and parenthetically entitled, "A TREATISE ON REBIRTH AND THE LAW OF CONSEQUENCE." Mixing biblical critique with theosophical pronouncement, it offers a new interpretation of the crucifixion that revives the event's forgotten racial import: Jesus "was not killed just Because of what He taught, but they wanted to get rid of Him Because He was not A white man, and they wanted a white Jesus And now they have one, He was not a white man, but A member of the Black, Brown, and Red skin peoples of the world."[37] Abraham recasts the crucifixion as the result of a supremacist show trial that served up a black martyr to consolidate white authority.

Jesus belonged to a dark-skinned race, as in strict biblical terms was true for all the patriarchs and prophets: "The Pale-skin man was a Black man Before he turned pale. We do not have any scripture any where that will Say that man was created from white Dust." Biblically speaking, white skin is a recent development, rendering racial difference a historical aberration better abandoned than accepted as fate: "there is always, in each Race, a danger that the soul may become too much attached to the Race; that it may become so enmeshed in Race characteristics it cannot Rise above the Race Idea and will therefore Fail to advance."[38] Abraham's ruminations on race, while not amounting to formal Thmei doctrine, sketch a racial theory that concedes historical difference to imagine the possibility of its ultimate transcendence. This is black activism beyond difference; the radicalism of political theosophy pushes social transformation past its historical prospects into the higher reaches of better living.

That meliorist program was its ultimate social aim, but Thmei's more immediate cultural agenda involved encouraging black creativity as a source of collective identity and pride. Reflecting later on these goals, Abraham admits they might not have been universally appealing:

The main purpose of this organization was to do some things to prove to the world that black people could do something worthwhile, that they could create things, they could do things that other nations would take notice of. It was not for everyone, but for those who know why they're here, not just living blindly and routinely. . . . It was for those who "know" (not those who say "no").[39]

Black uplift in this formulation comes through creativity fueled by an almost gnostic awareness that life involves more than routine living. Abraham's homonym (know/no) has large implications for Thmei's political activism. In preferring knowledge to negation, Abraham advances a politics of informed response to injustice, and in emphasizing creativity over antagonism, he makes culture the engine of social reform.

Thmei's activism offered an alternative to either passive resistance or open violence as a way of challenging the killing effects of segregation. Sonny, Abraham, and their fellow researchers responded to the limits of life on the South Side with a form of creative resistance, working culturally to build a better world for blacks. "Sonny wanted to do things not the right way, but *another* way, a *better* way"; Abraham thus testifies to Sonny's commitment to improving things without regard to the kind of moral precepts that would guide social reformers as different as Martin Luther King Jr. and Elijah Muhammad.[40] The better way is creative, a commitment to improving the lives of a segregated people by advancing their culture. Sonny, Abraham, and Thmei Research focused on blacks because white Chicago drew a line around their lives and left them to fend for themselves, perhaps to pursue consumerist dreams, perhaps to die trying to escape. Creative resistance thus meant racial resistance, as Sonny would say bluntly much later: "I was trying to uplift black people out of this condition they in and I only played for them. I [did not] play for white people."[41] For Sonny, only black culture could uplift black people. Music could build a better, blacker world.

Thmei provided collective support and intellectual inspiration to sustain this prospect. Its social agenda and spiritual impetus brought a new depth to Sonny's life and a new vitality to his music. He no longer needed to survive musically at the behest of others, comping at strip clubs or arranging for floorshows. His music might do something more than paper the walls of South Side ballrooms and lounges. It might lift their patrons toward a higher life. To mark this transformation, as deeply personal as it was musical, Sonny took steps. With Abraham's encouragement and the likely guidance of Thmei, he changed his name. He had been fiddling with the possibility for a while, as Szwed notes. "Sonny" was a nickname, after all, and in his early years he often played under the name "Sonny Lee." Soon after arriving in Chicago, he quietly queered his last name, adding a superfluous letter by spelling it "Bhlount."[42]

But the enrichment of his musical vocation required something more, a thorough reinvention in line with other African Americans who, renaming themselves, shed a collective history of subjugation and suffering to assert a promising future. In October 1952, Herman Poole Blount legally changed his name to "Le Sony'r Ra," trading his slave name for something more profound and dignified: not the title of a European aristocrat, as with Duke Ellington or Count Basie, or an American political official, as with Lester Young ("Prez"), but the name of a god, the Egyptian god of the sun, Ra. Sun Ra would be his patronymic, a cross-cultural self-synonym (Sun = Ra) connoting light, life, and divinity. Audacious! "'Ra' is older than history itself," he told one interviewer; "'Ra' is my spirit name," he told another.[43] In Sun Ra Sonny found a cognomen beyond human ken and reference, a sacred name out of black antiquity to inspire belief in a better tomorrow. Sun Ra would become widely recognized as a musician, poet, and sage. The precise significance of "Le Sony'r Ra," however, remains a mystery— as does much about Thmei's work as a secret society. Abraham and his posse of street intellectuals nevertheless provided emotional and intellectual support for creative resistance to segregation in Chicago. Thmei Research evolved a form of black radicalism that made culture its means of engagement and Sun Ra its presiding deity.

5

EGYPT

Ancient Egypt. Land of implacable sun and inscrutable ruin. The pyramids, the Sphinx, the Valley of the Kings. Sand stretching to infinity in a world out of time. A source of fascination for the West even before Napoleon's 1798 expedition (or invasion) and the ensuing twenty-three volumes of *Description de l'Égypte*. Ancient Egypt inspired a branch of Western knowledge (Egyptology) and genre of bourgeois architecture (Egyptian revival). Its somber gaze into death's vortex, its mummies, tombs, and hieroglyphics, its user's guide to immortality (the *Book of the Dead*): these conjure an antiquity of terrible, aloof wisdom. Even today, a stroll through any cemetery of substance yields sepulchers and tombstones etched in the hard lines of Egyptian motifs: sempiternal suns, animal-headed gods, kings seated in pharaonic profile. The land equally of death and immortality, ancient Egypt has haunted later ages like an animate dream. "In Chicago," Szwed relates, "intimations of Egypt were everywhere: in exhibits in the Field Museum, in the Oriental Institute, the libraries, the books sold by the street-corner Egyptologists on the South Side."[1] For a group of self-taught urban intellectuals, Egypt offered a ready-made alternative to an ostensibly enlightened culture of the West responsible for chattel slavery, racism, Jim Crow, and segregation.

Thmei Research made good use of it, but not simply because things Egyptian were ubiquitous in Chicago and elsewhere. The antiquity of Egyptian civilization proved a strategic advantage to a black radicalism that took culture for its means of social transformation. Egypt was much older than Greece and its rational philosophy, older than Israel and its jealous God. By the dawn of those belated civilizations, Egypt had witnessed millennia of social stability. Greece and Israel look like unsuccessful social experiments in comparison. In an interview conducted at Berkeley, Sun Ra describes the appeal of ancient Egypt as a model for politics, particularly given political unrest in America:

> America's just four hundred years old, and it's shakin' and quiverin'—they had a civilization—the oldest known civilization: ancient Egypt: five thousand years of precise, orderly government. So the world got to go back and see: what were they doing? What were they doing to have five thousand years of precise government, education; and the whole world, it revolves around Egypt, really.[2]

Along with the other members of Thmei, Sun Ra found in ancient Egypt a precedent for social stability and spiritual prowess. What was Greek democracy in comparison? What was Hebrew monotheism? Nothing but latter-day dabbling in political logistics. To account for their origins, Greece had mythology, and Israel had scriptures. Behind both, however, spiritually as well as historically, loomed an Egyptian antiquity whose longevity alone might undermine their sweet assurances of human rationality or divine entitlement. Furthermore, if the Western tradition of Abrahamic religion and Greek philosophy condones segregation and black debasement, then the times require a reevaluation of that tradition's self-congratulating assumptions. Ancient Egypt provided Thmei and its public persona, Sun Ra, with a historically viable and culturally powerful alternative to Western culture and its presumptuous politics.

Thmei's Egypt was black. Located in the northeast corner of the African continent, its ancient civilization rose to consolidate the wisdom, science, and statecraft of, as Thmei saw it, a native black population. White cultures came later, although not of course according to their own accounts. For Thmei, the West had traced its heritage back to Greeks and Hebrews in part to ensure the priority of whites as progenitors of civilization. A black civilization in ancient Egypt would force a reexamination of such claims to cultural anteriority and superiority, and it provided radicals such as those associated with Thmei an imposing tradition counter to the West's, with its built-in whiteness. To them, Egypt seemed not only an alternative to Western culture but, when considered more deeply, its unacknowledged origin. Long before Martin Bernal explored Greek retentions of Egyptian culture in his book *Black Athena* (1987), a variety of writers had taken Egypt for the true origin of both humanity and civilization. On their reading of history, whites derived—physically and culturally—from blacks. As early as 1791, in *The Ruins; or, Meditation on the Revolutions of Empires* (a book Sun Ra knew well), Count Constantin-François Volney argued that Africans gave birth to civilization and all its achievements: religion, law, literature, science, and art.[3]

Later writers followed suit, establishing a clear if unacknowledged intellectual legacy tracking humanity back to black Africa. That's the basic argument of a short book entitled *The Children of the Sun* (1918), by George Wells Parker.[4] Theodore P. Ford's *God Wills the Negro* (1939) similarly locates the birthplace of humanity in ancient Ethiopia and the flowering of black civilization in Egypt, describing its fall as having spawned a diaspora that scattered black Egyptians across Africa and eventually, thanks to the slave trade, America.[5] The British anatomist Grafton Elliot Smith, a resident of Cairo for thirty years, argues stridently in favor of an Egyptian genesis for civilization in *The Ancient Egyptians and the Origin of Civilization* (1923): "There can no longer be any doubt that the essential elements of civilization did really originate in Egypt."[6] While denying that ancient Egyptians were black,

Smith nevertheless attributes to Egypt an enormous effect on European cultures, doing so in terms deeply appealing to Thmei: "Egypt brought her influence to bear on the springs of European civilization, not by the violent imposition of an alien culture [. . .] but by raising the members of her own family group of peoples to a higher plane of knowledge and by inoculating them with the germs of her own culture."[7] Egypt diffused higher knowledge as if it were a benign pathogen, culturally invigorating an otherwise enervated Europe.

Most inspiring to Sun Ra and his fellow activists, however, was a book by George G. M. James entitled *Stolen Legacy: The Greeks Were Not the Authors of Greek Philosophy, but the People of North Africa, Commonly Called the Egyptians* (1954). Born in Guyana, James studied in London before coming to the United States and enrolling in a PhD program, probably in classics, at New York's Columbia University. He taught math, Latin, and Greek at several US colleges, most tantalizingly, for a time, Alabama A&M, where Sun Ra attended college for a year. Whether or not their time there overlapped, their ideas about the relationship between Egypt and Greece certainly do. In a relentless reevaluation of primary Greek texts, James hammers home his thesis: "Greek philosophers were not the authors of Greek philosophy, but the Egyptian Priests and hierophants."[8] The Greeks stole their celebrated philosophy from Egypt, and Western culture has since colluded in the crime, devaluing an ancient wisdom and its black proponents.

James's aim is not simply to exonerate that wisdom. More purposefully, it is to better the social condition of its black heirs: "We sometimes wonder why the people of African descent find themselves in such a social plight as they do, but the answer is plain enough. Had it not been for this drama of Greek philosophy and its actors, the African Continent would have had a different reputation and would have enjoyed a status of respect among the nations of the world."[9] James examines Greek philosophy not as truth but as drama, a power play that denigrated people of African descent, its true creators. As he systematically lays out the intellectual theft that he claims underwrites the works of the pre-Socratics, Plato, and Aristotle, he makes a compelling case for the Egyptian Mysteries as the foundation of Greek philosophical thought. And he does so for reasons that chime with Thmei's social agenda: "The aim of this book is to establish better race relations in the world by revealing the fundamental truth concerning the contribution of the African Continent to civilization." By emphasizing Egypt's contribution to a philosophical tradition mistakenly believed to be the sole property of the white West, James intended "to cultivate race pride in the Black people themselves and to offer them a New Philosophy of African Redemption."[10]

With pride comes parity. James sought to restore intellectual and cultural dignity to a people wrongly dismissed as uncivilized, cultivating "the realization and consciousness of their equality with all the other great peoples of the world, who have built great civilizations." James writes not simply as a critic but more inspiringly as a teacher advocating bold educational reform with a clear social agenda, "a world-wide dissemination of the truth, through a system of re-education, in order to stimulate and encourage a change in the attitude of races toward each other."[11] This aim neatly describes that of Thmei's activism and of Sun Ra's music, too: ancient Egypt as a countertradition through which to reeducate the world, composing fractious races into a new harmony. In James, then, Thmei's members found a strong advocate of both Egypt's ancient wisdom and its contemporary social promise. They would make creative use of his example, reviving, for instance, the potency of the implacable Egyptian sun: Sun Ra.

6

WASHINGTON PARK

He sat in the sun.[1] On a bench in Washington Park with a dozen books bearing strange titles splayed spine up or open around him: *Egyptian Magic, Anacalypsis, God Wills the Negro, Flying Saucers Have Landed.* He liked the park on a Saturday. It was packed with people, kids in strollers or short pants, old ladies carrying sacks of stuff, guys hungover from last night's spodie, maybe a couple on a blanket trying for some sugar while the world watched. Or didn't. Everybody seemed to be in motion, even people standing still. He liked the faint touch of cheap perfume that lingered after certain ladies passed, fake roses tattooed on the sinewy afternoon light. Now and then a breeze picked up and fluffed long skirts or jacket vents. Pigeons strutted the walkways in forced haste, resisting flight with iridescent head bobs. Grass and trees and sky and space. Walking the two blocks from his apartment and crossing busy Grand Boulevard, he felt like a traveler to another world. Things seemed possible here.

Washington Park was full of black people dreaming out loud— and not just kids squealing for penny candy or lovers longing for the night. Serious dreamers, too, with aspirations of uplift or salvation. He looked up from the old book balanced on his knee, pages riffling in the breeze. Far down the walk he could see the Communists with their table and their pamphlets. They usually drew a small crowd, some of them hecklers, but others hungry for promises. He had passed a clutch of Presbyterians on his way into the park, their hair groomed and shoes polished, touting a coming social in their church's basement. The local Democrats had a forum up the park a ways, and they loved to mix it up with hapless Republicans who strayed into range, as many had during the summer of conventions a few years back, when both parties had descended on Chicago. He liked the Black Muslims best. They took everything so seriously, from their skinny black ties and creased pants to their denunciation of white devils. He understood their fervor. They wanted a better world. He did, too—just not theirs. He wanted a world where the vibrations were different, not like planet Earth's. Washington Park made him feel good: preachers, hucksters, and visionaries haggling for the future. It was wonderful, a true democracy.

He returned to his book, studying in the sunlight. Clean green pants and a crisp shirt, sometimes a red fez: he liked to look presentable. He was a scholar. An intellectual. People should respect a student of wisdom. Occasionally a few curious passersby, intrigued by his pile of books and studious manner, would gather around and ask a few questions. He was happy to oblige but preferred reading to conversation. Sometimes when the spirit moved him, he would stand up and preach, at the ready a thick manila envelope of mimeographed handouts he had typed himself (he loved capital letters!). But now he was absorbed in *Anacalypsis*, pondering the greatness of Ethiopia and the blackness of so many ancient nations. If antique blacks once ruled great civilizations, why were their descendants living cooped up in segregated cities?

"My brother." A man leaned over the bench near his left shoulder. He wore the white shirt, dark trousers, and shiny shoes of the Black Muslims. "I notice you attract people. Just by reading—all by yourself on this bench. What you reading so hard?"

The voice in his ear was a faint buzz. A sixty-cycle-per-second hum.

"What? You talkin' to me? I ain't nobody's brother." He spoke softly and looked up from his book. A few people milled about, watching with curiosity: a lady with a pin in her hat, an old man with a grocery bag crumpled in his fist.

"Yessir, I'm talkin' to you. Why you read all them books? Why people interested in you if you only reading?"

"I don't want people interested. I don't pay them no mind."

"Well, they mind you. You come out in the park, like today, people see you just sittin' there readin', and they get interested. They leave where we set up down the walk a ways," he pointed a crooked finger, "and they come along here. I'd like to know why."

"Maybe cuz I don't want 'em. I don't care if they listen or not. Not much to hear when I'm readin' anyway." He turned his eyes back to the page.

The man in the suit leaned in a little bit farther. "It's the way you read. Like you in a trance. Like you know something they don't."

"Maybe I do. Maybe I don't. I'm just concerned with my research." He ran a finger down the page he'd been reading until he found the word he was looking for. "There." He resumed.

"You ever talk to people? Like we do, about Muhammad? You ever try to tell them what you believe?"

He looked up again. "On occasion. Yes. I communicate what I know. But I don't necessarily want to. I don't need to. You need to. I suspect."

"Yes, we do." The man walked around the bench in quick, nervous steps and sat down. A few onlookers took interest. "We offer hope to the black man, pride and dignity. We demand respect. In the name of Islam."

"You lookin' for people to lead. I'm looking for . . . nothin'. I'm studying, you see."

The well-dressed man looked at the books on the bench between them, put a finger on *Egyptian Magic* like it might bite. "We study too. The Koran. The words of Muhammad. Other books too. Secret books. Maybe like this one." A couple more people stopped to listen and nod.

"But that's what I mean. What good's the words of Muhammad or any other book if they ain't true? How do you know they true?"

The man twisted his ass and sat up straight, like he was in church. "They the words of *Muhammad*. Even older than that, too, go back to

Egypt and *Ethiopia*, when blacks was on top. They teach us we should reject the white man's world. Utterly and completely. Look what it done to us. Look how we be forced to live."

"Black people ain't nothin', I realize. How'd they get that way, I wonder? Who's responsible?"

"It's the white man did it. We got to live proud and apart. A nation apart. Of Islam." A murmur of approval flitted through the listeners.

"Maybe. But I'm just trying to see what's wrong with this planet. Maybe I can correct it."

"But who you?"

"You can call me Mister Ra. You can call me Mister-y. Makes no mind. I'm nobody. Gonna get back to my research now. Thank you for your conversation." His eyes returned to *Anacalypsis*.

The questioner rose and looked hard at the books scattered over the bench, feeling indignant without knowing why. He turned and walked toward the cluster of his cronies in the distance, working their little crowd of the bereft and the needful.

Nobody else moved. The sun poured down its warmth while birds swooped from branches to grass. Kids squealed. A faraway game hurled occasional faint shouts into the air.

It might have stayed like that all afternoon, him reading on the bench, the park pulsing with life. But the man returned, stepping right up to him and looming.

"My brother. Why don't you come and talk with us? My colleagues and I would like to hear your views about what's wrong with this planet. Maybe people need to hear what you have to say."

"I know they do, but do you think they want to?"

"Why don't we find out?"

"All right. I'll come. Help me with my books." They picked up a stack each and walked toward the cluster of white-shirted Black Muslims.

He wasted no time on introductions and stepped up on a park bench. "You want to hear what I have to say?" His voice was high and quiet. "You want to know what the Negro needs to do to improve the conditions of the Negro's life today? I'll tell you." He had the attention of the Muslim brothers, but of others, too. People stopped and gathered, intrigued by the quiet conviction of the man in the green pants and fez.

"Start with the Bible. I know many of you have read it your whole life—since you were a child—or heard it read at home and in church. It's the word *of* God, you've been told. But what kind of word *is* God? I can tell you: it's a bad word, one of the worst in the language. The God of the Bible created a world of death. How can he be anything but a bad God? How can you believe that his Bible is true?"

The size of the crowd grew as he talked, drawn in by his scandalous words, a few older folks stopping by, and then a family or two, a couple of Presbyterians from up the path.

"You been reading a bad Bible, a Bible of death. Is death your salvation? How can you believe it? How can you believe your creator wants you to die in order to live? You been taught to read the Bible in a way that makes you love death more than life. Who did that to you? Who taught you such things? Who keep you ignorant from the truth and the life that comes with it?"

Someone shouted, "The church! It's the church taught us how to read the Bible." Excitement grew and so did the crowd. This man was saying outrageous things.

"That's right. It's the church." He pitched his voice to the bystanders. "The leaders of your church want you to die. And you will if you stay ignorant—of the truth, of the true way to read the Bible."

"Who you call ignorant?"—"I know the Bible. I know Jesus."—"Praise Jesus."

The people roiled. Their numbers doubled, trebled.

"I say you're ignorant. And if you stay that way, you gonna die. You won't get credit for livin'. Look at you, don't nobody care what you done, how you lived. You're nothin'. You say Jesus cares, and maybe he does, but think about this. Jesus didn't get no credit when he was alive. He worked wonders, performed miracles—and what credit did he get? Crucifixion and the cross, death for his trouble."

Turbulence: the more people listened, the more they convulsed.

"Jesus saves!"—"They killed Jesus."—"God so loved the world . . .'"

"You folks just like Jesus. You don't get no recognition, you see. The one who came here and wasn't recognized, who healed the sick and raised the dead, was the one they call Jesus."

"Yeah!"—"Say it!"

"But who was it didn't recognize Jesus? It was *you* that would not recognize him. And you are over here in America and you gettin' no recognition for your good works 'cause he didn't get nothin' for his. Like Jesus. You get no credit and you the ones who refused to recognize him!"

"What?" The crowd, a hundred strong, began to seethe in confusion. "Who killed Jesus?"

"You killed Jesus. You the Jews who killed him and you the person they killed. And that's why you sufferin' today. You refused to recognize Jesus. So you not recognized today."

"But Jesus is my personal savior."—"He loves me."—"He died for my sins!"

By now a couple hundred crowded in to listen, maybe more. A fierce resistance was boiling up, anger in search of a target.

"You ignorant of the truth. And until you admit you didn't recognize Jesus, you won't be recognized by nobody, not the white man, not no one."

A chorus: "No!"

"Until you take responsibility for failing to recognize Jesus and condemning him to death, you will suffer likewise. And nobody will help you."

"No!"

"You must take responsibility."

Five hundred black people milled around as this man preached. They jumped up and down and shook the earth, shouting, "No, no, no, no!"

"Yes. It was you, all right." The crowd twisted and bucked. Fists clenched and teeth gnashed. The Black Muslims looked one to another in alarm, astounded.

"Brother," shouted the one who had invited him to speak. "We ain't never seen black folks worked up like this. You might be in danger. We don't know what's happening."

"The *truth* is what's happening," he said. But the Muslims gathered his books and, linking arms and beckoning him down from the bench, led him across Grand Boulevard and out of Washington Park. The crowd howled and clawed the air and slowly dispersed.

And the sun spilled its glory over the earth.

Washington Park runs from Chicago's Fifty-First Street to Sixtieth, ten blocks of green space bounded on the east by Cottage Grove Avenue and on the west by Grand Boulevard, now called Martin Luther King Drive. It lent life on the South Side a little openness and buffered the University of Chicago from the harder world due west. In the fifties it attracted people of all kinds, including those interested in debating problems and imagining solutions, whether religious, political, or just plain visionary. Sun Ra took pleasure in the scene, as he would later remark: "When I was in Chicago I would always listen to black people talk different things. I was in the park when the Black Muslims were talking. Everybody would be in that park. It was really wonderful in Chicago. Everybody was expressing their opinions. A true democracy in the black community."[2] Sun Ra was a full participant in that true democracy. A manila envelope marked "One of Everything," found years later among memorabilia in Abraham's house on the eve of its demolition, attests to his activism.[3] It contained a sheaf of typed papers, broadsheets meant for public distribution or declamation. Later edited by John Corbett and published as *The Wisdom of Sun Ra: Sun Ra's Polemical Broadsheets and Streetcorner Leaflets*, these homemade handbills illuminate Sun Ra's whole creative and political enterprise.

They are screeds from the sun. They bespeak a searing, searching intelligence devoted to transforming the lives of Chicago's blacks. In keeping with Thmei's political theosophy, the broadsheets offer a corrective to black reality grounded in esoteric reading and occult wisdom. They're maniacally typed, often in capitals, with occasional annotations in pencil or ink that, as Corbett suggests, probably indicate cues for oral delivery.[4] Ellipses and exclamation points dot the pages like secret code. Sun Ra took Thmei's wisdom directly to the people in Washington Park. He had considered himself a teacher since the year he spent as an education major at Alabama A&M. His tone shows him to have been a prophet, too, willing to declaim unpopular truths in the service of a higher vision. He uses a host of strategies to advance Thmei's agenda in the broadsheets: denunciation, shock, mockery, humor, wordplay, textual analysis, biblical midrash, and "equation" (in his idiosyncratic sense of the term—"THE MATHEMATICS OF WORDS," as he calls it).[5] Some broadsheets he signs in various ways, including "THE SUN," "RA," "We—Ra," "Raphael," or "EL RA." In Washington Park, Sun Ra became the public voice of Thmei's radicalism, calling South Side blacks to forsake ignorance and embrace a wisdom that might renovate their world.

However incendiary in tone, the broadsheets advance a surprisingly coherent if unusual vision for black uplift. Even Sun Ra's unorthodoxy is unorthodox. Sites shows how the broadsheets inhabit a legacy of antinomian critique that runs back through the American jeremiad to the English dissenting tradition of William Blake, Christopher Smart, and, before them, John Milton.[6] Indeed, if there is one artist whose vision most closely approaches Sun Ra's, it is Blake. Both men responded to a reality of rationalized confinement with a vision of creative excess. Both grounded their critique of that reality in a radical rereading of the Bible. And both praised art as a means of transforming the world, turning death into life. Like Blake, Sun Ra and Thmei understood the Bible to constitute the ideological superstructure of contemporary Western society, with the difference that Thmei directed its critique most pointedly toward *black* society, whites having gone the way of secular rewards, consumerist consolations, and imperialist dreams. "THE FOUNDATION OF THE WORLD IN WHICH NEGROES LIVE IS THE BIBLE"; this claim comes from a broadsheet bearing the title "*humpty dumpty*."[7] If blacks live in misery, and if the Bible is the foundation of their world, then it might be worth turning a critical eye on holy scripture.

And Sun Ra does precisely this, mercilessly. "THE BIBLE IS A DANGEROUS BOOK," he announces, "A DESTRUCTIVE FORCE PREPARED TO ENSNARE THOSE WHO HATE UNDERSTANDING OF WISDOM."[8] The problem lies not with the Bible per se but with how its readers interpret it: "MISINTERPRETATION OF THE BIBLE IS THE CAUSE OF THE WOES TROUBLING THE WORLD TODAY."[9] Contemporary social suffering, then, originates in the misinterpretation of scriptural truth. The critique here is troubling, for if the Bible is the foundation of black life, then blacks who read and teach it innocently appear to be implicated in their own subjugation. This point might be the hardest for Sun Ra's listeners to swallow, but it's fundamental to his vision. Blacks must accept some responsibility for their condition, in this instance for failing to plumb the Bible's true wisdom. "I MUST TELL YOU THAT THE BIBLE HAS MADE A FOOL OUT OF YOU, IT IS WRITTEN IN AN IGNORANT MANNER TO DIS-COURAGE YOU FROM READING IT."[10] The Bible is secret rather than sacred scripture, and blacks have been bamboozled by a long line of gullible readers, a tough judgment to pass on a Christian tradition that for many conjures the hope of salvation and social uplift. But Sun Ra's position promises hope of another kind: "THE PROPER INTERPRETA-TION OF THE BIBLE IS THE TRUTH, THE TRUTH WHICH WILL AUTOMAT-ICALLY FREE NEGROES"—and not only Negroes "BUT THE WORLD."[11] And what is this truth? What is the secret meaning of the Bible? The answer is simple, but only to those capable of interpreting truly: "AT THIS TIME IT IS DANGEROUS FOR ANY PERSON WHO IS TEACHING THE BIBLE NOT TO KNOW ITS SECRET MEANING, NAMELY, THE MEANING OF DEATH."[12]

For Sun Ra and his associates, the Bible is a book of death, at least as the text is traditionally interpreted. Thmei's target here is the black church, the institutional authority that sanctions a lethal misreading of scripture. It is the church and not the state that most directly and ruinously regulates black life: "THE FOUNDATION OF THE NEGRO IS AT PRESENT HIS CHURCH AND THE CHURCH IS RULING NOT THE GOVERN-MENT NOR THE EDUCATIONAL SYSTEM. THE NEGRO IS A PRODUCT OF THE CHURCH BECAUSE ALL OF HIS HOPES ARE PLACED IN THE WORDS OF HIS SPIRITUAL LEADERS."[13] Thmei and Sun Ra direct attention away from traditional targets of critique—whites and their various regimes of subjugation—and toward authorities that blacks can address directly and maybe dethrone. Little wonder, then, that neither Martin Luther King Jr. nor Elijah Muhammad would provide much inspira-tion for their radicalism. For Thmei, organized forms of black religion, whether Christian or Muslim, have failed to promote black life. On the contrary, they trade in death as the only means of salvation.

Sun Ra calls Christian doctrine a "monstrous creed." He accuses his audience of spreading it like a contagion: "Why are you telling the world that Death is the way to salvation?"[14] Such a belief makes Jesus a corpse to be swallowed, a human sacrifice to be mimed, a cadaverous dead god hawking a lethal salvation. "Jesus was the firstborn of the dead," Sun Ra declares.[15] A dead god is no more use than a dead man. What blacks fail to acknowledge in worshiping this dead divinity is their own responsibility for killing him: "The Black man is in torment and misery everywhere on the face of this earth. Why? Simply this. You are accountable to God for the death of Jesus."[16] To believe that the death of Jesus is the way to salvation is to kill him all over again— in the name of righteousness and truth.

Sun Ra advances an unusual historical explanation for this confusion. Christianity, he says, has stood divided into two churches since the Crucifixion, churches distinguished by their differing interpretations of Christ's death. One descends from Caiaphas, the Jew who wanted Jesus dead for political reasons. The other descends from Peter, the Gentile who defended Jesus at the risk of his own life. The former promotes "THE SALVATION DOCTRINE," which identifies death with heavenly reward.[17] Sun Ra prefers the church of Peter, a church of life where the simple force of living *is* salvation. Black suffering began with this division of churches: "THE NEGRO CHURCH ITSELF IS THE BEGINNING OF SEGREGATION AND SEPARATION."[18] Vanquishing "the salvation doctrine," then, might put an end to the belief that death offers a consolation for life's misery. Far preferable for Sun Ra and Thmei Research is the impossible imperative of *life*, life as its own salvation, here and now: "WE MUST SET OUR MINDS TO ACHIEVE THE ABSOLUTE IMPOSSIBLE . . . WE MUST CONQUER DEATH. IT IS OF THE UTMOST IMPORTANCE THAT WE CONQUER DEATH HERE AND NOW. WE MUST TAKE THE FIRST STEP FORWARD BY MAKING LIFE REAL."[19] Life against death: Thmei's social agenda is as simple, as harrowing, as impossible as that. But of course the possible has already been tried. Sun Ra urges his black listeners to recant familiar interpretations of the Bible in favor of a living wisdom.

Why should they reject something so historically central to their culture? Because "THE NEGRO RESURRECTED FROM HIS STATE OF IGNORANCE IS THE ONLY MEANS OF SALVATION LEFT FOR AMERICA."[20] On this view, ignorance is the condition most detrimental to contemporary blacks, and Sun Ra rails across many broadsheets against their acquiescence: "IGNORANCE IS THE CAUSE OF THE NEGROES PLIGHT IN AMERICA."[21] Sometimes his indignation lapses into rough humor, as in a broadsheet entitled *"wake up! wake up! wake up!"* when he proclaims that "NEGROES ARE DEFINITELY THE PEOPLE OF THE BIBLE BECAUSE THE BIBLE STATES THAT WISDOM WOULD DIE WITH THESE PEOPLE AND THE AMERICAN NEGRO IS THE DUMB DORA AND THE BIGGEST ASS ON THE PLANET EARTH."[22] Bible-thumping blacks cannot perceive their own alienation from biblical wisdom. Their ignorance begins in a lack of self-awareness, which Thmei's street-corner activism tries to correct.

To foster this self-awareness, the broadsheets advance a new genealogy for American blacks and with it a new history to transform their understanding of themselves. Their ancestors obviously came from Africa, but according to the broadsheets, not its western coast, as has been traditionally believed. The truth (of which blacks remain ignorant) is more surprising: "IN FACT VERY FEW NEGROES KNOW THAT THE PEOPLE THAT MOSES LED OUT OF EGYPT WERE BLACK-BROWN PEOPLE: THE ANCESTORS OF THE AMERICAN NEGRO."[23] This unsettling account has the historical appeal of associating American blacks with both Israel and Egypt, grafting Judaism onto a more ancient, austere—yet still African—past. In a move now familiar from Rastafarianism, Thmei insists on the blackness of the early Jews: "TO THIS VERY DAY THE RULER OF ETHIOPIA IS KNOWN AS THE LION OF THE TRIBE OF JUDAH, THIS TITLE IS A HEREDITARY ONE AND IT POINTS TO THE FACT THAT THE ORIGINAL JEWS WERE BLACK AND THAT THE JEWS IN THE BIBLE WERE BLACK."[24] On Thmei's account, the ancient Israelites were black people, and their culture owes a debt to Egypt: "these people called negro, are the flesh and blood descendants of the original ISRAEL."[25] American blacks remain ignorant of this history.

This account enjoys a twofold appeal. First, it positions blacks at the beginning of a culture—one based on Judeo-Christian underpinnings—that the white West claims for its own. White beliefs have black beginnings. Second and perhaps more important, it dislocates American black identity from whiteness as its defining condition, a condition that would remain in place as long as slavery and the slave trade continued to define what it means to be black in contemporary society. Thmei's proposed history as Sun Ra declaims it recovers for blacks a noble and unfathomable antiquity (passing through Israel and back to Egypt) that mitigates centuries of subjugation by whites. The broadsheets define being black not *against* being white but *beyond* it, a situation Sun Ra would later describe using the term "outer blackness." American blacks must no longer think of themselves as a subjugated people. Their history antedates that of whites and Western culture and in fact gave rise to that culture (as well as its horrors) through the errant destiny of the Jews. To remain ignorant of this history is to accept a legacy of subordination as a defining truth—in fact, to remain complicit in that legacy by failing to acknowledge (or imagine) an alternative.

From the perspective of this legacy of subordination, American blacks amount to very little. In a broadsheet bearing the date (typed in reverse) 11–14–1955 and signed "WE-RA," Sun Ra provides a surprising answer to the question, "Does the Bible contain anything about the Negro?"

> Yes. Jesus said, "Let the Negro bury the Negro." At least that is what he said in the original Greek Version of the New Testament. But according to Genesis C and G are interchangeable and for this reason the words of Jesus also reads [*sic*], "Let the Negro bury the Necro." . . . In present day language, the sentence just quoted reads: "Let the dead bury the dead." [. . .] Unfortunately for the Negro the word Negro means dead body.[26]

Unfortunate indeed. This passage is pure Sun Ra, from the bogus but provocative etymology to the demand that blacks take responsibility for transforming their lives. In scriptural terms, he says, blacks are already dead. In racial terms, they are nothing at all.

Playing mirthfully in another broadsheet with the phrase "Spodee O-dee," made famous by the blues guitarist and songwriter Stick McGhee's 1949 bowdlerized version of his song "Drinkin' Wine," Sun Ra runs it backward to make a remarkable discovery: "SPOITHE-OITHE is EHTIOPS. ETHIO-ETHIOPS. . . . (read it backwards). [. . .] ETHIOPS is the true identity of the American negro."[27] Even popular music, it seems, contains wisdom to edify black Americans, if only they have ears to hear it. In a related broadsheet, he pursues this insight further, tracking sound associations to a disturbing conclusion: "ETHIOPS IS OUDE

. . . OIHTE . . . OIHTE IS HOITE . . . . . HOOTE . . . . HOUT . . . . NOTHING. I DON'T GIVE A GOOT MEANS "I DON'T GIVE AN ETHIOPS" . . . ETHIOPS ARE NOTHING. NEGROES ARE NOTHING BECAUSE THEY ARE ALL NATIONS. ALL NATIONS ARE AS NOTHING TO GOD."[28] Sun Ra assaults conventional rationality and the bigotry it sustains through willfully associating sounds and substituting signs. The multimillennial African heritage of contemporary blacks comes to nothing if it yields only a fashionable nationalism. Nations mean nothing from a spiritual perspective, and from a cultural perspective, blacks don't even exist: "NEGROES ARE NOTHING . . . . . there is no such thing as a negro therefore negroes are symbolical of nothing . . [. . .] *there is a common expression 'A nigger ain't*—[shit]. *Less than that is nothing. Zero.*"[29]

Fade to black.

Sun Ra will exploit this empty status in his later poetry, myth, and music, attributing a positive content to "nothing" that associates it with infinity. In the broadsheets, he anticipates this move by pondering yet another name for "negro": "STOP! LOOK! LISTEN! WHAT PEOPLE ON EARTH CALL THEMSELVES SPOOKS? WHAT PEOPLE CALL THEMSELVES SPOOKS? IN WHAT COUNTRY DO SPOOKS DWELL IN WHAT COUNTRY DO THE SPOOKS DWELL? . . . IN AMERICA OF COURSE."[30] Blacks may be nothing, but they call themselves spooks, and in doing so, they unknowingly affirm a richer life than America allows them: "NEGROES ARE SPOOKS (SPIRITUAL PEOPLE). AND THERE ARE NO LAWS IN THE CONSTITUTION GUARANTEEING THE EQUALITY OF SPOOKS (SPIRITUAL BEINGS) TO MEN WHO ARE CREATED EQUAL. A SPOOK IS NOT A CREATION NEITHER IS A SPIRIT. ACCORDING TO THE DICTIONARY, SPIRITUAL MEANS IMMATERIAL, UNIMPORTANT, DISEMBODIED. WHITE PEOPLE KNOW THAT GOD IS A SPOOK."[31] Negroes = spooks = spirits = god. Listen to the words. Follow the equations. American blacks are spirits, and in this they incarnate a heritage leading back from their current subjugation through Israel, Ethiopia, Egypt, ultimately to the Creator. Blacks are NOT created equal. "EQUALITY IN A WORLD OF THIS KIND IS EQUALITY WITH CONFUSION."[32] They are spirits. Their better life lies elsewhere. In spiritualizing black experience—without recourse to scriptural authority—Thmei and Sun Ra announce a radicalism as ideologically extreme as it is spiritually absolute. Spooks shall inherit the earth.

But only if they heed Sun Ra's pronouncements and exchange ignorance for wisdom. To the question, "How can one stop being a Negro?" Sun Ra answers, "By the simple act of studying and understanding true life-giving wisdom."[33] Or again: "ONLY WISDOM OF THE FUTURE CAN SAVE THIS UNFORTUNATE RACE CALLED NEGRO."[34] Sun Ra's prophecy, this wisdom of the future, answers the death and nothing that blacks endure with an eschatological devotion to life: "It is time that you seek life not a life after death, but a real and true life here and now."[35] But how? How might life be made real, here and now, for South Side blacks? The answer for Thmei and Sun Ra is simply, audaciously, to create. Not religion, not politics, but culture offers the best means to transform a world of death into life: "WE MUST MAKE LIFE BEAUTIFUL. WE MUST CHANGE EARTH FROM THE HELL THAT IT IS AND MAKE IT THE HEAVEN THAT GOD INTENDED."[36]

This stress on beauty, on its almost apocalyptic potential, sets Thmei's radicalism off from most contemporary black activism. Here is resistance at its most creative, aiming at neither assimilation nor revolution but wholesale reinvention of reality. In a broadsheet entitled *"what must negroes do to be saved?*," Sun Ra describes Thmei's program for political activism as creative resistance. He begins by denouncing the complacency of black leadership: "NEITHER THE NAACP NOR THE NEGRO CHURCH HAS DONE ANYTHNG TO TEACH THE NEGRO AN APPRECIATION OF BEAUTY."[37] Nor does all the contemporary talk of brotherhood do much to make that beauty a reality: "SUCH A REALITY CAN BECOME REAL ONLY IF APPROACHED FROM THE POINT OF CULTURE AND ART."[38] Culture and art are the true means of Sun Ra's activism, and beauty becomes his index of a better world: "THE LOVE OF BEAUTY IS THE BEGINNING OF WISDOM."[39] So necessary is this commitment to creating beauty that relations between races depend on it utterly: "IF NEGROES WANT TO BE EQUAL TO WHITE PEOPLE THEY MUST PROVE THAT THEY ARE EQUAL BY PRODUCING SOMETHING BEAUTIFUL."[40] Not politics, not morality, but only art asserts equality. Thmei's radicalism turns art into activism.

Perhaps the most surprising aspect of such a stance, however, is its racial agenda: "I DO NOT APPROVE OF LEADERS WHO CAN NOT WIN THE

FRIENDSHIP OF WHITE PEOPLE BY CULTURE AND SINCERE GOODWILL."[41] The reason: "ART KNOWS NO COLOR LINE IN ITS HIGHER FORMS."[42] Sun Ra will not always appear so clear an advocate of a postracial reality, but art, culture, and the beauty they create nevertheless open a pathway to unknown worlds where black and white merge into a greater chromaticism. "THE TRUTH WILL FREE NOT ONLY NEGROS BUT THE WORLD."[43] Thmei's activism and Sun Ra's prophetic message begin with blacks on Chicago's South Side but open up to include all: "Proper wisdom is enlightment. It is the LIGHTNING that will ENLIGHTENEN THE WORLD."[44] Not enlightenment but *enlightment* will *enlightenen* the world. Sun Ra works old words in new ways to make space for better wisdom.

It would be a mistake, however, to conclude that Thmei took rapprochement with whites as a goal of its activism. On the contrary, it advocated black art for blacks' sake in the effort to transform the South Side from a racial death row to a place of life and beauty. Sun Ra betrays few illusions on the subject of black subjugation: "Negroes are in the low places," he says unapologetically; "that is what white people mean when they say for a Negro to stay in his place. They mean stay in your 'low' place."[45] Thmei's radicalism, however cultural its aims and artistic its means, sought to redress the wrongs blacks have suffered and continue to suffer in a white world. Sun Ra puts the point more pungently in an interview conducted much later: "Now white people telling black people, stay in your place. Sure, but where is that place? So now I have to get a place for them other than the cemetery."[46] Thmei's cultural activism and Sun Ra's creative resistance offer ways to resuscitate the dead. In Thmei's view, the South Side is one big cemetery. Blacks deserve a better place—to live. Sun Ra devoted the energy of his activism—his research, writing, and preaching in Washington Park—toward that simple if visionary prospect. Blacks must create a better world.

7

ARKESTRA

Thmei's street-corner activism, however strident, remained limited to the audience Sun Ra could gather on any given day during a stint in the park. Thmei needed a public address system, a means of spreading its message of building a better world through culture and art. Or maybe a medium that was the message, art that built the better world it announced. For Sun Ra, music was that art, a creative medium that could challenge reality and offer something better in the process: a new sound, a progressive sensibility, a bold promise that however ugly the world might be, a more beautiful one awaited those adventurers who could feel and respond to music's call. In the late forties and early fifties, Sun Ra devoted much of his creativity toward arranging the music of others, first the Dukes of Swing and then the Red Saunders Orchestra, both regulars at Club DeLisa. But he created his own sounds, too, as his private recordings reveal.[1] Sometimes these recordings would feature only himself on piano or organ; sometimes they included other musicians, too, among them the bassist Wilbur

Ware and the alto saxophonist John Jenkins.[2] Sun Ra's hunger for new sounds inspired a taste for unusual instruments and new technologies, including the celeste (a keyboard linked to hammers striking graduated metal bars), the Solovox (an early electronic keyboard), the electric piano (Sun Ra was the first jazz musician to play one on a record), and the latest in recording equipment (iron oxide tapes soon replaced the Sound Mirror's delicate paper). Create and innovate: Sun Ra's musical ambitions beautifully complemented Thmei's program of cultural activism.

Realizing those ambitions would require a big band. Sun Ra knew what a big band could do. He had heard many of them perform in Birmingham when he was younger. "The music they played," he once remarked, "was a natural happiness of love. [. . .] It was unmanufactured avant-garde, and still is."[3] The phrase "unmanufactured avant-garde" communicates Sun Ra's sense that when such music *happens*, it moves everything forward in a way that improves life more than just musically:

> In the Deep South, the black people were very oppressed and were made to feel like they weren't anything, so the only thing they had was big bands. Unity showed that the black man could join together and dress nicely, do something nice, and that was all they had. . . . So it was important for us to hear big bands.[4]

Big bands brought a sense of dignity and achievement to black life. For ten years (it must have seemed a lifetime earlier), Sun Ra led the Sonny Blount Orchestra, a twelve-piece outfit regarded by many as the best swing band in Alabama and staffed by players since inducted into the Alabama Jazz Hall of Fame.[5] It's a shame they never recorded, but southern territory bands were hardly fodder for record-industry profits. The Sonny Blount Orchestra provided a prototype for the kind of band Sun Ra would assemble in Chicago, with the added benefit of Thmei's activist agenda to enhance its capacity for improving black life.[6]

Sun Ra's new band would advance Thmei's agenda of black uplift, building a better world through music. New sounds would open new prospects for black culture and black people, transforming everyday life by the measure of unprecedented beauty. The ensemble would be both musically and socially progressive. It would be a working band, playing spaces that provided solace to South Side blacks, the lounges, bars, and clubs where music, booze, and dancing could conjure joy in a dreary world. Sites nicely describes the advantage of directing social activism into musical performance: "Operating musically in this black cosmopolitan milieu—the South Side of musical clubs, taverns, and community dance halls—reconfigured the combative political rhetoric of the broadsheets into a more slyly coded utopian appeal."[7] In this way, entertainment can become a vehicle for radical activism. A tune that inspires joy can also convey a sense of uplift, promise, and possibility. By coding political messages as intimate feelings, music can turn confrontation into consolation, confinement into release. It performs the possibilities it promotes, making the world feel like a better place, at least for a time. Thmei and Sun Ra were not the first to make music into a means of creative resistance and social transformation, but few other musicians (let alone political reformers) have invested as much hope in its effects as they did. In a world desperately in need of improvement, music might achieve what politics and religion could not: a wholesale change in the way people live that opens reality to wisdom and beauty.

It would take a special kind of musician to pursue this dream musically. Sun Ra's earliest gathering of kindred spirits was a small group he called the Space Trio, which served as a laboratory for his early experiments in sound. Laurdine "Pat" Patrick, a gifted musician who would remain a lifelong Sun Ra stalwart, played baritone sax in the group, with Robert Barry on drums, sometimes replaced by Bugs Hunter. A lone recording of Sun Ra and Patrick from a 1952 rehearsal provides some idea of the music that the trio aspired to play: standards with Patrick's sinewy baritone blowing over peculiar harmonies.[8] The Space Trio didn't play gigs, but according to Sun Ra, that wasn't its immediate aim: "It was for my own edification and pleasure because I didn't find being black in America a very pleasant experience, but I had to have something, and that something was creating something that nobody owned but us."[9] The allusion in the last phrase to Thelonious Monk's description of bebop shows how carefully Sun Ra targeted his own music to a black audience.[10] With Thmei's support, he would broaden its scope and compose for a big band, an ensemble large enough to both emulate the great black swing bands and exemplify collaborative black creativity aspiring to something larger than segregated life.

Sun Ra called this band the "Arkestra." People in Alabama pronounced the word "orchestra" that way, he claimed. But the name had the appeal of placing mirror images of "Ra" before and behind the sound "kist," which he believed meant "sun's gleam" in Sanskrit, forming a triple solarity.[11] When assembling the group, Sun Ra sought younger Chicago players, many of them associated with the exceptional music program run by the legendary Captain Walter Dyett at South Side's DuSable High School. Dyett, a model of disciplined creativity, inspired a generation of Chicago's greatest musicians. Pat Patrick studied under him, as did the gifted tenor saxophonist John Gilmore, who was born in Summit, Mississippi, but moved to Chicago as a child. After finishing high school, Gilmore served in the air force until 1953, when he joined Earl Hines's band, earning a reputation around Chicago for inventive phrasing and hard blowing. Sun Ra sensed his coming greatness and invited him on board. Personnel shifted frequently in the early Arkestra, not the least because Sun Ra's music was difficult and his rehearsals were demanding. He preferred younger players so that he could teach them the score. Early members included Dave Young and Art Hoyle on trumpet; Julian Priester on trombone; James Scales on alto sax; Johnny Thompson and occasionally Von Freeman on tenor; Charles Davis on baritone sax; Richard Evans, Wilbur Green, Victor Sproles, or Ronnie Boykins on bass; and Jim Herndon playing timpani.[12]

By late 1954 the Arkestra was well enough rehearsed to begin gigging, although its personnel continued to shift. An ad in the *Chicago Defender* for a late-December appearance at Duke Slater's Vincennes Lounge announces "LE SONYR RA & His Combo," featuring Robert Barry on drums, Earl Demus on bass, and "Swing" Lee O'Neil on tenor sax. An accompanying photograph features O'Neil so prominently that he looks like the combo's leader.[13] The band soon had a stable lineup that would include Patrick, Gilmore, Evans, and Barry, but others came and went. The Vincennes Lounge gig lasted six weeks, and with Alton Abraham acting as its agent, the Arkestra began to land work elsewhere, too: Shep's Playhouse for five weeks and an extended stint at the Grand Terrace, which ran ads featuring "Sun Ra, His Electric Piano And Band."[14] The year 1955 saw the Arkestra becoming established as a regular feature of the Chicago club scene, a status conducive to the Thmei agenda of advancing social change through cultural expression. Sun Ra was still active in Washington Park, but clubs and lounges now became places where he could practice what he preached, performing music with the Arkestra that fulfilled his unique prescription for black uplift: "WE MUST MAKE LIFE BEAUTIFUL."[15]

To Sites's description of the early Arkestra as "part avant-garde unit, part novelty act," another quality must be added: part activist organization.[16] The Arkestra was playing music to make a difference both aesthetically and socially. Sun Ra would remind them of it in rehearsal: "You look out at the world and you say, 'Something's wrong with this stuff.' Then you get so mad you can play it on your instrument. Play some fire on it. If you're not mad at the world you don't have what it takes."[17] Rehearsal for Sun Ra involved much more than reading charts and counting time. Practically speaking, it was a way of life. It was not unusual for the Arkestra to practice for eight hours, break to play a gig, and then return to their rehearsal space for even more practice. Sun Ra preached to his players like he did to his listeners in Washington Square. Rehearsals came laced with wisdom—about Egypt, space exploration, infinity—without which the Arkestra's music would have been just so much empty noise. He didn't require belief from his musicians; he asked only for understanding, so that they could feel where the music came from, how it should sound, and what it should do: "The world lacks for warriors," he would say. "You have to prepare yourself accordingly."[18]

Under Sun Ra's leadership, the Arkestra mounted a joyous musical assault on segregation in Chicago—or anywhere else. Szwed calls the band a "family" over which Sun Ra presided "paternalistically but benignly." Regarding Sun Ra's authority over his players, Pat Patrick once remarked wryly, "we're nobodies with the master."[19] This master's demands came in the service of a vision for bettering the world that began in demonstrating what blacks can do and how they should do it. In an interview conducted years later, Sun Ra communicated his sense of the Arkestra's purpose with arresting words:

> Well, it's demonstrating that some people in the form of men can stick together, [. . .] and they're not with me because I promised them anything, because I always said they're "in the Ra jail." And my jail is the best jail in the world, and they learn things in my jail. And that's what I express: they're in jail, and they're not going anywhere, because they can't . . .[20]

Coming from a man confined for his beliefs as a conscientious objector, the description of the Arkestra as a jail seems disconcerting. But it acknowledges not only confinement as the social condition of contemporary black life but also wisdom as its great compensation. The best jail in the world is the one that provides the opportunity to forsake ignorance and to learn. That's how Patrick later viewed his years with the Arkestra: "Sun Ra brought a lot out of me; he broadened my concept and helped me overcome certain inhibitions about playing. The music came to mean a way of life to me. On the whole, I have had a rare and priceless musical experience, one that you cannot go to school to get."[21]

Specifically, Sun Ra insisted that his players learn discipline. Discipline and precision: these are the watchwords of his music and politics. It may seem surprising, but this great experimentalist, often associated with free jazz, showed no patience for freedom as either an aesthetic or a political ideal. In a 1985 interview he insisted that discipline rules all:

> It's about one minute to midnight for this planet. [. . .] I'm not a politician and I don't believe in equality. And that makes me a

little different. I don't believe in freedom either because I've never had any. I have to work for the Creator whether I want to or not and that's discipline. I have to do like the Sun and the Stars in the sky. They have to be in the right place all the time. That's what I have to be. I don't know what people are talking about when they're talking about freedom. All superior beings have no freedom. They have to be obedient to the Creator. Talk about freedom. Biggest lie I've been told because it can't be you see. No one is free down here. They never have been and, really, they never will be because if they was free they would not choose to die. But since they die they're not free. So I'm talking about discipline you see. That made it kind of difficult for me in particular in this country that's talking about freedom. But I'm talking about discipline.[22]

Discipline was Sun Ra's alternative to all the colorful freedoms in the air during the fifties and the sixties, when the Arkestra was earning and learning its wings. Perhaps a legacy of his own confinement at Marienville, his insistence that such freedoms are illusory directs the focus of his music and politics—his music *as* politics—toward discipline as the means of mastering the creation of beauty under circumstances of constraint. From a cosmological perspective, all things have their place; all movement proceeds under determined impulse. Freedom belongs only to children (or whites) who can't apprehend the forces that regulate their lives. But a disciplined mastery of these forces, a precise recapitulation of the possibilities for creation that inhere within them—these are the great ends Sun Ra tried to cultivate in his musicians through interminable rehearsal. The Arkestra would be the best-disciplined band in show biz.

And it was a biz. The Arkestra could do little to spread the Thmei message of uplift through art and culture if it couldn't attract a crowd. It played music built for pleasure—dancing, drinking, strutting the stuff—mixed with bolder sounds to challenge the open listener. Sometimes described as a hard-bop combo or that elusive thing the bebop orchestra, the Arkestra proved capable of playing an extraordinary range of music. Because most of its players were young, hard bop was the thing they were initially after, the holy grail of hip. But Sun Ra's sound spectrum was too big to be reduced to rhythmic high jinks. Instead, his music encompassed low-register growls and dark harmonies, slithering midrange tones, a panoply of ludic percussion, twangs and squeals and tinkles and wails. Sun Ra, as musicians say, *had big ears*, and everything he heard (real or imagined) found its way into his compositions, from Latin rhythms to broad harmonies to dissonant chromaticism to exotic soundscapes. Little about his music is willfully alienating, however unfamiliar it may feel at first, and the Arkestra's early performances (like later ones, for that matter) mixed standards, bebop tunes, and originals in a manner meant to be conducive to *happiness*. "I don't think about nothin'," he would say later in Helsinki, "but reaching people with impressions of happiness."[23] That's where beauty starts and politics ends. "See, jazz is happiness," Sun Ra said elsewhere, "and you got very few people playing jazz on this planet."[24] The Arkestra's music all tended toward communicating happiness as the best evidence of a better world.

But this is not to say that the music always made for effortless listening. Even early performances challenged audiences with quarter-tone intervals, complex polyrhythms, unconventional tempos, modal scales, and unexpected transitions. This is difficult, inventive work. "The only way anybody could play my music," Sun Ra said, "I'd have to teach them." Hence the perpetual rehearsals. How demanding is his music? It might require a whole new sensorium to play: "I suppose it's the rhythmic feeling. It has sort of a two way thing going. Most jazz will lay over one rhythm, but my music has two, maybe three or four things going, and you have to feel all of them. You can't count it."[25] Music beyond meter: apparently you can feel more than you can know. This predilection for multiplicity (multiple rhythms, multiple tonalities) comes in the service of more than just aesthetic innovation. It advances the spiritual agenda that underwrites Thmei's activism, as Sun Ra makes peculiarly clear: "Superior beings definitely speak in other harmonic ways than the earth way because they're talking something different, and you have to have chord against chord, melody against melody, rhythm against rhythm; if you've got that, you're expressing something else."[26] Something else: that's what the Arkestra's music aspires to, another kind of life, a better world. It's entertainment *spiritualized*.

By the end of 1955, this avant-garde/novelty/activist ensemble was ready to make a bid for wider influence. In late March, Abraham booked Balkan Studios, at 1425 West Eighteenth Street, and the Arkestra recorded a session that yielded its first 45 rpm singles.[27] Although the labels of these and several other early recordings read "Arkistra," the spelling of the band's name settled into the familiar "Arkestra" within the year.[28] The tracks chosen for its first recording offer an accessible but representative introduction to its music. "Super Blonde," a Sun Ra composition, shows off the band's mastery of now-familiar bop conventions. It's a blues progression with the skittery rhythmic head typical of Charlie Parker's compositions. Sun Ra opens with a sly piano chorus before the band takes the jagged melody in unison, a big sound for bebop. The trumpet follows with a solo as first piano and then the other horns comp in chunky, deep phrases, making for bebop with a dark difference. Then the tenor swings for twelve bars, followed by a funky and dissonant series of phrases—sublimated traffic noise, an urban infarction. The piece returns to the trombone playing over a kitsch-cool walking bass, a softly preaching baritone sax, and a flirtatious piano; then it's back to the head, feeling now like an old friend. Pow, out: a carefully composed and disciplined ensemble blues. Two minutes and thirty-nine seconds of pure happiness.

"Soft Talk," a composition by the trombonist Julien Priester, shows off the Arkestra's section work, as the horns harmonize the head and trade phrases à la Ellington in staccato recitative. After a punchy eight-bar intro, it's the standard thirty-two bars more with solos by tenor, trombone, and trumpet. What's most notable is how *composed* this tune feels. There is no simple riffing behind solos; the horns serve up a variety of rhythmic figures and then sit out entirely behind the trombone (it's Priester's tune, after all). The band then returns to that filigreed head. Unadulterated joy! "Super Blonde" and "Soft Talk" announce the arrival in Chicago of an artful ensemble playing to exceptionally high standards of discipline and delight.

If this is politics, then let the revolution begin. In truth, it was already under way in the clubs, lounges, bars, and even rehearsal spaces where the Arkestra played, a revolution less overtly social than cunningly cultural. Sun Ra and this band of creative black men would transform the world through music, making it a better place through disciplined play and superior wisdom. They would harness the force of sound, drive life beyond its limits, and crash reality into the stars.

8

IMMEASURABLE EQUATION

New sounds blew through Sun Ra's head, sounds that exceeded the size and shape of more conventional jazz forms: swing, with its ensemble harmonies; bebop, with its jagged melodies and rhythmic tricks. It would take a lifetime to turn them all into compositions. Sun Ra now had a band of his own to express them freely and to share them with the world. But the sounds were not the whole of it. They chimed with ideas, longings, and visions that had visited him for years. Music was more than music. It stirred a philosophy in his bones, a deep wisdom he would orchestrate—eventually.

Sun Ra had been writing text, too, for quite some time. Words provided another way of expressing his beliefs and visions. While enrolled in teacher's training at Alabama A&M, in Huntsville, he had kept a journal in which he recorded his private thoughts and experiences, including the details of his alien abduction. One afternoon his roommates found it and read it to one another aloud, laughing and jeering mercilessly.[1] He threw his journal into a smoldering ashcan.

He would never again be played for a fool. But he continued to write when the mood descended, mostly poetry, sometimes vatic prose. He considered himself enough of a writer to list poetry among his serviceable skills as a conscientious objector. Although music alone made life livable, his poems helped him survive. They opened a space for spiritual reflection. Over the years, they would pile up to become a kind of user's manual for his compositions, instructions for better listening—and living—in a spiritual key.

It makes sense, then, to approach Sun Ra's poetry as a prelude to his music. The relation between the two bodies of work is as intimate as that between two common registers of the word "composition": a work of words or of sounds. Sun Ra worked in both. His lifelong activity as a writer provides a verbal commentary on a corpus of musical creation that remains utterly unique in jazz history, which typically relies on a tissue of reminiscence, research, and invention to convey a sense of the music's significance. While it would be naïve to read his poems as straightforward explanations of his music, they nevertheless offer slanted insight into its urgent, often strange sounds. His poetry crosses the music at oblique angles, or better, inflects it from within. "My music is words," he writes, "and my words are music."[2]

Sun Ra's words do not script his music. Rather, they recapitulate it in another idiom. Words equate with music, and vice versa, in a manner that communicates an abstract, ultimately spiritual wisdom: "My words are the music and my music *are* the words because it/is of equation is synonym of the Living Being."[3] The reversible phrase "my words are the music" provides an instance of the equation "it/is," which resolves distinctions into identity, a point Sun Ra makes semantically by equating the plural and singular form of the verb "to be." For him such an equation becomes possible only because Living Being underwrites it. Words = music = Being. To examine Sun Ra's poetry, then, is simultaneously to explore music and Being as well: words equating to music equating to spirit. A logic of equation guides the movement of Sun Ra's whole creative corpus. Poems accumulate in a verbal space (also a musical space) that expands to receive them. Over the course of a long career, with the exception of a few early experiments in a confessional mode, Sun Ra displays almost no development as a poet. His poems appear as if written in some deep past or distant future, on stone tablets, perhaps, or a Plutonian polymer. They arrive as if perpetually complete, and even when revised, they read like holograms of a higher world glimpsed *completely* in its scattered shards.

And they are scattered, those poems. Sun Ra's poetry has yet to receive treatment equal to the seriousness with which he wrote it. That seriousness was not lost on its few early proponents. The great progenitor of the Black Arts movement and theorist of black music Amiri Baraka (earlier known as LeRoi Jones) included several examples in the incendiary anthology he edited with Larry Neal, *Black Fire* (1968), and also printed an instance of Sun Ra's prose in his underground newsletter *The Cricket* (1968). A few poems also appeared in the important *Black Umbra* anthology (1967–1968) and even in a commercial collection of black verse entitled *The Poetry of Black America: Anthology of the 20th Century* (1973).[4] Sun Ra's reputation as a poet seems since to have sunk in proportion to his recognition as a musician. Its haphazard "publication" scattered the poetry across a hodgepodge of different media: record jackets, concert brochures, promotional flyers, business cards, and a variety of self-published booklets. Several recent collections from small presses offer gatherings of a corpus that can probably never be completely determined, so cavalier was Sun Ra's approach to publication. Editorially improvisational, these volumes nevertheless make a selection of the poems available to intrepid readers.[5]

The lack of a scholarly alternative leaves a collection whose subtitle gestures toward totality—*The Collected Poetry and Prose*—to serve as the standard edition of Sun Ra's written work. Compiled and edited by James L. Wolf and Hartmut Geerken, *The Immeasurable Equation* includes several essays, some by prominent scholars, that help dispel the confusion this poetry can arouse.[6] But even this edition amounts to little more than the work of earnest amateurs, the bibliographic equivalent of a fan-boy record collection. Sun Ra's poetry awaits serious editing. The near-universal neglect plaguing this singular musician and visionary's writings, which languish in slap-dash editions, attests to the skewed priorities of commercial and academic publishing alike.

Although Sun Ra sought to place his work with mainstream publishers, none would hazard such strange material. Undeterred, Sun Ra self-published his poetry in multiple editions of booklets bearing the cryptic titles *The Immeasurable Equation* and *Extensions Out: The Immeasurable Equation, Vol. II*. A title he used for a related, never-published volume from 1966, "The Magic Lie: Outer Universe Equations," shows how consistently he applied the term "equation" to his poems.[7] He printed the booklets privately and sold them at performances or through the mail.

Sun Ra later defended his decision to publish his poetry himself:

> I had to pay for it myself, 'cause in America, the main publishers said it might as well be written in a foreign language as far as they were concerned. It seemed to be poetry, in a sense. But it's not, it's equations, put in nice forms, just like putting some chocolate on top of it. It was just so strange to them, because of their fixed opinions.[8]

Sun Ra's disdain for a commercial idiom becomes clear to anyone who reads his poems. But note his unexpected assent to the opinion of America's "main publishers." They reject it for sounding as if written in a foreign language.

Rather than contest that opinion, Sun Ra corrects it. What those publishers took to be poetry is actually something else: "equations." The result is not poetry written in a foreign language but language written in a foreign idiom. "Equations put in nice forms"—in this disarmingly simple phrase Sun Ra announces a theory for composing poetry like little else in English, and maybe any other living language, too. The "fixed opinions" of commercial publishers blocked their capacity to perceive or value his poetry in its own terms. In a move deeply characteristic of much that he would create, Sun Ra decided to produce his poems himself, beyond the control of a culture industry blinkered by narrow opinion and guided by invoices. This is DIY meets avant-garde in a poetics of transposition that turns poetry away from traditional forms and toward new ones, "nice ones," forms for transporting people elsewhere.

"There is no place for you to go / But the in or the out. / Try the out": these words would ring out during musical performance in the attempt to provoke that transportation.[9] They provide a helpful motto for his poetry, too. "Try the *out*"; that little phrase goes a long way toward defining (or rather redefining) a poetics that works at purposes contrary to those of traditional verse. *Out* as in exteriority, a movement not inside but outside the self. Sun Ra turns lyric poetry away from personal identity as the ground of literary expression. But *out* as in improvisation, too, a movement not within but beyond chords. Sun Ra moves music past harmonic intervals as the foundation of sonic expression. This conflation of literary and musical connotation proves key to his artistic activity, which reaches beyond traditional forms to explore aesthetic possibilities that exceed them: playing out and beyond, playing *with* the beyond. Many of his admirers come to his music through this outside, his most *out* improvisations opening a door to new sonic possibilities—including his poetry. But *out* names a relationship as much as a movement, a space beyond that relates to forms that precede and propel its opening. It's important therefore not to take exteriority for the sole reference of either Sun Ra's music or his poetry. The relation of both to traditional forms, even where attenuated or transposed, helps situate their movement *out*.

It's difficult to describe this relation, however, which is one reason literary and cultural critics have neglected Sun Ra's poetry. It seems to fall from the heavens (or more likely Saturn) without much reference to terrestrial forms. Sun Ra eschews them; no sonnets, odes, couplets, blank verse, pastorals, or satires for him—though the formal eccentricity of his verse might align him with experimentalists. But he does have forerunners, however distant or indirect. Szwed allies his musical program generally with the tradition of European romanticism, and something similar can be said for his poetry.[10] Its true precursors (not progenitors; that would be overstating their influence) are poets of the British romantic tradition, in particular those prone to cosmological reference and mythic sweep.

William Blake provides an obvious example, one whose importance only increases with Sun Ra's turn to myth as a medium of expression.

Blake's unshakeable devotion to creative autonomy in his own historical moment of revolutionary fervor ("I must Create a System or be
enslav'd by another Mans / I will not Reason and Compare: my business
is to Create") aligns Sun Ra's poetry with a potent tradition of cultural
insurgence.[11] Like Blake, Sun Ra constructed an ideological architecture for his poems that enhances their claims. A myth sustains their
meanings. And like Blake, he worked as an artist outside the industry that would claim his labor. Blake, too, self-published his poetry—
engraving, printing, and illuminating his books by hand; selling them
to friends and fans directly; and living in obscurity for his reward. Sun
Ra took up a similar if not so completely uncompromising position
vis-à-vis the music industry, preferring to produce his most adventuresome music independent of commercial standards. Finally, like
most traditional poets, Blake situated his poems in direct relationship
to music (as the word "lyric" still implies). Sun Ra similarly explored
the affinities of poetry and music. Two of Blake's earliest collections
(*Songs of Innocence* and *Songs of Experience*) ally lyric poetry less with
individual speakers than with the songs they *sing* when speaking, a
relation developed even further by later artists who set those songs
explicitly to music (Allen Ginsberg, for instance, or Greg Brown). The
claim here is not that William Blake's poetry and myth provided direct
inspiration for Sun Ra's; rather, they unfurl a literary backdrop against
which the black musician's work acquires heightened visibility.

The British romantic poet whose work most closely resemblances
Blake's, Percy Bysshe Shelley, also offers an instructive corollary. Shelley shares with Sun Ra a less systematic approach to myth than Blake's,
manifest in a tendency to reverse inherited narratives rather than create new ones out of whole cloth. Shelley's most revered poem, *Prometheus Unbound* (1819), mounts a revisionist retelling of the Greek
myth of Prometheus, who filched fire to assist a suffering humanity and was rewarded with perpetual punishment (chained to a rock
with a raven pecking at his liver). In Shelley's hands, this old myth of
imperial indignation and curse becomes a new cosmo-drama of cultural insurgence and transformation. With unspeakable ease, Prometheus unbinds his tormentor's chains (as much his own), ushering

in new worlds of interplanetary music where stars and comets sing songs of celestial blessing. Shelley also proves a revealing precursor to Sun Ra at the level of poetic language. Compared to other poets writing in English, Shelley crafted poetry of unprecedented abstraction, not merely avoiding the concrete language typical of traditional poetry but willfully exhausting it in an effort to communicate something higher, more mystical, abstract. An instructive instance occurs in his poem "To a Skylark," where Shelley compares the song of a skylark ("bird thou never wert") to a series of sensory splendors until, all metaphors failing to convey its beauty, the song becomes a vehicle for the beyond ("Better than all measures / Of delightful sound").[12] Such an instance of poetic language as functional abstraction renders Sun Ra's poetry a little less weird, for the measure of Shelley's established achievement shows not only that poetry can serve a spiritual as much as an aesthetic or a political purpose but also that those aims might ultimately coincide. In the most spiritually ambitious poets of the romantic tradition, Sun Ra found, if not ancestors exactly, companions on the road to eternity.

But Sun Ra is a far cry from Shelley or Blake, most obviously in being black. The true tradition for his poetry is that of African American writing. It's disappointing, then, to note the dearth of critical response to his verse. The larger contours of his myth receive occasional notice, but not the poems that communicate them. Aside from prompting a few general comparisons between their content and more familiar African American images (swing low, sweet chariot), they have inspired little enthusiasm, dismissed as the left-handed work of a gifted piano player with two right hands.[13] If not tradition, then perhaps experimentation—maybe Sun Ra's poetry sounds best in the company of a literary avant-garde. But no, the critical study in which one would expect such treatment, Aldon Nielson's *Black Chant*, honors Sun Ra's poetry mostly by omission, preferring to poach a few phrases and titles instead of directly engaging its irremediable strangeness.[14] Sun Ra's most perceptive commentator remains a man who knew and worked with him personally, Amiri Baraka, whose collection of music reviews and essays called *Black Music* still offers the best place to begin a close encounter with the poet from Saturn.

In other words, not literature but music provides African American writing its most living legacy. The poet, essayist, and novelist Nathaniel Mackey, explicating Baraka, puts it this way: black music "serves many black writers as both a model and a highwater mark of black authority, a testament to black powers of self-styling as well as to the ability of such powers to influence others."[15] The higher authority to which Sun Ra's poetry appeals is not that of earlier British poetry or even African American literature but that of black music—the very music that Sun Ra himself composed and promoted. It circulates the dual effects of styling your own life and influencing the lives of others. Mackey offers a third source of that music's usefulness to black writers, its "longstanding status as a symbol of dissent, of divergence from conventional attitudes and behavior." As a "prod and precedent for non-conformist tendencies," black music unleashes a countertradition on the docile demeanors of majority culture, one irreducible to its romantic correlative because its insurgence originates with the most open, vile, egregious, and yet familiar form of human bondage, chattel slavery.[16] Black music inspires black writing by beating manacles into song.

But it is important to notice exactly how Baraka vindicates this music's creative insurgence. In *Black Music* he measures artistic accomplishment with an unapologetically spiritual standard. And what does he mean by spirit? What is its relationship to human life? "We are animate because we breathe. And the spirit which breathes in us, which animates us, which drives us, makes the paths by which we go along our way and is the final characterization of our lives. Essence/Spirit. The final sum of what we call being, and the most elemental. There is no life without spirit."[17] No life without spirit. Baraka's vindication of black music begins with breath, the breath that fills the lungs with air, the body with movement, the whole of human life with spirit. It is the element of true habitation, the medium of highest living. Whatever politics black music might advance, it aspires to realize this spiritual life. Physical life *doubled* by spirit, a double being: "What your spirit is is what you are, what you breathe upon your fellows."[18] It is in this sense of spiritual being—of spiritual breathing—that Baraka describes Sun Ra's vocation as artist: he "is spiritually oriented. He understands the 'future' as an ever widening comprehension of what space is. [. . .] So the future revealed is man explained to himself."[19] Black music explains man to himself, woman to herself, human beings to themselves, but in a spiritual idiom. Any politics that takes music in this sense for its medium will open a space of widening comprehension. So when Baraka writes that Sun Ra's music "seems to take up all available soundspace. All Nature," he celebrates its transformational force.[20] It fills the world with "total sound." It re-creates the world as abstract image: life as Nature, breath as Spirit. Black music spiritualizes reality. Poetry that it inspires will, too.

Here's why this is so. Consider first the strangeness of sound as a medium for artistic expression. Unlike paint, say, or marble, or even printed words, sound is intangible. It lacks substance, which is not to say that it doesn't physically exist, for clearly it *does*: stick strikes drumhead to propagate waves through air to strike a tinier drumhead in the human ear, translating them into nerve impulses that produce the sensory effect known as sound. Remove any part of this material circuit, including a medium for the waves—as could happen in the vacuum of space—and sound can't occur, which is why a small philosophical irony accompanies the common description of Sun Ra's music as "space music." Strictly speaking, space music remains a physical impossibility. Sound waves don't propagate in a vacuum. But Sun Ra would of course delight in the implication that his work achieves the impossible. "Everything that's possible's been done by man," he liked to say, "I have to deal with the impossible."[21] The very impossibility of space music enhances his achievement in having composed it.

More to the point, however, is the fugitive quality of sound. It disperses as it occurs. As sound happens, it passes away. To a large extent, sound lasts only as long as its source persists in making it. Unlike portraits or statues or books, it cannot outlive the moment of its occurrence. Even if recorded—on wax, vinyl, tape, or digital media—sound evanesces when reproduced. Recording achieves only an afterimage of its passing. This fugitive quality is nicely summed up in the word "decay," whose double signification (material rot/sonic fade) allies sound with dissolution. Perhaps better than more substantial media, sound reenacts the tendency for all living things to pass away.[22] *Decay*. As an artistic medium, then, sound introduces a hint of dissolution into the heart of creative activity, an undertone of annihilation that tugs toward silence. At its most extreme, this quality of sound gestures toward the priority of *nothing* as the basis of everything that occurs: music as the herald of *nothing*, the medium of *nothing*, the art of *nothing at all*. Sun Ra deeply appreciated the fugitive quality of sound and would make it basic to his understanding of both music and myth. Witness his poem entitled "The Sound I Hear": "The sounds I hear are nothing / They seem to be but are not." Such sounds dissolve reality, as the next lines attest: "These walls around me are nothing / They seem to be but are nothing."[23] The nothing of heard sounds erodes the walls of the real world.

So the nothing of sound is no simple absence but an active force that transforms the present. Sound offers Sun Ra not the truth of nothingness but an occasion for invention. In a positive sense, if that is possible, it annihilates the present world, as his poem proceeds to insist: "These seeming emotions, so real, so enlightening / That gently speak to me / Are nothing."[24] This untuning touch of sound opens the present to new possibilities. That is its effective force, as the poem's last lines indicate, wherein the present ("yesterday's now") becomes other to itself: "How unlike the days I would to be / How unlike the days I would to horizon-be the future. / But this is the alter-future I speak of. / The alternative is the key."[25] Punning on that little word "key"—a sign of what is necessary for change, the signature for a new musical mode or tonal center—Sun Ra inserts the conditional ("days I would to be") to transform reality through first negation ("how unlike") and then invention ("I would to horizon-be the future"). A new horizon opens a new world and, with it, a new "alter-future," a tomorrow discontinuous with the present and its constitutive past. Sound's *nothing* makes possible the impossibility of an alternative future.

Just where you might expect negation, Sun Ra swings the fugitive quality of sound toward invention of a better world. That's the gist of the following lines from his poem entitled "The Pure Sound":

Listen deeply to this and cogitate:
It is sound . . . . sound . . . sound
That makes the body sound . . . . .
    It is sound . . . . sound . . . . sound
    That makes the sound mind sound
It is sound . . . . sound . . . sound . . . sound
That makes the spirit besound . .
    A sound foundation is the key
    To locked-door fate's eternity . . .
    It is sound and sound again
    That makes the voice of silence heard.[26]

Poetry like this might be hard to read in the spirit of British, American, or even African American literature, but its abstract simplicity conveys with surprising clarity Sun Ra's commitment to the progressive effect of sound. The ritual repetition of the word "sound" lands, so to speak, first on a familiar register signifying health ("the body sound"), then on a double register signifying healthful sonority ("the sound mind sound"), and finally on an abstract register signifying an all-expressive spirituality ("the spirit besound"). The phrase "a sound foundation" assimilates health and strength to the *nothing* that is sound, which in turn is said to unlock an eternity hitherto sealed by fate. In the idiom of this poem, such is the force of "the voice of silence": an absent sound emerging in response to the imperatives "listen" and "cogitate."

This spiritual register of sound becomes central to Sun Ra's poetry, music, and myth. It's crucial to acknowledge this aspect of sound—all the more so in a world deeply skeptical of spirit. That it should thrive at the heart of Sun Ra's music, radiating outward toward other possibilities, is at least partly an effect of music's capacity to communicate at such a high level of abstraction. What, after all, does music communicate? Not, as with language, a set of meanings that, however potentially ambiguous, serve nevertheless to situate listeners in a socially coherent world. Music can certainly serve this linguistic function, as practices as diverse as listening to pop radio, downloading iTunes, and singing hymns or national anthems indicate. But some of its most interesting commentators claim that music can also invoke something higher. The early Friedrich Nietzsche, building on the work of Arthur Schopenhauer, identifies music with Dionysian instincts that celebrate the *deformation* (in pain, suffering, and even death) of life's beautiful forms. Musical decay here turns functional as the aesthetic correlative to suffering, transposing existential pain into joy born of sound. Baraka calls the saxophone, as wielded by Sun Ra's hard-playing peers such as Albert Ayler and Pharoah Sanders, a "howling spirit summoner."[27] They play not just to change the social world but to exceed it: "Oh, when the Saints go marching in." Blues and the abstract truth. Other planes of there. Sounds of transcendence. Sketches of infinity. Music communicates what philosophy only dreams.

Nathaniel Mackey helps explain how. "The world," he writes, "inhabits while extending beyond what meets the eye, resides in but rises above what is apprehensible to the senses."[28] In Mackey's description, the world exceeds our sensory apprehension of it. Sensation limits human understanding to a congeries of impressions. But what about everything that exceeds them, that "rises above the apprehensible"? Immanuel Kant quarantines such excesses, relegating them to the nouminal, the province not of understanding but of the speculative capacity of reason.[29] But Mackey, channeling Nietzsche, might whisper, "Immanuel, study music." His view contradicts Kant's: although apprehended via the sense of hearing, music captures and communicates the truth that lies beyond the world of sensation. It can do so because it operates at a level of abstraction commensurable with Mackey's "beyond" and "above."

Mackey draws upon the work of Viktor Zuckerkandl to describe how music can communicate what exceeds sensation. It all comes down to tone. Music

helps the thing "tone" to transcend its own physical constituent, to break through into a nonphysical mode of being, and there to develop in a life of unexpected fullness. Nothing but tones! As if tone were not the point where the world that our senses encounter becomes transparent to the action of nonphysical forces, where we as perceivers find ourselves eye to eye, as it were, with a purely dynamic reality—the point where the external world gives up its secret and manifests itself, immediately, *as symbol*.[30]

The intangibility of music ("nothing but tones") takes tone beyond matter and mere sensation to "a nonphysical mode of being" that exceeds both, "a life of unexpected fullness." Strangely, however, tone both is and is not "the point" where sensation becomes the means of apprehending the "purely dynamic reality" that exceeds it. Tone *is* that abstraction, but *as if it were not* a means of communicating it. That task seems reserved for the symbol as an immediate manifestation of that dynamic reality.

Tone remains allied to the fugitive quality of music. Here is Zucker-kandl again: "To be sure, tones say, signify, point to—what? Not to something lying 'beyond tones.' Nor would it suffice to say that tones point to other tones—as if we had first tones, and then pointing as their attribute. No—in musical tones, being, existence, is indistinguishable from, is, pointing-beyond-itself, meaning, saying."[31] As sonority beyond itself, tone signifies nothing beyond itself. Not merely its intangibility but more effectively this excess allows tone to communicate abstraction. And without sounding too mystical here, tone *is* what it communicates, which in Sun Ra's sense is nothing. Tone reaches and registers a level of abstraction that exceeds material reality and opens to "the final sum of what we call being," namely, spirit. And it does so as excess. As abstraction. As nothing. As tone science, which is an especially apt phrase Sun Ra uses to describe his music. Born of constraint, black music arises to resist confinement in material reality via an abstract spirituality forever beyond human understanding. As Mackey puts it, "immanence and transcendence meet" in such excessive sounds, "making the music social as well as cosmic, political and metaphysical."[32] Sun Ra's music operates on both registers, but it does so in such a way that the cosmic animates the political. Musical abstraction becomes mundane critique, cosmic tones for mental therapy.

Transfer this aesthetic to Sun Ra's poetry, and some of its weirdness begins to seem strategic, effectively so. Its abstraction turns
functional, the verbal equivalent of tone science. Sun Ra gestures in
that direction when he calls his poems "equations." In mathematics
and elsewhere, an equation is a statement establishing an equivalence
of two expressions. The particularity of each resolves into a higher
unity. By entitling his main book of poems *The Immeasurable Equation*, Sun Ra suggests that his poetry aspires to similar if more spiritual ends: equation beyond reckoning, abstraction as vast as the cosmos. Whereas conventional Western poetry celebrates particulars and
eschews generalizations, his does just the opposite, dissolving differences into abstract equivalence. His poetry of tone presses beyond
perceived distinctions to reveal spiritual prospects that exceed them.
Equations, not ideological convictions, set the terms for the social
agenda Sun Ra pursues through creativity. The purpose of his tone
poetry is to rediscover and resuscitate a life of spirit that exceeds
everyday sensation and its workaday words.

Not literature, then, but mathematics provides a model for this
kind of poetry. In an interview with Graham Lock, Sun Ra identified
its appeal:

> Mathematics is balanced; it proves itself. That's what that means:
> when you deal with equilibrium, balance, when a person loses
> their equilibrium, he can't even stand up. So if this planet lost
> equilibrium, it would do a flip. You've got to have equilibrium;
> that's why you got a right leg and a left leg, so you can stand up,
> you know. Really, a person's not really single, he's built in dual-
> ity, got two arms, you see, he got to balance himself, and that's
> the way it should be with doctrines and religions and philosophy.
> It should balance itself. If it can't balance itself, you shouldn't
> believe it, shouldn't follow it, because then *you'd* be unbalanced.
> "Unbalanced" also means mentally ill, so then it comes down to
> balance, and that's equation. It proves itself, you see. All you have
> to do is use intuition and reason, and you can see yourself what is
> needed: they need equilibrium, balance. They need sound truths

that deal with sound. [. . .] That's why you can hear it. If you hear sound that's not balanced or something, it not only hurts the ear; it hurts the body.[33]

These remarks contain the substance of Sun Ra's poetics. Mathematics in his gnomic summation is self-authenticating; it proves itself. He writes poetry that does the same, dissolving apparent differences through equivalence. Balance—equivalence asserted by the copula— becomes the ideal such poetry strives to produce and communicate. Moreover, balance possesses the abstract capacity to affirm life simultaneously in a variety of ways: physically, politically, psychologically, and spiritually. Its synonym "equilibrium" links people to the planet, and its antonym "unbalanced" confirms its value through inversion. Sun Ra's extended meditation on the proposition "mathematics is balanced" tracks associational nuance in so many directions that what begins as a quality becomes a universal value. Balance. In his closing move, Sun Ra turns equation toward music, just as balance promotes "sound truths [. . .] that deal with sound." Mathematical equivalence enhances bodily health as music communicates balance by force of sound. Sun Ra's poetry seeks to vindicate such purportedly self-authenticating claims, resolving difference through equation.

One of the challenges Sun Ra faces as a poet arises from the disequilibrium of his medium: language. Words serve as much to obscure as to illuminate existing equations. Sun Ra applies tone science to language itself, attempting to recover the balance it currently conceals. He explains its confused state with a familiar story from the Bible, a holy book of codes that in his view most readers fail to crack. In a lyric worthy of Blake, and rare for its use of rhyme, Sun Ra recalls the biblical account of the confusion of words at the Tower of Babel:

'Twas at Babylon they say . . . .
Ah, dread and drastic day . . . .
That God did something hitherto unheard
He confused the meaning of the word
He made the meanings thrice and double-twin

And helter-skelter-mayhem ruled since then.
Though you may roam yon here and there
You'll find confusion every where.[34]

Multiple meanings unhinge the world of words, scattering confusion to the winds. It's the familiar story of an unfortunate fall into polysemy, but without the usual assignment of blame to a prideful humanity. Instead, Sun Ra assigns responsibility for the babble of tongues to the biblical creator, who willfully alienates himself from sound ("did something hitherto *unheard*") and confuses meaning in the double sense of multiplying but also obfuscating it.

In an even more surprising twist, Sun Ra responds with a prescription for better speaking:

This is not to say
There'll never be a better day . . . . . .
Watch what you write, watch what you say!
    Some words lead to gloried shame
    Making innocence to blame
    Secret-sacred hidden lore
    Oftimes lead to deadly woe.
    Words substitute . . permutate
    Subtle tools of enwrit fate.
Tree of knowledge . . . Paradise
Led to needless sacrifice.[35]

Not the Holy Spirit but careful writing and speaking will undo the confusion of tongues. The poem traces a movement from sight to sound. The imperative to watch what you write and say shifts language from a verbal to a visual register, cultivating awareness of its fallen effects ("some words lead to gloried shame"). But it also opens a space for unperceived equivalence, as in the slant rhyme "lore" and "woe." Orthography dictates that these words do not rhyme. But a consideration of regional pronunciation raises the possibility that they do rhyme, especially for a speaker or reader from the southern United

States. Substituting auditory equivalence (full rhyme) for visual difference (slant rhyme) restores the abstract force of tone to a language untuned at Babel. A harmony of sounds supersedes a difference of meanings, equating what sight divides and redressing the confusion of words. Sun Ra's prescription for better writing and speaking involves close attention to the tonal possibilities of language: "Words substitute . . . . words permutate." Making substitutions and changing sequences become "tools" for fixing a fate "enwrit," written into words. Sun Ra's poetry both identifies and undoes the confusion that language inflicts.

As the short but instructive poem "To the Peoples of Earth" puts it,

Proper evaluation of words and letters
In their phonetic and associated sense
Can bring the peoples of earth
Into the clear light of pure Cosmic Wisdom.[36]

This little lecture telling us how to read also describes how to write poetry. Both involve judging words and letters with great care, particularly in regard to sound and association. This emphasis on sound, the phonetic aspect of words, allies Sun Ra's poetry with music and the intangible excess of tone. Sun Ra emphasizes and exploits the sonority of words independent of their apparent meanings. He writes a poetry of assonance, in which one sound leads to another and another and another, to identify equations concealed by the appearance of different meanings. Hence his emphasis on the "phonetic and associated sense[s]" of words, the sounds they make and relations among them that conventional attention to meaning deems insignificant. Word substitution becomes a strategy for reviving the force of sound, a tool useful for disrupting the limited fate enwrit by words. Assonance accumulates equivalence, whereas meaning distributes distinctions. As word substitutes for word, sonority displaces meaning, resolving differences by the measure of "Cosmic Wisdom," an abstract, intangible, fugitive excess. Assonance as additive sound: in poetry as much as in music, Sun Ra makes sound a vehicle for spirit.

Here is an example of the way Sun Ra works as a tone scientist of words. Follow him as he pursues the flight of sounds:

> This birth thing is very bad for people. The word should be abolished. Supreme beings have trapped humans with words and one of the words is birth. You see, birth is also spelled berth, which means a bed, and when they bury a person that's their berth because they're placed in a berth. So the day they're dead becomes their berthday. Birthday also has the phonetic word for earth in it—erth—so you could also say be-earthday.[37]

Birth/berth: two meanings, one sound. Their assonance provides the occasion for an equation that resolves difference—in this case, between life and death—into a unity that exceeds and subsumes them in a self-authenticating proof. Birth is berth, a premature burial. A birthday is a death day. Life is death. It's the kind of equation Sun Ra esteems, the terminal outcome of a mathematics of sound. In the interview just quoted, he continues to ponder the implications of the sound "erth," but does so visually, performing a permutation at the level of the letter: "erth" rearranged is "thre," which is "three," as in the third planet from the sun, or as he puts it in the revised version of a poem entitled "The Glory of Shame," "Ereth is eerth is earth is erth is thre is three."[38] Add to this equivalence several others ("tree" is "three" is "GIMEL . . . GAMMA . . . GE") and the conclusion becomes (for Sun Ra) clear that "earth" *is* "three": a "third heaven" (as the Arkestra chants on the recording *Soul Vibrations of Man*) confined to a limited orbit and destined for inevitable death.[39]

Sun Ra sums it all up in the compressed little poem "Be-earthed":

Those who are be earthed
Are be erthed
Burthed or berthed
They are placed
In their place
Now Ge is the earth

And Gesus is earthsus
And Ge's is earth's
Ge's us is earth's us
Consider Gheez and Gheezus[40]

Buried in common slang (the exclamation Gheez/jeez!) lurks an equation that identifies the Christian Son of God with death. Birth on
Earth is a living death for all of us, redoubled by our devotion to Jesus,
Earth's dying god. Equations born of sound substitution and semantic
equivalence (Je = Ge, Ge-earth, Jesus = Gesus = earthsus = earth's us)
create the possibility of an auditory alternative to the living burial of
life on Earth. Such is the force of sound in Sun Ra's poetry.

Sight can work similar effects. The visual register of Sun Ra's poetry
can reach a density characteristic of more recent L=A=N=G=U=A=G=E
poetry, as in his untitled poem called "[Point Equal Aim]," in which
equal signs after seven descending periods link them to the words
"aim," "end," "period," "time," "era," "age," and "cycle."[41] Any measure
of time, apparently, achieves equivalence with a point. Even more
visually arresting, however, is the poem entitled "Tomorrow Never
Comes," a serially permuting "word anagram":

Tomorrow Never Comes,
Comes Tomorrow Never
Never Comes Tomorrow
Tomorrow Comes Never
Never Tomorrow Comes
Comes Never Tomorrow.[42]

The poem unites two visual registers (a block of type with a series
of repeated words) that allow it to be read in any direction: across,
up, down, or diagonally. Sun Ra provides a rare written commentary:
"It is said that tomorrow never comes. Here is an equation with the
word never. The equation should read *Tomorrow comes never* or *Never
comes tomorrow*. Tomorrow here is associated with never."[43] Substituting "comes" for "is" replaces the copula with a dynamism, turning this

apparently static arrangement of type into a kaleidoscope of words. But nothing ever comes of all that movement. Like sound, like tone, like the sonic register of language, tomorrow is *nothing*. Tomorrow is *not* today. It *never comes*. Yet its equivalence with never bespeaks other prospects, an association that ever beckons, a permutation that never ends.

Association and permutation, assonance and rearrangement: these become Sun Ra's preferred strategies for creating poetic equations that resolve apparent differences in abstract equivalence. They can be auditory or visual: "The equations of sight-similarity / The equations of sound-similarity," as he puts it in his poem "Cosmic Equation."[44] Operating on different sensory registers, such "Subtle Living Equations" establish the conclusion that an abstract life of spirit exceeds appearances and, more radically, that music and poetry can convey it.[45] Sun Ra contests millennia of Western skepticism by practicing a counter-wisdom accessible to sound and identifiable by sight. His aim is not to flaunt the spirit, however, but to mobilize it toward the end of exploring new tomorrows, building a better world beyond this one. A poem entitled "The Outer Bridge" compresses these otherworldly aspirations into seven brief lines:

> In the half-between world
> Dwell they the tone-scientists
> Sound
> Mathematically precise
> They speak of many things
> The sound-scientists
> Architects of planes of discipline.[46]

Artists of abstraction, tone scientists dwell "half-between" living/ dying matter and impossible spirit. Sound is their medium, precision is their means, and what they speak of they build: abstract planes of sound/knowledge accessible through skill, persistence, and discipline. On a foundation of fugitive sound they construct nothing more than tone can sustain, command nothing less than the life of spirit.

Sun Ra frequently displays ambivalence toward language as a medium for this kind of creation. Only where it partakes of the fugitive quality of sound does it open to other worlds. More typically it prescribes confinement. Sun Ra shares with William S. Burroughs (beerthed the same year) a keen awareness that language can function as a means of control.[47] How then to write in a way that evades—or disrupts—this effect? In a poem entitled "The Enwrit," Sun Ra advances a critique of language—or more precisely, of writing that forces limits on life—but he offers an alternative, too. Writing by ear, as it were, with attention directed through the appearance of written words to their sound, he asserts an equation that will guide the meditation on language and control that follows:

> To beright is at times to bewrite:
> So that there is an equation
> Which through phonetic mathematics
> Makes right be write.[48]

Two words composed of the verb "to be" fused with a further single sound rendered in visually different ways (right/write) establish an equation that both reveals and disrupts the prescriptive force of words. Sun Ra works a small but willful violence on conventional language by resolving a difference in meaning into a similarity of sound. Right equals write—but why stop there?

> Through this summation or sum
> The idea of another three R's
> Assumes form
> Projecting the words right, write, and rite.[49]

Reading, writing, and arithmetic give way to a new kind of knowledge that assimilates verbal difference to abstract sound, in this case "rīt," identifying the social correlatives of law, language, and ritual and aligning their operation.

Writing prescribes rights by rite. Sun Ra immediately deploys this equation against language's tendency to assert control, but he does so in a way that might come as a surprise to easy advocates of social equality:

> *Those who in ignorance seek rights*
> *From the hand of man*
> *Receive rites.*
> *So that equal rights*
> *Are equal rites*
> *And equal writes.*[50]

The pursuit of equal rights betrays a nostalgia for subjugation to less congenial rites enforced by writing. Sun Ra's equation quietly invokes the whole tortured history of African enslavement and its deployment of writing (slave laws and black codes) to enforce ritual control over a people deemed inferior. An apparent commitment to social justice (which Sun Ra elsewhere permutes to "just is / the status quo")[51] conceals a longing for control enforced by language: "equal writes."

Sound abstracted from sense both identifies the problem and promotes a solution through the simple sonic force of negation.

> *Equal writes can be*
> *Equal written words.*
> *The right word can be considered*
> *As the write word; the written word.*
> *The negative abstract*
> *Is the unright, the unwrite*
> *And the unrite.*[52]

Sun Ra assaults the written word, with its built-in ritual control, through a simple act of negation, inserting yet another new sound ("un") as a prefix to words that usually work without one: "unright," "unwrite," and "unrite." That these are not canonical words—even when written—is part of his purpose. The sound of negation swallows conventional language, loosening constraints, unwriting rites and rights. Control cedes to sound that untunes its prescriptions. Nothing occurs instead, the nothing that opens rights, rituals, and writings to abstraction. And in this openness new worlds become possible.

Poems explicitly about music constitute a libretto, so to speak, that guides creation. By now, Sun Ra's basic strategy for composing should be clear: test what *is* against what is *not*, deploy abstraction to open new worlds, create sounds that can lead there. That is the simple program that his poetry outlines and his music performs. The poetry itself may be opaque to the point of obscurity or diffuse to the point of confusion. But for all its strangeness, it announces a coherent if abstruse theory of composition that brings a strong sense of purpose to music too often valued simply for being weird or fractious or unconscionably hip. Composition begins, then, with nothing: the negation of what is and the invocation of what is not, as the poem "The Music of the Spheres" instructs: "This music is of the outer spheres / Of the Kingdom of Not . . . the void / For it is of the unsaid words / Concerning the things that always are to be."[53] Music comes from an outside whose entrance is negation: words unsaid, sounds unheard—but not beyond reach. They reside not here and now but somewhere in the future, with words unsaid because yet to *be* said. The Kingdom of Not awaits its saying, its sounds.

Consider in this regard the wind, which *is not* and yet produces observable effects. In "Of Coordinate Vibrations," Sun Ra indicates how music sounds the unsaid, speaks (for) the future: "The wind is not / But the not is the note / And note permutated is tone. / Music is of the epi-cosmic ray point."[54] With the addition of a silent letter (signifying noth·ng?), what is not becomes something else, "note," the written sign of pitch and duration, which in turn—when turned—becomes "tone," the intangible excess that opens music to abstraction. What is *not* produces tonal prospects whose possibility boggles words ("ray-point") and leads beyond them to new worlds. As the poem puts it, "Music envisions and potentializes," and it does so out of nothing, since "The nothing is the whole note of music." Nothing, the full measure. The fugitive quality of sound becomes the vehicle of vision and creation, which becomes audible in music as "a grammar and a language / As well as a synthesizer."[55]

For Sun Ra, the new worlds that music synthesizes are better than what *is*, a conviction he conveys in the opening lines of the poem called "New Horizons" (which is also the title of an early musical composition by him): "Music Pulsing like a living heartbeat, / Pleasant intuition of better things to come. . . ."[56] This pleasant intuition provides the impetus for a political agenda as radical as anything either the civil rights or Black Power movements would have to offer. But Sun Ra's medium for transforming the world is neither moral conviction nor political indignation but, more boldly if surreptitiously, music, abstract sounds heralding new worlds:

> *Music spontaneous rapture,*
> *Feet rushing with the wind on a new world*
> *Of sounds:*
> *Invisible worlds. . . . vibrations . . . tone pictures . . .*
> *A new world for every self*
> *Seeking a better self and a better world.*[57]

A passage like this one renders Sun Ra's whole practice as tautology: a new world of sounds opens a new world for every self that seeks a better world. Repetition breeds abstraction and conjures intangible possibilities: invisible worlds, vibrations, tone pictures, what Sun Ra calls "the alter reality" in his poem entitled "The Skilled Way." Politics takes an otherworldly turn as he extends his reach to include art in its totality as "the skilled way . . . the skilled weigh," a practiced path to and adjudication of all that exceeds what is: "The Cosmos is the ever Eternal or the never / Ending immeasureable [*sic*]. That immeasureable / Beingness of the Cosmos is abstract art / Beyond compare."[58] The line-ending "never" is also "never Ending." New worlds alter reality by measure of the immeasurable. Music opens to abstraction. Abstract art is the Beingness of the Cosmos. Deep? Perhaps. But as Sun Ra writes elsewhere, "The unauthorized reality is celestial Being," a spiritual reality neither authored nor authorized by this world.[59] His practice as poet and musician breathes spirit into a world of death.

Sun Ra offers a summation of the tone science that guides composition in a poem he would reprint frequently over the course of his career, "The Neglected Plane of Wisdom." It's much more (or maybe less) than a poem in the traditional sense, comprising a series of declarative equations that read like aphorisms carved on the sarcophagus of a forgotten king. Their flat, serial presentation gives "The Neglected Plane of Wisdom" the weight and gravity of a manifesto, making it central to any understanding of Sun Ra's art. It gathers into a single sustained utterance many of the notions examined above and therefore deserves complete quotation:

> *Music is a plane of wisdom, because music is a universal language, it is a*
> *language of honor, it is a noble precept, a gift of the Airy*
> *Kingdom, music is air, a universal existence . . . common to all the*
> *living.*
> *Music is existence, the key to the universal language.*
> *Because it is the universal language.*
> *Freedom of Speech is Freedom of Music.*
> *Music is not material, Music is spiritual.*
> *Music is a living force.*
> *That which is of the soul is the greater light*
> *The light of greater instruction . . .*
> *The light of culture and beauty*
> *The light of intensity and living power.*
> *The name of Music is Art.*
> *The name of Music is played by infinite instruments.*
> *The name can lift dreams from nothing to reality . . .*
> *And keep them ever before the eyes . . .*
> *Like once silent voices burst into song, the name strikes the ear*
> *And the sound of it rushes like a wild thing and takes its place as the core*
> *of even the minutest part of being.*
> *Music has wings, it moves upon the wings of intuition and thought.*
> *Music is the Ambassador of the Airy Kingdom.*

Sound . . . Cosmic Vibration . . . Life
Pure life like pure blood is negative.
It is time to consider the negative plane of existence. It is time to consider
    Music as a plane of wisdom and a weapon of defense against the
    past and the condemnations of the past.
Blood when negative is pure.
The negative is the symbol of the pure.
The Music of the past is positive Music in the same way the past is
    symbolized by the positive.[60]

Characteristically, Sun Ra celebrates music as a negative wisdom, or more precisely, a plane of wisdom discontinuous with a positive past, cutting across it to disrupt its judgments and eradicate its evils (among them slavery and racism). Hence the disarming simplicity of Sun Ra's equations: music is not material; music is spiritual, a living force. Moving from negation to the life of spirit, music is abstract art. It comes from another kingdom, an airy, unapparent one where sound moves in vitalizing waves and breath communicates being. Most important among the equations this manifesto contains is the claim that music is a universal language. Sun Ra would repeat it frequently. Unlike written and spoken language, music is intelligible to everybody. It redresses the confusion wrought at the Tower of Babel by welcoming all who have ears to hear new worlds of sound. Universality offers Sun Ra a social correlative for abstraction. Music must be heard to be actualized, must sound to be-sound. It completes its work in people by transforming their perceptions in order, as he puts it in another poem, "That man might rise above the stage of man."[61]

In a press release published in Detroit in 1969 by the White Panther Party, Sun Ra explains the operation of music as a language:

How many times has it been said that music is a language? I want to say it agin [*sic*] in another way. COSMIC music is a cosmic language. Cosmic music is a plane of tomorrow, it is the dimension and the balanced perspective of tomorrow. It is the view of the living future of the living tomorrow. The music is rhythm, melody, harmony and precision. It speaks to the worlds of the greater potentials awaiting the peoples of the worlds at every future point on every future plane.[62]

As a universal—cosmic—language, music interrupts the present to introduce the prospect of a "living tomorrow." It speaks of "greater potentials" to transform reality through what is not: tomorrow, which never comes. It nevertheless transports its listeners to future points and planes where they become the people of those worlds. The universal language of Sun Ra's music enacts the absent future it communicates. And people change, making this a politics of sound.

To advance the musical agenda his poetry announces, Sun Ra would rely on the Arkestra, a living instrument for creating a living tomorrow. "I'm using the fellows who are playing the instruments as the instrument," he said once in an interview. "It's just a matter of transforming certain ideas over into a language which the world can understand."[63] Poetry is a personal expression, while Sun Ra's music has a public agenda. The Arkestra would conjure into existence his new sounds and the living futures they communicate. It played music to change the world.

EL SATURN

The Arkestra was a collective and a collaborative enterprise. Thmei Research provided its intellectual inspiration; Sun Ra, its spiritual and musical direction. Yet he frequently disclaimed creative authority over the music it made: "Every musician in the band was part of the composition process."[1] The Arkestra would never have taken flight, however, without the indefatigable energy of Alton Abraham. It is convenient to credit Sun Ra with the creative achievements associated with the Arkestra in its many avatars. After all, he composed and arranged most of its music, choreographed its performances, and even managed the lives of its most devoted members. Sun Ra deserves to be acknowledged for changing the history of jazz and arguably that of black culture in general. But Abraham deserves credit, too. As its business manager, he made the Arkestra an industry unto itself, a viable if shaky commercial venture that, against the odds, performed and recorded for forty years under Sun Ra's leadership—and continues to play to this day. Sun Ra and Abraham worked together like the two halves of a brain: Sun Ra the creative right hemisphere and Abraham the calculating left. They collaborated to extraordinary effect over the course of many years to make the Arkestra and its music an engine of cultural and social change.

If Abraham was an artist, then commerce was his medium. In some ways a true creature of Bronzeville, he brought an entrepreneurial spirit to Thmei's activist agenda and saw an opportunity to establish another kind of urban institution that could promote a better life for blacks. His experience as a member of the Knights of Music gave him connections that would benefit the fledgling band. Sites describes the wide variety of venues the Arkestra played in Chicago: "commercial music clubs, social dances, pageants, gay bars, churches"—wherever the band could make a buck.[2] Social clubs in particular sponsored a wide range of musical functions, and according to Sites, Abraham frequently booked the Arkestra to play for them. Traditional venues supporting large ensembles (such as the Grand Terrace and the Parkway Ballroom) were going the way of zoot suits and fedoras, good for an occasional night out but hardly the latest fashion. As clubs got smaller, so did the bands that played them, a point Abraham made years later in a note listing the core members of a stripped-down Arkestra: "It became necessary to use six men when clubs would not pay for a big band."[3] The business of managing a jazz orchestra at a time of economic retreat from large-scale entertainment proved challenging, particularly for a man whose day job earned him $350 a month.[4] The Arkestra was a labor of commitment and love.

Making records would be essential to the group's success as a musical and activist enterprise. Sun Ra devoted a lot of energy to recording in the early and midfifties, either scoring arrangements for other musicians in recording studios or rehearsing more personal projects at home. His interest in recording technologies was long-standing. In Alabama he acquired an early wire recorder, using it to record his own ensemble as well as more established units, such as Henderson's or Ellington's, when they played in the area.[5] In Chicago, his recording machines seemed to be rolling perpetually. The drummer Bugs Hunter, who would assume primary responsibility for recording the Arkestra some years later, remembers Sun Ra carrying some such device wherever he went and saving everything he recorded.[6] The habit would yield some interesting results. A home recording of "Deep Purple" made in 1948 with the violinist Stuff Smith eventually saw release, but not until 1973, on an LP with the same title.[7] Sun Ra experimented with small groups in his small space, recordings not meant for release but instead intended for the edification and advancement of the musicians involved.

The most inspired of these rehearsal recordings were made with several vocal groups. In the mid- to late fifties, probably at Abraham's urging, Sun Ra began working intensely with vocal ensembles, male groups with names such as the Lintels, the Nu Sounds, the Cosmic Rays, the Qualities, the Metros, and the Clockstoppers. These groups fell somewhere between Sun Ra's journeyman work as an arranger and the more experimental aims of the Arkestra. Abraham and Sun Ra were exploring the possibility of commercial success with singers. The Lintels sang doo-wop, tunes including "Blue Moon," "Blue Skies," and "Baby Please Be Mine." The Nu Sounds covered mostly standards, such as "Honeysuckle Rose" or "Nice Work if You Can Get It," newly arranged in sweet harmonies backed by Sun Ra's adventuresome piano. The most inventive of these groups was the Cosmic Rays, which occasionally performed with the Arkestra and was captured in that setting on a rehearsal tape from 1958 singing haunting minor harmonies on the Sun Ra originals "Africa" and "Black Sky and Blue Moon." Music from these rehearsal tapes appears on a compact disc released in 2003 and entitled *Spaceship Lullaby*.[8] It makes for enlightening listening because it reveals Sun Ra working not only with great promise in a popular idiom but also in the mundane way of a musical director: coaching Roland Williams of the Nu Sounds by singing his part to demonstrate its syncopation ("do-daboo-day") and playing the piano intro to "Holiday for Strings" to communicate its feel ("'cuz I want you to *hear* it"). Sun Ra taught his musicians by example and demonstration, call and response. He fit voices to parts, harmonies to words, in a way that communicates a comfortable mastery of popular vocal music.

But even here Sun Ra tinkered and innovated, following an expansive impulse that pressed beyond the boundaries of the pop song. This impulse is clearly on display in the two-part tune entitled "Chicago USA," possibly written as a contest entry for a new city song to replace Fred Fisher's "Chicago, Chicago, That Toddlin' Town."[9] Long thought lost, "Chicago USA" resurfaced on rehearsal tapes, confirming John Gilmore's recollection that "when you would hear the songs, they would depict Chicago perfectly. . . . The words make you feel it."[10] While Sun Ra was not a prolific lyricist, his writing for the vocal groups shows some skill. "Chicago USA" tracks the movement of public transport from the South Side's University stop, at 1200 East Sixty-Third, through the Loop and on to the much whiter world accessible from the Jackson, Monroe, and Washington stops. Sites reads the reversal of history implied by the order of these presidential stops as time travel, a return to national origins that attempts to erase the country's "brutal racial history."[11] But the track (think music as much as train) moves into the future, too, imagining an expansion of livable space for blacks that the Arkestra will also mutter, rollick, and scream to produce. Public transportation is a terrestrial spaceship propelling blacks from the South Side to alien worlds.

In 1954, Sun Ra copyrighted another song with a similar trajectory, "Bop is a Spaceship Melody," sung by the Nu Sounds. It anticipates his hard turn to space themes and hints at the dissonance to come. The title feels uneasy: is bop a spaceship? A melody? Both? By the midfifties, bop was a lot of things. Calling it a "spaceship melody" makes it a musical vehicle to worlds as barely comprehensible as that odd phrase. Another phrase that first appears in this song would become central to the Arkestra's extraterrestrial aspirations: "interplanetary harmonies, interplanetary melodies." Sun Ra would recycle it later in the Arkestra's more ambitious repertoire. His inventive work with small vocal groups thus splits the difference between commerce and culture. Regrettably, it would come to an end when the Arkestra started to take off.

Abraham understood the importance of recording to both the Arkestra's music and its mission. Rehearsal tapes were one thing, but the general public could not access them. The band needed to record commercially to spread the Thmei message as widely as possible. The obvious problem with that ambition was commerce, the bottom line. Black musicians generally fell prey to cultural exploitation: unscrupulous, white-owned record companies with their promises and their contracts and their neocolonial dreams of profit over people. The local blues factory, Chess Records, provided a blatant example: sure, the company recorded and promoted the masters of Chicago blues (Muddy Waters, Little Walter, Willie Dixon, and Howlin' Wolf, to name a few), but how big were the profits of those magnanimous Chess brothers? Did they run a recording studio or an analog plantation? The obvious solution was to follow the lead of Vee-Jay Records, Vivian and James Bracken's label based in nearby Gary, Indiana, a black-owned enterprise that offered black production of black music (at least initially) made by the likes of Jimmy Reed and John Lee Hooker. Why not found another independent black record label? It was a bold idea at a time when most black jazz musicians recorded for white-owned labels.[12] Sun Ra was clearly grooming the vocal groups for commercial success. His work with the Arkestra would follow suit. In 1956, Abraham and Sun Ra, with support from Thmei, registered an independent record company with the American Federation of Musicians: El Saturn Research. Saturn Records. A black label for black musicians playing music for a better world.

Sun Ra remembered the founding of El Saturn as an act of humanitarian generosity meant to sustain creative work that the commercial record industry might dismiss:

> It was backed up by some people who were unselfish, and some people who felt that what I was trying to do in music was being hampered by commercial folks and other people who said it was too far out, and about twelve people got together, some musicians and others, one of them is a rabbi, he's a black Hebrew, he's in Israel now—and they put up the money, and they established us a record company, Saturn, so that I would be heard regardless of commercial folks. They did that. So then the foundation

of it was for to get this music out there to people, and they put these records out, they put the money in it; they didn't ask for no money; it's the most unselfish organization ever been on this planet. They didn't ask for no money. They said this music should be heard by people.[13]

In Sun Ra's account of El Saturn's founding, stress falls on its social mission to reach an audience without being compromised by "commercial folks." This is not to say, however, that El Saturn would eschew commerce altogether. However generous its initial backers may have been (much about the company's financial operation remains mysterious), the label's purpose was to produce and sell records, even if the music on them was challenging. "I didn't want to go through all the starving in the attic and all that foolishness," Sun Ra said in a later interview. "I wanted to bypass that particular trauma they put on artists."[14] The point was to keep the business of recording this new music in the hands of the people who created it, an aim Szwed describes as "so daring, so unprecedented, as to be heroic in the music business."[15] Thmei members were at the helm and would remain so. Abraham served as the company's president, promoter, and chief recording engineer. Lawrence Allen managed record distribution.[16] James Bryant assisted on the business side as an authorized representative, signing invoices as "James Bryant III V.P."[17] El Saturn was the culture-industry wing of Thmei Research as an activist organization. It would promote Thmei's agenda commercially, or try to do so, directing business operations toward the ends of black enlightenment and advancement.

Saturn, the sixth planet out from the sun, a gas giant belted by rings: in astrology, the ruling sign of discipline, authority, and self-control; in Roman mythology, the god of generation, wealth, agriculture, and the Capitoline Hill; in Greek mythology (as Cronos), the youngest of the Titans, who ineffectually ate his children to avoid dethronement. Abraham and Sun Ra understood these associations, choosing Saturn for the name of their label to reap the advantage of this rich symbolism. Through a devotion to discipline and authority,

El Saturn would bestow personal and collective abundance, gilding commercial enterprise with occult wisdom.

Thmei took such symbolism seriously, as various publications in Abraham's possession indicate. Part of an astrological series entitled *The Books of the Planets*, Edward G. Whitman's pamphlet *The Book of Saturn* avers that "from a general standpoint Saturn can be said to govern the business side of life," granting "the quality of patience" to allow "proper time for the developing and maturing of plans" and influencing "the political and public sides of life [by] giving capacity for the rendering of service of a very high quality to the state and to people generally."[18] In a theosophically oriented publication, *Cosmic Voice: Aetherius Speaks to Earth*, the titular spirit master ("born on the Planet Venus—3456 years ago!" but now from Saturn, "the location of the Seat of Interplanetary Government") speaks of "magnetic energies radiated via Saturn" that will "help the world as a whole." He closes his message with a benediction: "May the Blessings of the Masters of Saturn and the Sun fall upon your heads this night, so that you may know that God dwells silently with you all."[19] Invoking Saturn with the name of their record label was no joke for Abraham and Sun Ra. "El Saturn Research" announced commitment to occult counter-knowledge as a means for producing a better life—by making and selling records.

It was a do-it-yourself organization for reinventing reality. El Saturn would manage the production, promotion, and distribution of the Arkestra's music, maximizing profits for the musicians, minimizing exploitation by executives, and advancing the Thmei message of better living through music. It would coordinate studio recording and small-batch record pressings with the mundane tasks of stamping jackets, pasting labels, filling orders, and booking gigs. However homegrown, El Saturn was a business. Rather than resist capitalism, Abraham embraced it in the spirit of Bronzeville, approaching it as the best available means for creating and sustaining a community of black artist-activists. Enlightened commerce to enlighten consumers: El Saturn products would become more than the mute hieroglyphics Marx claims commodities to be. They would *sound* and they would *sing*, often covered in Egyptian hieroglyphics. They would celebrate rather than exploit the labor that created them and inspire continuing creation. Sketches in one of Abraham's record books show his hopes reaching much higher than the top of the music charts, however. One depicts a four-story building with the words "El Saturn Wisdom Research Culture Art Foundation" in big letters on the ground floor. The second floor houses the "Department of Sound," the third bears the label "Space Communications," and the top floor is reserved for El Saturn's loftiest undertaking, "Cosmic Research."[20] El Saturn Records aspired to do more than press vinyl and make a buck. As Abraham imagined it, the company would function as the corporate sponsor and scholarly archive of Thmei's message and the Arkestra's music.

El Saturn's earliest records were singles, 45 rpm disks that could be produced cheaply in small numbers. The very first El Saturn single was long thought to be a recording of the Cosmic Rays with "Bye-Bye" on side 1 and "Somebody's in Love" on side 2. But Robert L. Campbell, Christopher Trent, and Robert Pruter show that the honor goes to the Arkestra's recording of "Super Blonde" and "Soft Talk."[21] More Saturn singles by the Arkestra as well as other artists would follow, most notably a side by a fringe R&B performer named Yochannan (also spelled Yochanan and also known as the "Muck Muck Man" for his Saturn single entitled "Muck Muck"), who wore open-toed sandals in all weather, sported crazy "sun colors," and claimed descent from the sun.[22] As the new standard medium for serious jazz recording, however, the LP loomed inevitably on Saturn's horizon, the main challenge being how to finance its more costly production.[23] Enter Tom Wilson, an African American with a Harvard degree who started a daring label called Transition that aimed to record the most progressive music going—and did so, signing Cecil Taylor, John Coltrane, and Sun Ra to their first sessions as leaders.[24] Abraham found Wilson's approach to financing record production attractive. It was, in Corbett's witty phrasing, "a bit of a pyramid scam," soliciting contributions from sponsors ostensibly to support particular recordings but in reality to sustain general operations.[25] In a letter to Adolph Hicks dated January 1, 1957, Abraham (like Sun Ra, a devotee of the caps lock) wrote, "WE, EL SATURN, ARE EXPANDING OUR BUSINESS, DUE TO DEMANDS FROM THE RECORD SHOPS AND RECORD DISTRUBUTORS."[26] El Saturn would produce LPs in the Wilson mode: "WE HAVE ADOPTED A SIMILAR PROGRAM TO TRANSITION." Abraham, however, promised investors a higher return ("MORE THAN THREE TIMES THE AMOUNT INVESTED"), *plus* the added Thmei bonus: "THEY CAN BUILD A BETTER FUTURE FOR THEMSELVES AND THEIR FAMILIES BY WORKING WITH OUR PROGRAM OF LP ALBUM INVESTOR SPONSORSHIP."[27] Investment with a progressive return: Abraham's business model turns a pyramid into the launchpad for a better future.

Transition recorded Sun Ra and the Arkestra at Universal Studios on July 12, 1956, yielding the Arkestra's first LP.[28] It was a willfully innovative session, nineteen takes yielding ten tracks, eight of them Sun Ra originals.[29] Transition released the LP in early 1957 under the title *Jazz by Sun Ra, Vol. 1*, auguring a second volume. Although recorded, it never appeared on the label because Wilson folded the company later that year, taking a job with United Artists Records.[30] An ad announcing *Jazz by Sun Ra, Vol. 1* in *Down Beat* dated December 26, 1956, celebrates the record's originality in sans serif caps: "FAR-OUT AS THE WEST COAST JAZZ . . . BASIC AS BASIE . . . LIVE CONCERT FI!!! A Fantastic New Jazz Conception by SUN RA, SUN God of Jazz."[31] Many of the tunes underscore the music's newness with forward-look-ing titles, for example, "Transition," "Future," and "New Horizons," the last a beautifully composed and hypnotically slow thirty-two-bar meditation that provided the LP its thematic focus and featured Art Hoyle on trumpet over spacious reed harmonies and Sun Ra's plunk-ing, angular piano.

Only one blues appears on the record, its sixteen-bar head strutting through minor changes and a melody that does not resolve so much as dangle over the coming solos. "Possession" takes a Harry Revel confec-tion (a waltz written for Les Baxter's *Perfume Set to Music* and arranged here in four by Eutrace U. ["Prince"] Shell) and adds some darker fla-vors to haunting effect. "Sun Song," the LP's last track, features Sun Ra's weird Wurlitzer with chimes and timpani, the trumpet playing evocatively over the tonal center. It's a tune without melody whose free-form piano interlude gives way to the return of those soothing chimes. Bells (credited to six of eleven musicians) splash transient colors across the whole LP, and chthonic rhythms add a register that feels as old as the arrangements are new. *Jazz by Sun Ra, Vol. 1* lives up to its advertising hype.

Maybe the most provocative thing about the record, however, is the booklet that came with it, a brief manifesto written by Sun Ra explaining his approach to music and its larger implications. This is an important, revealing document. It contains five poems to illustrate his claim that "music is only another form of poetry," one of which (in case you missed the point) bears the title "New Horizons," translating the song by that title into words that expand its imaginative prospects: "music pulsing like a living heartbeat, / Pleasant intuition of better things to come . . . / The sight of boundless space / Reaching ever outward as if in search of itself."[32] More is at stake in Sun Ra's music than simply making the latest in far-out sounds. Throughout the manifesto, emphasis falls on the *future* (another song title) as the destination this music seeks. His musicians "are dedicated to the music of the future," and Sun Ra declares that all should share their commitment: "*We must live for the future of music.*"[33]

This is the rhetoric of the Thmei broadsheets, but transposed into a singularly positive mode. Beauty remains the means to a better future, with life as its highest ideal, as Sun Ra claims in his opening paragraph, entitled "THE AIM OF MY COMPOSITIONS":

All of my compositions are meant to depict happiness combined with beauty in a free manner. Happiness, as well as *pleasure* and *beauty* has many degrees of existence; *my aim is to express these degrees in sounds which can be understood by the entire world.* All of my music is tested for effect. By effect I mean mental impression. The real aim of this music is to co-ordinate the minds of peoples into an intelligent reach for a better world, and an intelligent approach to the living future. By peoples I mean all of the people of different nations who are living today.[34]

This bold declaration sums up Sun Ra's whole vocation as composer and performer. Music is his chosen medium because, unlike language, it can be understood by everybody everywhere. The inclusiveness of this vision (all people living today) shows Sun Ra at his most optimistic, turning Thmei's activist agenda loose on the whole world.

The political potential of recording is such that dreams from Chicago's South Side can seek universal fulfillment. Music, by means of beauty, might coordinate all minds to produce a living future for all people. "I know," Sun Ra writes near the pamphlet's end, "that the dream they dream is *life*, and LIFE is the sound I seek to express." He writes as a teacher devoted to life and speaks as a prophet inspired by art: "*The well being of every person on this planet depends upon the survival and growth of civilization*; every civilization is determined, to great extent, by the scope and development of its ART FORMS."[35] These words evoke not only Sun Ra's broadsheets but also William Blake's prophecies. Like Blake, Sun Ra offers his texts with disarming simplicity and vulnerability, closing his manifesto with a poem cannily called "After-Thought":

> *I take my magic wand in hand and touch*
> *The mind of the world;*
> *I speak in sounds.*
> *What am I saying?*
> *Listen!*
> *These are the things spoken from*
> *My heart . . .*
> *These are of and are my intimate treasures,*
> *I give them to those who live and love*
> *Both life and living.*[36]

Few musicians ask so much of music as Sun Ra did. Few have so much to offer.

This tactic of using music to advance social and spiritual vision became a mainstay of El Saturn's business practices. With Transition defunct, this label assumed primary responsibility for recording the Arkestra and promoting its music. It's typical to approach music as if it were, well, only music. The Arkestra's music partakes of a whole material culture that gives it shape, weight, and significance. To advance the Thmei agenda through commerce and consumerist pleasures, Abraham exploits the supporting *matter* of music production. Not content to segregate Sun Ra's message in a manifesto, he also scatters it across company paraphernalia, encouraging more than just consumption, sowing seeds for the sun. Abraham and Sun Ra radicalize the dubious apparatus of commercial advertising by transforming promotional material for new music into ads for infinity. "My music demonstrates infinity," Sun Ra once told an interviewer. "Most people can't comprehend that."[37] Record jackets, catalogs, leaflets, flyers, posters, business cards—all the ephemera of commercial music—collude in demonstrating infinity as part of the process of music production.

In all these texts, a prophetic quality infects mundane business dealings and makes them portentous of new worlds to come. One business card asks, "Why buy old sounds? Buy new sounds from the future by Sun Ra & his Arkestra." Another, seasonally adjusted for Christmas, offers a blessing from "Sun Ra & Arkistra": "To You, Better Life Vibrations, For Always." A later one quietly recommends "Divine Cosmic Music from the Creator, Spiritual Intergalactic Divine."[38] Yet another depicting a solar boat promotes "Intergalactic infinite creative life spirit energies."[39] An El Saturn catalog from the late fifties, festooned in front with ankhs, eyes, and spaceships, presents the potential customer with an early version of Sun Ra's poem "The Neglected Plane of Wisdom." On the back appears a meditation on history as dead, frequently reprinted on flyers and record jackets, that includes a no-nonsense rejection all things past: "The past is DEAD and those who are following the past are doomed to die and be like the past."[40] A performance contract promotes Sun Ra's spiritual as well as musical qualifications: "Be good to your MIND'S MIND/EYE earthlings! . . . Give it a chance to do what all earthlings must do before it crosses the river styx . . . Be bombarded with LIVING-COSMIC-SOUL-FORCE-VIBRATIONS . . . of 'SUN RA AND HIS INTERGALACTIC INFINITY ARKESTRA'!!!!"[41]

Here the rhetoric of advertising ("buy one and get one free!") communicates a disarming promise of higher living, of a piece with the slogan that appears on much of El Saturn's printed matter: "Beta music for a Beta people for a Beta world." Sun Ra glosses this slogan in detail in a broadsheet entitled "the end":

The plane of wisdom will take those who desire to live to a BETTER DIMENSION of a BETTA LIFE. On the plane of Wisdom, the beta i am is the pilot. ALWAYS BETA IS TWO not one. Good, BETTER, Best. Better (Beta) is TWO. TWO is TO. TO is OT. OT is AUT or OUGHT (SHUD of SHD). SHD is the name of the ancient pre-Christian world.[42]

A simple business slogan freights a message grounded in antiquity that, read as equation, portends a better world. Abraham sums up the higher purpose of El Saturn in a later note written in pen on a mimeographed promotional flyer:

To bring to this universe, from the All Mighty Living Creator from the heart of All Universes Beyond the Central Sun, the Fruits of the greater impossible thru cosmic vibrating Music, Cosmic tones, Poetry and any other living means to give living cosmic Spiritual food to a spiritually starved and dying world. By permission of the All mighty Living Cosmic Energy Self.[43]

The signatories listed on this declaration, Alton E. Abraham, Sun Ra, Jihm Brihnt, and Adahm E. Abraham, endorse a business model that descends from above.

An El Saturn record was clearly meant to be more than just a patterned vinyl platter for storing sound. It was intended as a multimedia infinity machine that would coordinate the force of recorded music with visual art, poetry, mystical promises, and technological pronouncements to transform reality. As an independent record company, El Saturn pioneered DIY production in a way that anticipated, among other things, a punk aesthetic yet to come. It pressed records in small numbers and printed jackets to order, often by hand. El Saturn's first LP, *Super-Sonic Jazz*, set the pattern for its future production. The Arkestra recorded its tracks at Balkan Studios in March 1956 and RCA Studios that November, before and after the Transition sessions. El Saturn released *Super-Sonic Jazz* about a year later; the jacket combined Sun Ra's message with the Arkestra's music in a way that bound them intimately together. The front bears a spare, stark, red-on-white drawing of piano keys catching flame against a background in which music transforms the world: upraised piano tops stand in for mountains, and a thundering conga appears as the source of the wind, as a planetoid (the sun?) takes wing with stars atwinkle amidst a barrage of lightning bolts. The words "Saturn presents . . ." appear freely drawn above, with "SUN RA and his Arkestra" below. The cover's elusive designer, Claude Dangerfield, was an Arkestra acquaintance who, like many in the band, had graduated from DuSable High.[44]

The back cover replaces the usual jazz blather by some noted critic with words from someone, either the master himself or perhaps Abraham, beneath the phrase "21st Century Limited Edition." El Saturn presses the language of manifesto into the service of consumption, transforming jacket copy into jazz testimonial: "All compositions on this LP are designed to convey the message of happiness and hope, a living message from the world of tomorrow."[45] An ensuing song-by-song description teaches listeners how to hear them. "Advice to Medics" is "a leap forward into the better unknown." "Kingdom of Not" is "about a kingdom called Not which although it is not, yet is." "Medicine for a Nightmare" is "full of fiery counter rhythms," while "Portrait of the Living Sky" is "a tone poem, a sound etching of rare beauty and life." The music on this DIY release starts local and rockets beyond: "le Sun Ra's Arkestra is of CHICAGO origin" but plays "UNIVERSAL MUSIC, A FREE LANGUAGE OF JOY."[46] A promotional flyer for the record emphasizes its affinity with the future: "THIS IS TOMORROW KNOCKING AT YOUR DOOR . . . . . TODAY IS THE SHADOW OF TOMORROW BECAUSE COMING EVENTS CAST THEIR SHADOW BEFORE. / 'THIS MUSIC IS ALIVE' IT IS NOT THE SHADOW, IT IS THE REALITY IN A PREVUE FORM."[47] As El Saturn's debut LP, *Super-Sonic Jazz* wraps its joyous tomorrow tones in a weave of bold image and visionary text. Abraham

designed a product to signify infinity, spiritualizing the common pleasures of consumption.

Not that El Saturn customers could satisfy those pleasures in the
usual marketplace way. El Saturn took upon itself the challenge of distribution, too, making the records difficult to acquire. They weren't
available at a music store near you. To buy a Sun Ra LP, you had to
attend a performance or mail El Saturn directly and hope for the best.
As Szwed notes, local distributors or retailers would occasionally come
along: Roundup Records in Cambridge, Massachusetts, or Third Street
Jazz and Blues in Philadelphia.[48] But most sales came at the bandstand in a style of cash payment described by the sax player Danny
Thompson, who long managed such matters, as "no bullshit C.O.D."[49]
This quaint approach to capitalism obviously limited the profit that
El Saturn and the Arkestra could derive from recording. According to
Sites, "over the first half of 1957 the company's sales of 450 singles
and 78 LPs totaled all of $860."[50] Nobody played with Sun Ra for the
money. His style of compensation required a deep capacity for faith.[51]

Likewise for mail-order sales. El Saturn catalogs included an order
form on the back page, where customers could specify the records
they wanted "by LP number(s)," but orders also came in letters and
on postcards. Mrs. Inez Kelley, for instance, requested that record
208 (Secrets of the Sun) be sent to her apartment in Chicago; William
Koehnlein, from Long Island, sent a postcard asking for a catalog, a
sticker affixed to the front of the card reading "End war Viet-Nam
Now."[52] The poet John Taggart typed a request, written on Syracuse
University letterhead, that LP "reviewer" copies be sent to MAPS, the
magazine he edited.[53] A similar request, hand-written, arrived from
Nat Hentoff for his columns in Hi-Fi Stereo Review and Cosmopolitan.[54]
Jamey Aebersold wrote a card requesting "literature on any available
records by your company."[55] Henry "Ankh" Dumas, a young writer
whom Sun Ra would befriend in New York (fatally shot in the subway
by a policeman in a so-called case of mistaken identity), sent an order
on the catalog form followed by a letter of chagrin on Hiram College
stationery: "I think I failed to specify WHICH Sun Ra album I wanted"
(also no. 208).[56] Eventually such orders would arrive from all over the

world: England, Sweden, Japan, Mexico. A group of "Hungarian jazz lovers" sent in a typed letter describing the difficulties Eastern European fans had in obtaining records ("We can buy some old, second hand jazz records only on the black market for unbelievable amounts of money a 12 inch LP for 10 per cent of my salary for a month!!!") and asked (in red type) for "some of the records by Sun Ra advertised in Down Beat."[57] In the era before Internet downloads and viral hits, DIY record sales inspired heartfelt pleas and passionate attachments. One letter bore a celestial return address: "Earth (Western), Fourth [sic] heavenly body from the Sun in the Galaxy of Milky Way."[58]

Such correspondence indicates the public's receptiveness, however selective, to the higher aspirations of El Saturn's music. As a business, El Saturn would have to remain satisfied with spiritual rather than commercial success. At some point during its early years, Abraham drafted a disarmingly frank letter to James Petrillo, president of the American Federation of Musicians (Corbett suggests it was never sent), describing exactly what El Saturn wanted to achieve and asking for help.[59] Amid typical Thmei talk of the wisdom necessary to conquer death in a world "on the brink of disaster," Abraham shared his belief that El Saturn's music could breathe life into a dying world:

> The only solution that can save Mankind is the Kreation, by the original Kreators only, of a new music that is purposely designed to draw the evil attributes from the hearts and minds of men and to replace those attributes of death with attributes of life through music. During the past five years we have been experimenting with this ATONAL music from outter [sic] space on dope addicts, drunks, angry people, Mental-patience [sic], the depressed and even just plain stubborn fellows. The results obtained were remarkable. [. . .] The only way this world can be saved from being completely destroyed is through music. It must be a new music that is clean, unmarred with the evil thoughts of men, it must contain Life in the form which man has never known and most of all, it must be sent and directed by the "True Kreator (GOD) of All True Living of All Worlds." We have such a music. It is music from the True Living Kreator called "ATONAL music."[60]

El Saturn produced music that aimed much higher than commercial gain. For the people involved, the fate of the world depended on it, and not without reason. Five years of experimenting had proven its success. El Saturn produced and promoted music from the Kreator to save a troubled world: atonal music to retune humanity. "All of what you are reading may seem fantastic and unbelievable," Abraham admitted to Petrillo. But "the True Kreator works in ways unfamiliar to men."[61]

With time, El Saturn would find devoted fans, initially in Chicago and ultimately around the world. The Arkestra's regular gigging on the South Side in the late fifties made the band a fixture of the Chicago jazz scene. One group of boosters, likely with Thmei connections, sponsored Sunday-evening dances at the Pershing Hotel and styled themselves the "Atonites," a witty portmanteau moniker combining "Aton," the sun's disk of Egyptian myth (an aspect of Ra), with "atonality," musical expression with no defined tonal center. Surviving tickets from Atonite events attest to the delight these fans took in them. One reads, "*The Atonites* Present An Evening of OUTER SPACE MUSIC and DANCING *featuring* Sun Ra & his Outer Space Arkestra, Saturn and Transition Recording Artists." Another boasts, "*They're at it again . . .* THOSE ATONITES *that is* . . . Reaching 'way out of Space! / Bringing to you Earthlings / The Nu Sounds of *Sun Ra and his Arkestra.* / Dance the Outer Space Way."[62] The Atonites reached back to Egypt and ahead to the future, staging weekly events that opened the small space of a South Side lounge to mythological and extraterrestrial vistas. In the words of a later advertisement, "Sun Ra's group is what happens when Astrology meets technology in the 21st century."[63]

Atonite music shows up on *Super-Sonic Jazz,* where the Arkestra plays tunes that expand the traditional big band vocabulary. "India," the opening track, remains tonally centered throughout, but from the outset, Sun Ra's electric piano pursues the outré tones of commercial exotica, a trajectory rife with bright cymbals and rumbling drums that does not develop so much as flash a series of sonic images signifying "the East." It's a declaration of independence in keeping with the back cover's claim that "America is a composite nation and only a composite music can represent the real America."[64] "Portrait of the Living Sky" puts first a bass drone and then a recurring tonal figure into a tense and seemingly arbitrary relationship with a piano that skitters and cascades across this musical floor. "Advice to Medics" does something similar with a solo electric piano, as Sun Ra escapes terra firma entirely to flutter at will in the upper registers—until he returns to tempo if not quite to Earth. Maybe this was the tune that once provoked a longtime catatonic case to blurt (in sudden recovery?), "You call that music?"[65] It's hard to tell what key suits the head of the closing track on *Super-Sonic Jazz*, "Medicine for a Nightmare," so skillfully does the bass avoid the tonic and so gestural are the trumpet's short phrases stating something akin to melody. The Atonites' cherished band was in full swing. But it's important to remember that they sponsored *dances*. The Arkestra's music didn't only challenge musical conventions. It dislocated them to relocate them in spaces conducive to invigorated life and movement—like the Pershing on Sunday nights. The music El Saturn recorded and sold was entertainment too, turned artfully toward instruction to enrich the lives of its listeners. Beta music makes life beta. El Saturn Research was in the business of bettering the world.

10

ISOTOPE TELEPORTATION

Music moves. It transports. In transporting, it transforms. Music can transform worlds. Such is the vision of Thmei and its jazz messenger, Sun Ra. The various avatars of Sun Ra's Arkestras played during the second half of the century called the twentieth to transform this world. Or better yet, they played to transport people—black people—to a better one. Interplanetary transport: that was the practical purpose of Sun Ra's music, the transportation of a disfranchised mass from world to world, from planet to planet.

Politics, too, often comes down to transportation: in Europe, making the trains run on time; in America, designing interstate highways; in Chicago, plowing the streets to keep traffic moving, as Mayor Michael Bilandic discovered to his chagrin in the aftermath of the legendary snowpocalypse of 1979.[1] In Chicago, Sun Ra began composing the exhilarating ensemble music that would launch him, his musicians, and his myriad audiences on a sonic odyssey to other worlds.

In Chicago, he watched the civil rights movement rise like a waking giant. And in Chicago, too, he began to envision an alternative politics equal to that movement's aspirations. Where other leaders looked to oratory, spirituality, or resistance, whether passive or active, as a means to change, Sun Ra turned to music, approaching it as mass transportation, a politics of prophetic sound.

Sun Ra arrived in Chicago from Birmingham by train, leaving the Magic City from a station he knew well, having grown up in its shadow. He arrived in a city defined as much by public transportation as by lakeside views. And once he was in Chicago, he and Thmei laid the groundwork and built a launchpad for the Arkestra as a vehicle of creative insurgence. Important as Thmei was to the exploration of urban and intellectual space, however, the more material infrastructure merits consideration, too—for instance, the "L," Chicago's elevated train. Why not avoid street-level congestion by transporting commuters on a higher plane? As in so many other ways, Chicago is second only to New York in having the oldest elevated railway in America.[2] The Chicago and South Side Rapid Transit Railroad began operation on June 6, 1892, running 3.6 miles in a straight line from Congress Street to Thirty-Ninth. Among its striking features, the *Chicago Tribune* noted, was the diversity of its patrons, who ranged from "the lunch pail crowd" to passengers "appearing to be gentlemen."[3] Over the next fifty years, the "L" grew, flourished, and drooped until the Chicago Transit Authority acquired it in the 1940s and undertook an ambitious program of modernization. By the 1950s, all-metal PCC 6000 electric transit cars ran the "L" rails.[4] Sun Ra came to a city with sleek, modern trains running above the ground on elevated tracks. In Chicago, the iron horse had wings. Trains rumbled above the streets, kicking up a joyous urban cacophony.

Sun Ra captures some of this exuberance in a track from *Super-Sonic Jazz* entitled "El is a Sound of Joy." In the lower left-hand corner of the album's later cover the words "21st Century Edition," suggest transportation of and into the future. "L" sounds like "El," and Sun Ra would have known that "El" is a Semitic word meaning "deity," cognate to the Hebrew Elohim, father of all humankind, creator of all creatures. Interminable equations. In Chicago, the supreme deity is also a train. Sacred source of a sound of joy. Kevin Whitehead suggests that Sun Ra would have been "impressed with a city where a ride on the train system [. . .] might hurtle one through open space above the earth one minute and then into a subterranean netherworld the next—the realms of the angel and the demon in rapid succession."[5] And indeed, the tune plays a sinuous alto sax against a dark baritone groove. But Sun Ra's piano solo offers a punctuated dissonance that gestures toward something else, perhaps a future untempered by angels and demons alike. Joy. The sound of El.

Why this attention to mass transit? Sun Ra's supersonic jazz is more than a pastiche of futuristic sounds, for it explores the archaeology of a particular people's history, too. African Americans know a thing or two about transportation. Behind Sun Ra's conception of music as a means of travel, as *transport*, lies the memory of the Middle Passage, the marine voyage of expropriated Africans crammed into ships and sent across the Atlantic to an American marketplace of body and bone. The vehicular means of this mass transit was, of course, the slave ship, a floating factory of terror and domination. A technological wonder of its age, the slave ship transported dispossessed Africans from a familiar place to an unknowable space, a new and menacing world beyond their ken.[6]

It is beyond ours, too. When it comes to the Atlantic passage aboard a slave ship, our imaginations are probably limited to a few potent images, the most familiar no doubt being that of the *Brooks* (often rendered as "Brookes"), a Liverpool slaver that made ten successful voyages in the late eighteenth century, carrying a total of 5,163 Africans, 4,559 of whom lived to be sold in New World markets.[7] The familiar and disturbing abolitionist broadside depicting the laden *Brooks* shows 482 tiny black figures packed on the lower deck and half-decks installed specially to receive them—actually many fewer than the 609 or more the ship could accommodate when fully loaded. This is an image to demoralize the heartiest humanist. Those little black bodies look pretty cramped. Their color neither explains nor justifies their treatment.

But more interesting than the brute fact of this harrowing historical legacy is what Sun Ra does with it. Consider what happens when
the image of the *Brooks* rotates 90 degrees. It becomes a rocket—no
less cramped, perhaps, but ready to blast off for worlds other than an
American plantation. Perhaps these dislocated Africans weren't destined for subjugation after all. Perhaps other destinies are possible,
alternative destinies. In an interview published in 1984, Sun Ra made
the peculiar observation that there might be advantages to entering
the United States without a passport:

> Never in the history of the world has there been a case where you
> take a whole people and bring 'em in the country in the Commerce
> Department. Never before has that happened. It happened here.
> They bringing 'em in through the Commerce Department. It was
> possible for aliens and angels and devils and demons to come in
> this country. They didn't need no passport. So then they'd come
> as displaced people.[8]

The joke's on America. By trafficking in people, by admitting people
without passports through the Department of Commerce, to be then
bought and sold, America took aliens into its midst. No wonder they
seek new worlds. This one is not their home. Music, the sound ship of
Sun Ra's Arkestra, will become the means of transporting them, mass
transit for aliens seeking other climes and brighter futures.

This possibility, this alter-destiny, provides the subject of one of
Sun Ra's most playful, exuberant, kitsch-visionary tunes, "Rocket
Number Nine Take Off for the Planet Venus," recorded in late 1960
but not released until 1966, on the LP entitled *Rocket Number Nine
Take Off for the Planet Venus*, retitled *Interstellar Low Ways* three years
later.[9] It anticipates a celestial future for public transportation, updat-
ing the old kids' song "Engine, Engine Number Nine, Goin' down Chicago line."[10] Between it and the recording of "El is a Sound of Joy"
in 1956, Sputnik would ping its way around the globe, a Jupiter-C
rocket would hurl the first US satellite into orbit, and NASA would be
commissioned to assume responsibility for America's extraterrestrial

future. The Space Age would come to America. "Rocket Number Nine" celebrates its arrival by blasting mass transport into the cold, dark sky. The *Brooks* goes interplanetary, and the "L" along with it, running off the rails of joyful noise and heading toward more ethereal, abstract horizons.

After opening with a repeated piano figure and a clipped unison chant that some liken to Dizzy Gillespie's "Salt Peanuts" ("zoom, zoom, zoom, zoom, up in the air, up, zoom, up, zoom, up in the air [. . .] VenUS, VenUS, VenUS"), the tune morphs into a series of daring explorations of *space* punctuated by silence and followed with Sun Ra's rhythmically free piano. Astonishing among these explorations is John Gilmore's tenor saxophone solo. Blowing on the heels of several miraculous recordings from 1959 (Miles Davis's *Kind of Blue*, John Coltrane's *Giant Steps*, and Ornette Coleman's *The Shape of Jazz to Come*), Gilmore flies free of chord and form, playing lines of varying duration that finally rise in repetition to invoke a center that never arrives. Ronnie Boykins responds with what is less a bowed bass solo than a series of upper-register apologies for what once was music, now attenuated to the point of rumor, fading quietly into empty space. Here, then, is the place of Sun Ra's interplanetary transport: space. Here is music of astral mobility. It charts a historical course beyond history, from Africa to the Americas, from north to south, from planet to planet. Sun Ra transforms the fell history of the Middle Passage into deep-space exploration, mass transit for a dislocated and perpetually mobile people. Hear the call of the cosmic conductor; we travel the spaceways from planet to plant. First stop Venus. The second stop is Jupiter.

CRY OF JAZZ

The Arkestra was acquiring a reputation as Chicago's most cutting-edge ensemble, not primarily through recording (singles would remain El Saturn's main product for quite some time), but rather through live performance. It worked as regularly as Abraham could arrange, holding down a steady gig as the house band at Budland, formerly Birdland (the name changed at Sun Ra's suggestion when the esteemed New York establishment threatened to sue). Other venues included Duke Slater's Vincennes Lounge, the Parkway Ballroom, the Grand Terrace, Roberts Show Lounge, Club DeLisa, Casino Moderne, Queen's Mansion, 5th Jack Show Lounge, and the Wonder Inn.[1] The band's sound continued to develop as membership shifted, gaining fullness and drama when William Cochran replaced Robert Barry on drums and Victor Sproles played upright in place of Wilbur Green's electric bass.[2] The Arkestra recorded often enough to produce a fat body of material on tape, available for pressing when the time was ripe. Material for Transition's second volume of *Jazz by Sun Ra*, put to tape on

December 1, 1956, languished in limbo after the company closed.[3] The Arkestra played on, recording more singles, plenty of rehearsals, and some live sets at Budland and the Pershing Ballroom—work that culminated in a long studio session on March 6, 1959, yielding the second and last LP El Saturn would release during Sun Ra's years in Chicago, the remarkable *Jazz in Silhouette*. It was a willfully exploratory record, a harbinger of jazz to come. Enthusiasts were taking notice of the Arkestra's devotion to innovation, as did a writer for the *Roosevelt Torch*: "Their arrangements have been termed as the most advanced Modern Jazz yet devised."[4]

An interesting opportunity to promote the band's sound arose when the local filmmaker Edward Bland approached El Saturn and asked to use a few of the Arkestra's recordings in a movie he was making about black life and music in Chicago. Like Abraham, Bland had grown up on the South Side and knew its conditions firsthand. Like Richard Wright, he felt keenly the plight of urban blacks caught between dreams of a better life and a squalid reality. Part documentary and part drama, *The Cry of Jazz* would explore the relationship between jazz and black experience by juxtaposing real life images from the South Side with scripted conversation among a group of young fans.[5] Abraham and Sun Ra liked the idea and offered Bland free use of five of the Arkestra's recordings.[6] To avoid attracting union attention, Bland inserted a diversion in the film's credits: "music recorded in Europe."[7] It clearly wasn't. The Arkestra plays a prominent role in the film, providing musical and visual background for several extended meditations on jazz, its history, and its contemporary implications for black life in America.[8] Interspersed discussions occur among the racially mixed members of a Chicago jazz club, one of whom (a young black guy named Alex) knows whereof he speaks because he works as the arranger for "the Paul Severson Group."[9] Shot in noir-worthy black and white (menacing shadow/radiant light), *The Cry of Jazz* advances a view of jazz that, provocative in itself, serves as an illuminating foil to the very music it features—the Arkestra's.

The film offers an extended visual and verbal commentary on the significance of jazz as a form of American music. It opens with a familiar claim made unfamiliar by the addition of a single adverb: "Jazz is merely," says Alex, "the Negro's cry of joy and suffering." Merely? The word anticipates the film's critique of jazz as a form of contemporary black expression. According to the film, there is something limited—and limiting—about it, and Alex is determined to show just what. He acknowledges that only "Negroes" possess the history necessary to create jazz, but the remark provokes a predictable response from one of his white friends: "Jazz is American." So much for black history. America is so capacious! But Alex asks the group to consider the neighborhood around the place where his band jammed the previous day; the film then cuts to a slow, brutal montage of the South Side that continues for several minutes, depicting squalid tenements, abandoned cars, and junk piled in heaps. This is Richard Wright's South Side in living monochrome, the black urban space where jazz happens in Chicago. Bland's sobering images hang a disconcerting backdrop behind the little lecture Alex then gives his jazz-fan friends about the true source of the Negro cry of joy and suffering.

Jazz, Alex says quietly but with professorial authority, arises from a contradiction between freedom and restraint. This contradiction gets built into the music's fundamental form, which Alex understands to contain four basic components: two that are conducive to restraint (chords and chorus) and two that foster freedom (melody and rhythm).[10] Because the harmonic structure of the chords regulates a tune's progress, while the chorus inevitably recurs, jazz becomes a formula for endless repetition and constraint, an effect Alex interprets darkly: "This endless repetition is like a chain around the spirit and is a reflection of the denial of the future to the Negro and the American way of life."[11] Or again: "the Negro experiences the endless humiliation of daily American life [on the screen appears a sign that reads "For Rent: WHITES ONLY"], which bequeaths him a futureless future." Endless repetition recapitulates humiliation, trumpeting the hard fact that America denies blacks a future.

Melody, on the other hand, provides an occasion for improvisation, while rhythm induces the exuberant tension of swing. Both augur freedom: players improvise, and everybody moves. But a problem emerges with these formal freedoms, too. They remain too tightly bound to the present moment to offer much of an alternative to the futureless future of repetition. As Alex puts it, "Jazz is a musical expression of the Negro's eternal re-creation of the present." Denied a future, the present is all blacks have, and so the joys they celebrate in the freedoms of improvisation and swing turn out to produce another kind of constraint, that of confinement to the here and now. Under these circumstances, constant creativity is the only way for the Negro to feel free: "otherwise, the dehumanizing portrait America has drawn of him will triumph." Endless repetition meets the perpetual present; jazz reproduces the Negro's experience of contradiction between constraint and freedom in such a way that it at best becomes only "an unconscious holding action until he is also master of his future." Alex—with Bland behind him—implicates jazz in the social and cultural segregation that condemns blacks to a futureless future.

The implications of this impasse finally become clear in the last half of the movie, when Alex forces the issue with a blunt declaration: "Jazz is dead." An idiom that recycles constraint in the name of momentary joy becomes a hungry corpse and makes zombies of its listeners. Alex warms to his theme and delivers another lecture, this one on the development of jazz from New Orleans to bebop, in part to illustrate his claim that, given jazz's investment in endless repetition, no true growth is possible in its basic form. Evade the changes, and you lose the form; lose the form, and you kill the swing. Jazz seems formally committed to its own stagnation and death, becoming nothing more than "a genteel slavery." Alex predicts the same futureless future for jazz as faces the American Negro: "empty variations on obsolete themes, or worse." Unless . . .

Unless the Negro can continue to create in the *spirit* rather than the form of jazz: "The body is dead, but the spirit of jazz is here for a long time, just like the Negro." Hope for a future for blacks—and in fact for America—resides in the possibility that the Negro will forsake the dead form of jazz for the vital force of its spirit; it "depends on what the Negro does with the spirit of jazz. [. . .] The spirit of the Negro will remake serious music, but the sounds of jazz will not be used." Jazz is dead. Long live—something else. In the spirited conversation that follows, tensions between blacks and whites rise in a way that moves beyond the pointless joys of swing. America needs a future for the Negro in order to transcend constraints that produce an empty life for all. The death of jazz thus opens the possibility of new life, or so says Alex: "The death of jazz is the first faint cry of the salvation of the Negro through the birth of a new way of life." "The Negro and the rest of America," adds a black friend. Without a new future, all that most Americans will see "in tomorrow's mirror" (Alex's words) "is a Cadillac or a deep freeze." "Or," says his friend, "a man walking on the moon."

The Cry of Jazz offers a brilliant assessment of the state of jazz in the late fifties. But the band it uses to illustrate its thesis seems—in retrospect, at least—to have been an odd choice. Alex describes the Arkestra's music in a way that ties it to a terminal history:

> The newest sounds to come along in jazz are written by the composer and arranger Sun Ra out of Chicago. Sun Ra, among other things, fuses the snakelike bebop melodies with colors of Duke Ellington and the experimental changes of Thelonious Monk. The Sun Ra says of this music that it's a portrayal of everything the Negro really was, is, and is going to be, with emphasis focused on the Negro's triumph over the occurrence of his experience.

Bland samples five of the Arkestra's tunes to illustrate "the newest sounds to come along," but if the movie's discussion is to be the measure, that music appears destined either to die or to become something other than jazz. Bland presents the Arkestra in a way that visually anticipates the former. The ensemble and even individual players rarely appear as full images; instead, we see them only as fragments of a band: a reed section, a bassist, half a drummer, hands on a keyboard, fingers over valves. Shrouded in murk and shadow. Blank silhouettes. The Arkestra plays blues, swing, and bebop behind city scenes of black life, including a happiness church, a pool hall, and nightlife on the street. But when Alex starts his disquisition on the death of jazz, the musicians all fall out, leaving only abandoned instruments on the bandstand.

In an interview conducted years later, one hard not to read as a reference to *The Cry of Jazz*, Sun Ra states what he sees as obvious: "They said Jazz is dead. But no, Jazz isn't dead. The musicians are dead. They are the ones are dead. Jazz will never die."[12] Contra Bland and Alex, Sun Ra asserts that life will always belong to jazz. The Arkestra's appearance in *The Cry of Jazz* substantiates that claim, perhaps despite the film's overt message. The Monk-like intro to "A Call for All Demons" (think "Mysterioso") eschews traditional form, as does Sun Ra's comping during the snaky minor head. The Arkestra seems to be on the verge of giving old jazz new wings. Then there's the strange piano passage (actually played by Eddie Higgins over shots of Sun Ra's hands at the keyboard) that repeats a jagged phrase over and over again, ostensibly to demonstrate "endless repetition" and its "future-less future." Maybe so, but it also anticipates exciting new developments to come in jazz and popular music: minimalist seriality, digital sampling, and—most pertinent to Sun Ra's music—post-harmonic sonorities of noise. Bland's burial of jazz seems premature. The year *The Cry of Jazz* appeared, 1959, witnessed an extraordinary dawning of new horizons that pushed jazz beyond Bland's simple swing formula of constraint and freedom: the modal explorations of Miles Davis on *Kind of Blue*, the melodic odysseys of Ornette Coleman on *The Shape of Jazz to Come*, the harmonic invention of John Coltrane's *Giant Steps*, and the Arkestra's sonic "images and forecasts of tomorrow" on *Jazz in Silhouette*.[13]

It's a gorgeous, adventuresome recording, a joyous riposte to Bland's jazz obituary. Corbett ruminates evocatively on the title: "*Jazz in Silhouette*. It's not jazz, per se. It's the outline of jazz, the futuristic relief of jazz. [. . .] Jazz silhouetted: an absent space in which jazz can transform into something else"—while remaining jazz, Sun Ra would add.[14] Rather than bemoan the futureless future of blacks, Sun Ra devotes the considerable skill of his Arkestra to imagining the future—as music. Doing so involves combining the past ("Ancient Aiethopia"), the present ("Velvet," "Enlightenment"), and the future ("Saturn," "Images") and rejecting the linearity of Bland's analysis of jazz history. Music doesn't move from an absent past through a constrained present to a nonexistent future. It happens all at once, everywhere, everywhen. Hence the Gestalt figure-ground gimmick of the silhouette, multiple planes yielding reversible perceptions. What was, is—and will be.

"In tomorrow's world, men will not need artificial instruments such as jets and space ships. In the world of tomorrow, the new man will 'think' the place he wants to go, then his mind will take him there."[15] Listen to "MUSIC FROM TOMORROW'S WORLD."[16] Listen today. Time matters less than space, a future emanating sound. Can you get there? Can you hear tomorrow? "Ancient Aiethopia" rescinds chorus and chords, preferring a pure poetry of sound. "Saturn" harks back to swing and forward to polyharmony. The piano introducing "Images" just hangs like a shadow in space until the Arkestra (fore)casts it into form. Music of, for, by, beyond the future. "Music is the shadow of tomorrow / Today is the present future of yesterday / Yesterday is the shadow of today."[17] The future *happens*—as shadow—in the Arkestra's music. What can you hear? How does the future sound?

12

SPUTNIK

By the late fifties, the Arkestra did not appear to have much of a future in Chicago. An economic downturn blunted the prospect of black uplift as audiences grew thin. Its regular gig as the house band at Budland turned spotty after 1957. Abraham booked the band where he could, one-nighters at the Pershing Hotel or off-night jobs at Club DeLisa.[1] Queen's Mansion, a gay bar opening in the summer of 1958, offered steady work for a while, but between the dwindling of big-band dance venues and the rise of rock and roll, the Arkestra played less and less. Members split for better prospects: Hobart Dotson and Julian Priester, for the New York scene; Art Hoyle, to play with Lionel Hampton. Sun Ra returned to coaching vocal groups on the side, recording several Saturn singles with the Cosmic Rays backed by the Arkestra. He also taped a rock and roll song entitled "Little Sally Walker" as performed in rehearsal by a group called the Crystals, whose smooth harmonies somewhat understate the possibilities of the loopy lyrics: "Little Sally Walker, sitting in a saucer / ride Sally ride."[2] Those lyrics would eventually morph into a chant that became a favorite at

Arkestra performances: "Little Sally Walker, in a flying saucer." For now, the band seemed grounded in Chicago. Abraham eventually suggested that Sun Ra look for work elsewhere "because nobody was listening to him there . . . the Chicago newspapers ignored him."[3]

But something was happening to the music, too, broadening its scope, pushing its cultural reach beyond the confines of the South Side. To Thmei's occult message, with its Egyptian wisdom and Afrocentric philosophy, Sun Ra began to add a futuristic dimension, steadily enhancing the Arkestra's commitment to "the music of tomorrow." He retrofitted antiquity to the future. Space became a musical obsession, the space of rockets, satellites, and UFOs. As enthusiasts of things occult, Abraham and his Thmei brethren nursed a serious interest in the craze for unidentified flying objects that began in 1947 with Kenneth Arnold's high-altitude sighting of nine oblong lights over Mount Rainier. The *Chicago Sun* appears to have coined the term "flying saucer" in its report of that famous incident. Was Chicago peculiarly receptive to alien visitation? Abraham's library contained much material concerning UFOs, including the sacred scripture of alien-encounter texts, George Adamski's *Flying Saucers Have Landed*, published in 1953—the year to which acquaintances date Sun Ra's earliest public telling of his personal abduction narrative.[4] The Thmei insider and Saturn vice-president James Bryant recorded a sighting in 1965: "On the 30th October I had a vision their were five lights is in the north East dancing which look like Stars or Saucer lights flying then out of the South two lights" [*sic*].[5] For Thmei Research, ufology offered a culturally conducive way of conveying occult wisdom, particularly that of theosophy, given its emphasis on spirit masters from Venus and interplanetary communication. Adamski's book and others of its ilk promise wisdom through alien encounter, ostensibly authenticated by publications such as *Cosmic Voice: Aetherius Speaks to Earth* (with an image of Adamski's flying saucer printed in red on the pale green cover): "Many contacts with people from Mars, Venus and Saturn, are reported, as well as fairly detailed descriptions of Flying Saucers and Mother-Ships from these three planets" (Abraham—or was it Sun Ra?—underlined this passage).[6]

Sun Ra's interest in all things futuristic reached back to his Alabama days, inspiring both his curiosity about new developments in music and recording technology and his creativity, as early compositions with the titles "Thermodynamics" and "Fission" indicate. But over the course of the fifties it steadily increased. Although the Space Trio, his early group for experimental music, began rehearsing in 1951 or 1952, it took some years for space to become a defining preoccupation in his music. The titles of several of the Arkestra's first recordings gesture toward the future in a general way ("New Horizons" and "Future," from *Jazz by Sun Ra, Vol. 1*, and maybe "Saturn," from *Jazz in Silhouette*), but if an ideological agenda drove the early LPs, it primarily involved esoteric wisdom, as a great many of their tracks' titles suggest: "Call for All Demons," "Sun Song," "India," "Sunology," "El is a Sound of Joy," "Enlightenment," "Ancient Aiethopia," or "Horoscope." Things were different with recordings not intended for immediate release. During a small ensemble rehearsal in early 1956, Sun Ra recorded the Saturn single "Adventur in Space" [*sic*] (copyrighted April 25 of that year but not released for over a decade). Then, in April, possibly at Balkan Studios, he recorded "Blues in Outer Space" and "Space Aura" with a Space Trio sans drums that included James Scales on alto sax and Wilbur Green on electric bass.[7]

Space was working its way into Sun Ra's repertoire, initially more as a thematic than a musical gesture. "Space Aura," for instance, erupts in hard-bop overdrive, the head a blistering sixteen bars of harmony to squirm by. Nothing about the tune bespeaks space beyond its title, but citations of this sort will be one way Sun Ra puts the *space* in space music, creating words with which to hear its newness. "Adventur in Space," on the other hand, feels more experimental than the other tunes do, if not necessarily more space-like. This piano fantasy eschews melody, offering instead a procession of clumping chords over a vaguely Latin rhythm. Space here seems synonymous with adventure, a declaration of independence from traditional song forms and a premonition of things to come. Sun Ra's work was on the verge of a quantum leap forward in daring and innovation, heralded by the opening of the Arkestra's repertoire to include such compositions.

This development wasn't simply an aesthetic choice on the composer's part. By introducing notions of space into his music, Sun Ra was aligning it with larger cultural currents, in effect making a bid for wider impact, influence, and recognition. Black life on Chicago's South Side may have driven his interest in music of expansive possibility, but American culture more generally gave it wings, or rather fins, for flying into space. The language of space that found its way into Sun Ra's music referenced the preoccupations not simply of a black jazz composer in Chicago but of the entire nation and probably of the entire developed world. After all, postwar America had, with no little fanfare and self-congratulation, entered "the Space Age"; this phrase, widely familiar by the midfifties, had been coined to describe the opening of a new epoch and to mark an atmospheric shift in cultural climate. Its earliest use dates to the work of a British journalist named Harry Harper, who published a book in 1946 with the clairvoyant title *Dawn of the Space Age*.[8] That sun rose over America and shone for a quarter of a century. Sun Ra bathed his music in its light. He did so with increasing cunning, humor, and willfulness as the fifties unfurled. The booklet accompanying Transition's *Jazz by Sun Ra, Vol. 1* bore the title "Preparations for Outer Space." It names the purpose of music to come, redirecting the Thmei agenda from the urban space of Chicago's South Side to the outer space of American dreams.

Sun Ra's recollection of his days in Washington Park shows that he pursued this purpose deliberately, with care and imagination. It came to inform all aspects of the Arkestra's work, from the studio to the stage. At some point in the late fifties, Sun Ra introduced the space togs that would become the Arkestra's sartorial trademark: capes festooned with ringed planets and suns, metallic headgear, flowing silver-lamé shirts, and "moon boots." Costumes began to get florid when Abraham acquired the wardrobe of a defunct opera company, but Sun Ra exploited their cultural implications:

We started [wearing space-related costumes] back in Chicago. In those days I tried to make black people, the so-called Negroes, conscious of the fact that they live in a changing world. And because

I thought they were left out of everything culturally, that nobody thought about bringing them in contact with the culture, none of the black leaders did that . . . that's why I thought I could make it clear to them that there are other things outside their closed environment. That's what I tried with those clothes.[9]

Clothes as cultural pedagogy and creative resistance: the Arkestra's space-age wardrobe provided its audience with a visual tutorial in the preoccupations of American culture at large, pushing them imaginatively beyond the confines of the South Side into a world obsessed with outer space. What place (those clothes force the question) would blacks have in the Space Age as America imagined it?

The increasing urgency of that question, and Sun Ra's answer, becomes clear even in the production history of *Super-Sonic Jazz*, released by El Saturn in 1957. It isn't simply that the title refers to the wizardry of aviation. Sun Ra also celebrates outer space as a cultural and musical aspiration—overtly so on a redesigned jacket first used in 1961. Also created by Claude Dangerfield and known as the "void" cover for its mélange of disparate jazz images dancing in an abyss, it comes with a lesson in listening printed on the back: "With your mind's eye you are invited to see other scenes of the space age by focusing your eyes on the cover and your mind on the music. The scenes are from the space void."[10] Supersonic jazz requires listening with the eyes. The back of the void cover also bears two Sun Ra poems whose titles openly declare his newly expanded musical agenda: "Points on the Space Age" and "The Space Age Cannot Be Avoided."[11] Given Sun Ra's belief that his music transposes his poetry (and vice versa), these poems provide the word track, so to speak, to the sounds first released as *Super-Sonic Jazz*, unabashedly repurposed to a space-age agenda. Sun Ra's lyrics chart a course to the stars and beyond: "This is the music of greater transition / To the invisible, irresistible space age."[12] "Points on the Space Age" declares a break with musical history, consigning the music of the past to "museums of the past." A music of outer space will be every bit as "big and real and compelling"; it is the music of a future that already exists: "The music of the future is already developed / But the minds of the people of earth must be prepared to accept it." To the Arkestra falls the task, then, of educating Earth in a future already here, inserting its people into "the moving panorama of the outer spacite program."[13]

"The Space Age Cannot Be Avoided" provides the philosophical foundations of this education. Washington Park points to Saturn and far beyond: "the greater future is the age of the space Prophet, / The scientific airy-minded second man."[14] Sun Ra's message is simple tone science insofar as "The greater power of the future greater / Greater music is art." Future music, the Arkestra's music, will be (and is) greater by the power of two ("greater / Greater"). Sun Ra displaces the rhetoric of the Thmei broadsheets into a poetry of outer space and greater art: "Art is the foundation of any living culture" (a sentiment reminiscent of the broadsheets).[15] Then comes a canny riposte to Cold War jingoism: "The new measure of determination as to whether a nation / Is ready to be a greater nation is art. / A nation without art is a nation without a lifeline." By placing his space program for future music in a Cold War context, Sun Ra ushers onto the world stage a people—black people—whose main access to political agency is culture, the art they make, the music they produce. By implication, black art trumps the destructive wonders of technoscience, "because art is the airy concept of better living."[16] Sun Ra's poems—and the music they manifest—channel new worlds to come that have already arrived, a "Tomorrow beyond Tomorrow" that (*pace* American democracy) founds a new political order: "THE KINGDOM OF THE SPACE AGE."[17] Such is the creative force of Sun Ra's cultural politics, propelling the Thmei message of black uplift into the heart of American culture, with its imperialist ambitions and space-age dreams. Artfully and on a plume of music, Sun Ra blasts blackness into space.

Liftoff came in Chicago—not a bad place for imagining an alternative space program. The Manhattan Project, the technoscientific enterprise that did more than any other both to end World War II and to usher in the world that came afterward, took a major step forward at the University of Chicago, where, in 1942, Enrico Fermi and Leo Szilard engineered the first self-sustaining nuclear reaction in a laboratory made from a squash court under the stadium at Stagg Field.[18] The following year the Manhattan Project moved to Los Alamos, New Mexico, leaving behind seeds of the Space Age. Sun Ra's interest in outer space as a musical theme attests to their germination and astonishing growth: by the late fifties, the Space Age was culturally ubiquitous. It named a new era in which American society in general took space for a desideratum. Talk of the Space Age involved everybody, no matter how marginal or low. It provided Sun Ra with a spacious backdrop for Thmei's otherwise esoteric wisdom. It opened ancient Egypt and contemporary black America to national, international, even planetary concerns. *The Space Age cannot be avoided*, which is to say that black Americans, however confined to their ghettoes and defined by their past, nevertheless participated in a broader culture increasingly defined by the challenge of space. Blacks would have to create a place for themselves in the coming culture of the Space Age.

Between the old and new jackets of *Super-Sonic Jazz* (1957 and 1961, respectively), a sound from tomorrow's world greeted planet Earth. As J. G. Ballard puts it in his startled recollection, "the call sign of Sputnik 1 could be heard on one's radio like the advance beacon of a new universe."[19] Sputnik. Its launch by the USSR on October 4, 1957, challenged US claims to technological and political superiority. It affected the emphasis of the Arkestra's music, too, making the group's increasing preoccupation with space seem, if not inevitable, at least pertinent: a purposeful, maybe prankish response to a culture preoccupied with the "Red menace" now reaching its tentacles into space. Sputnik both completed an era in cultural history and inaugurated a new one, which is why the phrase "Space Age" doesn't appear in Sun Ra's poetry or music until after its ominous launch. Prior to October 1957, the technological mastery of space remained only a dream, one dreamed fiercely by politicians and scientists on both sides of the Iron Curtain but remaining nevertheless fantastical, the stuff of science fiction but not yet science fact. Sputnik made space real. It is no exaggeration to say that its successful launch and operation provoked the *invention* of outer space as an international if contentiously collaborative creative enterprise.[20]

Before World War II, space belonged to science fiction. Since the 1930s, tons of pulp paper and miles of celluloid had spread a popular gospel of adventures in space, mostly on alien planetscapes suffering incursions of viscid, bile-spitting BEMs (bug-eyed monsters). It wouldn't take much to interpret such fantasies as displaced propaganda for dreams of imperial domination. Combined with the relentless pursuit of rocketry by highly respected researchers including Robert Goddard in the United States and Konstantin Tsiolkovsky in the Soviet Union, such dreams bled easily into nationalist and imperialist aspirations on both sides of the Atlantic. World War II made them terrifyingly real. Not only did it demonstrate to ghastly effect that the wonders of technoscience could as easily destroy humanity as sustain it (first at Hiroshima and then at Nagasaki), but Germany's development of the V-2 as a means of delivering mass destruction at a distance also ensured that, following the Potsdam Conference, militarized rocketry would be assimilated to state policy, the war's victors having to differing degrees absorbed the remnants of Hitler's secret rocket program. The emergence of two superpowers in possession of nuclear weapons set the stage for the Cold War, which dominated foreign policy and domestic politics in both the United States and the USSR. Given these developments, one key to the future of both countries—and maybe the world—would be mastery of space, the medium through which the missiles guiding those policies would fly to rain atomic hell on enemy civilians.

A brief "Missile Age," then, preceded the Space Age, although that phrase appears with little frequency. In the decade before Sputnik, the world's superpowers fought the Cold War in rocket labs and on balance sheets, racing to perfect a missile capable of delivering a nuclear warhead between continents with enough accuracy to pose a viable military threat to civilian populations. Sun Ra's space music developed in the shadow of this lunacy and voices the resistance of a doubly vulnerable population (urban blacks) to the cultural logic of ballistic missilery. As the fifties unfolded, the Arkestra would come to play in a transcontinental theater of planned mass homicide that supplied both the thematic content of its space music and a larger target for its cultural activism. The history of powered missiles thus helped push the Arkestra toward space music by *creating outer space* as an arena of aspiration and contest.

Space became more than just medium for missile flight, however. Even more important, at least from an American perspective, was the possibility of spying from the sky, observing Soviet developments and reporting back unobserved: espionage and communications. US officials knew that the USSR possessed big rockets capable of boosting large payloads, but they knew, too, that those missiles were inaccurate. Rather than try to beat the Russians at their own heavy thrust game, US policy makers chose to focus on the smaller-scale technologies of guidance and communications. It was a gamble that presumed the planet to be wrapped in a kind of space open to new technologies of espionage and communications capable of monitoring Soviet research and development. After all, devices using these technologies would constitute much lighter payloads than nuclear weaponry. The United States could cancel the Soviet advantage in heavy thrusters with precision communications equipment. But doing so would require (and this may seem obvious) space through which such technologies could freely fly.[21] Was space a free medium for communication and its emerging technologies? Or did sovereign nations own the space immediately above them, and if they did, how far out?

It fell to satellites to adjudicate these questions—and missiles capable of carrying payloads into space. The stakes of the Missile Age, however unacknowledged as a phase of Cold War cultural history, involved the creation of space conducive to US propaganda and espionage. The nation devoted to defending freedom on Earth would defend freedom above it, too—which would be all the better for spying on other nations and communicating the results. Ideology may have fueled the race to launch a satellite into orbit, with both the United States and the USSR claiming superior political vision and technological prowess, but its effect would be the conceptual creation of *outer space* irreducible to national or territorial sovereignty. Perhaps this was the greatest eventual outcome of the "International Geophysical Year," which ran from mid-1957 until the end of 1958 and involved sixty-three countries in projects devoted to the advancement of geopolitically useful knowledge: space as a transnational medium for communication and flight.[22] While the United States ostensibly lost that race when Sputnik claimed kudos as the first satellite blasted into orbit, it mercilessly exploited a less obvious aspect of the Soviet victory, namely, the vindication of the freedom of space by the orbital flight of a 183.9-pound pinging object over multiple nations and airspaces.[23] The *scientific* profile of the Soviet achievement secured space as a free medium for producing knowledge—including knowledge, happily, of the state of Soviet missile technology.

An ensuing spate of policies and opinions consolidated this convenient outcome, which was summed up by a best-selling pamphlet produced by the President's Science Advisory Committee and entitled *Introduction to Outer Space* (1958). President Eisenhower prefaces this report on the implications of satellite flight with a word of caution: "This is not science fiction. This is a sober, realistic presentation prepared by leading scientists." He then announces his endorsement of a national and international commitment to space as a free medium: "We and other nations have a great responsibility to promote the peaceful use of space and to utilize the new knowledge obtainable from space science and technology for the benefit of all mankind."[24] Sputnik and other satellites (such as the United States' Explorer 1, successfully launched into orbit on January 31, 1958) *create* the free and open space they fly through, and in the words of those leading scientists, perhaps do much more: "These satellites cannot fail to reveal new sights forever hidden from observers who are bound to the earth. What these sights will be, no one can tell." Possibly they would reveal Soviet secrets as well. One thing is sure: the exploration of a free and open outer space would inspire earthlings "to try to go where no one has gone before."[25]

But where is that? *Introduction to Outer Space*, like US policy more generally, avoids defining the space it names. What *is* outer space? Where does airspace leave off and outer space begin? Such questions prove unanswerable in political or even scientific terms. A brief from 1958 entitled "Preliminary U.S. Policy on Outer Space" concludes that "the term 'outer space' has no generally accepted precise definition."[26] The proposed definitions include the Kármán line, the point at which a vehicle loses aerodynamic lift and becomes a spaceship; for a craft traveling at seven kilometers per second, that occurs at an altitude of roughly fifty-three miles.[27] Such a definition of outer space relies on stipulation arising from human interests, making space more a human construct than a fact of nature. Outer space is clearly as much consensual fantasy as reality. US policy makers in the late fifties came to prefer a functional definition that the USSR would follow: outer space begins at the point where satellites traveling seven kilometers per second or faster can achieve a stable orbit around the Earth.[28]

Tantamount to tautology, such a definition identifies outer space in terms of the vehicles used to explore it, rendering free orbital transit equivalent to the freedom of space itself. Construing outer space as free transit (irreducible to national territory or interest) provides a basis for declaring it a *res comunis omnium*, a common good for all humankind. That would become the US position, fundamental to Eisenhower's "Open Skies" policy, which served to maximize both ideological advantage and national prestige: outer space should be accessible to all nations, while the US would explore it for the good of humankind, also known as national security. This rationale led to the passage, in April 1958, of the National Aeronautics and Space Act, which established a civilian rather than a military space agency—NASA—in part to produce "general welfare and security," as stated in section 102(a): "Congress hereby declares that it is the policy of the Unites States that activities in space should be devoted to peaceful purposes for the benefit of all mankind."[29] By 1959, the United Nations Committee on the Peaceful Uses of Outer Space (boycotted by the Soviets) could advance as an international convention that "in principle, outer space is, on conditions of equality, freely available for exploration and use by all."[30] The consensual fantasy of outer space, functionally defined and politically deployed, opens freedom to infinity, but does so on the buried assumption that only nations, most obviously the United States and the Soviet Union, could acquire the capacity to explore its deeps and exploit its possibilities.

What if other players emerged to inherit the void? Nations in another sense, the black sense, or their cultural ambassadors to the universe—perhaps from the South Side of Chicago? The pervasive public language of the Space Age provides tools to build a kind of space different from the one that the two superpowers were racing to master. The Cold War appeared to set political terms for tomorrow's world, as it "expanded," in the words of Walter McDougall, "beyond nuclear weapons and espionage into a competition of entire systems, each claiming to be better at inventing the future."[31] But maybe neither liberal democracy nor communism exhausted the future's possibilities. Maybe the Space Age could open up another kind of space altogether, one irreducible to ideological agendas, even when advanced in the name of freedom.

That was Sun Ra's insight and gambit: that the public culture of the Space Age could lead beyond a politics of domination. Sun Ra would press space-age words and images into the service of a vision much bolder than either the United States or the Soviets Union could muster, one infinite in reach and inclusive in scope. He would build an alternative space administration, a visionary NASA, beholden only to blacks and powered by sound. He would conduct space exploration by means other than the heavy thrusters and miniaturized circuits of state-sponsored technoscience. He would invent a better future than democracy or communism could imagine precisely because he would *imagine* it, eschewing the language of policy and propaganda for a poetics of outer space. Music, poetry, performance, and recording would be his means of creating space for exploration. Sun Ra answered his own call to creative resistance with a space program marshaling all the resources of improvised music "to try to go where no one has gone before." As the fifties drew to a close, the Arkestra advanced its own definition of outer space every time it played.

If something seems funny about a group of intellectuals and crack musicians from Chicago's South Side womping up an alternative space program from the cultural detritus of the Space Age, it should. Describing the effects of his music, Sun Ra once stressed its playfulness:

There's humor in all my music [. . .] that sense of humor by which people sometimes learn to laugh about themselves. I mean, the situation is so serious that the people could go crazy because of it. They need to smile and realize how ridiculous everything is. A race without a sense of humor is in bad shape. A race needs clowns.[32]

Sun Ra clowns his way into outer space. Loopy harmonies, strained rhythms, weird costumes, quirky lyrics: humor hurls the Arkestra into orbit at a time when most blacks had little reason to laugh. In 1957, defense spending consumed 63 percent of the federal budget, and, thanks in no small part to Sputnik, Washington seemed oblivious to the realities of segregation.[33] In view of such circumstances, Sun Ra's humor could turn deadly serious: "Most people on this planet are lost, it's a limited existence. They get out there, there's no right or left, no right, no wrong, no up no down. That's outer space. So what do we have to go home to? Nothing."[34] Confinement to the South Side of Chicago or any other segregated place means inhabiting a world of nothing. Sun Ra's space program aimed at creating other possibilities: "Beta music for a Beta people for a Beta world."

Space music. Sun Ra composed it and the Arkestra played it—more and more as the fifties and the band's time in Chicago drew to a close. For Sun Ra, space is the place where better living becomes possible through music. So it is ultimately as a sonic metaphor that space acquires its greatest cultural force for Sun Ra. Szwed describes it as "both a metaphor of exclusion and of reterritorialization, of claiming the 'outside' as one's own, of tying a revised and corrected past to a claimed future."[35] Sun Ra's poetics of outer space unites a rehabilitated past (ancient Egypt) with a realized future (*Super-Sonic Jazz*) in just this manner. But it *moves*, too, in all senses of that word. Space as a force and form of sonic ballistics: it becomes as it sounds. Outer and other. Music moving beyond. Space outer, worlds better. A movement into or through the void. Here's Sun Ra:

When I say space music, I'm dealing with the void, because that is of space too; but I'm dealing with the outer void, because somehow man is trapped in playing roles into the haven or heaven of the inner void, but I am not in that. That particular aim/goal does not interest my spirit-mind and because of that it moves out to something else where the word space is the synonym for a multi-dimension of different things other than what people might at present think it means. So I leave the word space open, like space is supposed to be, when I say space music.[36]

Sun Ra takes space out. He moves beyond the inner life to outer space. And music propels him. Moves us. Space music. Into the open.

ROCKETRY

Sun Ra would soon leave Chicago, the place that gave birth to the Arkestra and its willfully futuristic sounds, and he would never return. Abraham had been casting about for gigs farther afield, maybe Birmingham or New York. A 1958 performance in Indianapolis turned out well—even if the band never got paid—yielding a lost but legendary recording with Wes Montgomery and a young Freddie Hubbard sitting in.[1] In July 1961, when the band got an offer to play a club in Montreal known as El Morocco, it seemed as good a reason as any to leave the South Side and its diminishing opportunities. Sun Ra gathered his core musicians—Gilmore, Boykins, and Marshall Allen (the indomitable alto saxophonist began his lifelong tenure with the Arkestra in 1958 playing flute)—and enlisted several others: Billy Mitchell on drums, Walter Strickland on trumpet, and the singer Ricky Murray.[2] After only two days, apparently, the club owner fired the band for playing unlistenable material, which he called "God's music."[3] Sun Ra refused to return to Chicago. The Arkestra found work at a mountain resort, Saint-Gabriel-de-Brandon, some sixty miles north, until a hip-ster coffee shop called The Place brought them back to Montreal for several weeks.[4] Canada proved a fickle patron. By the end of the year, the ensemble would relocate to New York.

The Arkestra left an astonishing stockpile of recordings behind in Chicago, fuel to propel them through the coming decade, if not quite the stratosphere. Abraham was a busy recording engineer in the late fifties, almost as inspired as Sun Ra. *Jazz in Silhouette* saw release on El Saturn in 1959, but the session it came from produced twice as many tracks. Masters from the doomed second Transition session were still looking for a home. Sun Ra usually ran tape at rehearsals, and the results often proved worthy of release. Such tracks pepper later El Saturn LPs. Live club recordings were a regular occurrence, sometimes disappearing only to surface again years later.[5] Abraham and Sun Ra used recording as much to document as to commodify the Arkestra's sound. In their hands, the tape recorder became a DIY mem-ory machine with commercial applications. About a year before leav-ing Chicago, the Arkestra recorded a marathon session at an unusual location, the Elks hall in Milwaukee, Wisconsin. An arduous day of playing yielded between thirty and forty tunes, enough for a spate of LPs. A quarter of the track titles betray an outer-space touch, with sev-eral of them copyrighted together under the title "Space Loneliness: A Sound Concerto."[6] Space provided Sun Ra room for innovative compo-sition. The recordings the Arkestra made before leaving Chicago reveal an ensemble launching to new heights of creativity, imagination, and excitement.

The release of those recordings obscures that impression, however. Completed by 1960, they would appear piecemeal or in small groups over the next decade on a variety of El Saturn LPs. Discontinuity gov-erns the relationship between the recording and the release of any given LP. Tunes recorded in Chicago might appear years later, long after the band had landed in New York, in 1961, or even Philadel-phia, in 1968. A kind of time travel characterizes these records. The "new" music they contain could be years old. In a sense, they play in *double* stereo, with both a temporal and an auditory channeling. An underlying discontinuity between now and then (release and recording) doubles that between left and right, an effect strangely enriching for the futuristic sounds of Sun Ra. New music is already old. Sounds from the future come from the past. Tomorrow's music loops through yesterday to arrive today, years after its creation. What does it mean to hear time's dissonance, the slippage of history into its future, our present? The time travel induced by El Saturn LPs released after the Arkestra's departure from Chicago disrupts history as a preferred means of receiving knowledge, even in musical form. Music of the past *and* future occur in a present that opens in both directions, dispersing the securities of historical knowledge.

Corbett rightly claims that Sun Ra preferred nonlinear modes of thought and expression: "A deep disturbance of temporal-historical relationships was perhaps what Sun Ra was after, aided by a somewhat disorganized and on-the-fly business practice."[7] The apparently haphazard release of El Saturn LPs containing music recorded years earlier defies time as a medium for both expression and, equally, cognition. Sun Ra sometimes defended Saturn's quaint habits of production and distribution by insisting that it would release music when the world was ready for it, not before. Convenient as that explanation is, it bears pondering. If the value of music derives from its relation not to the accident of its historical production but to its own potential, then time ceases to determine its efficacy. Music opens to space as the medium of its agency, the abstract space of its occurrence as sound. Space music disrupts time, diffusing history into the resounding force of recorded sound. El Saturn records launched the Arkestra through time into outer space.

And they did so at precisely the historical moment when America became engrossed in manned space flight. By the time the Arkestra reached Montreal, a Russian had reached outer space: Yuri Gagarin, whose 108-minute single orbit of the Earth on April 12, 1961, transformed the heroes of the Space Age from mindless drones (or cute animals) to living men. Satellites were out and cosmonauts were in, or so it seemed to a US administration fearful of losing the space race for good. With Gagarin's flight, the Soviets scored a second victory that left the United States decidedly in second place. As a payload, Vostok 1, Gagarin's craft, was massive in comparison to Sputnik 1. At 10,417 pounds, it approximated the weight of thermonuclear warheads, such as those intended for America's own intercontinental ballistic missile (ICBM), the Atlas, which in late 1958 had lofted the then heaviest artificial object into orbit, a communications satellite. But the Soviet rocket propelled a human being into space. Heavy ballistics now had a face, and it was Russian. The newly elected US president, John F. Kennedy, who rode into office in 1960 partly on a wave of resentment over Eisenhower's perceived humiliation by a bleeping metal spheroid (Sputnik), needed a bold initiative if the nation was to remain in the running for mastery in outer space, not to mention global politics. Project Mercury was months away from a manned orbital launch. Kennedy decided to commit his credibility—and the nation's resources—to a visionary goal that, if achieved, would bury the Soviet Union in its own rhetoric of technoscientific and political superiority.

Before a joint session of Congress on May 25, 1961, Kennedy unfurled a banner that would wave over America for a decade, declaring his belief that its future would be decided in space: "Now it is time to take longer strides—time for a great new American enterprise—time for this nation to take a clearly leading role in space achievement, which in many ways may hold the key to our future on earth."[8] A Soviet satellite, Luna 3, had circled the Moon on the second anniversary of Sputnik, beaming back to Earth the first photographs of the dark side of the lunar surface.[9] America could become a leader only by placing first in an enterprise grander than either manned Earth orbit or lunar reconnaissance. It should therefore, in Kennedy's decisive words, "commit itself to achieving the goal, before this decade is out, of landing a man on the moon and returning him safely to earth. No single space project in this period will be more impressive to mankind, or more important for the long-range exploration of space; and none will be so difficult or expensive to accomplish."[10] Kennedy stressed both the ambition and the expense necessary to rocket a man to the moon. His challenge to Congress and America would require a huge investment of labor and money in a cause that would indeed transform the nation—but for the better?

Sun Ra thought not. His own space program aimed at something higher than a lunar landing: blasting humans to infinity on a fiery counterthrust of sound. The Kennedy administration preferred more conventional aims and means. It would place a man first in orbit, à la Gagarin's mission, and then, more dramatically, on the moon. Doing so would require rockets, big ones, capable of lifting heavy payloads beyond the grasp of gravity. Such rockets had swarmed the technicolor covers of science-fiction magazines and paperbacks long before the first V-2 missile cleared the English Channel to fall on London in 1944. Engineering them to exceed escape velocity (about 25,000 miles per hour) while carrying the personnel and gear necessary for a moon shot would require extraordinary technological and scientific acumen. Building them would require technocratic coordination of labor and design. The Eisenhower administration had already inaugurated three programs devoted to the goal of manned spaceflight: Mercury, Gemini, and Apollo, involving one, two, and three astronauts, respectively. Kennedy's contribution was the deadline: a walk on the moon by the end of the sixties.

Rocket development was the key. Through skullduggery and luck, America had acquired the services of the great rocket designer and visionary Wernher von Braun, some of his associates, and a stockpile of V-2s when Allied forces captured Peenemünde, Hitler's rocket facility. Von Braun headed the Army Ballistic Missile Agency, located in Huntsville, Alabama, one of several teams scrambling to match Soviet advances in heavy ballistics. His design for the Redstone rocket, named for Huntsville's Redstone Arsenal, descended directly from the V-2 and would become the basis for a family of highly dependable rockets that included the Mercury-Redstone, used for the first two manned spaceflights (both suborbital), and the Jupiter-C, a modified and much larger Redstone that carried Explorer 1, the first US satellite, into orbit. The decision to use something other than a Redstone for the initial—failed—attempt to launch the first US satellite stemmed more from politics than from design considerations. Eager to give its space initiative a civilian profile, officials chose the US Naval Research Laboratory (more scientific than military in orientation) to develop a rocket for Explorer 1. But when the first Vanguard exploded after flying only four feet following ignition, von Braun's mostly German team received permission to take the next shot, despite its army and wartime credentials. Their consistent success would earn them transfer from military to civilian status with the creation, in 1958, of NASA, under whose auspices they would perfect a design for the largest launch vehicle in the US stable of rockets and the one destined for the moon shot, the formidable Saturn.

Von Braun himself named the beast—alas, not after a record company out of Chicago. But the happy coincidence shows how preternaturally Abraham and Sun Ra were tuned to the times. Both Saturn initiatives, rockets and records, required unprecedented coordination of invention and work. Just because the Chicago operation flew on a shoestring without much public awareness (let alone support) doesn't mean it lacked social significance. In fact, El Saturn Records provides an illuminating counterexample to the organizational methods necessary to the success of the Saturn rocket, the Apollo program, and the national commitment to land someone on the moon. That effort, building on innovations in the design and production of ICBMs, introduced unprecedented levels of administrative "command and control" into government management and therefore social organization. The battlefield language here seems apt, given Cold War realities. The US space program extended the administrative operations of war into peacetime by means of the complex efforts necessary to send a human to the moon.

Research and development would no longer be concentrated in the hands of prime contractors and concessionaires. It would be distributed among an array of subcontractors whose contributions could be coordinated, managed, and monitored to greatest effect.[11] Engineering and building a device as complicated as an ICBM required a new approach to operations management: "systems engineering," the design of networks to manage flow involving many parts and numerous personnel.[12] NASA served as the grand aggregator of the myriad systems involved in the design and production of the Saturn rocket and the pursuit of the moon, to the point that this project could be viewed as a model for social engineering more generally: "The space program promised a new era of great advances in the way large-scale efforts were managed, the encouragement of multidisciplinary efforts, new techniques and tools for the conduct of research in the social as well as physical sciences, and the manner in which they were applied to the solutions of age-old problems."[13] As James Webb, NASA's director under Kennedy, stated in 1963, "Every thread in the fabric of our economic, social, and political institutions is being tested as we move into space," and he would come to view the agency, in its capacity for coordinating diverse labors to induce social change, as a mechanism to advance "revolution from above."[14] The Saturn rocket and its moon mission helped consolidate a technocratic approach to US governance that vested authority in organizations such as NASA, agents of both continuous systems management and top-down social change. American technocracy would swallow the moon—and with any luck, Earth as well.

The other space program—El Saturn—operated by different principles, if that's the right word. Sun Ra might have run the Arkestra like a technocrat, leveraging expert knowledge to maximize precision, but he did so not to achieve political conformity and national prowess. Instead, the Arkestra played to transport people to other worlds, tomorrow's worlds. Sun Ra took that prospect seriously, however impish his performances in interviews or on stage could become. His band was a spaceship, his musicians were astronauts, and music propelled their audiences far beyond Earth orbit:

> I and my musicians are musical astronauts. We sail the galaxies through the medium of sound, our audience with us where we go whether they want to or not. The audience might want to be earth bound, but we being space bound we bind them to us and thus they cannot resist because the space way is the better way to travel. It keeps going out, and out, and further out than that.[15]

Sun Ra's emphasis on an absence of audience choice in the matter of astral travel chimes with his sense of the Arkestra as a space-bound jail. The prime mover of American liberalism, individual choice, plays no part in space travel as Sun Ra practices it. His play on the word "bound" (from "trapped" to "traveling") releases an individual into the impersonal flight of music: out and out, beyond America, beyond the Earth, the moon, the sun, even death. Utopian as Sun Ra's sense of space travel might seem, it remains the Cold War effect of a planned program of sonic ballistics, a willed improvement over conventional heavy thrusters: "We're like space warriors," Sun Ra says of his musicians. "Music can be used as a weapon, as energy. The right note or chord can transport you into space using music and energy flow. And the listeners can travel along with you."[16] That's not a promise NASA can make.

America's space program has been only a spectator sport, a spectacle that induces docility in its captivated audience. Sun Ra's offers participation that pays off in joy, often in the most mundane ways— the Arkestra's attire, for instance. Nicholas de Monchaux writes gracefully about the role clothes would play in NASA's pursuit of the moon, specifically, a space suit designed to keep US astronauts alive in the freeze-burning vacuum of space. The contract to produce it, after cutthroat competition, went to the Playtex Company, whose women's undergarments had achieved miracles in counteracting the effects of hostile environments on human bodies. De Monchaux's assessment of its success against corporate competitors in creating a livable space suit is profound: the human body, in its intimate and tender particularity, proves resistant to the imperatives of systems—and hence social—engineering.[17] So too do Sun Ra's astronauts, as their space-age hats and togs prove: "Astronauts are wearing hats like that. They could wear tuxedos in outer space but they wear space suits 'cause it's more suitable. So if I'm playin' space music, why can't I wear my celestial hats and things like that[?] But they want to chain a musician, where he just got to wear black all the time."[18] Sun Ra cut those sartorial chains so that his musicians can fly free. Such is the force of his poetics of outer space. Their space suits resist systems that would engineer docility: "A costume," as Sun Ra says, "*is* music."[19]

14

TOMORROWLAND

Space was everywhere during the Space Age. No longer the sole province of science fiction and its geeky fans, space provided popular culture in the fifties and sixties with a firmament of images, icons, narratives, and desires.[1] In Megan Prelinger's words, "Space was breaking out of the confines of genre-bound science fiction to become a mass civic object; it was becoming an inevitable and essential destination for human discovery."[2] The popularization of the outré visions of science fiction touched anyone who could attend movies, watch TV, buy appliances, or read. Well over two hundred science fiction movies appeared during the fifties alone, inspiring space-age hopes and fears with titles such as *Rocket Ship X-M* (1950), *It Came from Outer Space* (1953), *Invasion of the Saucer Men* (1957), *The Attack of the 50 Foot Woman* (1958), and *Teenagers from Outer Space* (1959).[3] Science fiction television programs beamed outer space into America's living rooms: *Commando Cody, Sky Marshal of the Universe* and the similar *Space Patrol*; *Tom Corbett, Space Cadet*; *Tales of Tomorrow*; and of course those two perennials, *Buck Rogers* and *Flash Gordon*.[4]

Space imagery infected the design of architecture and consumer goods: the ray-gun chic of drive-ins and gas stations, the futuristic ovoids of midcentury-modern furniture, the aerodynamic fins on Cadillacs and Chevys, and even the sleek look of refrigerators such as Hotpoint's "Space Age 18" (as advertised in the June 1960 issue of *Ebony*: it "brings you so many modern features"). By the early 1950s, science fiction publications had over two million readers.[5] Toys, games, costumes, comics, and windup robots seeded the popular imagination with dreams of a happy future in outer space.[6] More than Uncle Sam or Old Glory, the rocket became the privileged symbol of public yearning. Technicolor space vistas splashed across the covers of a thousand pulp magazines, providing the backdrop for a cosmic drama of good against evil in which Buck, Flash, and their interplanetary ilk generally triumphed, to the great happiness of humankind.

The rocketeers of science fiction's golden age (roughly 1930–1945) blasted into space to colonize the galaxies. They returned after World War II to colonize popular culture, but with a difference. The cosmic drama of outer space had turned all too real on planet Earth. World War II demonstrated that modern rocketry and big ballistics could be useful to state security, and with the advent of the Cold War, good and evil acquired a historical dimension. The detonation of the first hydrogen bomb (comfortingly named Mike) on Eniwetok Atoll in 1952, followed by Bravo on Bikini Atoll two years later, opened up the dark prospect of intercontinental delivery of thermonuclear warheads.[7] Missiles were so much faster than B-52s! The dreams of mass destruction that fueled the space race, a competition of planetary proportions, gave the astral adventures of movies, television, and magazines the gravity of real life. Science fiction had never before seemed so science factual, especially when it played by the rules of rocketry. Images of satellites, rockets, astronauts, atoms, moons, planets, and galaxies circulated truth among a postwar population hungry for something big to believe in. Religion couldn't unite a people constitutionally committed to religious toleration. The two-party politics of American democracy produced a divided polity except during times of open war. Science and its plausible fictions appealed across these divides, creating a basis for social unity that possessed strong ideological appeal. Rocket research and development helped launch the iconography of science fiction on a popular space odyssey that swept America and the world along with it.

Sun Ra's space program would fly on the fuel of popular culture but to ends far different from the ones science could then imagine. Mass-media accounts of the promises and perils of rocketry show how fifties science fiction ultimately blurs into Cold War fact. In the first of a famous series of articles appearing in *Collier's* magazine beginning in the spring of 1952, Wernher von Braun, fast becoming American's foremost science celebrity, explains in enthusiastic detail how a multiple-stage rocket could extend America's reach into outer space and all the way to the moon.[8] This glorious vision—straight out of the pages of golden-age pulp magazines—comes preceded, however, by an ominous editorial caveat: "What you will read here is not science fiction. It is serious fact."[9] The seriousness arises from its political implications, which render the *Collier's* material "an urgent warning": "The U.S. must immediately embark on a long-range development program to secure for the West 'space superiority.' If we do not, somebody else will. That somebody else very probably would be the Soviet Union."[10] When science fiction meets rocket fact, the former falls into a narrative of deadly ideological struggle. Visionary hopes had to pass political muster in the 1950s media ecology, subordinating the dreams of science fiction to *realpolitik*, which turned them terrifyingly real:

> A ruthless foe established on a space station could actually subjugate the peoples of the world. Sweeping around the earth in a fixed orbit, like a second moon, this man-made island in the heavens could be used as a platform from which to launch guided missiles. Armed with atomic warheads, radar-controlled projectiles could be aimed at any target on the earth's surface with devastating accuracy.[11]

Political terror regulated the dreams of rocket science, holding popular culture hostage to Cold War realities.

At least, some of pop culture fell prey to these anxieties. As science fiction accommodated the facts of Cold War rocketry, it often served a patently ideological function. Case in point: the British movie *Spaceways* (sound familiar?), released in 1953.[12] It hardly matters whether Sun Ra saw it, for the title resonates productively with his music. The story, presented in placid black and white, comes close to propaganda in its faithfulness to Cold War fearmongering. Dr. Stephen Mitchell, the handsome American head of engineering at Deanfield laboratory (located somewhere in England), designs rockets and discovers love—not for his shrewish British wife, Vanessa, who is confined to a military base that feels more like a concentration camp, but for his beautiful Slavic colleague, Dr. Lisa Frank, a mathematician with a fetching page-boy hairdo. The wife runs off (not an easy achievement under such close guard) with Philip Crenshaw, a suave biologist with a shadowy past—as a member of German intelligence. He has deviously infiltrated a crack team of scientists gathered by the British government, which seeks to win the race to become the first nation to place a satellite in orbit.

Personal and political intrigue in a context of technoscientific competition: *Spaceways* is science fiction at its most plausible and passionate. The rocket of Stephen's design comes straight out of *Collier's*, giving it von Braun's imprimatur as the latest in rocket technology. Footage of its fiery launch comes straight out of history: a German V-2 screaming skyward (perhaps from Peenemünde to London, a strange tribute to the ethnic origins of modern rocketry). It all adds up to a happy marriage between science fact and fiction—but not between Stephen and his wife, who, after her adulterous flight from Deanfield, accidentally finds herself on the business end of Philip's barking Luger. In a scenario too convoluted to explain clearly (involving unfashionably baggy but discreet spacesuits), Lisa cleverly maneuvers things so that she and Stephen end up alone on the first manned—or in this case, man-and-womanned—flight to outer space. It doesn't spoil the romantic ending to mention their safe return to Earth, implied in the final scene by a warm embrace over warmer controls (operational now after short-circuiting) and the happy words "we're turning back!"[13]

Like many B movies, *Spaceways* demonstrates with cringing clarity the ideological work that popular culture can perform. In its urgency to stay true to the facts of science, it purveys a science fiction that reduces its audience to ready boosters of imperialist adventurism—in the name of love, of course. Discussing the implications of a successful satellite launch, the project director, Professor Koepler, anticipates a near future when people will build the first space station, providing "a stepping stone to the moon, to the planets, to whole new worlds." "And if necessary," his interlocutor Colonel Daniels adds hastily, "a launching platform for atomic weapons." Hence the urgency of the work at Deanfield and the necessity of confinement to camp, provoking Vanessa's infidelity and her spiteful remark that Stephen and his colleagues are just "slaves in white uniforms." Given the history of rocket production at Peenemünde, which relied on slave labor, that remark throws a momentary shaft of light on the social effects of Cold War rocketry. Is Vanessa unfaithful to her husband or rather to the politics of Western rocket science? Her resistance to both marks her for elimination. You've been warned. The only way out of Deanfield appears to be up: the trajectory of love between Stephen and Lisa. Sun Ra would have appreciated the basic scenario, namely, escape from confinement through space travel. Stephen and Lisa survive to become the first heterosexual couple in space, solving in advance the libidinal implications of sending two men into space in close quarters. *Spaceways* is science fiction at its most socially serviceable.

The nadir (or inverted apogee?) of science fiction's fall into Cold War rocketry perhaps came two years later in an episode of the television program *Disneyland* broadcast on March 9, 1955. This episode, entitled "Man in Space," was presented as part of the recurring "Tomorrowland" series; the program's episodes were matched to the proposed theme park's various sectors, and the "Tomorrowland" series would eventually include "Man in the Moon" and "Mars and Beyond." "Man in Space" offers a contemporary look at the way science and its hucksters, Walt Disney foremost among them, appropriated the inspiring iconography of science fiction. It opens with Walt Disney himself sitting on his desk while holding a red-nosed model rocket and, in his avuncular voice, proffering sage clichés about the ubiquity of science: "In the modern world, everywhere you look you see the influence that science has on our daily lives. [. . .] Many of the things that seem impossible now will become realities tomorrow."[14] Sun Ra puts this vapid language to arresting use when he applies it to the force of sound. Here, folded within the idiom of an infomercial (Disney pitching "Disney"), the language is used to repeat one of the basic credos of science fiction deployed in the context of factual rocket science. More revealing, then, is the producer and director Ward Kimball's expressed intention of "combining the tools of our trade [film and animation] with the knowledge of the scientist." Kimball's remark is a declaration of pop-cultural imagination's dependence on the truths of science, a strategy of willed ideological design Disney would later call "imagineering."

A stirring sight for science fiction aficionados follows: the camera pans across a room full of seated designers surrounded by rocket mockups, some several feet long. The alluring imagery of innumerable sci-fi magazines suddenly takes material form, although it isn't clear whether those designers are rocket scientists or Disney animators. In a sense they are both, since the viewer's knowledge of rocketry comes pre-engineered by Disney's staff. A short history of modern rocketry serves to establish their authority, translating liberally interpreted "facts" into a past that merges the technologies of rocket science and cinema.[15] Jules Verne gets the show going with his 1865 novel *From the Earth to the Moon*, but the real originator of Disney history is Georges Méliès, whose 1902 film *Le Voyage dans la Lune* constitutes the first science fiction movie, complete with a cannon-fired moon shot.

Robert Goddard receives a brief homage as the father of modern rocketry and the American Rocket Society (no mention, of course, of the great Russian rocket scientist Konstantin Tsiolkovsky). Hermann Oberth, the German visionary, gets a nod primarily as the designer of the rocket in Fritz Lang's *Frau im Mond* (1930), foreshadowing the rise of German rocketry that comes to fulfillment in the vengeful V-2, seventy-five of which, the television audience learns, found their clandestine way to New Mexico's White Sands Missile Range near the end of World War II. But the real end of Disney's rocket history, the purpose that pulls it irresistibly forward, is a montage of American rockets, sleek and virulent, screeching upward in full color. Kimball's voice deadpans the ideological message for anyone who might have missed it: "A rocket firing is an awesome demonstration of tremendous power."

Under the sign of this tremendous power, "Man in Space" installs a new kind of celebrity as impresario of popular culture: the scientific expert, technocratic engineer of tomorrow. Listed in the credits as "scientific advisors," three such experts guide the television audience through the basics of contemporary rocketry. Dr. Heinz Haber handles the delicate business of placing a satellite in orbit. Willy Ley presents an introductory lesson (with prankster animation) in "Space Medicine," a survivor's guide to zero gravity. The renowned Dr. Wernher von Braun, impeccably coiffed, relates his latest thinking about rocket design for a successful journey to outer space and a return to Earth. These experts, all with German accents, take control of the popular imagination, directing the fantasia of science fiction toward "man's conquest of space." Willy Ley, for instance, speaking over the antics of an animated "common man" (a cigar-smoking, martini-swilling white guy in space), describes the new regime that awaits "*Homo sapiens extraterrestrialis*, or Space Man": "He must accommodate himself to an entirely new set of rules." Acceleration, weightlessness, vacuum, deep freeze: outer space environs prove inclement for terrestrial organisms.

No worries. Von Braun has engineered a vehicle to carry ten men safely into space, a four-stage rocket with a winged nose cone suitable for high-occupancy orbital travel and reentry through Earth's atmosphere. It's somehow comforting to hear all this from a man described as "one of the foremost exponents of space travel," whose military credentials ("Chief of the Guided Missile Division of the Army's research division at Redstone Arsenal") seem less imperious than his coy smile. Scientific experts such as von Braun, Ley, and Haber have taken command of the future, which will run smoothly on the astral rails of rocket science: "MISSION COMPLETED: Man has taken his first great strides forward in the conquest of space. His next goal will be the exploration of the moon, then the planets and the infinite universe beyond" (fade out to "When You Wish upon a Star"). Technocrats forever. Disney hands over popular culture to the engineers of futurity.

But here's the Disney difference—their future depends as much on the wonders of the media as on the wonders of science. "Man in Space" is more about film as the medium of popular rocketry than about the hard science of space travel. From the animated intro of Tinkerbell shaking stars from her wand over "Tomorrowland" to the closing segment of ten white men traveling the vacuum in von Braun's space bus, animation makes space imaginable. Disney teaches popular culture to think space in cartoons. Such is the force of television that it distributes the future en masse. Between experts and animation, the conquest of space seems guaranteed. It must be admitted that Disney is a powerful pedagogue. As a popular introduction to the fundamentals of rocketry, space medicine, and space conquest, "Man in Space" does an effective job of instruction. But it colonizes the minds it enlightens, too, authenticating an approved imagery for imagining tomorrow. Disney dreams the future for the audience of *Disneyland*, animating a tomorrow for popular consumption condoned by experts and sanctioned by broadcast. Science fiction turns factually plausible in the open arms of "scientific advisors," and Disney frosts it all in cinematic magic. For those hankering after even more reality, a visit to the physical Tomorrowland, which opened on July 17, 1955, at Disneyland, would materialize a future as only corporate America could imagineer it, with showcases sponsored by Monsanto, American Motors, and Dutch Boy Paint.

But not all science fiction was so cozy with the nationalist ambitions of technoscience. Some movies told cautionary tales that qualified the enthusiasm of Disney's vision. *Them* and *Godzilla*, both from 1954, confront the possibility of unanticipated horrors from nuclear fallout: the mutation of a colony of ants into carnivorous giants in New Mexico and the creation of the famous fractious reptile in Tokyo Bay. A classic of the genre, *The Day the Earth Stood Still*, from 1951, tests Cold War rocket-rattling against the possibility of an infinitely superior alien science—and the weaponry that would go along with it. The movie's opening sequence follows the reports of an unidentified and extremely fast flying object caught on radar. Calcutta, France, England, America: radios beam the news around the world. *The Day the Earth Stood Still* insists on a global rather than a national perspective on postwar geopolitics. To the alien if (mercifully) humanoid occupant of the flying saucer that lands on the mall in Washington, DC, American political interests and scientific aspirations seem partisan and petty. Klaatu, as he calls himself, has traveled millions of miles through space with an urgent message for planet Earth: its scientific achievements (atomic energy and rockets) threaten the security of other planets.

Much to the consternation of the US government, Klaatu refuses to speak to "any one nation or group of nations."[16] He requires the world's attention. This insistence on totality—implying that the advances of science touch *all* of Earth's inhabitants—leads to the unprecedented event of the movie's title, Klaatu's half-hour noontime interruption of all electrical activity the planet over (save where it would threaten life). Only such a demonstration of superior science holds any hope for uniting the people of Earth in Klaatu's simple, superior truth: "There must be security for all or no one is secure." Klaatu answers Cold War nuclear nationalism with a vision of total security, the prospect of a solidarity of planetary proportions. Both his vision and his language would make an impression on Sun Ra, whose music aspired similarly to transform the planet, appealing to science of a higher kind. Klaatu leaves Earth without receiving a commitment to his vision. Must the same be said of Sun Ra?

The skepticism that *The Day the Earth Stood Still* directs toward science and its wondrous achievements characterizes much of the pulp science fiction published in the wake of World War II. Ballistic missiles and nuclear weapons threw dark shadows over its brightly colored covers. The old pulp magazines from the thirties and forties, with titles such as *Science Wonder Stories* and *Astounding Stories of Super-Science*, gave way after the war to less wide-eyed publications, including *Magazine of Fantasy and Science Fiction* and *Galaxy*, both of which actively solicited stories less innocent than those of the genre's golden age. *Galaxy*, for instance, called for writing "too adult, too profound, or revolutionary in concept" to appeal to its creaky competition.[17] Writers seemed happy to oblige. Doomsday scenarios, inspired by the superpowers' pursuit of doomsday weapons, became familiar magazine material, and with the emergence of the paperback as a medium for such dreams (the pulp-novel publishers Ace and Ballentine both began operation in the fifties), science fiction acquired new seriousness as a genre. Some writers, Robert Heinlein chief among them, would keep the national faith in rocket science as a means to superior strength. His novel *Starship Troopers* (1955), with its militarized starships and weaponized space suits, presents a goose-stepping libertarian defense of perpetual preparedness for intergalactic war, which in his view the biological facts of species survival render inevitable.

Less jingoistic writers advanced sci-fi confrontations with an increasingly technocratic American society: Kurt Vonnegut, Clifford Simak, John Brunner, Philip K. Dick, and, soon thereafter, J. G. Ballard and William S. Burroughs. In their hands, science fiction, no longer content to sling amazing stories on behalf of super-science, became a medium of social criticism and resistance. A "New Wave" of science fiction built and crashed over a sixties society bent on landing men on the moon but bedeviled by social crises: segregation, racism, overpopulation, pollution, and an undeclared war in Vietnam. For all its Disneyfied complacency, science fiction also promotes countervisions that imagine prospects for popular culture other than technocratic triumph, worlds other than a corporate-sponsored Tomorrowland. Sun Ra and his music for a better tomorrow partake of this more critical lineage. His music allows the message of his Thmei brethren to serve as more than just fodder for South Side uplift. By wrapping occult wisdom in the colorful textures (and textiles) of contemporary science fiction, Sun Ra and the Arkestra aligned their music with a wider popular impulse to imagine worlds better than the one being built by rocket science and the Cold War. Why stop with the moon? Space music aims higher: planets, stars, galaxies, infinity.

Sonny Blount, early 1950s (above), and Sun Ra, late 1980s (below). On photocopies of these images, Alton Abraham wrote: "Before" and "After—I turned him into 'Sun Ra,' they say."

Sun Ra and his Arkestra performing in Chicago, late 1950s. From left to right: Ronald Wilson, Marshall Allen, unknown (standing), John Gilmore, Walter Perkins, Nate Pryor, Ronnie Boykins, Phil Cohran, and Sun Ra (in space helmet).

Claude Dangerfield, unused design for record jacket.

THMEI RESEARCH

RESEARCHERS IN SUBJECTS { COSMIC, SPIRITUAL, PHILOSOPHICAL, RELIGIOUS, HISTORICAL, SCIENTIFIC, ECONOMICAL *ETC*

"SEEK YE WISDOM, KNOWLEDGE AND UNDERSTANDING"

VOL. II, SECTION 18   INFORMATIVE, FACTUAL SERIES   ISSUED BI-MONTHLY   SUBSCRIBERS SEND MONTHLY DONATION   P. O. BOX 7124   CHICAGO 7, ILLINOIS

T
H
M
E
I

P. O. Box 7124 • CHICAGO, ILL. INOIS 60607 • (312) 373-6228

Thmei Research
cover stock and
Saturn Research
letterhead.

I DON'T GIVE A HOOT.........

AN OWL IS A CREATURE OF THE NIGHT.HE IS CALLED THE WISE OLD OWL YET HE DOESN'T DEMONSTRTE WISDOM...HE'S A HOOT OWL.HE IS KNOWN BY HIS HOOT. A HOOT IS SYNONYMOUS TO NOTHING.THE WISE OLD OWLS WORD IS NOTHING. NOTHING IS THE SAME THING AS SILENCE.THE WISE OLD OWL IS THE VOICE OF SILENCE.HIS WORD IS ####### CONSIDERED/AS NOTHING.A MAN IS TO BE JUDGED BY HIS OWN WORDS.A MAN'S OWN WORDS ARE THOSE WHICH ARE NOT THE WORDS OF GOD.A MAN WHO DOES NOT KEEP HIS WORD IS NOTHING BECAUSE THAT IS WHAT HE STANDS FOR.AS A MAN THINKETH SO IS HE.THOUGHTS ARE WORDS.IF A MAN'S THOUGHTS ADDS UP TO BE FOOLISHNESS# AND NOTHING..THE MAN IS LIKEWISE NOTHING...ALSO FOOLISHNESS....FOOLISHNESS IS VANITY... NEGROES ARE HOOT OWLS,THEIR WORD IS JUST LIKE THE HOOT OWLS WORD IN FACT THEY ARE A BETTER HOOT OWL THAN THE HOOT OWL. THE OWL IS WISE,SO ARE NEGROES:GOD SAYS THEY ARE WISE TO DO EVIL BUT TO GOOD THEY HAVE NO KNNOWLEDGE.Job says that wisdom perished with them.

KNOWLEDGE Job

anybody who robs the grave and feeds on the #flesh of the dead is a GHOUL. A GHOUL AIN'T NOTHING BUT A FOOL........F/GH.. A GHOUL lives off the FLESH OF THE DEAD.ARE YOU LIVING OFF THE FLESH OF THE DEAD CHRIST?IF SO,##### YOU ARE A GHOUL.

NEGROES BELONG TO THE RACE OF MU.ANOTHER WAY TO SPELL MU IS MOO.
MOO MEANS LOW.THAT'S THE COW'S WORD.NEGROES ARE MR. MOO.
WITNESS:....BLOW MR. LOW?,BLOW.....THE LOW SOCIETY CLUB.IS THE NAME OF A SOCIAL CLUB.. HERE IN CHICAGO
MOW...STORED....WHERE HAY IS STORED...mou.....
MU is MUT.....NEGROES ARE THE PEOPLE OF MU OR MUT.....
MU is the name of PAN signifying ground..MU is LEMURIA....
MU IS SUBMERGED IN PEACE...The "MY PEACE I GIVE UNTO YOU" MU IS FLOODED.
Gemma is L upside down..

THE THREE LONG EARS....JACKASS,RABBIT,OWL... symbolical of the negro...

I DON'T GIVE A HOOT.....I DON'T GIVE A HOOTE.......T/Te
HOOTIE is HOOTE.....######......HOITE/OIHTE...OUDE....EDUO...ETHIO...

THE ETHIOPS WERE KNOWN IN ANCIENT DAYS AS "the blameless ETHIOPS" NOW THE WORLD KNOW THEM AS THE BLAMED ETIOPS/ETHIOPS... ETHIOPS IS OUDE...OIHTE....OIHTE is HOITE......HOOTE....HOOT....... I DON'T GIVE A HOOT MEANS "I DON'T GIVE AN ETHIOPS"...ETHIOPS ARE NOTHING. NEGROES ARE NOTHING BECAUSE THEY ARE ALL NATIONS..ALL NATIONS ARE AS NOTHING TO GOD.. ALL NATIONS ARE AS NOTHING TO GOD...ALLNATIONS ARE AS NOTHING TO GOD ....ALL NATIONS ARE AS NOTHING TO GOD............... NEGROES ARE ALL NATIONS......NEGROES ARE ALL NATIONS......... ALL NATIONS ARE POSITIVELY,ABSOLUTELY,DEFINITELY NOTHING TO GOD..... THAT EXPLAINS THE POOR CONDITION OF THE NEGRO MENTALLY##### #SPIRITUALLY ECONOMICALLY AND SOCIALLY....THERE IS NO PLACE IN GOD'S UNIVERSE FOR NOTHING.....ALL NATIONS ARE AS NOTHING TO GOD....NEGROES ARE ALL NATIONS. HISTORY HAS PROVEN THAT ALL NATIONS (the negro) IS AS NOTHING TO GOD OR MAN THIS IS THEIR REWARD IN HEAVEN FOR THEIR DISOBEDIENCE AND REBELLION AGAINST GOD..ETERNAL SORROW AND SHAME AND SUFFERING...CRUCIFIXION DELUXE.
####

IS THERE ANY HOPE FOR THE NEGRO?....YES...ONLY WHEN THEY DECIDE TO ACCEPT THE TRUTH AND JUDGE FROM THE STANDPOINT OF TRUTH RATHER THAN FOR MATERIAL ADVANTAGES...IT IS A POOR BARGAIN TO GAIN THE WHOLE WORLD AND LOSE YOUR SOUL...IT IS FOOLISHNESS.........

Read

Sun Ra broadsheet, mid-1950s. Note the equation HOOT = NOTHING = ETHIOPS, yielding the conclusion that NEGROES ARE NOTHING.

The Artis Abrahams
BENEFIT DANCE
FOR MAYOR OF BRONZEVILLE
Sponsored by the
CAMPAIGN COMMITTE
Friday, Feb. 15, 1957   9 Till?
GRAND BALL ROOM   —   6351 Cottage Grove
Music by . . . S U N R A
(Sun God of Jazz)
DONATION $1.00
Bob Kelly, Campaign Mgr.   Geo. A. Jones, Bus. Mgr.

N? 246

The Atonites
Present An Evening of
OUTER SPACE MUSIC and DANCING
featuring
Sun Ra & his Outer Space Arkestra
Saturn and Transilina Recording Artists
At Budland   Every Sunday Evening
6412 Cottage Grove   4:30 p.m. to 8:30 p.m.
Advance Donation 75c   At Door $1.00

They're at it again . . .
THOSE ATONITES
that is . . .
Reaching 'way out of Space!
Bringing to you Earthlings
The Nu Sounds of
Sun Ra and his Arkestra
At Budland   Every Sunday Evening
6412 Cottage Grove   4:30 p.m. to 8:30 p.m.
Dance the Outer Space Way
Hear songs sung the Outer Space Way
by Clyde "Out of Space" Williams
Donation $1.00

Tickets to performances of Sun Ra and his Arkestra sponsored by the Atonites and the Campaign Committee for the Mayor of Bronzeville.

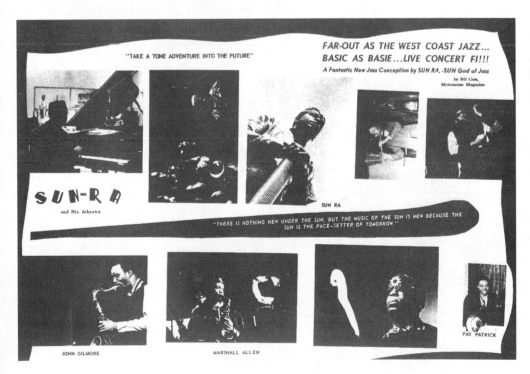

Promotional flyer for Sun Ra and his Arkestra.

Record jackets for *Super-Sonic Jazz* (the "void" cover, 1961) and
Jazz in Silhouette (1959).

Singles

By SUN RA ARKESTRA

from the World of ...

STATE STREET
SPACE LONELINESS
BIG CITY BLUES
BLUE SET
MEDICINE FOR
  A NIGHTMARE
SOFT TALK
SATURN
  CALL FOR ALL DEMONS
DEMON'S LULLABY
SUPER BLONDE
VELVET

S
A
T
U
R
N

RECORDS

The civilizations of the past have been used as the foundation of the civilization of today. Because of this, the world keeps looking toward the past for guidance. Too many people are following the past. In this new space age, this is dangerous. The past is DEAD and those who are following the past are doomed to die and be like the past. It is no accident that those who die are said to have passed since those who have PASSED are PAST.

Write:

SATURN RECORDS

P.O. Box 7124

Chicago 7, Illinois, U.S.A.

"THE DEAD PAST"

The civilizations of the past have been used as the foundation of the civilization of today. Because of this, the world keeps looking toward the past for guidance. Too many people are following the past. In this new space age, this is dangerous. The past is DEAD and those who are following the past are doomed to die and be like the past. It is no accident that those who die are said to have passed since those who have PASSED are PAST.

SUGGESTED RETAIL PRICES
200 SERIES $4.98
400 SERIES $5.98

— Prices and Contents of this Catalog Are Subject to Change —

Dealers Are Invited to Enquire Concerning Special Price Arrangements.

A NEW REVISED CATALOGUE IS BEING FORMULATED. THOSE ON OUR MAILING LIST WILL RECEIVE COPIES UPON ITS COMPLETION. IF YOU WOULD LIKE FOR YOUR NAME TO BE ADDED TO OUR MAILING LIST, PLEASE FILL OUT THE FORM BELOW AND SEND IT TO:

EL SATURN INC.
P.O. BOX 7124
CHICAGO, ILLINOIS
60607 U.S.A.

(A) Please add my Name to your mailing Lists.

(B) Enclosed is a Check or money Order for $................

Please Send LP Number(s) ....
As Listed in Your Handy Catalog.

NAME ....

ADDRESS .... APT. NO. ....

CITY .... STATE .... ZIP CODE ......

TELEPHONE NUMBER........................

ADD 50 cts. for handling.

FPO, APO ADDRESSES: WRITE FOR EXCLUSIVE OFFER

Permission For Reproducing portions of this "Handy Katalog" may be obtained, in writing, by contacting, SATURN "II" INC. Research Dept. Box 7124, Chicago, Illinois.

SATURN "II" INC. HANDY CATLOG No. B7S66Y

E
L
S
A
T
U
R
N

"Beta Music for Beta People for a Beta World"

Saturn Records catalog of singles and a "Handy Katalog," mid- to late 1960s (note the order form on latter).

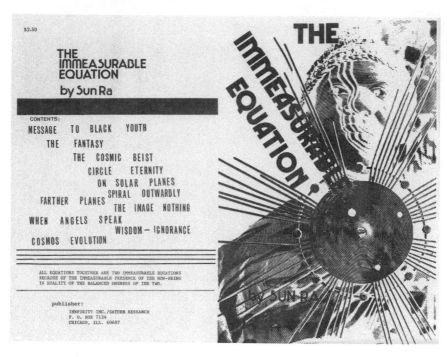

The cover to Sun Ra, *The Immeasurable Equation*.

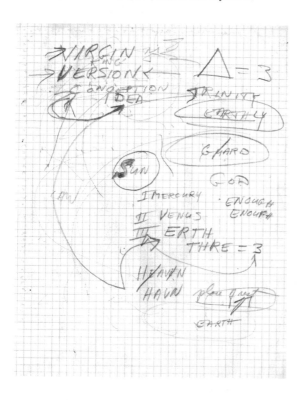

A page from a Sun Ra notebook, mid-1960s; note the verbal equations and permutations.

Sun Ra, mid-1960s. This image appeared on the
cover of *Fate in a Pleasant Mood* (1965).

Sun Ra and his Arkestra (and friends) parading in New York, 1966. From left to right, as identified on back of photo: Bernard Pettaway, Robert Cummings, Marion Brown, Marshall Allen, Ronnie Boykins, Sun Ra, and Danny Davis.

Record jacket, *Interstellar Low Ways* (1969; first released as *Rocket Number Nine Take Off for the Planet Venus*, 1966).

Promotional poster, Carnegie Hall performance, 1968.

Promotional poster for the film *Space Is the Place*.

Members of the Sun Ra Arkestra, early 1970s, among them James Jacson, Marshall Allen, June Tyson, Danny Thompson, John Gilmore, Cheryl Allen, Sun Ra, and Wisteria El Moondew (Judith Holton).

Sun Ra in Birmingham, Alabama, at the first *City Stages* weekend, 1989.

HARVEST ENTERPRISES, INC. PRESENTS

SUN RA
HEALTH BENEFIT CONCERT

MAY 15, 1993

8:00 p.m.
First Congregational Church
10th & G Streets, N.W.
Washington, D.C.

Program for a Sun Ra Health Benefit Concert.

15

INTERPLANETARY EXOTICA

Not technoscience but music would thrust Sun Ra into the future. His use of music as a medium for imagining tomorrow may seem eccentric, but it remained allied to powerful trends in popular culture. Science fiction movies of the fifties and sixties usually came with appropriately otherworldly or futuristic soundtracks. *The Day the Earth Stood Still*, for instance, splashes its title over images of stars and galaxies set to the music of a theremin, the electronic instrument patented by Léon Theremin in 1928, whose sound has since become a signature of outer space (as any *Star Trek* fan can attest). For technological newness and sonic frisson, electronics would define the sound of the future, especially in Hollywood. Case in point: *Forbidden Planet* (1956), the first movie to have a soundtrack produced entirely electronically.[1]

The soundtrack (including beeps, warfs, howls, and hums) provides a spare, spooky backdrop to a story set on the barren Altair IV, a world visited by the United Planets cruiser C-57D. The crew discovers it to be the home of the reclusive superscientist Dr. Morbius, who has only his daughter, Alta, to keep him company. Morbius devotes himself obsessively to mastering the stupendously advanced science of the vanished Krell (visionary roboticists, apparently, since their expertise inspires his creation of Robby the Robot). Unfortunately, Morbius has tapped into Krell technology that allows him to control matter with his mind, but he lacks any awareness that he harbors murderous subconscious impulses toward anyone who gets in his way. In this regard, it's *Frankenstein* in outer space, a scenario deeply critical of the human costs of unchecked scientific ambition. Morbius must die so that his daughter can live, of course, but not before sharing with his visitors a recording by Krell musicians made some half-million years earlier. The music sounds futuristic even today: warm, lyrical, diaphanous—and completely electronic.

This mix of past and future, of primitive and sophisticated, characterizes a genre of fifties and sixties popular music that left a lasting mark on Sun Ra's sound palette and the colors of his compositions: exotica. Looking "back" to the music of so-called primitive cultures for fresh rhythms, timbres, and instrumentations, exotica also looked forward in search of sounds in tune with the coming Space Age. The first recording of a theremin occurred in 1947 on Harry Revel's *Music Out of the Moon*, arranged and conducted by Les Baxter, the popular progenitor of exotica.[2] Although Sun Ra himself resisted the theremin (an unsuccessful encounter with one led him to conclude that "for black people, it ain't gonna play"), its spacey, wavering croon probably intrigued him.[3] Baxter achieved quick popular acclaim with the 1951 release of *Ritual of the Savage (Le Sacre du Sauvage)*, a brazenly exotic record, and not necessarily in the best sense.[4] Its cover sets the cultural agenda for the music it contains: colorful carved "African" masks and statues around a dancing couple, clearly from south of the border, she with a gardenia in her hair. Track titles reinforce the listener's sense that this music comes from *somewhere else*, outside the bounds of the familiar West: "Sophisticated Savage," "Jungle Flower," "Quiet Village," "Stone God," "Kinkajou," and "The Ritual," to name a few. Primitive sounds for sophisticated listeners. *Ritual of the Savage* promotes the illusion of a living-room encounter with exotic others, or at least their rhythms and cries.

Baxter found a formula that would ignite a popular craving for exotic music. Winds over congas: Latin rhythms to gesture toward a dimly lit but palpable African past. Rattles and flutes: sudden shifts in instrumentation or dynamics to pique and sustain interest. Unctuous strings: sweet melodies to soothe savage ritual with something familiar. Chattering brass: sectional narration to tell little stories of the strange. Baxter aimed to evoke feelings of something foreign, outside the everyday, maybe even a little dangerous. *Ritual of the Savage* may seem pretty tame in this regard, but in a slew of records to come (*The Passions* [1954], *Tamboo!* [1956], *Caribbean Moonlight* [1956], *Ports of Pleasure* [1957], and *African Jazz* [1959]), he codified a pop genre that delivered ersatz otherness to consumers hungry for a taste of difference but unable to stomach it by any means other than easy listening. In a sense, exotica provides an American soundtrack to the historical drama of decolonization. Its visually seductive record jackets and socially stimulating sounds persuaded fans of that era that other cultures were alive and well (however regrettable the legacy of colonialism), easily worth the price of Baxter's latest platter. Why not add the Caribbean to your collection? Dig those rhythms, Daddy? By the time Martin Denny recorded the album that gave the genre its name, *Exotica* (1957), it had settled into a stimulating mix of syncopated rhythms, extravagant dynamics, high-contrast arrangements, and (Denny's signature) vocalized animal sounds.[5]

Perfect for cocktails! The space that exotica explored was largely domestic. As Francesco Adinolfi notes in *Mondo Exotica*, "All these records were responsible for transforming domestic spaces into dark lounges like the ones in which the bachelor had lingered the night before."[6] Think of the bachelor here as an ideal demographic target: single, employed, hip, and horny. Exotica (note the feminine ending) entered his life and living room by commercial design. It was music scored for scoring—a doubly imperial confection. But just as the living room turned into a tiki lounge, so too did the bachelor become a vector of more public desires, those associated with the national longing for political superiority and victory in space. Exotica inevitably developed into "space-age bachelor-pad music," known more simply as "space-age pop," all these phrases being coined much later for commercial music calibrated to the climate of the times. As America prepared to explore space, exotica opened to the stars. Harry Revel's *Music from out of Space* (1955), with tracks titled "Jupiter Jumps," "Vibrations from Venus," and "Cosmic Capers," mixes sentimental strings with signature vocal glissandi (no theremin this time) to create a feeling of lyrical openness that can swerve suddenly into swing. Space here is a pastiche of stylistic possibilities. It slides effortlessly into the more terrestrial intensities of Baxter's *Tamboo!*, splicing and recombining to create a pop music for the Space Age that fuses highly textured lyricism with shifting rhythms and way-out sounds.

In the far background of this development stands *musique concrète*, Pierre Schaeffer's postwar experiments with found sounds intended to create a music of reality—except, of course, that the only thing real about the sounds of space in space-age pop was the money it took to buy them. There is, after all, no sound in space. Sound waves don't propagate in a vacuum. It seems fitting, then, that the great progenitor of space-age sounds, Attilio Mineo, composed *Man in Space with Sounds* in 1951, almost a decade before anyone heard it. It remains a time-warped masterpiece of space pop. Recorded in 1959 and finally released as the soundtrack, so to speak, to the 1962 World's Fair in Seattle, selections from *Man in Space with Sounds* played as ambient background on the famous *Bubbleator*, the fair's huge transparent elevator that transported visitors on a virtual tour of outer space. "Our first stop," the record's voiceover intones authoritatively, is "the Gayway to Heaven, that spins you skyward on the great space wheel, the fabulous Gayway, where you guide your own rocket and taxi to tomorrow."[7] The "sounds" of *Man in Space with Sounds* feel much more adventuresome than those of much space-age pop, ahead of their time (if sounds of tomorrow can be ahead of their time) in 1951, however familiar they might eventually become. The reverberating thunk of "Welcome to Tomorrow," the industrial grind of "Gayway to Heaven": these are the kind of barely musical sonic expressions that Sun Ra would explore in recordings from the sixties.

Mineo's long-silent masterpiece may not have given birth to space-age pop, but it should have. It reaches much further than did most commercial efforts to create a soundscape for the Space Age. That was the challenge, after all: to imagine and score a vacuum and then to persuade a generation of listeners (their kids and kids' kids) that the outer space of Vostok and Redstone rocketry, of Yuri Gagarin and John Glenn, and eventually Apollo and Soyuz, sounds like *this*. Sonically speaking, outer space was a blank slate. It could sound like anything, from an angelic chorus to a jet engine. Space-age pop created its sonic language and then taught listeners how to hear it. Pallid as much of it was, it bonded astral associations to particular sounds, fit together their connotations, and built a musical backdrop for a culture obsessed with satellites and moon shots. Early efforts offered little more than gestures toward this sonic tomorrow. The famous piano duo Arthur Ferrante and Louis Teicher released *Soundproof: The Sound of Tomorrow Today!* (it was also an age of exclamation points) in 1956. Its blue-tone cover image from *Forbidden Planet*, the United Planets cruiser C-57D scanning the bleak landscape of Altair IV, suggests something futuristic is happening here, as does the record's subtitle.[8]

The texture of the music on *Soundproof* and the technology used to record it (rather than the sounds themselves) account for the record's innovation. Its title refers to the studio conditions necessary to produce the natural reverb often engulfing one or both pianos.[9] A track like "Man from Mars" adds a sci-fi touch, but it's an exception to the more exotic numbers, such as "El Cumbanchero," "Baia," and "African Echoes." But the snapping reverb on "Dark Eyes" contributes directly to an overall futuristic feel—that and the seventeen microphones used to make the record. Part of the appeal of space-age pop derives from the new technological processes involved in recording it (called various things by various studios: high-fidelity mono, stereo, living stereo, and perfect presence sound). The sound of space arose as a technological effect, a sonic idiom perfectly tailored to technocracy. In just a few years, sound engineers would become as important as musicians, lending credence to Adinolfi's claim that "engineers and musicians seemed to work hand in hand with the technology of NASA."[10] When Ferrante and Teicher released *Blast Off!*, in 1958, the primary source of whatever space-ageyness it possesses aside from its title came from the studio effects that introduce the various tunes, plus a pervasive infatuation with reverb.

Such tricks of the studio trade, frequently with electronic embellishment, increasingly came to characterize space-age pop, not always to fabulous effect. *From Another World* (1956), by the arranger Sid Bass, gathers dusty popular songs with vaguely astronomical titles ("Old Devil Moon," "My Blue Heaven," "East of the Sun," "Stardust") and polishes them up with twangy electronic intros and outros. Gone, Daddio. More ambitious is a record by Pete Rugolo, the arranger for Stan Kenton; released in 1957, it was originally titled *Music from Out of Space*. Although little about it signifies outer space beyond the cover (which shows Rugolo in a red space suit and clear plastic bubble helmet) and the title of its first track (a blustery meditation called "Stereo Space Man"), the recording process makes up for what the music overlooks. Rugolo's technique in the studio, the notes on the back cover reveal, was "dependent on the willingness of the recording equipment—the mike, the tape machines, the play-back speaker—to go along with him."[11] Thank God for submissive equipment. Indeed, musicians on the record remain uncredited, but not so the machines; the microphones used include an Altec 21B, two Telefunken U47s, an Altec 639, and two RCA 44BXs. Wow. *Music from Out of Space* originates in a *studio* space equipped with the latest technologies to produce serious sounds for the serious audiophile, as the record's label attests: "A Stereophonic High Fidelity Recording."[12]

The annus mirabilis of space-age bachelor-pad music has to be 1958. Martin Denny released *Primitiva*, demonstrating his command of exotica and the commercial recolonization of Third World cultures.[13] Innovative sounds came from elsewhere, too. Juan García Esquivel, also known (inevitably perhaps) as Esquivel!, released *Other Worlds Other Sounds*, a record that took exotica's already rambunctious arranging and squared it, cubed it, tied it in knots, and set it spinning.[14] Born in Mexico, he amped up Latin rhythms to an ecstatic tumult, suffusing his music with variety, dissonance, disruption, perversity, and noise. The songs on *Other Worlds Other Sounds* did not in themselves gesture to some outer space beyond, but his treatment of them did, cued by a cover that puts a red-caped and leggy dancer on a provocatively lunar landscape. Old familiars such as "Begin the Beguine," "Night and Day," "That Old Black Magic," and "It Had to Be You" receive new arrangements so dynamic and bedazzling, so adventurous and bizarre, that they get pushed outside themselves, as if to become versions preferred on other planets by the advanced life-forms who inhabit them. "Primitive" cultures return here with a vengeance, looping through some undesignated future to command submission. Now! Esquivel said in an interview that he "wanted traditional instruments to play in a new and unusual way. [. . .] It was above all a game of microphones."[15] His exploitation of recording technology enhanced the imperious *jouissance* of his arrangements. On his next release, *Exploring New Sounds in Hi-Fi Stereo* (1959), the cover showing his arm draped over a telescope, Esquivel continues his adventures in otherness (and camp), importing, for instance, the electronic sounds of the Ondioline on the nutty—and popular—tune "Whatchamacallit."[16]

Space becomes an explicit sonic concern (sort of) in two other releases from 1958, Les Baxter's *Space Escapade* and Russ Garcia's *Fantastica: Music from Outer Space*. Baxter's record is pure "spaceotioca," a recombinant hybrid of lyricized exotica (plenty of strings) and space fantasy.[17] The cover does a lot of the space-age work. A cocktail-bearing astro-bachelor in a green space suit and bubble helmet is toasting his friends, a mixed gathering of three foreign/alien women (white, pink, and green complexioned) and another astro-bachelor, proud of his drink. Everyone is smiling, and why not? A carbon-dioxide fog covers the floor. Nobody seems to notice the ominous shadow of a missile on the wall behind them. The titles of Baxter's tunes ("Moonscape," "Mr. Robot," "The Commuter," "The Lady Is Blue," "Saturday Night on Saturn") tell a happy if vague story of a bourgeois future: moons rise; robots serve; and people work, love, imagine, and gather, usually on Saturday night, probably on Saturn. Not, however, Sun Ra's. Baxter's Saturn feels rushed and anonymous, a suburban shopping mall on a preholiday weekend. The gong that ends "Saturday Night on Saturn"—and the record—punctuates a space escapade notable more for emptiness than exploration, less a voyage to new worlds than just another party with exotic drinks. "With the aid of the music in this album," liner notes promise, "we can drift into the future's lovemist."[18] Baxter's space is neither urban nor outer; it's just a living room turned lounge, a place for easy listening and heavy petting.

Garcia's *Fantastica*, by contrast, starts with a countdown—"ten seconds till firing time, mark"—and dares to venture into space, or its sonic simulation.[19] The cover, a cloudless Earth in star-spangled black space beneath an ominous nonlinear graphic, promises "the ultimate in transistorized stereophonic hi-fidelity sound."[20] The record delivers. It's extraordinarily restrained, channeling *sounds* that seem to emanate from some pitch-black beyond: space. Garcia mixes occasional strings with a vast array of tones and timbres: harps, timpani, cymbals, bells, flutes, and electronic sounds whose infrequent, disturbing colors somehow communicate the chill of outer space. The spare arrangements, polar opposite to Baxter's, introduce space into musical composition in a new way, at least for pop, making it a constituent of the music, the instrument of absence, as if it were a player in Garcia's ensemble. The titles of *Fantastica*'s tracks, too, feel like something more than empty gestures toward fake worlds: "Into Space," "Lost Souls of Saturn," "Red Sand of Mars," "Frozen Neptune," "Moon Rise." Garcia builds on the known solar system to imagine its soundscape, one that is diaphanous, evocative, open, and speculative. Electronics enhance rather than punctuate the mood, allowing space into music as music opens to space.

Fantastica set the course for musical space exploration into the sixties. Its electronic oscillations and flutters extended the reach of the *Forbidden Planet* soundtrack into popular culture. Richard Marino's *Out of this World*, from 1961 (according to the jacket, "a unique and startling musical adventure"), spruces up star-themed standards such as "When You Wish upon a Star" and "Full Moon in Empty Arms" with space-toned warbles and sighs woven into the fabric of the arrangements.[21] Released in 1960, Marty Manning's *The Twilight Zone* ("a sound adventure in space") surfs the theme music of the TV show into an exoticized space turbid with Latin rhythms, vocal glissandi, and electronic beeps and colors supplied by an Ondioline and its keyboard cousin, the Ondes Martenot, both pictured on the record's back cover.[22] The great heir to *Fantastica*, however, is *Project Comstock: Music from Outer Space* (1962), a recording arranged and produced by Frank Comstock, who composed primarily for television and movies. Comstock retains the instrumentation of a light orchestra but remains faithful to *Fantastica*'s spaciousness. He fully integrates electronic sounds from a theremin and an electric violin into the soundscape he creates, described on the record's back cover as "the music of whirling satellites, brilliant galaxies, steaming comets, mysterious planets, and the eerie reaches of space in-between."[23] The slow dissonance of "From Another World" (fading into comforting strings) and the pizzicato tension of "Out of Space" (contrasting with a gliding theremin) create a space for relaxation as much as exploration—for the bachelor perhaps in recovery from one of the more turbulent outings of Baxter or Esquivel. Space-age pop, particularly in its most literal space-themed varieties, countered the darker preoccupations of technocratic culture—weapons, surveillance, communism, and superiority in space—with soothing sounds gesturing lightly toward other worlds. As Adinolfi puts it, "Space sound, like exotica, had a tendency to comfort listeners and suggest harmony and order."[24] It was music for dreaming—of a tomorrow that would always, for all its possibilities, resemble today.

The Space Age left its mark on mainstream jazz, too. The cover of Betty Carter's acclaimed avant-bop record *Out There with Betty Carter*, released in February 1958 just after the launch of Explorer 1, shows the singer gazing from a square widow on a round satellite, with a horizontal US missile (clearly a model) framed against a background of stars.[25] Also in 1958, Duke Ellington, fronting a nonet he called the Spacemen, which included Clark Terry and Paul Gonsalves, released an LP called *The Cosmic Scene*. It contained mostly up-tempo standards but also an Ellington original called, not surprisingly, "Spacemen." In an unpublished essay written about the same time, Ellington offered his opinion about the national rush to space superiority: "So, this is my view on the race for space. We'll never get it until we Americans, collectively and individually, get us a new sound. A new sound of harmony, brotherly love, common respect and consideration for the dignity and freedom of men.[26] Ellington here equates a new sound with dignity and freedom, qualifying the complacency of most exotica and space pop. Maybe jazz could innovate in ways they couldn't. Maybe jazz could explore space from a social as well as musical perspective. Whenever black musicians refer to space, they do so from a social place light-years away from that of their white peers.

The organist Sam Lazar recorded *Space Flight* (1960) in Chicago. The cover displays a missile fitted with a large payload lifting away from its launchpad. The promise of the record's title seems somewhat qualified, however, by that particular missile, which was designed for suborbital deployment.[27] Spaceflight here remains technologically impossible. And socially, too, perhaps? The question hovers around jazz recordings with similar titles, such as Grant Green's composition "Outer Space" (on *Born to be Blue*, recorded in 1962) or Lou Donaldson's "Spaceman Twist" (on *The Natural Soul*, also from 1962).[28] Such tunes respond playfully to the complacencies of space pop with a blues-based blast of improvisation likely to upset the bland satisfactions of any living room turned tiki lounge. John Coltrane, who would pursue the exploration of musical space with utmost seriousness, creates a free-jazz counterforce upsetting all listening considered easy; for instance, *Sun Ship* (recorded in 1965 but not released until 1971) sails forever away from the space of pop into an outer openness of free improvisation.[29] More representative of a jazz idiom in the early sixties is George Russell's *Jazz in the Space Age* (1960), which takes the Ferrante and Teicher trademark two pianos (played here by Bill Evans and Paul Bley) in concertedly new directions.[30] Three of the record's six tracks bear the title "Chromatic Universe" and interlineate the others: "Dimensions," "The Lydiot," and "Waltz from Outer Space." Here, it is formal rather than thematic innovation that renders space sonically. Eighteen musicians create a music centered more on individual tones than on keys, highly arranged and yet, as the pianos interpret and respond, improvised, too. Jazz in the Space Age will experiment with new forms, or so Russell's compositions appear to promise; they offer an intellectual exercise in advancing not so much new sounds as new arrangements of them.

When Sun Ra turned his music toward space in the late fifties, he did so in the context of a popular culture awash in space-age images and sounds. One of his responses to the confinement of blacks, segregated as they were in Chicago's South Side and other such urban spaces, then, involved deploying the cultural rhetoric of the Space Age toward the progressive ends of opening up wider vistas, new horizons. If blacks couldn't flourish in segregated cities, then maybe they could follow exotica into space. That Sun Ra and Abraham were deeply aware of space pop's wide appeal is the lesson of the cagey cover of *Jazz in Silhouette*, released not long before the Arkestra left Chicago. Corbett calls its depiction of topless African nymphets in orbit "300 space miles" above the surface of one of Saturn's moons "enormously strange."[31] But in the context of the musical genre it clearly references—exotica—the cover slyly charts the Arkestra's agenda of taking the music of so-called primitives far beyond the limits of popular expectation. Images of black women—on the cover of a record that blacks had produced—reverse the priorities, visually and musically, of recordings such as Esquivel's *Other Worlds Other Sounds* or Denny's *Primitiva*. Blacks already inhabited the (primitive?) new worlds of exotica, transported there by the power of music. Sun Ra listened carefully to exotica and took some of what it offered into his sound: tightly orchestrated arrangements, intense rhythms, dense percussion, transient noise, and unusual instruments, either homemade or from other cultures ("space harp," "Flying Saucer," "solar drum," Rhodesian bells, zither, violin-uke, tabla, etc.). But he eschewed its tricks of sudden contrast and campy commentary and depended instead on exuberant musicians to induce the unexpected through spirited improvisation.

Sun Ra took exotica on an odyssey that makes space pop feel like the auditory equivalent of *Lost in Space*. Given the time warps characteristic of El Saturn releases in the sixties, records belonging to the early days of his turn to space did not appear until long after the Space

Age was in full swing, giving them a sense of detachment from the cultural conditions that inspired them. But Sun Ra's early space music remains some of his best. He recorded a slew of it during the marathon 1960 session in Milwaukee, the summer before the Arkestra left for Montreal. A record containing some of that material appeared first in 1966, under the title *Rocket Number Nine Take Off for the Planet Venus*, and then again three years later with the new title *Interstellar Low Ways*. It offers an exhilarating trip to destinations to which space pop never dared to go. The later title plays a little joke on the Interstate Highway Act of 1956, combining interstellar travel with the ways of low folks (as Sun Ra referred ironically to blacks in the Thmei broadsheets). The tracks on the record all reference space pop, even the opening tune "Onward," which begins Sun Ra's explorations of space with a hip gesture toward what's to come. The head presents a savvy statement of urban cool that ends in punctuated dissonance. Prepare for takeoff.

The music conjures space in all its analog glory, with Sun Ra forgoing electronics to create an acoustic structure for musical space travel. Three tunes unfold to an evocative spaciousness. "Somewhere in Space" offers Gilmore a vehicle for sinewy flight, Sun Ra toggling up and down a half-step while the horns harmonize microtonally. Wherever this somewhere is, it's dreamy and unresolved, fading quietly to nothing. The tune "Interstellar Low Ways" could be pure exotica, but its title puts it between the stars. In good Baxter form (but thankfully without strings), a flute dances over a jungle rhythm that, were it any less restrained, might parody exotica's parody of the primitive. The tune meanders for over eight minutes through an astral garden of sounds, creating space for speculation with a lone drum or bass. This is interstellar travel by underdrive to destinations unknowable. After a funereal opening statement, "Space Loneliness" becomes a minor blues of unutterable wistfulness, backed by Sun Ra's shimmering yet discordant piano and leading to no particular consolation. Loneliness as big as space, a feeling communicated almost painfully by a haunting, recurring, reverberating *snap* over the melody.

"Interplanetary Music," on the other hand, is unabashed happiness. Over the squeal of a bowed violin-uke and the clunk of an on-the-beat cowbell, the band half sings and half chants, "Interplanetary, Inter-*plan*-etary, Interplan-etary Music"—hilarious and fun. Then comes the chorus: "Interplanetary Melodies, . . . Interplanetary Harmonies," the bass walking and the piano flirting. The Arkestra advances a plan for conquering the cosmos through sound and a sense of humor. The violin-uke breaks into a tortured, shrill solo while the bell clunks on. Then it all cycles again until they all head out: "MUSIC, . . . Music, . . . music." Never has space pop achieved such untempered joy. There's more to space than technological superiority and shaken cocktails. "Space Aura" picks up the pace two tunes later, a double-time romp through harmonies stacked and leaning like they are about to fall over. Postbop, anybody? Sun Ra's spare chords give Gilmore space to soar vertically before the Arkestra reconverges on an orchestrated chorus that feels accidental and sharp. Then the raucous finale: "Rocket Number Nine Take Off for the Planet Venus." What a record! *Interstellar Low Ways* launches space pop to heights unimaginable in purely popular terms. Improvisation as antigravity: the extraordinary feeling and technique of the Arkestra's musicians derange exotica to reassemble and extend its possibilities somewhere—else—in space.

Sun Ra had in mind an agenda higher than either space pop or NASA could sustain. "Space music," as he would later put it, "is an introductory prelude to the sound of greater infinity. . . . It is a different order of sound synchronized to a different order of Being."[32] Good-bye primitivos and space-capaders. Sun Ra aimed to transform the planet. Joining his space program will require serious preparation for outer space, and music provides the only education:

In this age of Outer Space challenge, People will have to change their tune, i.e. they will have to be tuned up or down (according to what is necessary) another way. The intergalactic counsil has a different tuning system. The insistent idea is that people will have to change their tune and that tuning should be in tune with the intergalactic outer universe, which is everything which is not yet in. And this is the meaning of the Kingdom of Not and its phonetic note. Note![33]

In Sun Ra's music and words, the language of science fiction converges with the sonic possibilities of space music to retune people so that they may inhabit worlds yet to come. From the South Side of Chicago to infinity: Sun Ra plots a course for blacks and anyone else who can keep up with him through outer space to a new tomorrow.

16

SPACE MUSIC

Interstellar Low Ways contains a message from Sun Ra to his listeners printed in caps on the back cover: "THE IMPOSSIBLE IS THE WATCH-WORD OF THE GREATER SPACE AGE. THE SPACE AGE CANNOT BE AVOIDED AND THE SPACE MUSIC IS THE KEY TO UNDERSTANDING THE MEANING OF THE IMPOSSIBLE AND EVERY OTHER ENIGMA."[1] Sun Ra expected the Arkestra's music to do more than flock the walls of a space-age bachelor pad. In his hands, the commercial idiom of space pop became a vehicle of insight and change, a means of understanding the "meaning of the impossible" and living accordingly. In this way, music becomes more than music, transfigured into philosophical inquiry, social criticism, and a way of life. Space music explores possibilities other than those endorsed by contemporary preoccupations, however scientifically plausible or socially progressive they appear. It pursues aims higher than that of landing humans on the moon or even achieving equality among them on Earth. It aspires to nothing less than transforming reality. Space music *performs* the impossible, transporting people to better worlds. "When I talk about outer space," Sun Ra once said, "people listen. People are sleeping, and I'm here to wake them up from their slumber. The right music can wake people up."[2] And the right music is space music, which moves people by force of *sound*: "You got to reach people with all kinds of sounds now. Sounds. That's what they need. They got to have sound bodies now. Sound minds."[3]

As Sun Ra and the Arkestra, including its chief studio engineer, Abraham, understood things, sounds produce remarkable effects, and not merely as a function of the latest recording technologies. For all their playful jacket testimonials of recording technique ("Solar Fidelity," "Galaxtone," etc.), El Saturn records mostly remained low-tech fare compared with their commercial counterparts. Sound, not the equipment reproducing it, could touch and transform minds and hearts—physiologically and in real time. The long and wandering manuscript typed on Mount Sinai Hospital letterhead contains an interesting commentary on the "tone science" that informs the Arkestra's approach to music. It ponders in detail the force of sound as vibration: "these invisible sound-vibrations have great power over concrete matter. They can both build and destroy." The writer, likely Abraham, illustrates this principle by describing how powder on a brass plate assumes "beautiful geometrical figures" when a violin bow drawn across its edge causes the plate to vibrate.[4] Then the author draws a revealing human parallel:

> If one note or chord after another be sounded upon a musical instrument, say, a piano, or preferably a violin, for from it more gradation of tone can be obtained, a tone will finally be reached which will cause the hearer to feel a distinct vibration in the back of the lower part of the head. Each time that note is struck, the vibration will be felt. That note is the "key note" of the person whom it so affects. If it is struck slowly and smoothingly it will build and rest the body, tone the nerves and restore health. If, on the other hand, it be sounded in a dominant way, loud and long enough, it will kill as surely as a bullet from a pistol.[5]

The shift in the first sentence from "note" to "tone" (a favorite Sun Ra permutation) registers the agenda of the Arkestra's space music. The fundamental unit of Western music, the note, cedes here to tone, less a precise (and written) point of pure sound than a smear, a *gradation*, whose "distinct vibration" produces bodily effects. There might be more to sound than meets the ear. The vibrations it communicates can be conducive to health—or harm. Sounds build bodies, tune them up or turn them out. New sounds might build better bodies or transport them to better worlds.

Sun Ra's space music flies far beyond space pop to become tone science. It explores the effects of sounds on human bodies and being, experimenting with their capacity to induce physical and therefore social change. Long before rappers started "droppin' science" to hip their listeners to urgent issues, Sun Ra's tone science advanced a method for creating new futures through music. The Arkestra's players became *tone scientists*. "Not musicians," Szwed emphasizes: "They were exploring sound, experimenting, not re-creating what already existed."[6] These were tones for people in need of special care, as is suggested by *Cosmic Tones for Mental Therapy* (the title of an El Saturn recording made in 1963). New sounds to propel them to better worlds. Sounds for the Space Age. Such therapeutic tones would not necessarily sound pretty, nor would the music made from them, in the usual sense, sound musical. "I like all the sounds that upset people," Sun Ra said in an interview, "because they're too complacent, and there are some sounds that really upset them, and man, you need to shock them out of their complacency, 'cause it's a very bad world in a lot of aspects. They need to wake to how bad it is: then maybe they'll do something about it."[7] Tone science shocks in order to awaken its listeners and change them, mentally *and* physically. James Jacson, who started playing percussion regularly with the Arkestra in New York, put it this way: "What Sun Ra had to do was reverse the state of bodily control, and he would demonstrate it with music and the Arkestra."[8] Space music subverts control, opens bodies to a life better than the one contemporary America has provided, especially for segregated blacks.

But there's also something soothing about its sounds, precisely because they create an opening to other worlds. Abraham once described Sun Ra's turn to space music as inaugurating "the period of the Major Greater Spiritual Musical Art Forms."[9] Space music communicates a hope so vast it surpasses human understanding, as the following remark by Sun Ra suggests: "Now, my music is about a better place for people, not to have a place where they have to die to get there, I'm not talking about that."[10] So much for the morbid consolations of Christianity. Any place where death is the price of entry is no place for Sun Ra. Space music aspires to transport people to a better place, not beyond death, but simply without it, the space of music itself, or music of the Arkestra's kind. If (to reiterate) "space music is an introductory prelude to the sound of greater infinity," it remains a preliminary gesture, a first-stage booster.[11] Not itself the sound of infinity, space music offers a prelude to it, different sounds synchronized to a higher order, sounds expressing the *prospect* of infinity: "I'm actually painting pictures of infinity with my music, and that's why a lot of people can't understand it. But if they'd listen to this and other types of music, they'll find that mine has something else in it, something from another world."[12] Sun Ra's tone science tests this world against sounds from another one, a place where space opens to infinity. Space music challenges listeners to pursue those vistas mindfully: "The real aim of this music is to coordinate the minds of people into an intelligent reach for a better world, and an intelligent approach to the living future."[13] Music after infinity: space travel with Sun Ra requires collective aspiration for a life defined not by its end but by its continuation. "I am not of this planet," said Sun Ra. "I am another order of being."[14]

A music more fully synchronized with that different order of being began to emerge after Sun Ra arrived for an extended stay in New York. The story goes that the Arkestra intended to return to Chicago by car, but a collision with a taxi marooned the band in the city with the most innovative jazz scene in the country.[15] It would prove a productive accident. Szwed describes in detail New York's vitalizing effect on Sun Ra. The city felt like Chicago turned upright and inside out.

The wide expanse of Lakeshore Drive narrowed into Broadway, cutting through Manhattan like a valley of concrete shadow. The segregation of the South Side gave way to new urban possibilities, particularly on the Lower East Side, where the band took up residence at 48 East Third Street in 1962. Once America's most crowded slum, the East Village was becoming a space of extraordinary diversity, attracting a wide variety of bohemians interested in living creatively and cheaply. Szwed calls it "the closest thing to an integrated community that America could produce," however fleeting it might have proved to be as the sixties unfolded.[16] The East Village offered black artists a space to create and interact, and they responded by forming musical groups, theater companies, writers' circles, and publishing ventures—in such numbers and with such energy that Szwed suggests the collective results should be considered yet another renaissance for African Americans.[17] The names of the musicians involved, many living within blocks of Sun Ra's residence, add up to a who's who of the sixties black avant-garde: Archie Shepp, Ornette Coleman, Sonny Simmons, Henry Grimes, Sunny Murray, Cecil Taylor, Wayne Shorter, Sonny Sharrock, Albert and Don Ayler, and a young saxophone player from Arkansas named Farrell Sanders, whom Sun Ra rechristened Pharoah. Uptown in Harlem, LeRoi Jones, soon to change his name to Amiri Baraka, conjured the Black Arts movement out of indignation and word magic. An urban ecology more conducive to sound research—tone science—could hardly be built to order.[18]

The Arkestra first performed in New York as the Outer Spacemen at Café Bizarre in January 1962.[19] A gig at the Charles Theater soon followed, with advertisements for it announcing "Outer Space Jazz" performed by "Le Sun Ra" and his "Cosmic Jazz Space Patrol."[20] Work was intermittent at first but became increasingly steady, and soon the Arkestra secured a regular place to rehearse and record, the Choreographers' Workshop at 414 West Fifty-First Street.[21] Here the band would make many of its most challenging recordings, moving beyond the thematic engagements with space of the Chicago years (as evidenced by titles of records and tunes, commentary on covers, chants, and costumes) to create sounds commensurable with space as a musical medium. Bugs Hunter, Sun Ra's drummer from his days working Calumet City's strip clubs, had already moved to New York. He began playing regularly with the Arkestra and took responsibility for recording at the Choreographers' Workshop, creating the thick reverb, familiar from exotica, that characterized El Saturn's New York releases.[22] Ever the experimentalist, Sun Ra encouraged Hunter to explore how even low-end recording technology might contribute to sound production, turning machines into new instruments in the Arkestra arsenal. The New York records take tone science to new heights.

This is where the serendipity of El Saturn's approach to release and distribution muddles—or at least complicates—any sense of the Arkestra's development as a vehicle for space music. Thanks perhaps to the trials of relocation, to personal tensions between Sun Ra and Abraham, or to shaky financing—really, to any number of unclear causes—a lot of material recorded in Chicago didn't see release until years later, after the band had evolved into a much different, more aggressively experimental ensemble. As mentioned earlier, the music on *Interstellar Low Ways* was recorded in 1960 but was not released until 1966. *Sun Ra Visits Planet Earth*, also released in 1966, contains material recorded ten years earlier.[23] The 1959 session that resulted in *Jazz in Silhouette* also yielded the music on *Sound Sun Pleasure!!*, which was not released until 1970.[24] Rehearsal recordings from Chicago provided the tracks on *Lady with the Golden Stockings*, released in 1966 and retitled *The Nubians of Plutonia* in 1967.[25] Finally, enough music remained from the marathon Milwaukee recording session of 1960 for two more records, *Fate in a Pleasant Mood* and *We Travel the Spaceways*, El Saturn releases of 1965 and 1966, respectively.[26]

Given El Saturn's improvisational sense of advertising (the Arkestra's performances were its main means, backed by mail-order catalogs), it is not as if these records enjoyed a huge demand. But Sun Ra's goals did not include commercial success. "My music is self-underground," he said once, "that is, out of the music industry: I've made records with no titles, primitive, natural and pure."[27] While selling a few records inspired hopes of sustaining the Arkestra and its experiments, the music industry did not do the same, and El Saturn avoided it and its usual practices. The anonymity Sun Ra associates with his music—its primitiveness and natural purity—all gesture toward the importance of sounds that arise not from popular demand but from more abstract resources. The New York recordings pursue that agenda with the enthusiasm for research implicit in El Saturn's full name. They constitute a series of experiments in sound.[28] Alongside the time-lapsed Chicago recordings, then, appears a string of innovative records that double interplanetary exotica with advanced research in tone science.

These were not the first records Sun Ra made in New York. In 1961 he recorded *The Futuristic Sounds of Sun Ra* for the Savoy label and *Bad and Beautiful* for El Saturn, both outings notable—the former, for pushing jazz-ensemble harmony way beyond bebop, and the latter, for scoring standards in low registers with warmth and imagination.[29] But beginning in 1962, the Arkestra took flight on a trajectory that would lead it through spaces previously unexplored by jazz musicians. *Secrets of the Sun* served as a launchpad. It exaggerates an iconoclastic tendency audible in Sun Ra's music from the start: an attention to transients (all the sonic variations that blur a pure pitch), which vastly extend the range of musical possibility. At the same time, though, it remains faithful to cultural influences, as Sun Ra's penciled notebook draft of possible jacket copy indicates:

> This is the music heralding and reiterating the presence of another age . . . the Space Age. Congratulations to those who have taken photographs of the moon at close proximity and too, this album is dedicated to them & to others who feel a change is in the air & who know that life will never be the same again upon this planet called earth. How rapidly we are moving, and splendidly so, for we have a rendezvous with a better destiny than [scribbled deletion] those former roles we have played in the dream called life.[30]

Sun Ra refers here to Ranger 7, launched in 1964, which was the first American probe to return photographs of the lunar surface. The Soviet Union's Luna 3 had already done one better in 1959 with its dark-side photographs.[31] Sun Ra's draft dedication unites Cold War adversaries in an impressive if unevenly shared accomplishment. *Secrets of the Sun*, as Luna 3 had done before it, follows a bolder trajectory into hitherto unknown space, returning audible impressions of things unseen. Fresh experiments followed with impressive frequency, always to exciting and often provocative results. The Arkestra recorded both *Secrets of the Sun* and *Art Forms of Dimensions Tomorrow* in 1962, releasing them in 1965.[32] Other tracks recorded in 1962 and 1963 appeared on *When Sun Comes Out* (released remarkably quickly in 1963) and *The Invisible Shield*, a rare record that didn't appear until 1974.[33]

More sessions from 1963 yielded *When Angels Speak of Love*, out in 1966, and *Cosmic Tones for Mental Therapy*, out the following year.[34] In 1964, the band recorded *Other Planes of There* (released in 1966) and taped a live recording (not released until 1974) featuring Pharoah Sanders, who played with the Arkestra during Gilmore's stint with Art Blakey's Jazz Messengers.[35] In 1965, the Arkestra completed the two volumes of *Heliocentric Worlds of Sun Ra* for the ESP label, which brought them out in 1965 and 1966—the Arkestra's wonder years, with an astonishing total of thirteen records seeing release, six from Chicago and seven from New York sessions, the latter including *The Magic City*, a miracle of musical invention.[36] In 1966, the Arkestra also recorded the beguiling *Strange Strings* and *Outer Spaceways Incorporated* for El Saturn, plus performances for a live set entitled *Nothing Is* on ESP (these records saw release, respectively, in 1967, 1974, and 1969).[37] More recordings were to come in New York, but perhaps this is the moment to pause and ponder some fundamentals of space music, the fruits of this marvelous series of sonic researches.[38]

Three qualities seem worth emphasizing. They are not necessary criteria for space music, nor is that music any less "spacey" without them. They certainly appear in flashes and shards in the Chicago recordings. But the New York work bears witness to a vast expansion and exploration of their possibilities. First among them is openness. Recall this cryptic remark from Sun Ra: "The word space is the synonym for a multi-dimension of different things other than what people might at present think it means. I leave the word space open, like space is supposed to be, when I say space-music."[39] Space is open. Openness *constitutes* space music, both thematically, as a metaphor plucked from the public language of outer space, and musically, as a suspension of traditional conventions, in particular those regarding time. It may seem odd to say that space music involves the suspension of time, but that's how space *happens* musically, as a dilation of regular—and regulated—pulsation. In the Chicago recordings, Sun Ra creates this feeling of suspension during introductory passages such as the one from "Images," on *Jazz in Silhouette*, where his piano flirts with time before the band enters at a formal tempo. In New York, flirtation turns habitual, opening space for dilation and play. A quick comparison of two versions of "Space Aura," one from *Sun Ra Visits Planet Earth* (recorded in 1956) and the other from *Secrets of the Sun* (recorded in 1963), illustrates what is happening. By significantly slowing the tempo of this once hard-bop blow fest, space opens up for soloists, Gilmore especially, to spiral and drift. Suspend tempo even further and you get the soundscape of *Other Planes of There*, a recording that seemingly hangs the Arkestra in space to move with currents of the solar wind. When *Down Beat* reviewed the record in 1966, it acknowledged this quality of the Arkestra's sound as the trace of "an age-old transcendentalism" and gave *Other Planes of There* a rating of four and a half stars, "not only for the beauty of the music when the moment has been seeded [. . . , but] also for Sun Ra's persistent activism within the void—his undaunted perseverance in recording the unrecordable. Transcendental as Sun Ra's music is, it somehow works to involve us more in the everyday."[40] Sun Ra calls space music "the introductory prelude to the sound of greater infinity," but it leads back to social space as the place where its life and ours *happens*—all the time.[41]

Second among the defining qualities of space music is multiplicity. Sun Ra expresses it best when he says space is synonymous with "a multi-dimension of different things."[42] It opens to a multiplicity of musical possibilities that occur without reference to a single regulative order. Sun Ra can work, for instance, with multiple rhythms in a way that makes Stan Kenton, who also explored unusual time signatures and rhythms, seem timid: "Sometimes I might have a 5/4 against a 7/4 against a 3/4 in one measure. It looks like a computer thing on paper."[43] Perhaps multiplicity functions as a corollary of openness: once regular tempo gets suspended, a multitude can crowd in. Sun Ra heads in this direction on "Music from the World Tomorrow," recorded in 1960 and released on *Angels and Demons at Play* in 1965: strings, piano, and snapping percussion march, so to speak, to their own drummers.[44] The true potential of multiplying tempos in such a way suffuses "Reflects Motion," on *Secrets of the Sun*. Boykins's jittery, freewheeling bass opens over an irregular pulse, followed by a lone traps drummer (Scoby Stroman) playing in three until Boykins returns, soon to be overlaid with Sun Ra's unmeasured piano and Gilmore's jagged saxophone in and out of unison with Allen's flute.[45] The tune is a hurtling bundle of tensions, incommensurable rhythms interacting and pulling apart to create a multisphere of sound. Similar tendencies disrupt musical continuity even further, spreading time over multiple consecutive rhythms to summon space into music like an absent deity, as on "Celestial Fantasy" (1963), released in 1966 on *When Angels Speak of Love*.

The third quality to emphasize about space music may be the most familiar: improvisation. It's de rigueur to think of Sun Ra as a master of it, as both a soloist and an ensemble player. All the constitutive qualities of space music come together in improvisation, for such music opens space for multiple members of the Arkestra to improvise, often simultaneously. One of the most compelling aspects of Sun Ra's later music especially is the intensity of improvisation it sustains: Marshall Allen's freak-show solos, Gilmore's flights of stratospheric frenzy, Boykins's bass ravings and harmonics squeals, and Sun Ra's own turbulent keyboard storms. But improvisation as Sun Ra understands and (perhaps oddly) *composes* it does not occur as individual virtuosity in a collective ensemble context. Theorizing the improvisational break as a musical "space between" that "fills and erases itself" in the midst of collective playing, Fred Moten equates the ensemble with "the improvisation *of* singularity and totality *through* their opposition."[46] But improvisation in Sun Ra's space music isn't oppositional; rather, it becomes (as) the space of music itself. The opposition between soloist and ensemble falls to the music's collective occurrence; "everything is happenin'" all the time.[47] This is the sense in which Sun Ra insists that he composes even the most chaotic sounds his musicians make: "I can write something so chaotic you would say you know it's not written. But the reason it's chaotic is because it's written to be. It's further out than anything they would be doing if they were just improvising."[48] Sun Ra can script a collective chaos that exceeds mere improvisation.

His music breaks down the traditional distinction between improvisation and composition. Marshall Allen provides a revealing description of the way Sun Ra conducted recording sessions in New York:

> Sun Ra would go to the studio and he would play something, the bass would come in, and if he didn't like it he'd stop it, and he'd give the drummer a particular rhythm, tell the bass he wanted not a "boom boom boom," but something else, and then he'd begin to try out the horns, we're all standing there wondering what's next. [. . .] A lot of things we'd be rehearsing and we did the wrong things and Sun Ra stopped the arrangement and changed it. Or he would change the person who was playing the particular solo, so that changes the arrangement. 'Cos he knew people. He could understand what you could do better so he would fit that with what he would tell you.[49]

People were Sun Ra's instruments. He arranged what they could do, which included improvisation in the conventional sense. So instead of performing a deviation from scripted material, improvisation constitutes the material, an approach that also collapses the distinction between soloist and ensemble.

It becomes possible, and even inevitable, that improvisation becomes the province of the *ensemble* rather than its soloists—as prelude to infinity. "When the band reaches a certain point," Sun Ra confessed about the Arkestra in performance, "the creative forces join us and they play. It's a romance of two worlds, you might say. They play the instruments . . . sometimes I hook up with the cosmos. And then out of the cosmos comes this sound. And then that is, like, food for people, when they hear that sound. It's enlightening, it's encouraging."[50] Improvisation opens musical arrangement to higher creative forces, producing sounds that sustain and enlighten the Arkestra's listeners. Sun Ra's approach to improvisation moves worlds beyond bebop's variations over changes. The recorded results are magnificent beyond reckoning: *The Magic City*, quite simply the most moving, evocative, and sustained group improvisation to come out of the sixties; its exact contemporary "The Sun Myth" from *Heliocentric Worlds, Volume 2*, whose sequential studies in tone and transience hang sounds in deep space until they erupt in collective chaos that tapers into silence; and *Strange Strings*, the uncanny beauty of whose willed illiteracy (the Arkestra playing unfamiliar stringed instruments) stirs unsounded depths of feeing.

The composer Sun Ra plays the *Arkestra* as his instrument, with multiple tonal registers and harmonic possibilities sounding in real time to transcend time, pushing time into space. Often during performance, when he felt the call to move a composition in fresh directions, he would direct the Arkestra to play a "space chord," a cacophonous collective disruption that cleared space for new sounds.[51] Improvisation extends what openness and multiplicity invoke: space as the medium of collective aspiration for better worlds. In a magnificent bid for public acknowledgment and acceptance of these exhilarating sounds, the Arkestra played Carnegie Hall on April 12 and 13, 1968. The show's printed program announces a call to adventure: "THE SPACE MUSIC OF SUN RA: *a free form excursion into the far reaches of sound and sight—*."[52] The performances occurred on a dark stage lit intermittently by projected images of the moon, Saturn, and abstract shapes. Twenty instrumentalists in robes of green, red, and orange blasted and swooped through the full spectrum of Sun Ra's compositions, accompanied by onstage dancing and offstage singing. Two experimental films added visual luster: Phill Niblock's *The Magic Sun*, an abstract short built up from negative black-and-white close-ups of the Arkestra in action, and Maxine Haleff's *The Forbidden Playground*, the backdrop for dancing performed by the Edith Stephen Dance Theater.[53] Although the *New*

York Times promoted the event with a two-page notice, fewer than five hundred people turned out, only a handful of them African American. Sun Ra had the ill fortune to open at Carnegie Hall only a week after the assassination of Martin Luther King Jr., and he blamed that atrocity for the show's poor attendance. But he would continue to enrich the visually dramatic elements of the Arkestra's performance to the point of mythological depth and grandeur.

A poem entitled "The Outer Bridge," which serves as an epigraph in the Carnegie Hall program, describes a world somewhere between reality and abstraction:

In the half-between world
Dwell they, the tone-scientists
Sound
Mathematically precise
They speak of many things
The sound-scientists
Architects of planes of discipline[54]

As tone scientists, the Arkestra's musicians dwell in music, a bridge to other, outer planes. Space music follows its own science, building abstract worlds of sound.

MYTH-SCIENCE

The Arkestra's move from Chicago to New York took its music out of the lounge and into deep space. Sun Ra marked the transition with new christenings: the Arkestra became, variously, the Solar Arkestra, the Myth-Science Arkestra, and the Astro-Infinity Arkestra.[1] More names would follow depending on the mood of a given project, but these three appear on most of the music released in New York, including material recorded years earlier in Chicago. More time travel: by modifying names, Sun Ra disrupted his ensemble's relationship to time, further complicating the notoriously difficult business of crediting particular musicians to particular recordings. Although Sun Ra might have intended these terms as generic markers, it's impossible to tell how. Recordings made in both places come out under sometimes one name and sometimes another. "The Myth-Science Arkestra" first appeared in 1963 on *Secrets of the Sun*; "The Solar Arkestra," in 1965 on *Art Forms of Dimensions Tomorrow*. "Astro-Infinity Arkestra" is the clear latecomer, first appearing in 1967 on *Strange Strings*.[2] "Solar" indicts the paltry lunar ambitions of NASA, and "astro-infinity" charts the ultimate course of space music. But "myth-science"? What can Sun Ra possibly mean?

Only everything. "Myth-science" describes the form that knowledge takes as space music. Under all its names, but this one explicitly, the Arkestra creates knowledge running counter to normal science and its positivist presumptions. Music as science and science as myth. Myth-Science. A clue to the way it works emerges from the records credited to the Myth-Science Arkestra: their release dates attest no particular attention to the historical time or place of their production. *Interstellar Low Ways* and *Cosmic Tones for Mental Therapy*, recorded three years and half a continent apart, both testify to myth-science, and not because they display continuity in style or personnel.[3] The when and the where of their production seem not to have mattered to Sun Ra, since history doesn't exist, at least not from the perspective of the music or its packaging. In fact, the packaging communicates this point with disarming directness. In a blurb that appears often enough on El Saturn record jackets and catalogs to make it a miniature manifesto, Sun Ra declares a moratorium on history:

> The civilizations of the past have been used as the foundation of the civilization of today. Because of this, the world keeps looking toward the past for guidance. Too many people are following the past. In this new space age, this is dangerous. The past is DEAD and those who are following the past are doomed to die and be like the past. It is no accident that those who die are said to have passed since those who have PASSED are PAST.[4]

The Space Age demands the abolition of history. If today's civilization arises from those of the past, it will inevitably repeat their failings. History amounts to a cinema playing the same old horror show, interminably. Sun Ra's myth-science turns away from the past as a foundation for knowledge, away from the zombies of civilization. It resists the call of the dead and aspires to a higher life.

Myth becomes Sun Ra's vehicle to infinity. But it's a tricky rocket to ride, not least because it isn't there. Myth appeals to Sun Ra precisely because, unlike the observable, measurable, substantial constituents of normal science, it doesn't *really* exist. Or more precisely, its contents do not. It's hard to confuse Zeus with Newton's apple. Zeus is an image, a fiction, a phantasm of the ancient Greeks. Newton's apple was real, possessing weight and density enough to knock some sense into him and inspire modern physics. The story of the apple hitting Newton, however, might itself be a myth. Sun Ra finds the nonexistence of myth deeply attractive and, for his music (as tone science), profoundly functional. A quick turn to his poetry (remembering his dictum that "words express music and music expresses words") illustrates the force of myth:[5]

> *The kingdom of not . . . . .*
> *A realm of myth. [. . .]*
> *It is not but yet is . . . [. . .]*
> *Thus it is not of the past*
> *And hence is not of the passed*
> *Consider the hidden presence [. . .]*
> *Of the kingdom of not . . . .*[6]

The realm of myth—literally—*is not.* It does not exist and never has. To that extent, it offers a solution to the problem of history, whose pastness scripts a dead present. In a functional sense, however, myth does exist. Its effects influence life, as myths of Zeus influenced the Greeks. The force of myth, efficacious in nonexistence, gives it a "hidden presence": "it is not, but yet is." Nothing as negation acquires a positive value as pure potential, or as Sun Ra puts it in another poem ("Music of the Spheres"), "Nothing comes to be in order that / Nothing shall be because nothing / From nothing leaves nothing."[7] Read generously, these lines turn absence into potential presence, or rather the presence of potential as the condition of creation. Out of nothing.

The efficacy of myth became important to Sun Ra because it exactly matches the operation of music: "This music of the spheres / Music of the outer spheres / This music came from nothing, / The void, in response to the / Burning need for nothing else."[8] Like myth, music does not exist. It resembles Zeus more than it resembles Newton's apple. It possesses no substance. It lacks a medium. It dissipates *as it* happens, coming to presence in the midst of its passing. And yet the force of this absencing creates the truth of sound, as these lines from "Black Prince Charming" suggest:

The strange truth of Eternal myth
Is the Sound; It is the
Sound truth . . . Music Sound
And there always is music
The music always is
Whatever is.[9]

The strange truth (the *notness*) of myth occurs as *sound*, the sound truth, which "always is / Whatever is." Nothing becomes everything. The passing force of music potentiates time ("always"), transfiguring it into space ("Whatever is"). Sun Ra puts the point more directly in a series of remarks entitled "The Air Spiritual Man" published in *The Immeasurable Equation*: "Music envisions and potentializes."[10] It produces effects from no apparent cause, as naturally as the wind: "The sound is of the wind, the wind is not but the not is the note and the note permutated is tone."[11] Out of wind, sound. Out of not, tone. Permutations of equivalence turn nothing into whatever is through sound. Or again: "Nothing is the whole note of music, within that nothing is the divisional-manifestations of the elements of rhythm, and the analyzation quintessence of the melody."[12]

The nothing of myth and music served to ground the magic city of potent fictions that built up around Arkestra as it played, its astro-black mythology. Sun Ra has been called the great progenitor of Afrofuturism for his exploration of both tomorrow's world and the new musical technologies that could take him there.[13] But it is useful to examine closely his understanding of the relationship between blackness and myth. His days with Thmei as a street-corner activist in Chicago taught him the urgency of black uplift. Space music and myth-science direct activism toward infinity, amplifying its spiritual sonority. Sun Ra remained a black activist at heart, as lines from his arresting poem "The Visitation" show:

In the early days of my visitation,
Black hands tended me and cared for me;
I can't forget these things.
For black hearts, minds and souls love me—
And even today the overtones from the fire
Of that love are still burning.[14]

Loving hands create a history of the heart to counter the horrors of civilization. But in Sun Ra's efforts to ameliorate suffering through music, blackness slides inevitably into myth. An observation he made during an interview shows how it happens. Discussing the social value of blacks, he says in his verbally frisky way, "They're priceless. They have no price. They're worthless. Which makes them priceless. They ain't worth nothing."[15] Socially considered, blacks are nothing. But that condition associates them with myth and music. From that nothing, perhaps, can come everything ("worthless" turning "priceless").

Blackness becomes space, becomes music. Between them, the two versions of a poem entitled "The Outer Darkness" chart Sun Ra's heading: "Black is space: THE OUTER DARKNESS," reads the opening line of the first version. "The music of the outer darkness is / the music of the void. / The opening is the void: but the / opening is synonym to the / beginning."[16] The nothing of black space—the void—opens to a (new) beginning. That Sun Ra means these terms racially becomes clear in the revision: "Natural Black music projects the myth of Blackness / And he who is not Black in spirit will never know / That these words are true and valid forever."[17] Black in spirit: Sun Ra changes the race game from skin tone to sound tone. Music projects myth, and both are black, as black as space. This is blackness of a deeper shade:

I speak of different kind of Blackness, the kind
That the world does not know, the kind that the world
Will never understand
It is rhythm against rhythm in kind dispersion
It is harmony against harmony in endless coordination
It is melody against melody in vital enlightenment

And something else and more
A living spirit gives a quickening thought.[18]

Note that the qualities of this "different kind of blackness" mimic the multiplicity characteristic of space music. By assimilating blackness to space to music, Sun Ra potentiates "nothing," remaking it into "living spirit." This is activism (to quote Stevie Wonder) "in the key of life," no longer agitating in the confined space of segregation on the South Side but orchestrating spiritual flight into the space Sun Ra calls "Black Infinity."[19]

Sun Ra formally announces this spiritualized political agenda in a poem frequently chanted at later Arkestra performances, the stirring invocation entitled "Astro Black":

Astro-Black Mythology
Astro-Timeless Immortality
Astro-Thought in Mystic Sound
Astro-Black of Outer Space
Astro Natural of Darkest Stars
Astro Reach Beyond the Stars
Out to Endless Endlessness
Astro-Black American
The Universe is in My Voice
The Universe Speaks through the Dawn
To Those of Earth and Other Worlds
Listen While You Have the Chance
Find Your Place among the Stars
Listen to the Outer World
Rhythm Multiplicity
Harmony, Equational
Melody Horizon
Astro Black and Cosmo Dark
Astro Black and Cosmo Dark
Astro Black and Cosmo Dark.
Astro Black Mythology

Astro-Timeless Immortality
Astro Thought in Mystic Sound
Astro Black Mythology.[20]

From nothing to infinity: astro-black mythology answers segregation and racism and bigotry and hate with sounds (in the most exhilarating and exuberant sense) for the Space Age.

Lest Sun Ra's astro-black myth, with its mystic sound and timeless immortality, seem too abstract to address worldly concerns, consider the poem in which he speaks directly to the coming generation, "Message to Black Youth." It begins surprisingly: "Never say you are unloved / I love you."[21] Rarely one for open declarations of affection, Sun Ra offers young blacks a blessing. He is also quick to explain what might appear to them as neglect: "If I deny you / It is only love / Seeking a way to make you hear / The thought essence of being."[22] Love moves through its apparent absence to make essence audible— yet another instance of what is not becoming what is. "Your beauty to me is your discipline," Sun Ra writes to challenge stereotype. "No one could ever care more / Than I."[23] Through "discipline-precision" he promises them "an abstract tomorrowness myth / A triumph of otherness love." Astro-black mythology conveys and bestows love as a constituent of tomorrow in a way that opens toward otherness, as the poem's final line suggests: "Other youths if real in the myth shall partake."[24]

As Sun Ra pushes reality into myth, he takes blackness far beyond the more mundane registers of his Chicago activism. One of his favorite puns—almost a homonym, really—shows the height of his hopes for blacks:

See how the black rays of the black race
Have touched the immeasurable wisdom
And therefore the unknown quantity
See how they are not understood
And as what they know is what they are
See the unlimited freedom of the black rays.[25]

"Race" becomes "rays" when heard in a different way. A limiting social distinction unfurls to unlimited freedom. The desideratum of so much traditional activism arises to hand as black rays touch immeasurable wisdom. "The alternative to limitation," Sun Ra wrote in a concert program, "is INFINITY."[26] As blacks realize what they already know, they become a power source, beaming a wisdom that exceeds social confinement.

So decisive is this transformation that Sun Ra postulated a new race to distinguish its new being, the "angel race," which he describes in detail in an essay called "My Music is Words," published by Amiri Baraka in his newsletter *The Cricket* in 1968:

> My measurement of race is rate of vibration-beam . . . rays. . . . Hence the black rays is a simple definition of itself/phonetic revelation. [. . .] [B]ecause in the scheme of things even the least of the brothers has his day, and when you realize the meaning of that day, you will feel the presence of an angel in disguise.[27]

Out of the least, then, the most: from South Side black to space angel. Sun Ra holds this conviction so dearly that he repeats it, intensifying its meaning: "If you do not understand anything else, understand this . . . that the least of the brothers in his humbleness and understanding of the weakness and the strength of everything is the initiator and the interpreter of the dimensions of the infinity . . . and that is why there is a black angel race of beings or soul-mates."[28] The black rays of angels interpret infinity to a dead planet. When, later in the essay, Sun Ra describes himself as "the least of the brothers [. . .] as far as popular jazz is concerned," he affirms both his membership in the angel race and the infinite prospects of space music.

Sun Ra often distinguishes himself from humans altogether. In a Detroit television interview, he makes his position clear: "You got the angel race and you got the human race. That's where I make a distinction. I'm not human because to err is human. I don't. [. . .] I'm talking about precision and discipline, human beings are talking about freedom and other things. It don't concern me."[29] Angels don't err, and neither does Sun Ra—that's the point of discipline and precision. By holding himself and the Arkestra to a higher than human standard, he opens its music to other worlds. Nor is he alone in his aspirations. Others share it, as did, for instance, the blacks weeping openly at the funeral of Albert Ayler, the dazzling saxophonist. An African in attendance reported to a mutual friend an unusual sight: "some black people, black Americans, they were crying. The angels were crying and he saw." Sun Ra recognizes them as kindred spirits: "I've been saying that I'm an angel, like all along and I've been saying a lot of black people are angels and there are some white angels too. But this man from Africa say he saw some angels crying. So it fits right in."[30] Sun Ra recognized these mourning blacks as kindred spirits. The angel race exists in the midst of the human, and their example can inspire a deeper reach into infinity.

Astro-black mythology lifts history out of time and opens space for new creation. It assimilates ancient Egypt as readily as modern America, solar boats as effortlessly as Cold War rockets. Thmei's esoteric wisdom meets Space Age aspiration in a recombinant mixological myth that crosses antiquity with futurology. Sun Ra's Egypt, paying little homage to either history or its scholarly interpretation, enters astro-black mythology as a stockpile of material useful to the task of creating better worlds for blacks—and angels. Responding to the Arkestra's initial performances in France, critics noticed the homemade quality of its Africana. One wrote, "It was interesting precisely for this invention of Africa by blacks from Harlem and elsewhere. But it was a mythic Africa, a bricolage." To which another replied, "A drugstore-styled Africa."[31] The names of tunes like "Ancient Aetheopia" or "Pyramids" or even the name of Sun Ra himself (double solar deity) bespeak an Africa built to order, one whose force is not a function of its truth, historical or otherwise. Myth, as Sun Ra saw it, is "something that's greater than the truth. . . . Myth was here before history. That's what everybody was dealing with before history"—and then he adds, "I'm talking about space."[32] Myth antedates history but includes space; it *is* space—namely, the space where ancient Africa and contemporary America intersect. Astro-black mythology thus reinvents Africa and African Americans for the Space Age. In this view, as Brent Hayes

Edwards says in arguing against taking Sun Ra for a black nationalist, "black people are mythic, ancient, or *cosmic*. They are the race for space."[33] Blacks are the true astronauts (afronauts?), astro-blacks inhabiting a myth irreducible to the linear time of history or the confined space of segregation. Astro-black mythology, Sun Ra believed, could inspire a reinvention of politics along impossible lines: "I really prefer mythocracy to democracy. Before history. Anything before history is myth. . . . That's where black people are. Reality equals death, because everything which is real has a beginning and an end. Myth speaks of the impossible, of immortality. And since everything that's possible has been tried, we need to try the impossible."[34]

What better way to perform the impossible than to incorporate infinity as a business? In 1967, as if to make astro-black mythology a material and economic reality, Sun Ra, Alton Abraham, and Almeter Hayden, an old Thmei crony, filed papers of incorporation in Cook County, which includes Chicago, for "Saturn 'II' Research," whose purpose appears most clearly in a draft application Abraham typed in his beloved caps:

TO PERFORM WORKS OF A HUMANITARIAN NATURE AMONG ALL PEOPLE OF EARTH, TO HELP STAMP OUT IGNORANCE DESTROYING ITS MAJOR PURPOSE, TO OWN AND OPERATE ALL KINDS OF RESEARCH LABORATORIES, STUDIOS, ELECTRONIC EQUIPMENT, AND ELECTROMECHANICAL EQUIPMENT, ELECTRONIC EQUIPMENT RELATED TO AUDIO AND VIDEO DEVICES AND AUDIO AND VIDEO DEVICES THEMSELVES INCLUDING SOUND RECORDINGS AND TAPES AS WELL AS VIDEO RECORDINGS, TELEPORTATION, ASTRAL PROJECTION DEVICES, MIND CLEANSING SOUND DEVICES, MAGNETIC COMPUTERS, ELECTRICAL AND ELECTRONIC DEVICES RELATED TO ALL PHASES OF ENTERPLANETARY SPACE TRAVEL, INCLUDING SPACE SHIPS WITH SPEEDS BEYOND THE SPEED OF LIGHT, INCLUDING ENTERPLANETARY COSMONETIC DEVICES OF AN ASTRO INFINITY NATURE, TO OWN REAL ESTATE AND ALL OTHER FACTORS RELATED TO REAL ESTATE INCLUDING, LAND, BUILDINGS, WATER, INCLUDING AIR SPACE ABOVE SAME, TO USE THESE VALUES FOR THE ADVANCEMENT OF ALL PEOPLE OF EARTH . . . . .[35]

Although Abraham toned down the language on the actual application, Saturn "II" Research originally included the impossible in its articles of incorporation. Astro-black mythology served an economic as well as a conceptual purpose. It sustained the Arkestra's explorations of space.

Explore they did. As NASA sent Mercury, then Gemini, and then Apollo rockets into space, the Arkestra released album after album, shooting higher and journeying further on an explosive mix of myth and sound. On July 20, 1969, Apollo 11 touched down on the powdery surface of the moon, with Neil Armstrong's "giant leap" meeting JFK's challenge to land a man there by the end of the decade. At the time it seemed an incredible achievement, and in some ways it still does. But how does it compare to the Arkestra's achievement as tone scientists exploring space with musical instruments? Soon after the lunar landing, the Arkestra recorded a chant that urged an awakening: "Them folks been walkin', a-walkin', they're walkin' on the moon, / If you wake up now, it won't be too soon."[36] Perhaps the world has indeed awakened. The moon circles Earth now like an abandoned dream. Apollo touched it, as did the Soviet Union's Luna and, most recently, China's Chang'e. But it no longer fires the desire of millions or the rage of nations. It's a silver dollar lost in the night sky. NASA, which once hurled mighty Saturns into the heavens, later focused closer to home, driving a fleet of low-orbital space trucks until July 21, 2011, when the last shuttle returned to Earth for good. And yet the Arkestra continues its explorations every time it performs or someone dusts off an old El Saturn LP or slots its CD reissue into a playback system. The Space Age lives on in music created to meet its challenge: Sun Ra's sounds of outer blackness, the Arkestra's "images and forecasts of tomorrow."

"The beauty of music," said Sun Ra in a statement worth a thousand moons, "is that it can reach across the border of reality into myth. Impressions never known before can be conveyed immediately."[37] New worlds open as music reaches into myth. If, as Sun Ra once insisted, "the synonym for myth is happiness," then music ultimately aims to convey it.[38] As Neil Armstrong, Buzz Aldrin, and Michael Collins flew toward the moon during the summer of 1969, *Esquire* magazine asked Sun Ra (among others, including Ayn Rand, Kurt Vonnegut, Truman Capote, and Vladimir Nabokov) to compose a few lines suitable for touchdown. The poem he wrote for the occasion views the event as a promissory note for impossibility:

> *Reality has touched against myth*
> *Humanity can move to achieve the impossible*
> *Because when you've achieved one impossible the others*
> *Come together to be with their brother, the first impossible*
> *Borrowed from the rim of the myth*
> *Happy Space Age to You . . .*[39]

As other impossibilities now beckon, happiness does, too. That might be the greatest gift of Sun Ra's myth-science and astro-black mythology, the prospect of a happy tomorrow.

18

BLACK MAN IN
THE COSMOS

Sun Ra and the Arkestra left New York a year before humankind first landed on the moon. According to Szwed, the quiet gentrification of the East Village meant that the noise of rehearsals on Third Street began to attract frequent police attention, so that when the building that housed the Arkestra's core members went up for sale, Sun Ra felt the pull of other possibilities. Marshall Allen's father owned property in Philadelphia—"the city of brotherly shove," as Sun Ra called it— and proved willing to rent a row house in Germantown on generous terms.[1] So in the fall of 1968, Sun Ra and his closest Arkestra associates moved to 5626 Morton Street, some of them (including Sun Ra) for the rest of their earthly lives. Through their devotion to space music and the communal life it inspired, the place soon came to be known as the House of Ra. Marshall Allen still lives there and has kept the Arkestra alive and flying since 1993, when Sun Ra left the planet.

The move coincided with a number of changes already reshaping the Arkestra. Typical of a large ensemble, the membership beyond the inner orbit (Gilmore, Allen, Jacson, and a few others) saw frequent changes, many players unwilling or unable to sustain the discipline and precision necessary to play Sun Ra's music. Several key and seasoned musicians left as the sixties rolled to a close, without much more to show for the Arkestra's efforts than an astonishing series of innovative, unpopular records. Pat Patrick, the great baritone saxophonist who had played with Sun Ra (with a little time off to get married) since the Space Trio, began gigging seriously with other bands— a big loss on the low end. But a bigger one came with the departure in 1966 or 1967 of Ronnie Boykins, the extraordinarily nimble and creative bassist who had laid the foundation for Sun Ra's space music. Both would play intermittently with the Arkestra in coming years, but without their particular contributions in the lower registers, its sound would Doppler shift to the blue, as if approaching rather than receding. Moving to Philadelphia meant filling empty chairs with local players, compromising the collective intuition of an ensemble once capable of unutterably sensitive, surprising, and inspired improvisation. Bugs Hunter, who ran tape machines for much of the music recorded in New York and remained with the Arkestra long afterward, remarked in less than flattering terms about the effect of losing old hands: "You'd have these other musicians to take their place, but they couldn't read. They couldn't read Sun Ra's music anyway. So he had to put on a show, so he would have John [Gilmore] and Marshall [Allen] play and the drummers [who] knew the arrangements."[2] Sun Ra often worked without a bassist because he couldn't find one to play his arrangements. In the previous remark, what Hunter lacks in generosity he may make up for in honesty. Sun Ra found himself with musicians whose abilities changed what the Arkestra could do, but not necessarily for the worse. He always claimed that people were his instruments. Different people inspired different sounds.

Hunter implies that the quality of those instruments affected Sun Ra's "show," and he's right. Not long before leaving New York, Sun Ra added new elements that enhanced the Arkestra's live performances. Space costumes, poetry, audience participation, even the occasional windup toy had sparked the Arkestra's shows since its nights at Chicago's Wonder Inn and Queen's Mansion. But those were club dates. Rock and roll may have helped euthanize large jazz ensembles, but it also provided means for resurrection. In mid-June 1967, the radical music critic and promoter John Sinclair booked a show at Wayne State University's Community Arts Auditorium that put Sun Ra and his Myth-Science Arkestra on the same bill with MC5, the proto-punk band of headbangers schooled in anarchism, amplification, and the avant-garde. And why not? MC5 admired the Arkestra's dedication to improvisation and outer space. Sun Ra might gain a new generation of listeners, on a scale that made the New York loft scene look like microcircuitry. Miles Davis saw it, too: rock venues amped musical performance to previously unimagined levels of excitement, celebrity, and maybe even money.[3] The MC5 show was successful enough to secure the Arkestra an extended residency in Detroit two years later. Sinclair could wax enthusiastic about space music and its astral architect: "One Sun Ra is worth 10,000 astronauts, one million Richard Nixons."[4] Something clicked that June night at Wayne State. The Arkestra discovered that it could mesmerize rockers as forcibly as hipsters and in larger numbers. Sun Ra proved his crowd appeal, at least to young whites. By April 1969 (wearing slit-eyed shades, a tiger-striped tam, and a Mona Lisa smile), he would stare them down blankly from a yellow-tinted cover of *Rolling Stone*.[5]

Sun Ra adapted to larger spaces by enlarging the dramatic aspects of performance, purposefully enhancing the visual, linguistic, and mythological registers of the Arkestra's music. Astro-black mythology became more than a conceptual framework for outlandish activism. It provided a cosmic backdrop for any given musical performance that enlarged it to operatic proportions. The Arkestra aimed no longer merely to play space music but to perform musical rituals that would immerse listeners in the cosmo-drama of astro-black mythology. The times required it, and the venues encouraged it. Documents indicate that Abraham took an active role in booking the Arkestra in large halls across the United States and soon in Europe, and the definitive discography, *The Earthly Recordings of Sun Ra*, attests to a permanent spike in the frequency of live recordings after 1968.[6] That was also the year when Sun Ra added a new dimension to the ensemble, one that would modify its look and sound in a way that made space music more accessible and challenging at the same time.

Through the recommendation of Lem Roebuck, who occasionally arranged gigs for the Arkestra in New York, Sun Ra auditioned and enlisted its first female member, June Tyson.[7] The Arkestra had developed as a boy's club—or fraternal order—not merely as a function of jazz tradition. As a confirmed bachelor, Sun Ra harbored a deep distrust for the influence women could wield over his musicians. But allowing Tyson a role onstage, and an important one at that, brought vitality and *drama* to performances that, for all their costumes and improvisation, might otherwise have felt distant or cerebral. Tyson focused the ensemble's energy and the audience's attention in ways that allowed the music to pivot rapturously around her. Her crystalline voicings doubled Sun Ra's gibbous exhortations with *intensity*. Her dynamic dancing crossed the Arkestra's incipient chaos with coherence. Tyson's rapt but regal female *presence* blessed astro-black mythology with living evidence that its other worlds included otherness as a means to apprehending them: blackness with a female difference. Szwed notes, too, that Tyson "helped liberate Sun Ra from the keyboards," allowing him to come forward on stage as the guiding force of the Arkestra and audience alike.[8]

With the addition of the singer and dancer Vertamae Grosvenor (and others when occasions called—sometimes seven or eight), the Arkestra's visual dimension burgeoned to sustain a cosmo-drama that became the mainstay of performance. Szwed describes it in the lush detail available to one who witnessed it repeatedly.[9] For those born too late (or too provincial) to participate, that cosmo-drama lives on in the dreams of other media: recordings, transcriptions, videos, films, breathless memories, third-hand rumors. Its content remained consistent, but its presentation could vary with the venue, audience, band membership, or mood. The basic premise resembled many a Baptist sermon, but served up in space-age bunting: death appears on the brink of triumphing over life on planet Earth, and only a profound change of heart among its inhabitants can save them. The

cosmo-drama offers salvation through music, song, dance, and spectacle. Perhaps a lone percussionist would begin, and then other musicians would enter singly or in groups, building to a torrent of sound
that would suddenly fall silent with the entrance of Sun Ra, usually
accompanied by Tyson.

The ensuing show might include a call-and-response homily, chanted
melodies and poems, turbulent forays into space music, precise renditions of old swing standards, freaking solos by individual musicians
or the whole Arkestra, whirling dancers, shimmering lights, flicker-
ing films, or jugglers and tumblers—all framed conceptually by the
images and ideals of astro-black mythology. Space costumes flashed
through projected images of Egyptian pharaohs. Electronic squeals
sliced through rumbling thunder from ancient drums. The Outer
Space Visual Communicator splashed kaleidoscopic colors across the
stage.[10] The cosmo-drama had a purpose, which was to awaken its audience to the greater potentials of another kind of life. "I hate everyday
life," Sun Ra said in an interview. "This planet is like a prison. I'm trying to free people. I've observed this planet from other planets and
I've experienced what I saw in my music."[11] Performing it for big audiences in large spaces suffused with sounds, movements, and images
might bring myth to life, altering the destiny of an imperiled planet.
As Sun Ra puts it rather more abstractly in "My Music is Words," "The
neglected mathematics of MYTH is the equation differential potential
impossible potential potential potential otherness alter-issness."[12]
Cosmo-drama gives that neglected mathematics living vitality.

Sun Ra took the show on the road—internationally—with concerts
in England, France, Finland, the Soviet Union, Mexico, and, to his undying delight, Egypt, where he and other members of the Arkestra visited
the Valley of the Kings and the Great Pyramid of Giza. Ra came home—
if such were possible on planet Earth. The Arkestra increased its reach
far beyond either South Side lounges or East Village lofts, promoting
a planetary vision for an ailing planet. In a sense, Thmei uplift went
global after Sun Ra left New York. Globalization and decolonization
(two faces of the same phenomenon) saw to it that astro-black mythology, grounded in the wisdom of Egyptian antiquities and propelled by

space-age aspirations, could appeal widely across national boundaries. America possesses no monopoly on either blackness or death. A planetary perspective on black suffering and human subjugation would provide globalization with a conscience irreducible to national identity or imperial ambition. "When I play something," Sun Ra said, "it obliterates nationality."[13] Astro-black mythology spans nations and dwarfs empires. It boggles common sense, laying a foundation for global— and globalized—interdependence. "Well," Sun Ra said to a skeptical interviewer, "what I represent is totally impossible. It affects every nation on the planet—on this planet. It affects governments, it affects schools, it affects churches; the whole thing has got to be turned to another kind of thought. A blueprint for another kind of world."[14]

This kind of talk crosses Christianity with utopian science fiction, but with an indelible difference. Sun Ra is black. And so is his blueprint. While it makes sense to notice with Szwed that "Sun Ra's views on race and the role of black people on Earth change[d] strikingly over the years," those changes never removed the black from astro-black mythology.[15] They may have indicated dismay at the Arkestra's neglect by black listeners. They may have opened space music to whites capable of hearing it. But his tendency in later years to chastise black audiences more interested in disco or hip-hop than in cosmo-drama ("I couldn't approach black people with the truth because they like lies. [. . .] I don't think of Negroes as my brothers") does not lessen Sun Ra's devotion to the cause of black uplift.[16] A planetary perspective forced the issue of a black future at a moment when American popular culture started to acquire global appeal. Cosmo-drama, both now and then, inserts blackness into a mediascape that distributes images of the future to a hungry world. Hence the curious description of his activity that Sun Ra offered in the program for a concert staged to benefit a pan-African study tour for university students: "Cosmo-Drama Intuition Infinity Ambassadorial Communications of Sound, Movement and World Chromatics."[17]

Try a thought experiment: what cultural difference would it make if the entire cast of *Star Trek* had been black, if the Jetsons had been a black family, if Neil Armstrong had been a black astronaut, if the

Beatles and the Rolling Stones had been in actual fact, as both tried so hard to become, black bands? Would the planet be a different place? A black planet, perhaps? Sun Ra's astro-black mythology and cosmo-drama address a planet teetering on the verge of permanent white-ness. Black people may not hear the message, but black myth declares its necessity: "You go to black people in America and say, show me your myths. How many do they have? None. They got a vacuum and a void in their life. [. . .] They should correct it. Speedily."[18] Sun Ra filled that void with space music and cosmo-drama. Black uplift on a planetary scale requires new invention, perhaps even of a new race to transform the old ones, created in Sun Ra's image: "I'm in the form of a man, but I'm an angel you know because man has tried a long time to do things. He couldn't do it. But you know an angel can do a lot of things"—like imagining a black planet or cosmos.[19]

Sun Ra's reputation as activist and thinker would win him an unusual appointment in 1971: that of lecturer at the University of California at Berkeley in the newly opened Department of Afro-American Studies. Whether on a concert stage or behind a classroom podium, Sun Ra took seriously his task as educator, a vocation that he first embraced in his year studying education at Alabama A&M University. The course he proposed and taught had a title worthy of his planetary ambitions: "The Black Man and the Cosmos." It mixed music (often performed by members of the Arkestra) with wisdom delivered as lectures in Sun Ra's soft, sly, southern accent, punctuated by his favorite interpretive strategies: equations, permutations, puns, and critical exegesis of everything from the Bible to yesterday's news. A recording of one such lecture survives online for those eager to study with the astro-black master.[20] It's an astonishing lesson, not an exposition so much as a performance of black counter-knowledge incommensurable with conventional academic learning.

Sun Ra's syllabus gives some sense of his agenda. It comes straight out of Chicago: *The Egyptian Book of the Dead*, Theodore P. Ford's *God Wills the Negro*, Yosef A. A. Ben-Jochannan's *Black Man of the Nile and His Family*, Volney's *Ruins of Empire*, and works by Blavatsky and Ouspensky, as well as suggested reading in hieroglyphics, slave narratives, and the Rosicrucians. Contemporary titles included politically bold black writing: *Ark of Bones*, by Henry Dumas, and *Black Fire*, the collection of African American writing edited by LeRoi Jones (Amiri Baraka) and Larry Neal.[21] Transported to the Berkeley classroom, Thmei wisdom acquired an institutional authority it never had in Washington Park. In content and style, Sun Ra's course advanced black counterknowledge through an unapologetic (and often humorous) critique of American culture. It probably lent his agenda credibility that the Black Panther Party had originally invited Sun Ra and the Arkestra to Oakland, where they lived in a house the Panthers owned, until ideological differences forced the musicians out after a few months. Sun Ra's stint as an academic proved vexed. He claimed never to have been paid for his lectures, attributing the insult to their incendiary content.[22] The academy appeared unready, even under the rubric of Afro-American studies, to sustain a curriculum so visionary, so heretical, as Sun Ra's.

The Arkestra's California sojourn yielded an even more important opportunity to educate the planet, however. According to Szwed, a film producer named Jim Newman approached Sun Ra about the possibility of making a documentary of the Arkestra to air on PBS. Somehow the project morphed into feature-length film to be directed by John Coney and called *Space Is the Place*. Szwed calls it "part documentary, part science fiction, part blaxploitation, part revisionist biblical epic," and the film is all that and more; most important, it is a vehicle for astro-black mythology disguised as the low-budget cult classic it would become.[23] Szwed cautions against identifying *Space Is the Place* too closely with Sun Ra's own beliefs, crediting the screenplay—as the movie does—to Joshua Smith. But Smith didn't sign on until after production began, and the way Sun Ra, master of improvisation, delivers his lines makes it pretty clear that much of the time he's channeling Sun Ra, master of improvisation. Nothing if not a canny student of contemporary media (after all, El Saturn served to distribute an activist message disguised as music), Sun Ra seized the chance to make a movie that might reach a wide audience, and with a star like Ray Johnson from *Dirty Harry*, a black audience at that.

As usual, Sun Ra's motives involved more than notoriety for himself or his music. Several years later, in a lecture at New York's Soundscape, Sun Ra would indicate (however casually) why film was such an important medium for his planetary message: "You just like over in a science fiction film now. You've outlived, you might say you outlived the Bible, which was your scenario."[24] It's a remark worthy of William S. Burroughs, and it shows how seriously Sun Ra took popular media as a means of ordering human life. As a scenario for living, the Bible is obsolete. Another kind of narrative has taken its place, this one not so sacred. Sun Ra was informing his audience not that they are watching a science fiction film but that they're *in* one, *living* one. The film they live is the life they lead. By making a science fiction film of his own, Sun Ra aimed to change the scenario its audience lived by. He was offering them, in place of the Bible, astro-black mythology: *space is the place*.

SPACE IS THE PLACE

The movie's scenario is simple, best rendered in the précis circulated by its production company, North American Star System:

> Sun Ra, black poet, prophet and master of the keyboard, has been trying to tell us for years that there's a place in space for the people of planet Earth. Now, in the new feature film from San Francisco's North American Star System, he brings his music and his message to the screen.
>
> Ra travels through space and time with his Inter-galactic Myth-Science Solar Arkestra. He stops by Chicago, 1943, to do a gig as a boogie pianist for the tap dancing "Ebony Steppers" at a southside Cabaret; then, after literally destroying the club with his frenetic keyboard work, he is left face to face with his long-time adversary, the king pimp Overseer. Magically teleported to a desert plain, they begin a cosmic card game in which the stakes are the end of the world and the very souls of its black people. The choice is made

clear. One can opt for SUN RA's "alter-destiny" and tune into the frequencies of the cosmos through his music or choose the Overseer's way of life and death as usual on planet Earth.

While SUN RA takes his message to the people and prepares for his final world concert, the Overseer connives to upset RA's plans and eliminate, once and for all, this threat to his own power. He attempts this through manipulation of a variety of type-cast characters, government agents, prostitutes, idealistic youths, ultimately to no avail. Finally RA departs the doomed planet, taking a few souls on a cosmic trip into space toward peace and the "alter destiny."[1]

Astro-black mythology faces off against worldly pleasure in a game to claim the souls of black folk. The new scenario of this science fiction film is hauntingly biblical in envisioning an end to human captivity. *The Seventh Seal* meets *Superfly*, and the fate of the planet hangs in the balance.

Space is the place. But in what sense can *space* and *place* coincide? It's a truism of contemporary social criticism that the two realms are distinct: the former is an abstraction (outer space, for instance, or its digital descendant, cyberspace), and the latter, vividly particular (the South Side of Chicago in the fifties or downtown Oakland in the seventies). Yet the copula of the movie's title fuses them together: space is the place. More than hippy-dippy dictum, the phrase announces the aim of Sun Ra's cosmo-drama and the space music that sustains it: to envision an abstract space conducive to everyday life. Through myth— the abstract nothing that yet is and produces living effects—space and place might come to coincide. The movie offers a solution to the problem posed by its title, staging an encounter between outer space and inner city that only astro-black mythology can resolve. As Sun Ra and the Overseer cut tarot cards to determine the fate of planet Earth, myth confronts reality with a new scenario for a better tomorrow, the "alter-destiny" of the synopsis. Sun Ra retailors the Thmei message for planetary consumption, delivered not by broadsheets in a city park but by film to a mass audience. At least that was the hope.

The movie opens with a bulbous, bright-orange spaceship flying through the spangled darkness of outer space. Then comes June
Tyson's brassy voice with a wake-up call that reveals time, too, to be
medium for travel:

It's after the end of the world,
Don't you know that yet?
It's after the end of the world,
Don't you know that yet?[2]

Space Is the Place begins by transporting its viewers to a point in time
after the end of their world—and therefore after the movie they are
watching, forcing them to reflect on life from a posthumous, or maybe
posthuman, perspective. A second dislocation follows immediately,
transporting viewers to another planet whose lush, lunatic foliage
might have been imagined by Max Ernst. A guide appears, a black man
wearing a pharaoh's headdress: Sun Ra. Cocking his head as if to listen,
he speaks in a gentle voice. "The music is different here, the vibrations
are different. Not like planet Earth." Sun Ra explores a place that is *not*
(utopia = "no place"), yet nevertheless *is*, an abstract, ideal, fictive—
mythic—place where people might live out an alternate destiny.[3]

Nature in its whimsical abundance characterizes life on this planet,
a circumstance fundamental to Sun Ra's understanding of the way
space and place might coincide. Their disjuncture on planet Earth
testifies to a baleful destiny. In "My Music is Words," Sun Ra aligns
nature with other worlds: "My natural self is not of this world because
this world is not of my not and nothingness."[4] Everyday reality is too
present to be natural, too unequivocally real to yield a better future:
"the potential impossible is [. . .] calling softly to the natural selves of
nothingness according to the standards of infinity nature and infinity nature's BEING."[5] If nature includes the nothing that gives rise to
impossibility and myth, infinity nature (reading "infinity" as "never
finished") involves never-ending creativity. Freedom exists, then, but
not in this world: "FREEDOM TO ME MEANS THE FREEDOM TO RISE
ABOVE A CRUEL PLANET AND TRUE PROTECTION IS PROTECTION BY

THE BROTHERS OF NATURE AND NATURES [*sic*] GOD."[6] Protection (continued living) comes through alignment with a higher nature, which is exactly how Sun Ra understands the way he works as a musician: "What I am playing is my natural way of playing. It is of, for and to the Attributes of the Natural Being of the universe of which is, and it is to everything that should be is, because to me it is natural."[7] Sun Ra's sense of nature collapses the potential into the actual, what is not yet into what is natural. When the impossible coincides with the present, space and place align, as in the name "Sun Ra," an Egyptian deity *and* a jazz musician. The living myth. "I have to do like the sun and the stars in the sky," he said not long before he left this planet. "They have to be right in place all the time. That's what I have to be."[8] Space is where sun and stars and people realize the impossible by always being in the right place—naturally.

Sun Ra imagines such a place on the planet he explores as *Space Is the Place* opens. In a reversal of history, he proposes setting up "a colony for black people here. See what they can do on a planet all their own, without any white people there." The steely black activism of his years in Chicago returns here to underwrite the alignment of space and place. Only a black planet can ameliorate ills wrought by racism and segregation. What appears to be separatism, however, opens to myth as Sun Ra sheds history as a condition for racial identity. "Equation wise," he says in his arcane way, "the first thing to do would be to consider time as officially ended. We work on the other side of time." With the official end of time comes the end of a history that includes African slavery and all the miseries of the dead—an obvious impossibility but for that very reason the province of another kind of knowledge, that of myth, which works on time's "other side." Sun Ra's Egyptian headdress combines with the prospect of space travel to produce an astro-black solution to historically enforced injustice. When Sun Ra describes how he intends to create his extraterrestrial colony, his real (impossible) agenda becomes clear: "Teleport the whole planet here through music." *All* planet Earth; Sun Ra's musical teleportation holds out the potential for everyone on Earth *to become black*. No longer merely a historical identity, blackness becomes a transformative effect of space music, the cultural means of inhabiting a new world. Blacks may be in the best social position to make the most of this opportunity, but *Space Is the Place* holds it open to others, too, at least theoretically. Astro-black mythology can transport people to a brave new black world.

Or it can take them back in time. At this point, the scene shifts to "Chicago 1943" and a lounge called Byron's, with a can-can stage act featuring the scantily clad Ebony Steppers. "Sonny Ray" beats out a boogie-woogie accompaniment to entertain a racially mixed and uppity audience. The situation resembles Sun Ra's sweaty nights working clubs in Calumet City, except that time (officially ended) seems somehow out of joint, for in 1943, Sun Ra (then Herman Poole Blount) spent thirty-nine days in a Birmingham jail and several weeks confined to a work camp for conscientious objectors in Marienville, Pennsylvania. Apparently club gigs in Chicago amount to particolored imprisonment. When the smiling black Overseer enters the lounge, wearing a luminous white suit with a blood-red rose boutonnière and a woman on each arm, it becomes clear who rules this roost. "He sees something he wants," says one of the cigarette girls, "he gets it." Desire and its satisfaction make him a swaggering, brash, domineering force. The Overseer (played by Ray Johnson) accepts material reality on its own terms and exploits its every potential for worldly gain and happiness. Music offers little more than a soundtrack to his self-indulgence, and when it doesn't flatter his libido, he makes his dissatisfaction known to everyone: "This piano player sounds like shit!"

Working "the other side of time" allows Sun Ra—here playing both the piano *and* Sonny Ray—to escape his confinement to Byron's and his subjection to the Overseer. The anachronism of Sun Ra's dress signals his disregard for history; from the wide lapels of his double-knit jacket to his knitted cap to his chrome-rimmed shades, this piano player comes from the future—the seventies, to be precise. The music he plays follows suit. It begins as boogie-woogie, but as the Ebony Steppers make their entrance, Sonny Ray decides to show the Overseer what his music can do. Blues changes slide into improbable dissonant harmonies in rhythms uncongenial to the ebony steps of the confused dancers. Sun Ra unchains melody to create a *wind* of sounds that blows through the bar at gale force, taking with it patrons, dancers, cigarette girls, and ultimately even his piano, which spins smoking across the proscenium. Music as mere entertainment? Sonny Ray demonstrates the capacity of his playing to transform reality, rearranging space so it will admit new possibilities. "Are you ready to alter your destiny?"

Sun Ra's question hangs in the air as the scene shifts again to reveal the ideological divide that shapes black life on planet Earth. Sun Ra and the Overseer now vie to determine its destiny, drawing cards at a table engulfed by empty desert. A better tomorrow or a squalid today? Myth meets history to contest the future. The Overseer's identity indicates that, historically considered, life for blacks occurs on a plantation of now planetary proportions. The best they can hope for is the dubious reward of proxy domination, the Overseer's black rule over blacks, sustained, of course, by a white state and its security network. Alter-destiny advances an astro-black alternative, spiritual in aspiration and mythological in means. True to his Thmei roots, Sun Ra appeals directly to the black community to change its ways and choose between the terminal pleasures of today and a more challenging call of tomorrow. He draws an ominous card—Judgment—bearing the image of his spaceship and portending the imminent arrival of the Arkestra from outer space.

And arrive they do, a few minutes later, to an awed reception by a curious crowd, among them members of the news media. In a scene that parodies the initial appearance of Klaatu in *The Day the Earth Stood Still*, a door on the throbbing double-eyed spaceship slides open to reveal Sun Ra and his musical astronauts: "I am the alter-destiny, the presence of the living myth." The crowd surges and the journalists bristle. In answer to a question about the power source of his strange craft, Sun Ra answers, "Music. This music is all a part of another tomorrow. Another kind of language. Speaking things of nature, naturalness, the way it should be. Speaking things of blackness, about the void. The endless void." Sun Ra's spaceship *is* music. The Arkestra's musicians travel the spaceways on waves of sound, a means of propulsion somehow commensurable with the *void* even though sound waves can't propagate through outer space. Music transports, but it arises out of nothing, to arrive—in the best possible sense—nowhere:

> music's a language, and it's telling people they have to become nothing in order to survive in the Kingdom of Nothing. See, nothin' can't hurt nothin', nothin' plus nothin' equals nothin'. [. . .] You can't go into outer space unless you count down to zero. Everything started from zero, you see. You count down to zero, then you can go into outer space. They do it, NASA does it every day, they count down first.[9]

Sound transports the Arkestra through empty space to planet Earth as music and astro-black mythology conjure an impossible future out of nothing.

As if to emphasize the perversity of this enterprise, an interior shot later reveals the navigation console of Sun Ra's spaceship to consist of technologically advanced musical instruments, including a Minimoog, the portable analog musical synthesizer designed in 1968 by the engineers at Robert Moog's factory in Trumansburg, New York, and put into production in 1970. Sun Ra's relationship to the Minimoog and its synthesized rainbow of auditory vibrations shows how sound in the widest sense propels the Arkestra through space. The latest advances in keyboard instruments inspired his constant experimentation; Sun Ra was an early player of the Solovox, the Clavioline, the Clavinet, the Kalamazoo K101, and the Rock-Si-Chord, among others, which he credited on his records with names such as "Solar Sound Organ" or "Intergalactic Tone Instrument." He coaxed sounds out of them beyond the tolerances of their intended designs, taking the keyboards in strange new directions, as on the tumultuous LP *Atlantis*, recorded in 1967 and released a year later. After exploring a forbidding planet of keening bleeps and storming intervals, the record ends with the Arkestra happily chanting, "Sun Ra and his band from outer space have entertained you here."[10] In the mid- to late sixties, when analog synthesizers began to open up a new spectrum of

sonic possibilities (or perhaps impossibilities), Sun Ra showed immediate interest. By 1969 he was making his first recordings with a synthesizer, one of Robert Moog's modular beasts complete with patch
chords and amplitude pots, programmed on the fly in the studio by
the early Moog enthusiast and virtuoso Gershon Kingsley.[11]

Sun Ra's devotion to the synthesizer as an instrument perfectly
suited to space music coincided with the development of Moog's
most influential model, the Minimoog. Simple to operate and easy to
transport, it quickly became the performer's choice for creating a vast
array of electronic sounds live and in the studio. The story of Sun Ra's
acquiring his first Minimoog, an early prototype known as "Model B
Min Moog," is worth hearing from Robert Moog himself, who told it
to Peter Hinds in an interview: "Well, it was a prototype. That's basically the story. We loaned it to him and Sun Ra's way of working is
that when you loan something to him you don't expect to see it back
(laughs). So that's really the only story."[12] Sun Ra drove to Trumansburg in 1968 to procure the Minimoog while it was still in development, bringing the Arkestra with him: "His whole band came by to
this small upstate town in New York. It was, you know, I don't know,
14 or 15 people and they came up in cars, I don't know, three or four
cars and each one was older than the other."[13] One of Moog's engineers, Jon Weiss, remembered the impression they made: "This was
a fairly rigid, straight-laced, little sleepy New York state town. And
here's this bizarre looking black guy with, you know, robes and all
this stuff in the local ice cream parlor!"[14] The Arkestra came in quest
of new sounds and found them, sounds to drive space music further
than ever into outer blackness.

Synthesized sounds: part of the appeal of the analog synthesizer,
particularly in comparison to other keyboard instruments, comes
from its sonic spectrum, which is almost infinite, practically speaking,
because a player can vary any given tone's pitch continuously rather
than only through the meager twelve increments of the Western chromatic scale. And the variety of tones available is vast, many of them
patently unmusical in a Western sense. The sonic palette of the Moog
synthesizer opens a creative space as vast, seemingly, as the cosmos.

Sun Ra played myriad sounds between those that "count" in conventional composition. As for the Minimoog itself, it proved capable of creating whole new registers of possibility: a viscid bass that stirs the entrails, a tonal warmth that solicits well-being, a cringing static that conjures animal fear, a piercing screel that commands almost spiritual submission. How the Minimoog produces these effects (and affects) remains part of the mystery of musicianship and engineering. Bill Hemsath, another of its designers, pointed out that because the Minimoog uses three oscillators (responsible for tone production and thus tuning) that tend to drift slightly in pitch, they never "lock," or become perfectly synchronized, remaining slightly out of tune with one another and creating the device's distinctive analog frisson.[15] Hemsath's colleague Jim Scott added information familiar to vacuum-tube devotees: overdriven by design, the Minimoog's circuitry slides gradually toward distortion, creating the warm overtones felt along the arteries and associated with a "fat" sound. He also offered a somewhat mysterious explanation of the way inaudible ultrasonics can have audible effects: "there were things that happen up in the ultrasonic range that can cause inner modulations and distortions, [and this] reflects back and can be heard in the audible range."[16] Heard melodies are sweet, but those unheard beseech infinity. In the right hands, the Minimoog's huge spectrum of sounds might transport people, materially and spiritually, to unknown worlds.

Sun Ra had those hands—and ears. The engineers who created the Minimoog built it from the ears up, tinkering until it produced inspiring sounds for Sun Ra and other musicians to play with. His discoveries riveted and roiled and soon showed up on recordings. Beginning with *My Brother the Wind, Volume 2* and *The Solar Myth Approach*, volumes 1 and 2 (portions of both recorded in 1970), the Minimoog would increasingly come to power the Arkestra's exploration of space. In 1970, as if to mark the next phase after the successful moon landing, Sun Ra began labeling his ensemble the "Astro-Infinity Arkestra" on record jackets, designating not so much a new departure as a higher flight, as he explained to Henry Dumas: "Astro-Infinity music is just one aspect of my music. It is heavenly and eternal, no beginning and no ending. The highest aspiration for man on earth is freedom. Astro-Infinity music is beyond freedom. It is precision, discipline. It is not just freedom. It is coordination and sound interdependence. It is the design of another world."[17] The Minimoog helped push space music into new zones of discipline and precision—but not because its designers provided new charts to follow. Weiss visited Sun Ra in New York to check the performance of his borrowed prototype: "I happened to hear this machine, and he had taken this synthesizer and I don't know what he had done to it, but he made sounds like you had never heard in your life, I mean just total inharmonic distortion all over the place, oscillators weren't oscillating any more, nothing was working but it was fabulous."[18]

Sun Ra played—and played with—the Minimoog, taking its sonic possibilities far beyond the limits imagined by its designers. It makes perfect sense, then, that the Minimoog features prominently in the navigation console of Sun Ra's spaceship in *Space Is the Place*. It navigates infinity, boldly going where no jazz has gone before—taking black folks along with it. This is synthesized music as interstellar transport. The Moog's historians understand this potential: "Great musicians like Sun Ra could always do the impossible."[19] Such as, for instance, saving the planet, as Sun Ra testifies he must do in an interview with *Newsweek*: "I have astro-infinity gifts to offer, solutions for all people and all nations concerned. I'm playing for the whole planet. I'm supposed to do the impossible, demonstrate to the people that there is something beyond the God they have been worshiping. My music is about friendship."[20] To the crowd in *Space Is the Place* that gathers to greet him on his landing, he offers consolation and promise born of the friendship such music cultivates: "Earth doesn't fall— it's the music. Vibrations. Your music too. You all astronauts. Everyone is supposed to be playing their part in this vast Arkestrey of the cosmos."

Just before he utters this benediction, June Tyson's clear, exhortatory voice chants a canticle that serves to plot the course of the film's coming cosmo-drama:

The satellites are spinning
A new day is dawning
The galaxies are waiting
For planet Earth's awakening.

Oh we sing this song to
A brave tomorrow.
Oh we sing this song to
Abolish sorrow.

The satellites are spinning
A better day is breaking
The galaxies are waiting
For planet Earth's awakening.[21]

Galaxies await Earth's awakening. This is the language of Percy Shelley's *Prometheus Unbound* (1819), updated and now made imaginable by the legacy of Sputnik. The reference to spinning satellites is no mere sop to space-age imagery. By the time *Space Is the Place* was made, they consolidated a legacy far greater in social effect than the moon landing provided. Satellites circling the Earth weave an orbital warp for global communications. Their "spinning" creates a network that makes it possible to broadcast sounds on a planetary scale. Thanks to those satellites and the whole machinery of heavy ballistics that lifts them aloft, space music can go global and more; it can become interplanetary, intergalactic, hurling toward astro-infinity.

Space Is the Place proves to be perceptive about the role mass media plays in contemporary life. The crowd around Sun Ra's spaceship includes a famed radio announcer named Jimmy Fey (played by Christopher Brooks), whose celebrity in the black community derives from his employer's market saturation: "Channel 5 Stone Jive, the all-black station for the all-black people with all the news that grooves at noon. Live from Oakland." The Arkestra arrives on the outskirts of Oakland not to commemorate the group's stint at Berkeley but, more radically, to make the black community there a test case for the transformative force of space music and cosmo-drama. Oakland resembles the South Side of Chicago after a twenty-year time lapse: empty storefronts, languid street life, black poverty and persistence in a segregated urban cityscape—all the squalid imagery of *Cry of Jazz*, but remixed in living color. One big difference, however, appears in the person of Jimmy Fey and the keen attention he devotes to this band of travelers from outer space. Media coverage offers a means to spread Sun Ra's message both within and beyond the black community. It links the place of segregation with the space of infinity through Fey's live coverage and commentary broadcasting the arrival of the "black musician and thinker" Sun Ra: "He is reported to have disappeared while traveling in Europe in 1969, reputed to have been traveling in space all this time with his Intergalactic Solar Myth-Science Arkestra."

The centerpiece of Sun Ra's sojourn in Oakland is a visit he pays to a youth development program at a black community center. As if to underscore the parallel to Chicago's South Side (with all due deference to the latest fashion), a group of Afro-coiffed, slim-fitted, and bell-bottomed young men sing doo-wop around a pool table: "That's the way love is, oo–oo–oo–oo." Young women talk urgently as a few youths read quietly, surrounded by wall-hung posters depicting black activists: Angela Davis, Malcolm X, LeRoi Jones. Then something weird happens: Sun Ra beams into their midst—big red moonboots appearing first—wearing the headdress of an Egyptian pharaoh and flanked by life-sized living images of the gods Horus and Thoth: "Greetings black youth of planet Earth. I am the ambassador from the Intergalactic Region of the Council for Outer Space." Reasonably enough, the black youth respond with skepticism: "How do we know you ain't some old hippy from off Telegraph?" "Is he for real?" The latter question prompts Sun Ra to utter one of the central statements of both the movie and astro-black mythology itself:

How do you know I'm real? I'm not real—just like you. You don't exist in this society. If you did, your people wouldn't be seeking equal rights. You're not real. If you were, you'd have some status among the nations of the world. So we're both myths. I do not come to you as a reality, I come to you as the myth. Because that's what black people are: myths. I came from a dream that black man dreamed long ago. I'm actually a presence sent to you from your ancestors. I'm gonna be here till I pick out certain ones of you to take back with me.

Sun Ra schools the black youth of inner-city Oakland in the fundamentals of astro-black mythology. He comes from outer space. He appears out of the deep black past. Like his audience, he lacks reality on planet Earth. But being nothing, he and they become myths. And as myths, these black youths together with their intergalactic antique black mentor might create worlds beyond the reality that neglects them, worlds hitherto unknown but not beyond the force of myth to imagine. Sun Ra arrives to take those he chooses, those who have ears to hear the music, back to the outer blackness of infinite space.

Through music, astro-black mythology moves toward eschatological possibilities. In the segregated Oakland of *Space Is the Place*, the means of salvation are multiple. "If you find Earth boring / Just the same old same thing / Come and sign up with Outer Spaceways Incorporated"; one means of salvation is thus an employment agency. Down a busy street of closed and boarded-up storefronts stands a freshly painted door whose sign announces unusual hours: "Eternally Open." Sun Ra's Outer Space Employment Agency offers full-time work for qualified applicants. Several stop in for interviews with the agency's chief officer, Sun Ra himself, who sits behind a half-door in a small office loaded with musical and other communications equipment. Thoth handles the telephones as a dancer gyrates in the background. A nervous, middle-aged white man appears at the doorway. Kurt Rockman, an unemployed NASA engineer specializing in guidance-systems design, desperately needs a job so that he can support his wife and seven kids and avoid—uh, you know—*welfare*.

In response to Rockman's offer to take a cut in pay, Sun Ra explains what should be obvious: "We really don't have salaries in our division. We creators never receive anything for our work." Then he describes his own methods of space travel in a joyous parody of scientific jargon:

"Multiplicity adjustment, readjustment synthesis, isotope teleportation, transmolecularization, repolarization, intergalactic realm of eternal darkness, intergalactic realm of eternal blackness darkness, white darkness, infinity incorporated." Confronted with this technical counter-vocabulary, the white engineer turns a little whiter and hurries away. Another applicant, this one black, poor, and drunk (played by the porn star Johnnie Keyes of *Behind the Green Door* fame), presents his credentials: "I been doing nothing." "You must be an expert at it," says Sun Ra, "we'll hire you to do that."[22] But salary again becomes an issue: "How much will I get paid, man?" Sun Ra, deadpan, responds, "Nothin'." Already *nothing* but unwilling to work for it—to inhabit his condition as an occasion for myth—this black hustler turns away with indignation: "I gotta have somethin'." Employment by Sun Ra's space program requires commitment—to nothing and its potential for creation—by white and black applicants alike. Most leave empty-handed.

A more potent means of astro-black salvation comes through the Arkestra's music. *Space Is the Place* generates narrative momentum through the ultimate goal of Sun Ra's terrestrial visitation, a "world concert" to be staged in Oakland and broadcast live around the world. Jimmy Fey arranges the details of time, place, and media coverage ("I've got my fingers out to the entire communications network in this country, every TV, radio, movie house, newspapers, magazines, you name it"), while the Overseer does his damnedest to see that the event flops, colluding with the FBI in a plot to kidnap and interrogate Sun Ra as a dangerous black agitator (agents tie him to an armchair and force earphones on him blaring "Dixie"). The plot unravels thanks to the just-in-time intervention of three black youths from the development program, one of whom—initially skeptical ("I think this whole big concert business is a by-product of the Eurasian-Occidental conspiracy")—takes an FBI bullet meant for Sun Ra. Shot in the chest, he dies onstage as Sun Ra readies his keyboards, to be resurrected in and through the music that drives the Arkestra through space.

The cosmo-drama must go on! And it does. The great and activist purpose behind *Space Is the Place* was to stage it in a mass medium—film—that might achieve planetary circulation and a global market for astro-black mythology. A show unfolds that, however beyond description, remains as close to cosmo-drama as those who never witnessed it can come. Space chord: a clangor, clash, and cacophony fill the air of the theater, wrestling, beating, struggling against tempers tuned to other, less vital vibrations. A long, stentorian call and response erupts between Sun Ra (leaning swiftly into and away from his microphone) and June Tyson (standing behind him), the effect of which is to catechize listeners in the fundamentals of astro-black mythology and inspire their participation:

> *We are another order of being*
> *We bring to you the mathematics of an alter-destiny*
> *Look up, see the greater universe*
> *Everything is in place, every star, every planet*
> *Everything is in place but you, planet Earth.*

A call to awakening: cosmo-drama proceeds through confrontation to affirmation, offering the example of Sun Ra as living myth, arising out of nothing and nowhere (the South Side of Chicago) to journey through outer space (infinity). Another space chord: a nuclear detonation of noise within noise to trouble and provoke the spirit. Then Sun Ra sets to testifying:

> *I am the brother of the wind*
> *I cover the Earth and hold it like a ball in my hands*
> *I can take away others to another galaxy*
> *I will take you to new worlds*
> *I will take you to outer unseen worlds*
> *That are more beautiful than anything the earth presents*
> *If you are fearful you will die in your fears*
> *If you are fearful you have the futile persuasions*
> *We are the pattern for the spirit of man!*

Cosmo-drama fulfills the street-corner activism of Thmei's black intellectuals in the performance of a total work of art, as dancers swirl and sounds howl and lights strobe and voices command.

Sun Ra builds toward a wholehearted rejection of the worldly ways of Earth, driven by blasts of gale-force music:

> *I the wind come and go as I choose*
> *And none can stop me*
> *I hate your reality*
> *I hate your reality*
> *I hate your positive absolute reality*
> *We refuse to be a part of your life, your . . . death.*

A hurricane descends, a perfect storm of synthesized sounds, sizzles of lightning, thunderous rumbles, keening blistered banshees soaring stratospheric to inaudible heights, plunging parabolic in leviathan dive beneath the weeded deeps of subsonic seas. All sounds happening, all the time. In space. Through music. The world concert must finish, and Sun Ra must forsake a planet recalcitrant to his message of discipline, precision, and wisdom.

But before he sets the controls of his Minimoog for astro-infinity, Sun Ra reclaims the black souls of those receptive to his sounds. "My kingdom," he tells Fey earlier in a radio interview, "is the kingdom of darkness and blackness, and none can enter except those who are of the black spirit." Sun Ra finds them and spirits them away in his spaceship; the elect include a drug-addict pimp, the youths who saved him, a group of whites (cut from the movie to avoid the wrath, Sun Ra said, of the NAACP), and even the "black part" of Jimmy Fey, whose "white part" lives on to scorn the Overseer: "You colored people never learn, do you?"[23] For all his streetwise, badass cool, the Overseer can never be *of* the black spirit. His is the kingdom of reality. He wins the world but loses the cosmos. Astro-black mythology offers an alter-destiny that he—and planet Earth—refuses. So Sun Ra and the Arkestra must bid this doomed world good-bye: "Farewell, earthlings. You just want to speak of realities. No myths. Well, I'm the myth talking to you. So it's farewell." The spaceship Arkestra blasts off from a planet destined to explode on this side of time.

But on the other side, the time of astro-black mythology, the Arkestra plays on and awaits human awakening:

> *In some far off place*
> *Many lightyears in space*
> *We'll wait for you.*
> *Where human feet have never trod*
> *Where human eyes have never seen*
> *We'll build a world of abstract dream*
> *And wait for you.*[24]

The cosmo-drama of *Space Is the Place* answers the hopelessness of human destiny with a hope born of myth, music, and outer space. Sun Ra and the Arkestra will wait for you.

In the meantime, they will keep performing space music. *Space Is the Place*: Sun Ra also released an LP under that title in 1972; *Astro Black*: another LP, this one released in 1973; *Discipline 27-II*, also from 1973: maybe the greatest of this great spate of records, in quadraphonic format.[25] In these recordings, the Arkestra's music becomes a mythic enterprise, disseminating the vision of a better tomorrow through the media of mass communications. Myth transmutes the Arkestra's recordings and myriad national and international performances into an interstellar network of teleportation capable of transporting all those who are black of spirit to a place called space.

Transcribed by an unknown typist (perhaps Abraham), a ten-page document entitled "intergalactic correspondence" and "dedicated to those seeking the many treasures of the universe" presents several of Sun Ra's recitatives from various performances, creating a brief script (or scripture) that summarizes cosmo-drama and illuminates its aims. Out of antiquity speaks a voice of black command: "Well I'm old Pharoah [*sic*] and I'm not going to ever let you go."[26] It announces a new understanding of the past that liberates it from whips and chains:

Your ancestors didn't enter this country legally
Your ancestors didn't leave Africa legally
That is why you have no legal status here
Might as well say you are from Saturn
Who can prove that you are not
Who can prove that your ancestors didn't come from Mars Venus,
    Neptune and Pluto too [. . .]
Let them prove you aren't from outerspace.[27]

Not Africa but Saturn, not Egypt but Mars: a history of terror and dislocation opens blacks to new worlds and otherwise impossible identities. The wisdom of antiquity antedates that history and pivots upward, into space: "you need to listen to your black ancestor who said / swing low space chariot coming for to carry me home / your home is among the stars."[28] A solar boat awaits those who heed the ancestral voice of Sun Ra soliciting a better tomorrow: "And so here I am again my people saying space is the place / While nations around you fight for a place in space."[29] And why space? "I want to open up to you the regions of the outerspace eternal immeasurable and endless so you may have a better way of life than you have ever known."[30] The final lines of this fortuitous libretto crystallize the whole of Sun Ra's life's work in music and myth: "come my brothers out into the blackness of outerspace / there is no limit to the things you can be."[31] From Herman Poole Blount to Le Sony'r Ra, from Thmei activism to astro-black mythology, from the South Side of Chicago to astro-infinity, from inner city to outer space: Sun Ra and the music of the Solar Myth-Science Astro-Infinity Intergalactic Research Omniverse Arkestra herald and create a better tomorrow. "Beta music for a Beta people for a Beta world."

Sun Ra remained committed to that prospect until 1993, when he left the planet. Space is the place for achieving the impossible, and if NASA could help, why not exploit its resources? At a moment when an orbital space station seemed a plausible national venture, Sun Ra completed a questionnaire created by a NASA space station task force "to measure interest in the idea of allowing a wide range of artists to use the NASA Space Station."[32] It solicited suggestions for "Programs of Artistic Merit in Space." How could Sun Ra resist? On the line for "Name of Organization," he wrote, "Sun Ra Omniverse Arkestra." On the lines following "Type of Organization," he entered, "Music," "Tone Science," and "Poetry/Literature." Responding to the form's request for specific ideas for artwork, he remarked, "Without the proper type of music your program will be more difficult than need be." But a bigger question follows: "What kind of technology, process or facilities do you or your group employ that might have artistic application relevant to an Art in Space program?" Sun Ra's answer bears pondering: "Music that enlightens and space orientate discipline coordinate." The technology relevant to an "Art in Space" program is music. Space music. It enlightens. Orientates. Coordinates. Induces discipline. Sun Ra's sounds for the Space Age make space the place for creating new words and better worlds.

20

TOKENS
OF HAPPINESS

From the start, with the founding of El Saturn Research in 1954, music served Sun Ra as the vehicle for his vision, and the music business, independently conducted, served as the means of distributing it. The film *Space Is the Place*, however, provided opportunities to reach audiences far wider than those possible through El Saturn, with its mail-order vagaries and cash-on-the-barrelhead operations. Blue Thumb Records (founded in 1968 and home to such well-known artists as Captain Beefheart, the Crusaders, the Pointer Sisters, and Hugh Masekela) expressed interest in recording the Arkestra's boisterous sounds. For two days in October 1972, Sun Ra and his Astro Intergalactic Infinity Arkestra occupied Chicago's Streeterville Studios, producing enough music for four LPs. The session yielded *Space is the Place* for Blue Thumb, as well as a second LP that was never issued and whose master disappeared.[1]

This foray into the commercial music industry came with no small business vigilance. According to the producer Ed Michel's liner notes for a reissue of *Space is the Place*, Blue Thumb's contract with Sun Ra set conditions that only an entrepreneur with his foresight could have negotiated. Paragraph 5, concerning the "actual ownership of masters," stipulates, "Company shall have the exclusive and perpetual right to manufacture, advertise, sell, lease, license or otherwise exploit the same throughout the planet Earth." Paragraph 6, with an eye to other markets, claims "similar rights on planets other than Earth," namely: "Company agrees that all rights discussed in paragraph 5 above, as well as all rights of distribution and retail sales, on planets other than Earth (including but not limited to Saturn, Pluto, Jupiter, and Mars) shall belong to Sun Ra."[2] Sun Ra clearly anticipated wide audience appeal for *Space is the Place*.

An even bigger opportunity knocked when ABC/Impulse! approached Abraham and Sun Ra. Working through Michel, the label tendered a proposal to reissue the bulk of the El Saturn catalog and record several new LPs. It was an appealing deal, especially considering ABC's marketing and distribution capabilities. The Arkestra might finally see commercial success in the house that Trane built (Impulse!). But Abraham and Sun Ra proved to be wily contract negotiators. In the liner notes for a later Evidence CD, Michel describes how they responded to ABC's "standard Artist's Contract ('Everything You Have Is Ours . . . ,' spelled out in some detail over seven pages)."[3] Abraham put the contract in his briefcase and took it home to examine. Michel continues: "This is the place to remind ourselves that the business of making and selling records in the '70's (or now whathehell) isn't exactly Rocket Science. But the business of Sun Ra is, more or less, Rocket Science. One definitely needs to be on one's toes. Or, perhaps, someone else's."[4] Abraham revised or rather "simply retyped the contract, turning everything on its head, with ABC, rather than Saturn, at the short end of the stick."[5] Abraham had been running a record company too long to be duped by the paper promises of industry executives.

ABC began issuing new pressings of old El Saturn recordings in colorful new covers (*Jazz in Silhouette*, *Angels and Demons at Play*, *Nubians of Plutonia*, *The Magic City*—the contract called for thirty reissues).

It recorded several entirely new LPs, too: *Astro Black*, *Pathways to Unknown Worlds*, *Cymbals* (unissued), and *Crystal Spears* (also unissued).[6] But without explanation, ABC suddenly canceled the contract, relegating released work to the cutout bins and unreleased work, for a time, to oblivion.[7] The Arkestra ultimately realized little gain, financially or otherwise, from the arrangement. Sun Ra waxed bitter over the outcome of this bid for commercial viability: "Impulse was going to spend almost a million dollars in publicity. They were going to put out fourteen LPs at one time. Something happened where they didn't keep their contract."[8] Szwed suggests that the debacle with ABC/Impulse! at least broadened Sun Ra's audience and earned the Arkestra more reviews and greater press.[9] Be that as it may, Sun Ra returned to the DIY ways of El Saturn Research, flirting only occasionally with mainstream media exposure and fame. On May 20, 1978, he and the Arkestra made a guest television appearance on *Saturday Night Live*, and a decade later they played joyously on David Sanborn's *Night Music*, on CBS.[10] But mass celebrity eluded them. They remained a gorgeous curiosity, these musicians from outer space. The National Endowment for the Arts named Sun Ra a "Jazz Master" in 1982, making him among the first to receive that distinction.[11] Birmingham would welcome back its errant son in 1987, when he accepted induction to the Alabama Music Hall of Fame.[12] But Sun Ra's renown remains muted in relation to his vast achievement.

The music remains misunderstood, too. A tendency persists among critics and fans alike to dismiss Sun Ra's turn, or rather return, to the swing music of his early days as the quaint nostalgia of an aging jazz master or even the taming of a once tempestuous imagination. Wikipedia proves representative: "Beginning in the 1970s, Sun Ra and the Arkestra settled down into a relatively conventional sound, often incorporating swing standards." The article then offers a quotation from Sun Ra almost obligatory in this context: "They tried to fool you, now I got to school you, about jazz, all about jazz."[13] The implication is obvious. Sun Ra turns pedagogue in his later years, more concerned with transmitting tradition than transforming the world. Never mind that contemporary reviews of later performances stress the sheer invention of his return to swing, such as this one from the *Philadelphia Inquirer* regarding an outing in 1988: "The Sun Ra specialty is taking standards and presenting them in the manner of an extraterrestrial on a New Year's Eve jag. His use of harmony, melody, rhythm, timbre and electronics defies the commonplace—even the avant-garde, as most of us understand it."[14] Some listeners heard continuing experimentation in Sun Ra's rendering of swing tunes. Later performances mixed past and future without regard to "tradition" in some honorific sense, "capering," in the words of a critic writing two years later in the *Chicago Tribune*, "through free-blowing collective improvisations, honking and bleating backward through time to odd renditions of Ellington, Monk, Cole Porter, and the mentor Fletcher Henderson; kicking in the hyperspace to ethereal tunes from the 21st Century."[15] Sun Ra was no swing traditionalist reviving an antiquated style to preserve it perfectly in auditory amber.

One of the reasons for his "return" to swing is so obvious it's hard to see: only later in his career, with his increasing opportunities to play for large—and paying—audiences, was he able to sustain the large ensemble swing requires. Economics partly drove the chamber-scale experimentalism of the New York years. Bigger crowds and venues demanded and rewarded bigger bands, whose ideological importance to black culture Sun Ra never overlooked. He unambiguously bemoaned the passing of those ensembles: "That's one thing very bad about the black race that they don't have any big bands. They used to have some, but the wrong kind of black folks got in charge and they downgraded music."[16] The Arkestra resuscitated swing to re-upgrade the music and restore dignity and grace to blacks as creators. But Sun Ra had never left swing very far behind. The course of his recording career shows him releasing LPs focused on standards even in the midst of intense invention: *Sound Sun Pleasure!!* (recorded in Chicago in 1958; released in 1970), *Holiday for Soul Dance* (recorded in Chicago in 1960; released in 1970), and *Bad and Beautiful* (recorded in New York in 1961; released in 1972).[17] The overall number of recorded originals may exceed that of standards over the course of the Arkestra's career, but the latter never fell out of its repertoire; their number simply dwindled to fit its diminishing size. Even the early live recording made at the Wonder Inn in 1960 contains old familiars: "'S Wonderful," "It Ain't Necessarily So," and "How High the Moon."

The better documentation of later performances (especially all those audience tapes made after recording technology became easily portable) seems to show the Arkestra increasing its commitment to swing, but little comparable evidence of early set lists exists. What can be said with confidence is that, from the seventies onward, the Arkestra had a wide array of swing tunes in its repertoire. *The Earthly Recordings of Sun Ra* shows over fifty in regular rotation, with another sixty-plus called occasionally—and over twenty played, according to best available information, only once.[18] The late Arkestra was, to say the least, swing literate. Legends of note-for-note rehearsal of recorded standards—including mistakes—find confirmation in its enormous (for lack of a better word) erudition.[19] Some of these tunes had, like "'S Wonderful," been in the Arkestra's repertoire from the start, but they reentered it with a vengeance in the midseventies: songs such as "Yeah Man!" and "Big John's Special" from the Henderson book; Ellington's "Prelude to a Kiss," "Sophisticated Lady," and "Take the 'A' Train"; Coleman Hawkins's "Queer Notions" and the song he made famous, "Body and Soul"; the old favorites "King Porter Stomp" and "Limehouse Blues"; Brooks Bowman's "East of the Sun"; and Hoagy Carmichael's "Stardust."

These and a legion of other standards found a lasting place in the late Arkestra's sets, a strategic one, if lists lifted from audience tapes provide any indication. A typical set from the band's last two decades would begin in cacophony with collective improvisation, move through a few space-themed originals, settle into a series of swing standards, and return (players refreshed?) to more space titles confirming the Arkestra as "Sun Ra's band from outer space." Swing provided a center of gravity around which it fell into and out of orbit—often playfully. Sun Ra had a soft spot for novelty tunes—witness his 1966 appearance (with John Gilmore and Pat Patrick) on the LP *Batman and Robin* or the late Arkestra's frequent performance of "I'm Gonna Unmask the Batman."[20] Nowhere does he give his pop impulse fuller reign than in his flirtation—or maybe temporary infatuation—with the Disney songbook. It began in earnest with the Arkestra's 1988 recording of "Pink Elephants on Parade" for *Stay Awake*, a collection of Disney tunes by various bands, and fulfilled itself the following spring in a series of Disney tributes on the West Coast by "Sun Ra and his Disney Odyssey Adventure Arkestra."[21] Not simply swing standards but, more impishly, omnipopular Disney songs maintained open communication with a planet still far from infinity.

The resurgence of swing and even pop in the late Arkestra's performances attests to a renewed interest in accessibility and, for lack of a better word, fun. Believing too strictly in those tales of note-for-note rehearsals makes the band seem like a mechanical memory machine. Closer to the truth is a remark that John Gilmore, Sun Ra's devoted tenor player, made regarding European fans of the Arkestra's later shows:

> The audiences were running around talking about big bands being alive, big band is back after they heard us. They were saying that 'cause it was hot. We're not able to rehearse all the time, 'cause guys live all over the place, so it's not as tight as when we were in Chicago. But it is so fresh—no telling what might come out.[22]

The big band is *alive*: Sun Ra didn't relapse into swing; he resurrected it. According to Gilmore, the late Arkestra was no longer the impeccably drilled unit it had been in Chicago, but that was the source of its vitality. Anything might happen—which is to say that even swing arrangements provided an occasion for the unexpected joys of improvisation. Testimony to the excitement that the late Arkestra still inspired appears on a handbill for a performance for the "Alternative Concert Series" at Haverford College near the end of Sun Ra's sojourn on planet Earth: "An evening with Sun Ra and his Cosmic Swing Arkestra is an evening of mystery, joy, pageantry and a trip through space, time, dreams and layers of music that add up to an experience unlike any other, part sanctified church, part boody-bump-beautiful-business, part mystic giggles and satire, part swing *to the max!*"[23]

Recall Sun Ra's dictum that jazz at its best *is* happiness. The late Arkestra's swing repertoire, both live and recorded, produces happiness in abundance. There's nothing retrograde about the joy that Jelly Roll Morton's "King Porter Stomp" adds to the astral flight of otherwise original compositions on *Live in Paris at the "Gibus,"* recorded in Paris in 1973 and released in France in 1975. The Arkestra plays with New Orleans abandon and interactive cunning to deliver two minutes and fifty-three seconds of unapologetic pleasure.[24] A review from a performance in Chicago almost twenty years later makes it clear that part of that pleasure derived from the creativity of the swing renditions: "Virtually everything that the Arkestra played, from straight-ahead swing arrangements recalling the '40s to high-decibel, high dissonance improvisations out of the '60s, recalled Ra's consistent sense of innovation."[25] Sun Ra put that sense of innovation nakedly on display on a live solo piano recording entitled *St. Louis Blues*, made for Paul Bley's Improvising Artists Incorporated in 1977.[26] The title track travels back to the beginnings of jazz to discover everything that would emerge later in Sun Ra's piano playing: clumping chords, surging rhythms, and dissonant harmonies, all over a walking boogie-woogie left hand. Fats Waller's "Honeysuckle Rose" becomes a dalliance with the familiar standard rather than a cover, Sun Ra stating the famous first five notes, then retreating, stating them again, and falling silent for a time, turning this rollicking standard into an etude of itself that forecasts the music of tomorrow.

The full force of the Arkestra's creativity in a swing idiom comes marching in on an especially vibrant live recording made in Greece, *Live at Praxis, 1984*.[27] It features a broad selection of the Arkestra's swing repertoire, making up over half the material on two LPs. "Yeah Man!," written by Noble Sissle and made famous by Fletcher Henderson, was an Arkestra staple, recast in a careful rendering that wildly exaggerates the tune's rhythmic possibilities. Sun Ra sets a blistering tempo with his plunky intro and snaps his sections to attention, reiterating Henderson's rhythms with stuttering bravado until their chunky swing gives way to an explosive drive toward broader horizons. "Cocktails for Two," written by Arthur Johnston and Sam Coslow and recorded in 1934 by Duke Ellington, introduces a cluster of standards by showcasing their possibilities for improvisation. Sun Ra's piano and Marshall Allen's alto take this one as a duet, in the process using familiar swing changes to clear space for something else. Rhythmically fluid comping allows Allen to explore improvisational cacophony in a relaxed context. At turns winsome, floating, and grisly, he slides and screeches in solo phrases as beautiful as they are frightening.

Sun Ra goes solo to explore "Over the Rainbow" (by Harold Arlen and E. Y. Harburg), turning its timid longing for a world where "skies are blue" into a thundering demand for infinity. Dissonant chords harry the melody, mounting and crashing until they undo it altogether, allowing it eventually to return chastened and refreshed. As John Litweiler would later remark in the *Chicago Tribune*, Sun Ra's "Over the Rainbow" communicates "a remarkable piece of self-revelation, for the song's hope is certainly seductive—and the cruel, angry phrases were an admission that those sentiments are clearly impossible."[28] With *Live at Praxis, 1984*, the full Arkestra returns to droll treatment of more standards (Horace Henderson's "Big John's Special" and Duke Ellington's "Satin Doll"), always with an eye to the happiness they inspire—which is nowhere more apparent than on the mordant Kurt Weil–Bertolt Brecht tune "Mack the Knife." Recording it here for the first time, the Arkestra whomps up all the fun the song's icy lyrics work to subvert, James Jacson singing them with a Satchmo growl as Sun Ra croons gently in response. If swing is square, long live the Arkestra!

The Arkestra's traditional practice of relegating swing and space music to different studio-produced LPs began to break down on late recordings, as two from 1986 indicate. *Reflections in Blue* contains mostly standards, with the exception of Sun Ra's early composition in straight swing idiom, "State Street Chicago," first recorded in 1960, and the twelve-bar title track, with its sumptuous section playing.[29] *Hours After* mixes Gershwin's "But Not for Me" and "Beautiful Love" (by Wayne King and others) with the Sun Ra originals "Dance of the Extra Terrestrians," "Love on a Far Away Planet" and "After Hours."[30] The tendency to interlineate space with swing music reaches a glorious apogee on *Blue Delight*, recorded for A&M in 1988 for its Modern Masters Jazz Series.[31] This imaginative exploration of sounds moves effortlessly from one plane of musical possibility to another, as if time has indeed officially ended and space is big enough to include old and new without acknowledging such distinctions. The title track sounds like blues outside history, the horns playing so beautifully as a section as to disavow all trace of arrangement. "Gone with the Wind" (by Allie Wrubel and Herb Magidson) and "Days of Wine and Roses" (Henry Mancini and Johnny Mercer) fit easily alongside the throbbing ambience of Sun Ra's "They Dwell on Other Planes" and the diffuse sonorities of "Sunrise."

Sun Ra eschewed the either/or of space and swing his critics sometimes require of him. Happiness unites them, as he insists on *Blue Delight*'s back cover: "The reason I haven't been playing my compositions for the last five or six years is because I've been doing tunes by people who had very nice minds as far as pleasantry and happiness goes. These composers left something of value, little tokens of happiness."[32] If space is the place, happiness is how you get there, the happiness inspired by music played with precision and discipline. But Sun Ra never abandoned space music as a primary propulsion system, as the spirited recording entitled *Purple Night* demonstrates.[33] Made in 1989, it features twenty-four musicians, including Don Cherry on pocket trumpet, reprising and reinventing a friendly galaxy of Sun Ra compositions. Sun Ra's creativity seems as infinite as the Creator's, a possibility he once professed playfully: "They asked me what albums I'm putting out next? And I said there's one I've been holding back for some time. It's music from the private library of God."[34] Sun Ra would curtail his adventuresome, divinely inspired composing and recording only after the Creator began calling him to other worlds: coyly at first, with a stroke in 1990, and for good with another stroke in 1992. Sun Ra would leave this planet far richer than he found it. However transformative his adventuresome space music may be, it seems fitting that his last recorded work appears on a tribute to Stuff Smith, the great swing violinist with whom he made his earliest home recording, "Deep Purple," in 1948 on the South Side of Chicago.

21

CONTINUATION

The Arkestra lives on in many ways, most powerfully in the work of the musicians it continues to inspire. Still, Sun Ra's music deserves—and let's hope will receive—much wider attention than it enjoys among the general run of listeners. Lady Gaga thinks so, too, apparently. The single "Venus," from her wildly popular album *Artpop* (2013), opens with a riff that references a familiar Sun Ra title: "Rocket Number Nine take off to the planet . . . to the planet . . . *Venus*."[1] Lady Gaga's Venus remains light-years away from Sun Ra's (the distance between simple sensual satisfaction and "a Beta World"). While few of her millions of fans the world over might recognize the allusion to Sun Ra, her song inserts a meme into the global transmission of musical awareness. Memes do their work, and if even a small percentage of those fans become sufficiently curious to look up those words' origins, Sun Ra's reputation could spread fast. They might also discover that the phrase "Rocket Number Nine" has enjoyed a surprising afterlife among other musicians; for example, it provides a name for both a British drum and synth duo (RocketNumberNine, made up of Ben and Tom Page) and an EP by the French electro-pop duo *Zombie Zombie* (Etienne Jaumet and Néman Herman Düne). Similarly, they might learn that the Arkestra's rap/chant call-and-response composition "Nuclear War" receives a hipster reprise on Yo La Tengo's recording by the same name.[2] Sun Ra's creative audacity, his commitment to the impossible, has inspired far-flung innovation in a wide variety of musical genres, from free jazz to funk to hip-hop to deep house. A brief survey of music that channels Sun Ra's astral influence provides a fitting if incomplete homage to a great artist fiercely devoted to better living through the transformative force of sound.

FREE JAZZ AND FURTHER OUT

Sun Ra's involvement in the Lower East Side music scene of the sixties resulted in his deep and lasting influence on avant-garde jazz. That influence reaches back to Chicago through his impact on progressive musicians who fell under his tutelage, among them the tenor saxophonists Sonny Rollins and Yusef Lateef and the bassists Wilbur Ware and Richard Davis (not to mention more regular members of the Arkestra). Nor were the influences solely musical. For example, in the midfifties he gave a broadsheet entitled "Solaristic Precepts" to John Coltrane; this may not wholly explain the sax giant's spiritual turn, but the language of this text does chime with many titles of Trane's later music, such as "Out of this World," "Sun Ship," or *Interstellar Space*.[3] "Warning," the broadsheet reads; "this treatise is only for Thinking 'Beings' who are able to conceive of the Negative reminiscences of Space-Time, as is expressed in Is, Are, Be and reconcepted 'AM' which to the initiate is–, a symbol of Not or Non."[4] Sun Ra's abstract spirituality fueled space music from the start and made an indirect but indelible contribution to the musical avant-garde in New York.

Sun Ra's relationship with the insurgent music known as "free jazz" or "the New Thing" remained uneasy, though he clearly played a major part in its emergence. He involved himself deeply enough in Amiri Baraka's Black Arts movement to hang and harangue at its

Harlem headquarters and accept funding to add players to the Arkestra when necessary.[5] In 1968, he scored and recorded *A Black Mass*, Baraka's radio play about the Nation of Islam's myth of Yakub, the demiurge who supposedly created the evil white race.[6] But for all Baraka's reasonable insistence on spiritual affinities between Sun Ra and other New Thing innovators—"What Trane spoke of, speaks of, what Ra means, where Pharaoh wd like to go, is clearly another world. In (w)hich we are literally (and further) 'free'"—Sun Ra himself kept a cautious remove from the province of free jazz.[7] That little word "free" gave him pause. Not freedom but discipline and precision—those were the virtues he offered his musicians. As mentioned before, he may have given Farrell Sanders the name "Pharoah" and groomed him to replace Gilmore in the Arkestra, but not in the name of freedom.[8] An infinite distance separates space music from the New Thing, as Sun Ra insisted in a remark worth recalling again: "Space music is an introductory prelude to the sound of greater infinity. It is not a new thing project to me, as this kind of music is my natural being and presentation. It is a different order of sounds synchronized to the different order of Being."[9] That different order of being distinguishes Sun Ra's music from less aspirational excursions beyond the confines of musical convention, giving space music a force that exceeds formal experimentation.

Still, anyone accustomed to the cacophonies of both genres can hear the affinities between the music of the New Thing ("the New Black Music," as Baraka called it) and that of the Arkestra.[10] Albert Ayler's primordial invocations, Ornette Coleman's "harmolodic" flights, Archie Shepp's guttural plunges, Coltrane's microtonal trespasses: all occur in the openness of a musical space freed from traditional constraint. All occur, too, in an ensemble setting anchored by a diffuse rhythm section holding that space open for solo exploration (as on Ayler's *Spiritual Unity* [1965], Coleman's *Free Jazz* [1961], Shepp's *Four for Trane* [1964], or Coltrane's *Ascension* [1965]).[11] Although the difference between such free-jazz excursions and Sun Ra's space music doesn't reduce simply to ensemble size, the larger number of members in the Arkestra certainly multiplies possibilities for improvisation. Improvisation, the soul of the New Thing, proceeds more collectively for Sun Ra. While soloists play an important part in producing the sonic ambience of space music (Allen's screeches, Gilmore's filigrees), improvisation occurs in the midst of an *ensemble* that moves all together: in, out, and beyond.

Phil Cohran, a trumpet and string player with the Arkestra in Chicago from 1959 to 1961, affirms the collective character of its improvisation in the emphasis he places on the first-person plural: "We didn't have any models, so we had to create our own language. It was based on sound. It wasn't just something you could pick up and physically deal with. *Space is a place*, and you had to think space, to expand beyond the earthly plane—that's why everyone was so creative."[12] Only an ensemble schooled tirelessly in discipline and precision could improvise so extensively—and beautifully—*together*, the hallmark sound of the Arkestra during the New York years. Terry Moran notes the results with approval in a review of *The Heliocentric Worlds of Sun Ra* (1966) for *Sounds and Fury*: "Sun Ra presents, here, the first new-thing big band, and his music sounds almost entirely improvised."[13] Moran finds improvisation of such consistency in a large ensemble a remarkable achievement: "This is demanding music for the players, and a new musical world for the listeners."[14] This new musical world's difference from the world of everyday life—even reimagined as a space of freedom—sets Sun Ra spiritually apart from many of his free-jazz compatriots. Another review from 1966, this one in *Down Beat*, crystallizes the difference: "Sun Ra plays from a place beyond everyday consciousness. He senses other planes of existence known to musicians, poets, and sorcerers for as long as there has been man. [. . .] If the music has any value to those outside, it is as a bridge to this other state of being."[15] Collective improvisation, precise and disciplined, conjures other planes of there.

Sun Ra nevertheless inspired a rising generation of musicians to explore the possible and impossible worlds of open sound, particularly in Chicago. Cohran remained behind when the Arkestra made its move to New York, but he became an important circuit routing its musical approach to new receivers. He would always remain devoted to Sun Ra: "He taught me the one thing that really made a difference in my life, and that is: whatever you want to do, do it all the time."[16] Cohran played in Chicago with his own band, the Story Tellers, as well as occasionally with Muhal Richard Abrams's Experimental Big Band. When jobs grew scarce and musicians fled in large numbers to the coasts, Cohran seized the initiative; in 1965, he and his fellow musicians Abrams, Jodie Christian, and Steve McCall formed the Association for the Advancement of Creative Musicians (AACM), aspiring (in the words of its charter's first principle) "to cultivate young musicians and to create music of a high artistic level for the general public through the presentation of programs designed to magnify the importance of creative music."[17] The organization remains to this day an active source of musical support, inspiration, and education. It quickly attracted the participation of a host of innovative musicians, among them Henry Threadgill, Anthony Braxton, Jack DeJohnette, Chico Freeman, and Wadada Leo Smith. Cohran established a new band for its first performance, the Artistic Heritage Ensemble, which would eventually regroup around several session players at Chess Records and release two important LPs on Cohran's own independent label, Zulu Records, both in 1968: *On the Beach* and *Malcolm X Memorial*.[18] Through the ministrations of Maurice White, whom Cohran tutored musically, the Artistic Heritage Ensemble eventually morphed (without its founder) into a band that achieved much greater renown: Earth, Wind, and Fire, whose predilections for Egyptian iconography and elaborate stage shows payed clear homage to the Arkestra.[19]

One of the most vital—and vitalizing—effects of the AACM was the emergence of the Art Ensemble of Chicago, in some ways the streetwise, terrestrial counterpart to the Arkestra's cosmic space machine. Roscoe Mitchell (saxophone), Lester Bowie (trumpet), and Malachi Favors Maghostut (bass) initially played together in the Roscoe Mitchell Sextet, the title of whose first record set an agenda in good keeping with Chicago's Arkestral heritage: *Sound* (1966). The band soon became known as the Roscoe Mitchell Ensemble, but in 1967, with the addition of Joseph Jarman (saxophone) and Phillip Wilson (drums), its named changed again after ads for a performance in Paris billed them as the Art Ensemble of Chicago. Fiercely committed to moving beyond musical convention, the Art Ensemble innovated in several ways, adding "little instruments" to the jazz arsenal (bells, whistles, noisemakers, percussive objects, etc.), opening the whole field of composition to improvisation, and incorporating noise into the sonic palette of serious music. Its members' frequent performances in African headdresses, masks, or face paint evoked the antic spirit of the Arkestra, but without overt reference to antiquity or astral black futures. The Art Ensemble of Chicago pursued the possibilities of unfettered sound into the deeps less of outer than of urban space. A family resemblance to the Arkestra's music nevertheless characterizes recordings as different as the ambient *People in Sorrow* (1969) and the much funkier "Theme de Yoyo," from the soundtrack album *Les Stances à Sophie* (1970).[20] Not astro-infinity but ethnic vicinity: the Art Ensemble has remained true to the task of musical insurgence *in situ*.

Another important group that took inspiration from Sun Ra's music and stage performance is the underappreciated ensemble called the Pyramids, founded in the early seventies by the saxophone player Idris Ackamoor along with Kimathi Asante and Margaux Simmons, all of them students at Antioch College in Yellow Springs, Ohio. Ackamoor felt himself "attracted to the theatricality of Sun Ra" and conceived of the Pyramids similarly, as a musical troupe with a cultural mission.[21] A year studying abroad, first in Europe and then in Morocco, Senegal, Ghana, and Kenya, gave Ackamoor direct experience of African cultures.[22] The way they combine music, theater, and dance made a lasting impression and helped to inform the Pyramids' theatrical approach to playing music with an African feel, one that that included colorful costumes and dynamic dance. In the tradition of El Saturn, the band released three self-produced LPs with black-and-white covers on their own label, Pyramid Records: *Lalibela* (1973), *King of Kings* (1974), and *Birth/Speed/Merging* (1976).[23] By turns raucous, meditative, and stately, the music on these records (which quickly became underground classics) fully earns its recent description as "Afrofuturistic psychedelic spiritual jazz."[24] Much of it appears on the 2009 compilation *Music of Idris Ackamoor, 1971–2004.*[25] Although the Pyramids disbanded in 1977, and Ackamoor moved west to found the renowned San Francisco performance company Cultural Odyssey, a recent return to touring and the studio put the ensemble back in the spotlight in a way that reinforces its debt to Sun Ra. A recent release by the Pyramids bears the auspicious title *Otherworldly.*[26] Ackamoor describes it in terms that honor the Arkestra's space-age legacy: "It basically goes beyond the confines of Earth, in the sense that it really gives the feeling of 'extra'—of interplanetary music, a music that you could hear on another planet."[27] Space music continues to inspire new innovation.

And it has done this for decades, even outside the orbit of jazz. The Arkestra's whole approach to making and performing music—do it yourself on a shoestring and never mind the bollocks—provided an example to punk musicians who shared its commitment to imminent change and to noise as a means of provoking it. No band took the lesson more to heart than Detroit's MC5, the hard-rock/proto-punk unit whose members listened carefully to Sun Ra's music and liked what they heard. In 1967, their good friend and future manager John Sinclair suggested they play a gig with the Arkestra at the Community Arts Theater auditorium at Wayne State University.[28] Sinclair worked as a jazz journalist (writing for *Down Beat, Vibrations,* and *Guerilla: A Newspaper of Cultural Revolution*) and political activist (founding the White Panther Party, a parallel to the Black Panthers).[29] His interest in Sun Ra and the music of the New Thing generally took an openly political form, which he encouraged MC5 to advance in their music and onstage. Witness the White Panther News Service press release from 1969 that, channeling Sun Ra, reveals a readiness to make music that "speaks to the worlds of the greater potentials awaiting the peoples of the worlds at every future point on every future plane."[30]

MC5 may have been more concerned with demanding conventional freedoms on this particular planet, but Sun Ra's space music drove the band's creativity to extraordinary rock and roll heights—and volume. The long closing track "Starship," on *Kick Out the Jams* (1969), pays glorious, chaotic tribute to the Arkestra's inspirational improvisations, taking harmonic distortion into spaces only Jimi Hendrix could navigate safely. Sinclair again booked Sun Ra and the Arkestra to perform with MC5 for several shows in 1969, arranging their stay in a house next door to the rockers, whose "sex, drugs, and rock 'n' roll" antics eventually tried the patience of the high priest of discipline and precision.[31] Sinclair's bust for marijuana possession later that year put any formal association between the bands to an end, but MC5's redirection of the Arkestra's sound remains a crucial link between it and a commercially viable, Detroit-based youth culture that would include Iggy Pop and the Stooges.

Sun Ra's rock influence treads a politically progressive line. Thurston Moore of Sonic Youth tells how a late-blooming interest in jazz led him into the deeper reaches of improvisational music—next stop Mars! Moving to New York in the midseventies, Moore became alert to extensions beyond the boundaries of traditional black music: Sunny Murray, Albert Ayler, Archie Shepp—the whole New Thing. He came to know Sun Ra's music initially through MC5: "The first real Ra thing I heard was on *Kick out the Jams*. That track 'Rocket No 9.' [. . .] That was such an amazing track."[32] Moore began buying El Saturn records and attending Arkestra performances around New York—in Tompkins Park, for instance, or at the Knitting Factory, where, Moore recalls, Sun Ra would often hold forth on subjects of his peculiar, imperative interest:

> the way he did this talk was, you could hear him talking coming down the stairs to the stage, so the whole place went silent. It was like this matinee lecture by Sun Ra. And then he just walked onstage mid-speaking and he stood on stage and he would just go off on all these tangents about jazz musicians being angels, the messengers. He talked about race politics, about why Americans need to put their bad energy down and listen to the messages from the angels, from the antique blacks, because that's where the true information is as far as like saving the world.[33]

Through musicians such as Moore, Sun Ra's wisdom passed to a new generation and a new genre. Moore attests to the importance of a compilation of the Arkestra's New York material entitled *Out There A Minute* and produced by Blast First Records (1989): "That was a heavy record for a lot of people you know, for a lot of people in my world, that was the first time they had heard him."[34]

Sun Ra took a liking to Moore, another young rocker open to new tomorrows. In 1992, the Arkestra and Sonic Youth shared a stage in Central Park for one of Sun Ra's last gigs before he left the planet. Moore remembers it with gentle awe:

> It was a heavy gig. It was really a magical gig. [. . .] Ra comes out, they play first and then Sonic Youth plays, and getting ready there's a downpour, within ten minutes of their set, the clouds move out and the sun comes out. And we're just looking at each other thinking, "Is this for real, can he really be doing this?" And he was already in a wheelchair. [. . .] He still had the orange beard and a smile on his face but he wasn't talking. His motor skills were a bit challenged. And when he came out there, the sun came out. Crazy[35]

Even in physical decline, Sun Ra could change the world.

The joyful noise he bequeathed persists today in the freer registers of collective improvisation. New York continues to sustain a community of Lower East Side musicians devoted to sonic exploration, although economic realities make it ever harder for it to stay alive. With the closing in 2010 of the club Tonic, on Norfolk near Delancey, many musical experimentalists and cross-cultural hackers lost a place that had sustained their spaceflights. No one has been more devoted to pursuing that community—and the legacy of improvisation that Sun Ra helped bequeath—than the noisecore guitarist Marc Ribot, whose various bands (Prosthetic Cubans, Ceramic Dog, and Spiritual Unity) cross florid improvised sounds with divergent musical lineages: the Latin combo, the power trio, the free ensemble.[36] In the context of free jazz, Ribot's work with Henry Grimes, the famed New Thing bassist who played with Albert Ayler, among many others, takes improvised music past all musical form and into a space where feelings, freed from reference, rise, torque, soar, and dissipate. The Arkestra's legacy resounds forcefully in Spiritual Unity: space music rushing to infinity. Others received it, too, the spirit as it spread: in Philadelphia, the noisy experimental collective Need New Body, one of whose members as a child knew Sun Ra, the elder man's music the soundtrack of higher innocence; in London and Stockholm, The Thing, a lean trio churning and growling toward something postapocalyptic; in Japan, the Shibusashirazu Orchestra, whose blaring brass section warps soul jazz into kabuki chaos; in Brooklyn, Paris, and Brazil, the recombinant researches of Amayo's Fu-Arkist-Ra, which fuses Chinese Lion Dance rhythms, kung fu, and Nigerian Afrobeat.[37] These bands receive and relay the Arkestra's musical example to yet unknown worlds as they continue the drive into outer blackness.

AFROFUTURIST DIVERSIONS

Sun Ra frequently receives homage as the father of Afrofuturism, the cultural and creative movement driven by African Americans with "other stories to tell about culture, technology and things to come."[38] While he never used the term himself (it wasn't coined until the year he left the planet), his devotion to tomorrow's worlds, to astro-black mythology, and to the latest advances in keyboard technology lends credence to his stature as progenitor of this prolific line of contemporary black creativity.[39] The stories Sun Ra told about things to come may contain spiritual vibrations stronger than those of his Afrofuturist heirs, but they set a course for the future using musical technologies of propulsion and life support that provided an inspirational precedent for later instrumentalists and afronauts. The Arkestra's music, myth, and theatrics proved powerfully provocative to Afrofuturist imaginations, including those better attuned to terrestrial than intergalactic frequencies. Their futures may not always resemble Sun Ra's in spirit, but these musicians inherited his charge to change a world uncongenial to black aspirations.

George Clinton responded by envisioning a future built by and for blacks with thick bricks of funk. His bands Parliament and Funkadelic preach uplift on the downbeat, imagining a better tomorrow in unapologetically earthly terms. Their big bottom end and heavy rhythm ground funk in the viscera—the body's proof against captivity, the source of its life, its own infinite potential. Clinton and company create a funkier tomorrow in which blacks live out the riches of sensation, led by a music that heals what ails them individually, producing unison *on* the beat. As the title of one tune puts it, "Everything Is on the One."[40] Clinton redirects Sun Ra's space program back to this world. Asked about his cosmic precursor, Clinton once quipped, "This boy was definitely out to lunch—same place I eat."[41] But they probably ordered from different menus. Clinton strips astro-black mythology of its interplanetary thrusters and lands it safely on planet Earth. The sprawling collective of musicians and singers that became known as Parliament-Funkadelic (or more commonly, P-Funk) after Clinton merged his two bands resembles the Arkestra in the vitality of its message and theatricality of its performance. Interestingly, they began in the fifties as a doo-wop group, running a course parallel to Sun Ra's, if ultimately one more popular and profitable.

In a string of extraordinary recordings from the midseventies (*Chocolate City* [1975], *The Mothership Connection* [1975], *The Clones of Doctor Funkenstein* [1976], and *Funkentelechy vs. The Placebo Syndrome* [1977]), Clinton sketches a musical blueprint for a near future in which blacks turn majority and regulate their lives through the powers and possibilities of funk.[42] It's alien invasion with a difference, as the opening of *The Mothership Connection* makes clear: "Do not attempt to adjust your radio," smooth-talks the black announcer; "we have taken control as to bring you this special show. We will return it to you as soon as you are grooving."[43] Then comes an homage to Sun Ra, togged in fur cape and platform shoes: "Welcome to radio station WEFUNK, we-funk, or deeper still the Mothership Connection, home of the extraterrestrial brothers, dealers of funky music, P-Funk, uncut funk, thuh *bomb*."[44] Clinton's Afrofuturism, another instance of the genre that antedates its definition, forgoes spiritual exploration for the more worldly ambition of reanimating black life through P-Funk, deploying, where necessary, "specially designed afronauts capable of funkatizing galaxies."[45] They've landed—and they're black!

What Clinton loses in philosophical nuance, he gains in crowd appeal, as is joyously documented in the film *George Clinton: The Mothership Connection* (1998), which shows thousands of fans roaring as they watch the mothership itself (shaped peculiarly like the Apollo mission's lunar lander) descend on the auspicious site of Houston, home of NASA's Mission Control.[46] The door slides open and out struts Dr. Funkenstein—in white fur. Clinton reverse engineers astro-black mythology for popular consumption, forsaking space music for heavy-hoofing Earth tones. If imitation is a form of flattery, however, maybe Sun Ra offers Clinton the greater homage. His own rollicking funk album, *On Jupiter* (1979), pays knowing tribute to Clinton, most directly on the track "UFO," whose unison chant over a solid groove ("UFO, . . . where you go?") sounds like Parliament in jazz drag.[47] Clinton may take Sun Ra's music places it doesn't usually go, but Sun Ra takes it back and launches funk into outer space.[48]

The Afrofuturist impulse found its way into hip-hop almost from the start. While Sun Ra himself may not have found the idiom entirely to his liking (on a panel with Ice-T at a music journalism conference in New York, he remarked that it "concerns itself far too much [with] material necessities"), his example opened a space where musical activism and innovation could meet.[49] One of the great originators of hip-hop, Afrika Bambaataa (born Kevin Donovan in the South Bronx), stepped into that space with the commanding twelve-inch single "Planet Rock," recorded with his group Soul Sonic Force in December 1981 and released early the following year. The planetary scope of its refrain, "You gotta rock it don't stop it," and its electronic foundation (a mélange that spans from Germany's Kraftwerk to Japan's Yellow Magic Orchestra) align "Planet Rock," however loosely, with Sun Ra's spacious experimentalism.[50] Bambaataa also shares the instinct to view music as part of a larger social initiative, consolidated in his case under the cultural banner of the Universal Zulu Nation. His efforts on behalf of both hip-hop and black uplift in the Bronx have yielded him heavy recognition as "Amen Ra of Hip Hop Kulture," making Bambaataa a direct descendant of the Sun God of jazz.[51]

Afrofuturism of a vaguely Arkestral kind also fueled other important hip-hop projects. Kool Keith (Keith Thornton), whose career began with the pivotal outfit Ultramagnetic MCs, pursues alternative tomorrows in his music under a number of aliases, among them Dr. Octagon, Dr. Doom, Black Elvis, and Dr. Ultra.[52] His work as Dr. Octagon most closely parallels the Afrofuturist prospects of space music, if not its aspirations to infinity. Dr. Octagon, in the words of Wikipedia, is a "homicidal, extraterrestrial, time-traveling gynecologist and surgeon"—a far cry, perhaps, from the cosmic, free-form pharaoh, but a creature nevertheless capable of viewing earthly life from an astral perspective.[53] When "rap moves on to the year 3000," as Dr. Octagon chants on the semi-eponymous compact disc, the present dwindles to a point of insignificance, and other futures become imaginable, even necessary (*Dr. Octagonecologyst*, 1996).[54] A group (really a supergroup) that extends this Afrofuturistic impulse to the ambitious task of imagining a whole future world consists of the producer Dan the Automator, the rapper Del the Funky Homosapien, and Kid Koala on turntable. They call themselves Deltron 3030. Their 2000 release by the same name, set in the year 3030, narrates the resistance of a "mech" (i.e., mechanical) soldier and computer whiz against a hauntingly familiar (as if impossible to unimagine) New World Order.[55] Sun Ra's Afrofuturist speculations may remain in the realm of myth, but Deltron 3030 puts black science fiction to the shared cause of inventing alternatives to racist containment.

Sun Ra makes a direct, exhortatory appearance in the remarkable work of Madvillain, the fierce hip-hop duo consisting of MF Doom (Daniel Dumile) and Madlib (Otis Jackson Jr.). Their debut recording, *Madvillainy* (2004), contains the track "Shadows of Tomorrow," which samples portions of the Arkestra's tune by the same name, as well as lines from the film *Space Is the Place*, in a manner that acknowledges the urgency of Sun Ra's wisdom.[56] Other artists, too, make heavy use of Sun Ra. The most thoughtful of these uses perhaps come from DJ

Spooky, in recordings such as *Viral Sonata* (released under the name Paul D. Miller, 1997) and *Celestial Mechanix* (2004), or more recently, Azealia Banks, whose track "Atlantis," from *Fantasea* (2012), samples "Twin Stars of Thence."[57] Janelle Monáe makes Afrofuturism a mainstream pop commodity on *ArchAndroid* (2010) and *The Electric Lady* (2013).[58] Sun Ra's Afrofuturist influence continues to inspire new possibilities among a wide range of producers, rappers, and performers.

FUTURES OF ELECTRONICA

For all his jazz stature, Sun Ra's greatest current influence may reside in the digital deeps of electronica. The inheritance makes technological sense. From the Sound Mirror to the Minimoog to the elusive Crumar Mainman, Sun Ra conducted a lifelong exploration of the possibilities, musical and cultural, made available by the latest technologies of sound production and reproduction. He was among the first (as was Ray Charles) to record using an electric piano (1955), and in 1990 he won *Down Beat*'s annual International Critics Poll for synthesizer.[59] For all his love of the analog Minimoog's volcanic sound palette, he proved masterly at adapting to less flexible devices, as on the legendary late-1970s recordings made in Italy for the Horo label, *New Steps* and *Unity*.[60] Captured in an unusually spare quartet format (sax, trumpet, drums, and keyboards), Sun Ra used the Crumar Mainman heavily, apparently having stumbled upon it stashed in a closet at the Rome studio. Working without a bass, he played his own bottom lines on the synthesizer, programming it for live performance (as can be heard on El Saturn releases *Disco 3000* and *Media Dreams* [both 1978]).[61] But it isn't only as an instrumentalist that Sun Ra deserves electronic homage. The Arkestra's vast discography preserves a seeming infinity of material for sampling and remixing. Unknown worlds remain to be built, modeled, and remodeled from these unbounded reserves.

An exhaustive account would be—exhausting. A few salient instances of Arkestra-inspired electronica should suffice, followed by closer encounters with several master practitioners. Charles Cohen deserves mention as an analog virtuoso (he favors rare Buchla instruments), as his *Music for Dance and Theater* (2013) testifies.[62] Sun Ra's example taught him that the synthesizer could serve well for live performance. Early instances of sampling occur in work by the Frenchman Frédéric Galliano (*Nangadef Maafric* [1996], which samples "When There is No Sun," from *Soul Vibrations of Man*) and the Australian group the Avalanches (*Electricity* [1999], which samples "Say," from *Strange Celestial Road*).[63] *Sonic Fiction* (2003), by Portugal's Spaceboys, owes a general debt of inspiration to the cosmic aura of Sun Ra's electronic sounds, as do the more recent offerings from RocketNumberNine, such as *MeYouWeYou*.[64] The Dining Rooms, an Italian ambient/electronica/jazz duo, covers "Astro Black" on their album *Tre* (2003) in gorgeous deep synthetic sound currents, the breathy soprano of Anna Clementi sitting in for June Tyson.[65] Tyson's version rings out over a dance beat on a remix of "Astro Black" by Freedom Satellite on an Austrian compilation entitled *Vienna Scientists V: The 10th Anniversary* (2009).[66] A stirring electronic tribute by the producer Mono/Poly (Charles E. Dickerson) entitled "Ra Rise," from *Golden Skies* (2014), communicates, hauntingly, the awe that dawns with a new world.[67] Tellingly, the creators of these tracks hail from many lands, including France, Portugal, England, Italy, Austria, and the United States, which documents the global musical flows Sun Ra's space music induces. Space is the Arkestra's place, but its music wraps the planet.

The shimmering taffeta that synthesizers, drum machines, sequencers, and mixing boards weave in response to that influence might constitute the Arkestra's most potent musical legacy. Electronica receives and reinvents space music more urgently than do other idioms, even jazz, which reveals something important about Sun Ra's example. It isn't simply that it provides content for samples, covers, or wholesale homage—as it does in the haunted psychedelia of Sun Araw (*Beach Head* [2008], for instance), whose independent Sun Ark Studios pays obvious respect to the spirit master, or the radicalized lyrics of the rapper Sun Rise Above, aka Sun R.A., who like many others dons the mantle of black musical activism (as he does on "Every Day I Wake Up on the Wrong Side of Capitalism").[68] The Arkestra's music falls (un)naturally into electronica. The radical commentator Kodwo Eshun helps explain why. In regard to the relationship between technology and sound, machines and music, Eshun credits electronica with a science of its own: "Machine Music doesn't call itself science because it controls technology, but because music is the artform most thoroughly undermined and recombinated and reconfigured by technics."[69]

Technology reconfigures music. Sun Ra used technology to recombine and invent sounds. He practiced a science of creating new musical possibilities. In this sense, space music is not really *about* the future. It *is* the future come to trouble the present by measure of its difference, artifice, and *alienness*. In Eshun's words, "It alienates itself from the human; it arrives from the future. Alien Music is a synthetic recombinator, an applied art technology for amplifying the rates of becoming alien. Optimize the rations of excentricity [*sic*]. Synthesize yourself."[70] Become Sun Ra. Herman Poole Blount did. Electronica acknowledges and reconceptualizes the alien in space music. No longer something to be feared or resisted, the alien (arriving perhaps from Saturn?) offers a model for a new kind of life and another kind of creativity: sampling, sequencing, and synthesizing recombinant sounds. Electronica advances the emancipation from musical form that Sun Ra initiated, harnessing machine rhythms to drive open-ended explorations of sounds with no necessary trajectory, purpose, or destination beyond their own recursive occurrence.

Some of the best producers of such music working today credit Sun Ra with an inestimable influence. Osunlade, a musician and producer from St. Louis who is also a Yoruba priest, takes Sun Ra for an example of a wholly spiritualized creativity, as alien in its devotion to infinity as it is in its pursuit of Afrofutures.[71] Sun Ra suffuses the spirit of Osunlade's music and occasionally its content, too, as he does on the track "Satellite beneath the Stars," from the 2013 double LP *A Man with No Past Originating the Future*, whose title provides a synopsis of the great Saturnian's career.[72] Sun Ra presides over this music like an ancestral presence. He similarly informs the work of Mike Huckaby, the reigning deity of Detroit techno whose devotion to the art of the mix has led him to become a major educator of machine music. Hucka-by's admiration for the masterly management of audience feeling that Sun Ra displayed in performance provides a surprising link to the club scene where techno thrives: "He could introduce a sense of tension or calamity within a chord progression, and easily resolve it with a sense of beauty."[73] Perhaps surprisingly, the Arkestra's music can inspire sustained dancing. In recognition of this unexpected potential, Huck-aby devotes the first two volumes of his *Reel to Reel Edits* (twelve-inch tweaks of jazz recordings) to Sun Ra tunes including "UFO," "Antique Blacks," and "Space is the Place," gently "restructuring the original's instrumental elements so that they're more DJ-friendly and dance-able."[74] However strange the thought of clubbing with the Arkestra, the technologies of electronica allow Huckaby to reproduce its music for a new crowd of listeners and dancers.[75]

The same holds for producers whose work owes Sun Ra a deep con-ceptual debt. The British electronic duo Africa Hitech (Mark Pritchard and Steve Spacek) make their allegiance clear on their debut album from 2011, *93 Million Miles* (the distance from the Earth to the sun).[76] It's eclectic fare, ranging across multiple territories but centered (or maybe decentered) on Arkestral spaces, as the titles of various tracks indicate: "Future Moves," "Cyclic Sun," "Light the Way." The last-named track samples "When There is No Sun," from the Sun Ra Quartet's *New Steps* (1978). The phrase "Light the way" counterpoints "When there is no sun" over ambient electronics with enough insistence to con-travene nothingness with nothing more than synthetic sound. The Arkestra provides similar fortitude to the music of Flying Lotus (Ste-ven Ellison), a Los Angeles producer who, as a relative of Alice Col-trane and her grandson Ravi, provides a living link to the freer pas-sages of jazz. The track "Arkestry," from *Cosmogramma* (2010), asserts a heavy musical pedigree that other tracks confirm: "Intro//A Cosmic Drama," "Sateliiiiiiiitee," and "Do the Astral Plane."[77] Synthetic sounds weave and warp alternative worlds in service to Sun Ra's message of uplift, as Flying Lotus confirms in an interview: "I really think if we're going to send out vibrations, they should be positive. Try and uplift the people."[78] Recombine vibrations in the Kingdom of Not. Keep it unreal. The Arkestra achieves a synthesized and sampled afterlife in the digital archives of electronica.

And the Arkestra lives on nowhere more potently than in the extraordinary music of another Los Angeles producer, Ras G (Gregory Shorter Jr.), also known as Ras G and the Afrikan Space Program. The full *nom de synth* answers the question put to a captive Sun Ra by FBI agents in *Space Is the Place*: "Is there an African space program?"[79] Indeed there is, one run by Ras G. Much more aggressively than most of his peers do, Ras G explores the deep space of sounds freed from the constraints even of instrumentation. The Arkestra's joyful noise morphs into spattering hiss and ambient skittering, as on the first track from *Back on the Planet* (2013), and the Afrikan Space Program voyages into worlds beyond human tolerances ("we have a whole nother world up here, a whole nother planet") where only electronics can go.[80] Afrikan electronica. Ras G quotes the visual symbolism of Sun Ra's ancient Egypt (the pharaoh's headdress, the ankh, the eye of Horus) and overwrites it with the stylings of a more contemporary Afrophilia, the Rasta's locks, beard, and shades—*Ras Tafari!*

This Rasta betrays little nostalgia for African roots, however. He routes ancient Egypt through Ethiopia through empty nothing and outer darkness to desolate effect on tracks such as "Asteroid Storm," which is utterly bereft of musical bearing, or to more hopeful prospects on "All Is Well," a digital gesture in Sun Ra's general direction, and "Find Ya Self (ANU Wrld)," where synth sonics and intermittent rhythms accentuate spoken phonemes or fragments of a phrase until a full one emerges ("you caught me off guard"). When Sun Ra appears *in propria persona*, as on "Natural Melanin Being . . . ," Ras G displays a fully virtual wit and wisdom, sampling the Black Pharaoh at his natural blackest over an organ loop: "get to be your natural self. Now the minute you become your natural self, you gonna be alright. Because there isn't anything better than your natural self. There isn't anything more beautiful than a black person who is a natural."[81] This natural fact, indisputable and true, comes scratched, transcoded, and remixed in a technodelic ecology as artificial as it is real: digital wisdom at its most direct.

So pervasive is Sun Ra's presence in the oeuvre of the Afrikan Space Program that Ras G becomes a self-appointed priest in the virtual church of Ra, custodian of the master's memory, officiant of theophanies. Or better, perhaps, he serves as a translator, coding space music into digital tongues. This aspect of his work as a producer appears clearest in long mixes, excursions through sonic space that can last an hour or more. Under such conditions, form turns infinitely additive, a sequencing of sequences that spirals into trance: the auditory armature of infinity. That's how "Cosmic Tones 4 Mental Therapy" works—a forty-five-minute digital "translation" of Sun Ra's 1967 El Saturn LP by the same title. As with any connotative leap from one language to another, this one communicates the original not literally but by inference, rendering Sun Ra's open and dilating psychedelia through an array of sonic allusions: a child's voice, a typewriter, backward speech, electronic drones, sung samples, fades, whorls, and then, at the twenty-one minute mark, June Tyson's clarion-crisp "Calling planet earth! . . . Calling planet earth!," followed by a spoken Sun Ra loop, again celebrating "your natural self."[82] In and out, up and beyond, cosmic tones transliterated—not through music, exactly, but via something more primal and prior, sound's viscid substrate heard by the entrails before the ears. Just as the release from musical constraints feels complete, a sung loop over organ restores the memory of harmony with flutes and cello: those days of clarity and comfort. But Ras G moves effortlessly elsewhere ("smokin' it up," spoken over a Latin bass groove), into—where else?—infinity, or so Sun Ra returns to explain: "I'm using it as a synonym for myth [. . .] because it can't be measured, [. . .] it can't be proven to exist."[83] Can you prove it? Ras G follows Sun Ra to the edges of an infinity electronically measurable as myth, the nothing that is not there. And is.

HOMESICK ALIEN

"Sometimes I miss Chicago. It's a very strange place but it's a big city. It's more cosmopolitan than New York. It's better where you can stretch out more. New York have to go up. It can't stretch out."[84] Sun

Ra's remark, like so much of his music, comes as a surprise. Chicago more cosmopolitan than New York? The city of segregation so complete it contained within itself a separate black metropolis? Sun Ra remembers Chicago as a place superior to others in its openness to the cosmos, space stretching out rather than up, reaching toward new horizons. Chicago today remembers Sun Ra, too, doing so more variously and vitally than any other place on the planet, at least in regard to music. The Arkestra's legacy infuses diverse musical adventures, sometimes so thoroughly that its influence can be hard to detect. It pervades Chicago's music like the memory of a dream. It isn't simply that Sun Ra's example helped establish a lasting local devotion to improvisation and experimentation, institutionalized in the Association for the Advancement of Creative Musicians and sustained by a diehard circle of tone scientists. Sun Ra's sounds for the Space Age—and the new worlds they create—seep into the colors of *Chicago's* sonic palette, opening infinite vistas for innovation.

From the angular free blowing of Von Freeman (a sometime Sun Ra sideman) to the word-sound-image fusions of Freeman's fellow saxophonist Matana Roberts (raised on the South Side), Chicago sustains a musical openness conducive to experimentation.[85] It shapes the evocative work of Tortoise (as on *TNT* [1998]), an indie ensemble that crosses rock, jazz, and electronica to create soundscapes of alluring depth and intensity.[86] The guitarist Jeff Parker provides a link between Tortoise and the experimental Chicago Underground Trio, one of several "Chicago Underground" avatars that push avant-garde jazz into new territories. Centered in the fierce playing of the cornetist Rob Mazurek and the imaginative drumming of Chad Taylor, the Chicago Underground groups (Duo, Trio, or Quartet) open traditional jazz improvisation to ambient electronic sounds and sampling to create a music strangely suited to a contemporary life saturated by infotech and digital communications (witness *Boca Negra* [2010] or *Locus* [2014]).[87] Space exploration now involves a laptop as much as a Minimoog.

Another Mazurek initiative, the Exploding Star Orchestra, pays clear and joyous homage to Sun Ra's Arkestra in both size (up to fourteen members) and substance; its first recording, *We Are All From*

Somewhere Else (2007), narrates a story that begins with a star's explosion and moves through a series of cosmic transformations that turn a stingray into a rocket into a new-born star.[88] Mazurek mixes natural sounds (of electric eels, for instance) with those of traditional and electronic instruments in a setting of group improvisation. As if colluding with the Arkestra, this music evokes unknown worlds, opening new possibilities for what used to be called jazz. The Exploding Star Orchestra keeps faith with such futures in *Stars Have Shapes*, from 2010, which harks back to Roscoe Mitchell's early sonic explorations and reaches forward to Sun Ra's abstract infinity.[89]

Less insistently experimental, perhaps, but more directly in the Arkestra's lineage is the music of Ken Vandermark, a formidable tenor saxophone player and MacArthur Fellow deeply devoted to free improvisation. Vandermark makes the unusual move of covering what might be called the standards of free jazz: Cecil Taylor's "Conquistador," Eric Dolphy's "Gazelloni," Ornette Coleman's "Happy House," or Sun Ra's "Saturn" (*Free Jazz Classics*, vols. 1 and 2 [2001]).[90] His trio with Hamid Drake on drums and Nate McBride on bass, Spaceways Inc., openly celebrates the Arkestra's achievement and follows it into Funkadelic's. This group's *Thirteen Cosmic Standards by Sun Ra and Funkadelic* (2000) mixes loving covers of the master's Chicago-era space music with a barrelful of cosmic slop to make the case for a musical countertradition worthy of the respect reserved for jazz "classics."[91] The Vandermark 5, the saxophonist's main group from 1997 to 2010 (from *Single Piece Flow* to *Annular Gift*), receives Chicago's legacy of improvisation like a birthright, churning and chattering hot blasts of sound for the sheer delight of relaying their intensities.[92] They proliferate new forms of life.

The direct descendant and living heir of Chicago's unmanufactured avant-garde, Tiger Hatchery (the saxophonist Mike Forbes, bassist Andrew Scott Young, and drummer Ben Baker Billington) incarnates the future of Sun Ra's better tomorrow. The group's music recombines torrential free-jazz improvisation with incendiary postpunk noise, creating dissonance that seethes, roils, and convulses in staggering mutations of (dis)organized sound. Sun Ra presides over the trio's work in sovereign splendor. Tiger Hatchery's debut recording, *Sun*

Worship (2013), performs its title with unapologetic precision, producing an impossible sonic density and dynamism.[93] If Tiger Hatchery provides any indication, the future of space music is now.

Like Borges's aleph, Chicago seems somehow to contain the whole planet, musically speaking. It harbors one of the most canny, creative, and courageous producers working today: Hieroglyphic Being, aka Jamal Moss. Moss mixes with relentless momentum and programs his machines for hyperspace, splicing (in the words of an interviewer) "the legacies of house music and Sun Ra into abrasive and acutely psychoactive takes on club music, noise, and industrial."[94] Born in Chicago in 1973, Moss grew up in the company of the local electronic idiom that became known as "house" (Chicago's equivalent to New York hip-hop and Detroit techno). He seems to have artfully absorbed it all, turning electronica into a medium for sonic exploration and experimentation of the highest order. Moss approximates Sun Ra's subtlety as a sound artist, doing so more closely than producers in pursuit of sales and celebrity can. The name "Hieroglyphic Being" references the master almost directly, as do the titles of many mixes, recordings, and their associated images: *ANKH* (2010), *The Sun Man Speaks* (2010), *Cosmo Rhythmatic* (2011), *Strange Strings* (2011), and *Seer of Cosmic Visions* (2013), the last of which includes the tracks "Nidhamu" and "Outer Nothingness," which are also Sun Ra titles.[95] Moss releases most of his work on his own label, Music From Mathematics, making Chicago the place where space and spirit suffuse electronica.

Moss came to Sun Ra's music through his adoptive parents' record collection, learning to appreciate it through its influences:

> When it came to finding out that Sun Ra influenced people I thought were cool, then Sun Ra became cool—because, you know, Earth, Wind & Fire or George Clinton or P-Funk, all those cats. And then come to find out that Sun Ra influenced a lot of punk bands or industrial bands I didn't know, so—you see what I'm saying—that's part of the evolution of his energy still transforming itself, even though he's crossed over.[96]

Moss now has a hand in evolving that energy. His uncompromising attention to the timbre and texture of technologized sound brings unusual discipline and precision to his style of production. A Hieroglyphic Being track, for all its fractal static, can feel like a philosophical disquisition, digitized Socratics. Among all producers, he stays truest to the spiritual register of space music, rendering it in a manner faithful to infinity, as potentially endless sonic tapestries signifying, in Sun Ra's sense, nothing. That's the celebratory wisdom of "Space Is the Place (But We're Stuck Here on Earth)," from the double LP *A Synthetic Love Life* (2013).[97] However earthbound his audience may feel, Hieroglyphic Being produces music that opens sonic passages from Chicago to heliotropic worlds, their impossible possibility. Sun Ra lives on digitally, his energy ever evolving.

Sun Ra may have left the planet, but his music remains potently creative. Its influence will only grow, multiplying musical possibilities and transforming people's lives. Let a musician, then, restate the main motifs of his lives, times, and legacies: Fhloston Paradigm, former member of Digable Planets and resident of Sun Ra's neighborhood in Philadelphia:

> Sun Ra said he that was from outer space, and I really believe that. He was the first one that took the context of science fiction, and appl[ied] it to black people in America. He spoke of alienation within our own country, and trying to get out of this hypnotic funk that programmed us to act a certain way. "You're black, so you must like this." Afrofuturism is a hope, a hope for an alternative to how life is here on earth. You can still apply it to the now—you first have to change your trajectory.[98]

"Beta music for Beta people for a Beta world": the possible has been tried, and it failed.

Try the impossible.

EXTENSIONS OUT

Sun Ra lies in a bed at Baptist Medical Center in Birmingham, Alabama, with a few friends in attendance. In lieu of speaking, he clutches their hands.[1]

I'm an angel, you see. I belong to another race, the angel race. Angels don't die. Humans die. To err is human, and I don't err. I got to be like the sun and the stars. Always in their places, where they should be. Where I am, everything happening, all the time. I'm a free spirit. I see myself as P-H-R-E not F-R-E-E. That's the name of the sun in ancient Egypt. I'm not really a person at all . . . immortal spirit. They talk about freedom in America. First creative artists have got to have the freedom to play for people. It's ridiculous for America to even talk about freedom when all the artists are in chains. Life on this particular sphere is nothing but imprisonment. A lot of people begin to see it. I wouldn't be caught dead on a planet like this. My *real* self is somewhere else. There have been times when people have seen my real self. If I feel ill like I do now in this hospital bed, my other self will stand right there in the room watching me, like it is now. Over there. My other self is darker, but absolutely the same. So I do have what the Egyptians call a double. I'm connected with ancient Egypt. I'm connected with the pharaoh. I could feel it when we played there, Egypt. The vibrations were different there. Not like Chicago or New York or Philadelphia. They got the pyramids. Giza. The Sphinx. They didn't want to let me in because of my name. On my passport. But Sun Ra is not a person, it's a business name. I made it official. And on the certificate (it's a business certificate which was gotten in New York City), they didn't notice that I didn't have down there what my business was. They stamped it, notarized it, and they filed it. So therefore, it's a business name, and my business is changing the planet. I can talk all the ancient Egypt anybody knows. Hieroglyphics. So they let me in, the Egyptians, and the next day we played at a friend's house in Heliopolis. Then the Balloon Theater. You might say jazz came from the priests of Egypt. The whole world revolves around Egypt, really. And there we were. I wanted to play my compositions in the pyramids. I'm going to play my music. So then we went to see the Great Pyramid, just three of us, and I brought a tape recorder and some tapes we made of our performances. Our guide was an old man in a white robe. He led us upstairs and down corridors until we got to the King's Chamber. I could feel the ancientness, five thousand years of precise government, education. So right there, me and Bugs start chanting "Sun Ra, Sun Ra," and when we hit the ninth "Sun Ra"—all the lights went out. Pitch black. A sea of darkness. Antique blackness. So you see. Now they have to deal with phonetics. "Sun." That is the sound of God and not the son. This is the sound. Because it's the voice, you see. The sound and the voice and it comes right back to one word. Namely Ra. Because that represented the mouth or the voice that named Ra, you see. Now, they got to get back to Egypt. Because they had the truth too. And they talking about immortality and infinity. The world is talking about something else. I'm dealing in equations, uh, I'm a cosmo-scientist. Equational scientist. Now, I'm an equational equationist scientist. If people want a better world, then they have to get the formula to have a better world. If they want eternal life, they must get a formula. You can't get it without equations. It's nothing but equations. That's all they need now. Another tomorrow they never told me of came with the abruptness of a fiery dawn and spoke of Cosmic Equations: the equations of sight-similarity, the equations of sound-similarity, subtle Living Equations, clear only to those who wish to be attuned to the vibrations of the Outer Cosmic Worlds, subtle living equations of the outer realms dear only to those who fervently wish the greater life. The equation Ignorance equals bliss deserves due consideration. In the beginning God created the heaven and the Earth and the Earth was waste. In the undertaking God created the haven and the oath and the oath was waste. All equations together are two immeasurable equations because of the immeasurable presence of the nonbeing in the duality of the balanced openness of the two. You may be sure that my conclusions about the whole thing will be balanced justice . . . precision sincerity. *Hold my hand.* There. I have to deal with the people. They're not manmade, you know. They're instruments in a sense. And so they got to be tuned up. They got to be tightened up like they do a piano. If you tune them up to the Creator they'll be in communication. If you tune them up to Saturn, they'll be in communication there. Wherever you tune them, that's where they gonna be. But right now they in the department of death. The realm of death. All in the realm of death is nothing but peace. Its inhabitants have all received equal rights because they received equal rites. But if death is the absence of life, then death's death is life. But when it comes to music, man is god up there in the octave. The music comes from the void, the nothing, the void, in response to the burning need for something else. And if music is in your heart, you can't do anything wrong. Friendship is what I'm talking about. Friends are not friends for any reason whatsoever but it's very beautiful, friendship. Like one of my songs is Friendly Galaxy. I'm talking 'bout friendship. I don't think about nothing but reaching people with impressions of happiness. I'm actually painting pictures of infinity with my music. It has something else in it, something from another world. *Hold my hand.* I opened up the Space Age. See, nothing happens on this planet unless somebody from somewhere else allow and give permission to man to do it. So I've chosen intergalactic music or it has chosen me. Intergalactic music concerns music of the galaxies. It concerns intergalactic thought and intergalactic travel. The intergalactic music is in hieroglyphic-sound: an abstract analysis and synthesis of man's relationship to the universe, visible and invisible. This music is of the realm of the alter-destiny. It touches upon the realm of myth of the outer-alter potential. The eternal endless mythology spectrum hieroglyphic parallel/duology presence. HOLD MY HAND. All that I am is a visitation, and that is the meaning of the natural alter-self. . . . The alternative to limitation is INFINITY.

Sun Ra departed planet Earth on May 30, 1993.
He travels the spaceways from planet to planet.

ACKNOWLEDGMENTS

Conversation can be dangerous. Maybe it should be. *A Pure Solar World: Sun Ra and the Birth of Afrofuturism* originated in a long, vexed conversation with my friend and colleague Billy Joe Harris. Our talk, about black music that makes for hard listening, led to team-teaching a course on free jazz, and that experience piqued a passion for Sun Ra's music that refuses to abate. I can't thank Sun Ra enough. He revealed a pathway to unknown worlds. Still, I have had a lot of help and guidance traveling it. Some gifted young researchers lent a hand when the going got rough: Jason Shafer, Alexandra Newsome, and Misho Ishakawa. This book is better for their suggestions, particularly regarding Sun Ra's influence on contemporary music. Connie Fasshauer proofed and polished the manuscript, and it shows—or rather doesn't. She saved me from many a howler. My colleague Adam Bradley pointed the way to publication, and I deeply appreciate it.

Anyone interested in studying Sun Ra with the seriousness his amazing body of work deserves will sooner or later find a way to the

Alton Abraham Collection of Sun Ra held at the Special Collections Research Center of the University of Chicago Library, an indispensable archive for solaristic research. Its staff is without equal. I am especially grateful for the assistance of Diana Harper, Oscar Chavez, and Barbara Gilbert. Judith Dartt handled image requests with grace and patience. Several small but generous gestures lifted my spirits during long hours of research: a cup of coffee with John Corbett, an e-mail from John Szwed, a midnight tour of the Loop with Marta Ruiz Galbete. Tom Choate let me crash at his house and again at his condominium, cutting research costs. I appreciate the kindness. I am grateful, too, to the bartenders and servers in Chicago who made my several visits all the more pleasant for their anonymous company. It's an affable city. Generous support for research came from the Center for Humanities and the Arts at the University of Colorado. The staff at the University of Texas Press (Robert Devens, Sarah McGavick, and Nancy Lavender Bryan especially) provided inspiration when I needed it most.

More personal thanks are harder to put into words. I wrote the early chapters of this book in Kingston, Jamaica. My friend and collaborator Fran Botkin provided thoughtful support—intellectual and medical—during several hot, languid weeks; I owe her my undying thanks. I am grateful to the staff members of St. Andrews Hospital for their dispassionate attention, particularly nurse Doily. Ossie Osman and Shaneka Johnson kept me in food, drink, and good vibes. Evan Williams of Red Bones recalled hiring Sun Ra in the early sixties to play a club he ran in Brooklyn. All this hospitality has been a blessing. Some thanks seem beyond expression, and those go to Arlene Passley.

Closer to home are the friends and family whose company, not to put too fine a point on it, keeps me breathing: Caitlin Rose, Cecil Giscombe, Jeff Cox, Tom Daly, Thora Brylowe, Kieran Murphy, Erika Polson, and Talissa Ford. I wanted to write a book my mother, Joanne, would enjoy. She's no longer around to read this one, but maybe her friend Thelma Bivens will.

NOTES

INTRO: WONDER INN

1. Sun Ra, "Space Aura," *Music from Tomorrow's World: Sun Ra and His Arkestra, Chicago 1960*, Atavistic ALP 237, 2002, CD. Recorded live at the Wonder Inn.

2. Sun Ra, "It Ain't Necessarily So," by George and Ira Gershwin, on *Music from Tomorrow's World*.

CHAPTER 1: ALIEN

1. Details of Sun Ra's sojourn on planet Earth come largely from John Szwed's biography *Space Is the Place: The Lives and Times of Sun Ra* (New York: Da Capo, 1998), as well as scattered interviews, transcriptions, and video.

2. Ibid., 6.

3. Ibid., 6, 11.

4. Ibid., 11.

5. *Brother from Another Planet* is the title of Don Letts's documentary film about Sun Ra (BBC4 broadcast, October 28, 2005), but the title comes from John Sayles's film of that name. Letts offers an exhilarating introduction to Sun Ra's life and work. He combines footage from Robert Mugge's 1980

documentary about Sun Ra, *A Joyful Noise*, and John Coney's film *Space Is the Place* (1974) with interviews of a number of Sun Ra's musicians and admirers, including Marshall Allen, Luqman Ali, Danny Thompson, Michael Ray, Archie Shepp, and Amiri Baraka.

6. The standard discography lists over two hundred LPs and compact discs and contains almost eight hundred entries beginning in 1946 and including many live-audience recordings. See Robert L. Campbell and Christopher Trent, eds., *The Earthly Recordings of Sun Ra*, 2nd ed. (Redwood, NY: Jazz Cadence Books, n.d.). For an even closer examination of Sun Ra's early recordings, see the website compiled by Campbell, Trent, and Robert Pruter, "From Sonny Blount to Sun Ra: The Chicago Years," http://myweb.clemson.edu/~campber/ sunra.html. This site adapts information available on the gathering of early recorded material compiled by Michael Anderson in his collection *Sun Ra: The Eternal Myth Revealed, Vol. 1*, fourteen discs, Transparency 0316, 2011, CD. Much of Sun Ra's poetry and related writing appears in Sun Ra, *The Immeasurable Equation: The Collected Poetry and Prose*, comp. and ed. James Wolf and Hartmut Geerken (Norderstedt, Germany: Waitawhile, 2005). Sun Ra's work as a visual artist can be found among the images in John Corbett, Anthony Elms, and Terri Kapsalis, eds., *Pathways to Unknown Worlds: Sun Ra, El Saturn and Chicago's Afro-Futurist Underground 1954–68* (Chicago: WhiteWalls, 2006).

7. Szwed, *Space Is the Place*, 308. Scholars and critics who offer especially helpful commentary on Sun Ra's music, poetry, and politics include the following: John Corbett, *Extended Play: Sounding Off from John Cage to Dr. Funkenstein* (Durham, NC: Duke University Press, 1994); John Corbett and Aye Aton, *Sun Ra and Aye Aton: Space, Interiors and Exteriors, 1972* (New York: PictureBox, 2013); Evan Crandell and Lisa Lorenzino, "Nurturing a Joyful Noise: Examining Sun Ra's Philosophies as a Model for Music Education," *Canadian Music Educator* 54, no. 3 (2013): 25–29; Kodwo Eshun, *More Brilliant Than the Sun: Adventures in Sonic Fiction* (London: Quartet Books, 1998); Krin Gabbard, ed., *Jazz among the Discourses* (Durham, NC: Duke University Press, 1995); Daniel Kreiss, "Appropriating the Master's Tools: Sun Ra, the Black Panthers, and Black Consciousness, 1952–1973," *Black Music Research Journal* 28, no. 1 (2008): 57–81; Daniel Kreiss, "Performing the Past to Claim the Future: Sun Ra and the Afro-Future Underground, 1954–1968," *African American Review* 45, nos. 1–2 (2012): 197–203; George E. Lewis, "Forward: After Afrofuturism," *Journal of the Society for American Music* 2, no. 2 (2008): 139–153; Graham Lock, *Blutopia: Visions of the Future and Visions of the Past in the Work of Sun Ra, Duke Ellington, and Anthony Braxton* (Durham, NC: Duke University Press, 1999); Tadhg O'Keeffe, "Street Ballets in Magic Cities: Cultural Imaginings of the Modern American Metropolis," *Popular*

Music History 4, no. 2 (2009): 111–125; Nathan Ragain, "A 'Reconcepted Am': Language, Nature, and Collectivity in Sun Ra and Henry Dumas," *Criticism* 54, no. 4 (2012): 539–565; T. Griffith Rollefson, "The 'Robot Voodoo Power Thesis': Afrofuturism and Anti-Anti-Essentialism from Sun Ra to Kool Keith," *Black Music Research Journal* 28, no. 1 (2008): 197–215; Stevphen Shukaitis, "Space Is the (Non)Place: Martians, Marxists, and the Outer Space of the Radical Imagination, *Sociological Review* 57, no. 1 (2009): 98–113; John Swenson, "Images of Tomorrow Disguised as Jazz," *Rolling Stone*, March 4, 1993, 63; Marcel Swiboda, "Re Interpretations: Sun Ra's Egyptian Inscriptions," *Parallax* 13, no. 2 (2007): 93–106; Aurelien Tchiemessom, *Sun Ra: Un noir dans le cosmos* (Paris: Harmattan, 2004); Lorenzo Thomas, "'Classical Jazz' and the Black Arts Movement," *African American Review* 29, no. 2 (1995): 237–240; Lorenzo Thomas, "The Mathemagic of Sun Ra," *Ann Arbor Sun*, April 5–19, 1974, 16–17; Gayle Wald, "Soul Vibrations: Black Music and Black Freedom in Sound and Space," *American Quarterly* 63, no. 3 (2011): 673–696; Alexander Weheliye, *Phonographies: Grooves in Sonic Afro-Modernity* (Durham, NC: Duke University Press, 2005).

8. Sun Ra, "[I always called myself Sun Ra]," in *The Immeasurable Equation*, 457.

9. Szwed, *Space Is the Place*, 29. The story appears frequently in reviews and interviews.

10. Ibid., 29–30.

11. Ibid., 351.

CHAPTER 2: MARIENVILLE

1. Szwed, *Space Is the Place*, 39–40. The word "colored" was abbreviated "col." in the notices. For a discussion of the Sonny Blount Orchestra, see Campbell, Trent, and Pruter, "From Sonny Blount to Sun Ra."

2. Szwed, *Space Is the Place*, 41.

3. Ibid., 40.

4. Office of the Comptroller General, *Decisions of the Comptroller General of the United States*, vol. 24, July 1, 1944, to June 30, 1945 (Washington, DC: Government Printing Office, 1946), 646.

5. Szwed, *Space Is the Place*, 41.

6. Ibid., 41, 42.

7. Ibid., 44.

8. Ibid., 44. I base the following imagined exchange between Sonny and the judge on Szwed's description of the encounter.

9. Ibid.

10. Ibid., 45.

11. Ibid., 46.

12. Sun Ra, "The Neglected Plane of Wisdom," in *The Immeasurable Equation*, 250.

CHAPTER 3: BRONZEVILLE

1. Arnold R. Hirsch, *Making the Second Ghetto: Race and Housing in Chicago, 1940–1960* (Chicago: University of Chicago Press, 1998), 17.

2. Dempsey J. Travis, "Bronzeville," in *Encyclopedia of Chicago*, ed. Janice L. Reiff, Ann Durkin Keating, and James R. Grossman. Chicago: Chicago Historical Society, 2005. www.encyclopedia.chicagohistory.org/pages/171.html. Gentry apparently coined the term "Bronzeville." He had earlier sponsored an annual Miss Bronze America beauty pageant.

3. Dominic A. Pacyga, *Chicago: A Biography* (Chicago: University of Chicago Press, 2009), 324.

4. Thomas Dyja, *The Third Coast: When Chicago Built the American Dream* (New York: Penguin, 2013), 23.

5. Ibid., 24.

6. Ibid., 83.

7. Alan Ehrenhalt, *The Lost City: Discovering the Forgotten Virtues of Community in the Chicago of the 1950s* (New York: Basic Books, 1995), 158.

8. Qtd. in ibid., 156. Bronzeville hosted a half-dozen large insurance companies. As Ehrenhalt (158) notes, the *Defender* annually published this tribute during National Negro Insurance Week: "I am the destroyer of poverty and the enemy of crime. I bring sunshine and happiness wherever I am given half the welcome I deserve. I do not live for the day nor for the morrow but for the unfathomable future. I am your best friend—insurance."

9. For a detailed account of this second African American renaissance, see Robert Bone and Richard A. Courage, *The Muse in Bronzeville: African American Creative Expression in Chicago, 1932–1950* (New Brunswick, NJ: Rutgers University Press, 2011).

10. On Wright and the Chicago Renaissance, see Robert Bone, "Richard Wright and the Chicago Renaissance," *Callaloo* 9 (1986): 446–468.

11. Szwed, *Space Is the Place*, 59.

12. Ibid.

13. For an extended meditation on Chicago jazz and its effects on local life, see Gerald Majer, *The Velvet Lounge: On Late Chicago Jazz* (New York: Columbia University Press, 2005). Majer's chapter on Sun Ra is the best piece of writing on him and the Arkestra's music.

14. Dyja, *The Third Coast*, 35.

15. Ibid., 5–6.

16. Hirsch, *Making the Second Ghetto*, 25. For a distressing fictional representation of these conditions, see the opening scene of Richard Wright, *Native Son* (1940; repr., New York: Harper Perennial, 1992), 7–12.

17. Gwendolyn Brooks, "kitchenette building," in *Selected Poems* (New York: Harper and Row, 1963), 3. Reprinted by consent of Brooks Permissions.

18. This paragraph is loosely based on various descriptions and photos of kitchenettes.

19. The most thorough account of Sonny's earliest recording and group performances appears on Campbell, Trent, and Pruter's website "From Sonny Blount to Sun Ra." Michael Anderson's fourteen-CD compilation *Sun Ra: The Eternal Myth Revealed* provides invaluable musical context for Sun Ra's earliest recordings, as well as previously unavailable tracks.

20. Qtd. in Szwed, *Space Is the Place*, 57.

21. Campbell, Trent, and Pruter, "From Sonny Blount to Sun Ra."

22. Szwed, *Space Is the Place*, 56.

23. Dyja, *The Third Coast*, 135.

24. Szwed, *Space Is the Place*, 59.

25. I heard this story from the guitarist Bill Kopper, who had it from the Chicago trumpet player Brad Goode.

CHAPTER 4: THMEI

1. Szwed, *Space Is the Place*, 47. Campbell, Trent, and Pruter's website "From Sonny Blount to Sun Ra" contains many details about early gigs and recordings. Information from this indispensable work appears throughout this section.

2. See Campbell, Trent, and Pruter, "From Sonny Blount to Sun Ra," for more detail regarding Sonny's encounters with Hawkins. A recording was apparently made of their initial after-hours encounter (1948) and may still exist. Two tracks from the Hawkins session appear on disc 11 of Anderson, *Sun Ra: The Eternal Myth Revealed*.

3. Bugs Hunter tells of Sonny's attachment to recording machines, which he took wherever he played and used to record everything, even the Calumet City gigs; see Peter Hinds, conversation with Tommy Hunter, April 9 and 13, 1998, *Sun Ra Research* 32 (February 2001): 63, 76. Paper tapes broke easily, and Hunter confesses to having thrown out a lot of early material. The Brush Development Company first manufactured the Sound Mirror BK 401 in 1946; see Szwed, *Space Is the Place*, 34, and, for a picture, *Sun Ra Arkive*, June 6, 2008, http://sunraarkive.blogspot.com/2008/06/brush-sound-mirror-bk401.html.

4. Wright, *Native Son*, 3.

5. Ibid., 164.

6. Ibid., 109.

7. Ibid., 23, 24.

8. Ibid., 84–85.

9. Ibid., 392.

10. Ibid., 364, 366.

11. Ibid., 366, 368.

12. Ibid., 335.

13. These tunes as well as the poem can be heard on Anderson, *Sun Ra: The Eternal Myth Revealed*, discs 3–5.

14. Campbell, Trent, and Pruter, "From Sonny Blount to Sun Ra."

15. Qtd. in Szwed, *Space Is the Place*, 364, 100.

16. William Sites, "Radical Culture in Black Necropolis: Sun Ra, Alton Abraham, and Postwar Chicago," *Journal of Urban History* 38, no. 4 (2012): 691. See also Sites's essay "'We Travel the Spaceways': Urban Utopianism and the Imagined Spaces of Black Experimental Music," *Urban Geography* 33, no. 4 (2012): 566–592.

17. Alton Abraham Collection of Sun Ra, 1822–2008, box 51, folder 15, Special Collections Research Center, University of Chicago Library (hereinafter cited as AAC).

18. Ibid.

19. John Corbett, "From the Windy City to the Omniverse: Sun Ra's Chicago Life as Street Priest and Father of D.I.Y Jazz," *Down Beat*, December 2006, 36.

20. AAC, box 19, folder 21. See also AAC, box 21, folder 7.

21. Sites provides a detailed description and assessment of this secret society in "Radical Culture."

22. Sir Gardner Wilkinson, *The Manners and Customs of the Ancient Egyptians*, 3rd ed., 5 vols. (London: John Murray, 1847), 5:29.

23. Ibid.

24. Sites, "Radical Culture," 692.

25. AAC, box 14, folder 2.

26. Ibid.

27. Wright, *Native Son*, 364.

28. Sites, "Radical Culture," 697.

29. Gardiner H. Shattuck, "Wallace Fard," *American National Biography Online*, www.anb.org/articles/08/08-00457.html.

30. Szwed, *Space Is the Place*, 105–106.

31. See ibid., 106–107.

32. The allusion here to Carl Schmitt is meant to emphasize Thmei's emphasis on a sovereignty descending from above. See Schmitt's *Political Theology: Four Chapters on the Concept of Sovereignty*, trans. George Schwab (Cambridge, MA: MIT Press, 1985).

33. Qtd. in Szwed, *Space Is the Place*, 313.

34. AAC, box 18, folder 6.

35. AAC, box 14, folder 1.

36. AAC, box 13, folder 12. The word "Better" was added by Abraham himself.

37. AAC, box 15, folder 9.

38. Ibid.

39. Qtd. in Szwed, *Space Is the Place*, 75.

40. Ibid.

41. In John Hinds and Peter Hinds, conversation with Sun Ra, October 13, 1984, *Sun Ra Research* 19 (October 1998): 3.

42. Szwed, *Space Is the Place*, 79.

43. Ibid., 86, 85. For a fuller discussion of the significance of the name "Sun Ra," see ibid., 79–87.

CHAPTER 5: EGYPT

1. Szwed, *Space Is the Place*, 65.

2. Jennifer Rycenga, "Interview with Sun Ra," transcr. and ed. Dan Plonsey, [1988], www.plonsey.com/beanbenders/SUNRA-interview.html.

3. Constantin-François Volney, *The Ruins; or, Meditations on the Revolutions of Empires; and the Law of Nature*. Baltimore, MD: Black Classics, 1991.

4. George Wells Parker, *The Children of the Sun* (1918; repr., Baltimore, MD: Black Classics, 1981).

5. Theodore P. Ford, *God Wills the Negro* (Chicago: Geographical Institute Press, 1939).

6. Grafton Elliot Smith, *Ancient Egypt and the Origins of Civilization*, rev. ed. (1923; repr., Freeport, NY: Books for Libraries, 1971), xi.

7. Ibid., 26.

8. George G. M. James, *Stolen Legacy: The Greeks Were Not the Authors of Greek Philosophy, but the People of North Africa, Commonly Called the Egyptians* (New York: Philosophical Library, 1954), 3.

9. Ibid., 5.

10. Ibid., 7, 158.

11. Ibid., 153, 155–156.

CHAPTER 6: WASHINGTON PARK

1. This scenario is based on Sun Ra's reminiscence of his days in Chicago's Washington Park as recounted in John Hinds and Peter Hinds, conversation with Sun Ra and Carl LeBlanc, October 31, 1988, *Sun Ra Research* 15 (February 1998): 8–9. I have tried to stay very close to the facts presented there and the sentiments contained in Sun Ra's broadsheets.

2. Qtd. in Szwed, *Space Is the Place*, 78.

3. To John Corbett goes the credit for rescuing this priceless hoard of memorabilia after fortuitously learning that Abraham's house was scheduled for demolition. To the University of Chicago go the thanks for housing and cataloging it all at the Special Collections Research Center. An article by Barry McRae corroborates Sun Ra's activist commitments: "He is held in very high esteem by all of the Chicago modernists that I have met, not only as a musician but also for his extra musical activities. As his nomenclature suggests he is deeply interested in the universe and senses that the whole spectrum of human knowledge will be expanded now that interplanetary travel can be realistically predicted. On a more mundane level he is a true product of his background, and the deprivation on Chicago's South Side has made a deep impression on him. He has always felt resentment, not only of the conditions themselves, but also the blind resignation with which they are accepted. During the late fifties he became, almost by accident, the leader of an organization determined to see improvements. His practical philosophies earned him many followers outside the musical field, and, with their help, he set out to better the lot of the poorer Chicagoans. He distributed pamphlets that expounded a doctrine of self-improvement to the Negro population"; see Barry McRae, "Sun Ra," *Jazz Journal* 19, no. 8 (1966): 15.

4. See John Corbett's introduction, "one of everything: blount hermeneutics and the wisdom of ra," in *The Wisdom of Sun Ra: Sun Ra's Polemical Broadsheets and Streetcorner Leaflets*, ed. John Corbett (Chicago: WhiteWalls, 2006), 5–6. For the originals, see AAC, box 15, folder 10.

5. Sun Ra, "keys to understanding the hidden meaning of the bible," in Corbett, *The Wisdom of Sun Ra*, 122.

6. Sites, "Radical Culture in Black Necropolis," 695–696.

7. Sun Ra, "humpty dumpty," in Corbett, *The Wisdom of Sun Ra*, 119.

8. Sun Ra, "united states at the crossroads," in Corbett, *The Wisdom of Sun Ra*, 112.

9. Sun Ra, "humpty dumpty," 120.

10. Sun Ra, "keys to understanding the hidden meaning of the bible," in Corbett, *The Wisdom of Sun Ra*, 123.

11. Sun Ra, "humpty dumpty," 120; Sun Ra, "[illegible title] it is time to discuss," in Corbett, *The Wisdom of Sun Ra*, 117.

12. Sun Ra, "united states at the crossroads," 113.

13. Sun Ra, "[illegible title] it is time to discuss," 116.

14. Sun Ra, "why don't you turn again!," in Corbett, *The Wisdom of Sun Ra*, 109.

15. Sun Ra, "satan," in Corbett, *The Wisdom of Sun Ra*, 139.

16. Sun Ra, "why don't you turn again!," 109.

17. Sun Ra, "zoroastrianism," in Corbett, *The Wisdom of Sun Ra*, 138.

18. Sun Ra, "the truth," in Corbett, *The Wisdom of Sun Ra*, 130.

19. Sun Ra, "the poor little rich one: the prince of this world . . . ," in Corbett, *The Wisdom of Sun Ra*, 102.

20. Sun Ra, "the bible was not written for negroes!!!!!!!," in Corbett, *The Wisdom of Sun Ra*, 90.

21. Sun Ra, "united states at the crossroads," 111.

22. Sun Ra, "wake up! wake up! wake up!," in Corbett, *The Wisdom of Sun Ra*, 89.

23. Ibid.

24. Sun Ra, ". . . solution to the negro problem . . . ," in Corbett, *The Wisdom of Sun Ra*, 114.

25. Sun Ra, "the god of Israel," in Corbett, *The Wisdom of Sun Ra*, 110.

26. Sun Ra, "jesus said, 'let the negro bury the negro,'" in Corbett, *The Wisdom of Sun Ra*, 66. No tenable etymological connection exists between "Negro" and "necro," but Sun Ra uses such associations of sound to disrupt the conventional meaning of words. In this case, auditory similarity reveals what a difference in meaning obscures: that black people suffer social death as a legacy of enslavement.

27. Sun Ra, "the true way to life," in Corbett, *The Wisdom of Sun Ra*, 87.

28. Sun Ra, "I don't give a hoot," in Corbett, *The Wisdom of Sun Ra*, 96.

29. Sun Ra, "johnny one note," in Corbett, *The Wisdom of Sun Ra*, 105.

30. Sun Ra, "satan is the god of the spooks / negroes are the children of the 'devil,'" in Corbett, *The Wisdom of Sun Ra*, 72.

31. Sun Ra, "the bible was not written for negroes!!!!!!!," 90.

32. Sun Ra, "humpty dumpty," 120.

33. Sun Ra, "jesus said, 'let the negro bury the negro,'" 66.

34. Sun Ra, "humpty dumpty," 119.

35. Sun Ra, "why don't you turn again!," 109.

36. Sun Ra, "the poor little rich one: the prince of this world," 102.

37. Sun Ra, "what must negroes do to be saved," in Corbett, *The Wisdom of Sun Ra*, 126.

38. Ibid., 128.

39. Ibid.

40. Ibid.

41. Ibid., 127.

42. Ibid., 128.

43. Sun Ra, "[illegible title] it is time to discuss," 117.

44. Sun Ra, "the end," 141.

45. Sun Ra, "why don't you turn again!," 110.

46. Jennifer Rycenga, interview with Sun Ra, November 2, 1988, part five, *Sun Ra Research* 26 (December 1999): 8.

CHAPTER 7: ARKESTRA

1. Sun Ra's early years in Chicago receive meticulous examination in Campbell, Trent, and Pruter, "From Sonny Blount to Sun Ra"; and Anderson, *Sun Ra: The Eternal Myth Revealed*.

2. Campbell, Trent, and Pruter, "From Sonny Blount to Sun Ra."

3. Szwed, *Space Is the Place*, 17.

4. Ibid.

5. Campbell, Trent, and Pruter, "From Sonny Blount to Sun Ra."

6. In *Sun Ra: The Eternal Myth Revealed*, Michael Anderson shows how important big bands remained to Sun Ra during the Chicago years, even as smaller ensembles became de rigueur. The Fletcher Henderson Orchestra was only the most influential. Other big bands of great importance to Sun Ra's musical growth include ones led by Lionel Hampton, Jimmie Lunceford, Benny Carter, and Cab Calloway, as well as the bop-oriented ensembles of Billy Eckstein and Dizzy Gillespie. See Anderson, *Sun Ra: The Eternal Myth Revealed*, disc 2.

7. Sites, "Radical Culture," 700.

8. Campbell, Trent, and Pruter, "From Sonny Blount to Sun Ra." This recording appears on Anderson, *Sun Ra: The Eternal Myth Revealed*, disc 6. Patrick would eventually play with other jazz greats, including John Coltrane, Blue Mitchell, Mongo Santamaria, and Thelonious Monk. Deval Patrick, the governor of Massachusetts from 2007 to 2015, is his son.

9. Szwed, *Space Is the Place*, 88.

10. In a 1954 essay in *Melody Maker*, the great jazz pianist Mary Lou Williams, writing of the origins of bebop, quotes Thelonious Monk as saying, "We're going to get a big band started. We're going to create something they can't steal, because they can't play it." See Rob van der Bliek, *The Thelonious Monk Reader* (Oxford: Oxford University Press, 2001), 12.

11. Szwed, *Space Is the Place*, 94.

12. Ibid., 93; Campbell, Trent, and Pruter, "From Sonny Blount to Sun Ra." Such a list is hardly definitive. With some notable exceptions, the Arkestra's personnel would shift dramatically throughout its extraordinary history.

13. The picture appears in Campbell, Trent, and Pruter, "From Sonny Blount to Sun Ra."

14. Ibid.

15. Sun Ra, "the poor little rich one: the prince of this world," in Corbett, *The Wisdom of Sun Ra*, 102.

16. Sites, "Radical Culture," 703.

17. Qtd. in Szwed, *Space Is the Place*, 100.

18. Ibid.

19. Ibid., 97, 116.

20. Rycenga, "Interview with Sun Ra" [1988].

21. Transcription of an interview with Pat Patrick, AAC, box 56, folder 3.

22. Peter Hinds and John Hinds, conversation with Sun Ra and Charles Bass, November 15, 1991, *Sun Ra Research* 1 (May 1995): 3.

23. Sun Ra, "Sun Ra Interview (Helsinki 1971)," http://nuvoid.blogspot .com/2012/04/sun-ra-sunday_22.html.

24. Qtd. in Bret Primack, "Captain Angelic: Sun Ra," *Down Beat*, May 4, 1978, 41.

25. Qtd. in Chris Cutler, "In the Realm of Lightning," in *Omniverse Sun Ra*, ed. Hartmut Geerken and Bernhard Hefele (Wartaweil, Germany: Waitawhile, 1994), 81.

26. Qtd. in Szwed, *Space Is the Place*, 128.

27. Details gleaned from Corbett, "From the Windy City," 35; Campbell, Trent, and Pruter, "From Sonny Blount to Sun Ra."

28. See Campbell, Trent, and Pruter, "From Sonny Blount to Sun Ra," for a close and careful accounting of the singles that constitute the Arkestra's earliest recordings. Both sides of the first single reappeared on the Arkestra's first Saturn LP: Sun Ra, *Super-Sonic Jazz*, Evidence 22015, 1991, CD; original release, Saturn H7OP0216, 1957, LP.

CHAPTER 8: IMMEASURABLE EQUATION

1. Szwed, *Space Is the Place*, 29.

2. Sun Ra, "My Music is Words," in *The Immeasurable Equation*, 469.

3. Ibid., 468.

4. The poems included in the latter were "The Plane: Earth" and "Primary Lesson: The Second Class Citizen." See Arnold Adoff, ed., *The Poetry of Black America: Anthology of the 20th Century* (New York: Harper and Row, 1973).

5. Two handy if editorially improvisational collections of Sun Ra's poetry have recently appeared on an imprint called Kicks Books: Sun Ra, *This Planet Is Doomed: The Science Fiction Poetry of Sun Ra* (New York: Kicks Books, 2011), and Sun Ra, *Prophetika* (New York: Kicks Books, 2014), both edited by Miriam Linna. Neither offers insight into the publication circumstances of the poems they include. Kicks's affiliated record label, Norton Records, has released several vinyl albums of poetry read by the master himself: Sun Ra, *Strange Worlds in My Mind: Sun Ra and His Arkestra*, Norton CED 365, 2010, CD; ED-365, 2010, LP. Sun Ra, *The Sub-Dwellers: Sun Ra and His Arkestra*, Norton CED 366, 2010, CD; ED-366, 2010, LP. Sun Ra, *The Outer Darkness: Sun Ra and His Arkestra*, Norton CED 367, 2010, CD; ED 367, 2010, LP. Sun Ra, *My Way is the Spaceways: Sun Ra and His Arkestra*, Norton CED-391, 2014, CD; ED-391, 2014, LP. Szwed published several examples of Sun Ra's poetry in *Space Is the Place*; see in particular pp. 319–329. Sun Ra's poetry can be found on the Internet, of course, in various states and guises.

6. Essays are by James L. Wolf, Hartmut Geerken, Sigrid Hauff, Klaus Detlef Thiel, and Brent Hays Edwards; see Sun Ra, *The Immeasurable Equation*.

7. A typescript for "The Magic Lie" exists among the material in the Alton Abraham Collection, AAC, box 13, folder 4.

8. See *Sun Ra Research* 17 (1998), inside front cover.

9. As can be heard on Sun Ra, *Concert for the Comet Kohoutek*, ESP Disk' 3033, 1993, CD. This live performance was recorded at Town Hall in New York on December 22, 1973.

10. "He was the bandleader as prophetic leader, the music arranger as arranger of the world. Such a program was enough to qualify him as a European romantic." Then Szwed adds an important qualifier: "But his was an African-American romanticism, its goal a collective metaphysical experience" (*Space Is the Place*, 383).

11. William Blake, *Jerusalem*, pl. 10, ll. 20–21. From Blake, *The Complete Poetry and Prose of William Blake*, rev. ed., ed. David V. Erdman (Berkeley: University of California Press, 1982), 153. I have retained Blake's spelling and punctuation.

12. Percy Bysshe Shelley, "To a Skylark," in *Shelley's Poetry and Prose*, ed. Donald H. Reiman and Sharon B. Powers (New York: Norton, 1977), 226, 228.

13. An exception is the perceptive work of Graham Lock, who senses keenly the persistence in Sun Ra's poetry of African American tropes and themes; see his *Blutopia*. A helpful introduction to Sun Ra's poetry appears among the essays in Sun Ra, *The Immeasurable Equation*: Brent Hayes Edwards's "Race for Space: Sun Ra's Poetry" (29–56). The poetry's importance is understated in even so celebratory a gathering of essays as John Corbett, Anthony Elms, and

Terri Kapsalis, eds., *Traveling the Spaceways: Sun Ra, the Astro Black and Other Solar Myths* (Chicago: WhiteWalls, 2010).

14. See Aldon Lynn Nielson, *Black Chant: Languages of African-American Postmodernism* (Cambridge: Cambridge University Press, 1997).

15. Nathaniel Mackey, *Discrepant Engagement: Dissonance, Cross-Culturality, and Experimental Writing* (Cambridge: Cambridge University Press, 1993), 7.

16. Ibid., 8.

17. Amiri Imamu Baraka [LeRoi Jones], *Black Music* (1968; repr., New York: Da Capo, 1998), 136.

18. Ibid.

19. Ibid., 198.

20. Ibid., 129.

21. This is a favorite sentiment of Sun Ra's. This version appears in Szwed, *Space Is the Place*, 295.

22. I am drawing loosely here on Friedrich Nietzsche, *The Birth of Tragedy*, trans. Douglas Smith (Oxford: Oxford University Press, 2008); and Paul D. Miller, *Rhythm Science* (Cambridge, MA: MIT Press, 2004). For explorations of sound from a variety of cultural perspectives, see Kara Keeling and Josh Kun, eds., *Sound Clash: Listening to American Studies* (Baltimore, MD: Johns Hopkins University Press, 2012).

23. Sun Ra, "The Sound I Hear," in *The Immeasurable Equation*, 346.

24. Ibid.

25. Ibid.

26. Sun Ra, "The Pure Sound," in *The Immeasurable Equation*, 318.

27. Baraka, *Black Music*, 194.

28. Mackey, *Discrepant Engagement*, 323.

29. See Immanuel Kant, *Critique of the Power of Judgment*, trans. Paul Guyer and Eric Matthews, rev. ed. (Cambridge: Cambridge University Press, 2001). For a succinct exposition, see Gilles Deleuze, *Kant's Critical Philosophy*, trans. Hugh Tomlinson and Barbara Habberjam (Minneapolis: University of Minnesota Press, 1985).

30. Qtd. in Mackey, *Discrepant Engagement*, 232.

31. Ibid.

32. Ibid., 235.

33. Qtd. in Szwed, *Space Is the Place*, 306.

34. Sun Ra, "The Confusion of Words," in *The Immeasurable Equation*, 104.

35. Ibid.

36. Sun Ra, "To The Peoples of Earth," in *The Immeasurable Equation*, 390.

37. Jennifer Rycenga, interview with Sun Ra, November 2, 1988, part one, *Sun Ra Research* 2 (July 1995): 8.

38. Sun Ra, "The Glory of Shame" (1980), in *The Immeasurable Equation*, 185.

39. Sun Ra, *The Soul Vibrations of Man*, Saturn 771, 1977, LP. The recording was released without track titles. "Third Heaven" appears on side 1.

40. Sun Ra, "Be-earthed" (1972), in *The Immeasurable Equation*, 75.

41. Sun Ra, "[Point, Equal, Aim]," in *The Immeasurable Equation*, 306. On L=A=N=G=U=A=G=E poetry, see Bruce Andrews and Charles Bernstein, eds., *The L=A=N=G=U=A=G=E Book* (Carbondale: Southern Illinois University Press, 1984).

42. Sun Ra, "Tomorrow Never Comes," in *The Immeasurable Equation*, 391.

43. Qtd. in Szwed, *Space Is the Place*, 304.

44. Sun Ra, "Cosmic Equation," in *The Immeasurable Equation*, 110.

45. Ibid.

46. Sun Ra, "The Outer Bridge" (1965), in *The Immeasurable Equation*, 293.

47. On language as a control machine and the word as virus, see William S. Burroughs, *Nova Express* (1964; repr., New York, Grove, 1992); William S. Burroughs, *The Job: Interviews with William S. Burroughs* (New York: Penguin, 1989). Burroughs shares Sun Ra's sense that disrupting conventional associations and substituting new ones can open up new possibilities for life.

48. Sun Ra, "The Enwrit" (1972), in *The Immeasurable Equation*, 155.

49. Ibid.

50. Ibid.

51. Sun Ra, "Discernment," in *The Immeasurable Equation*, 137.

52. Sun Ra, "The Enwrit," 155.

53. Sun Ra, "Music of the Spheres," in *The Immeasurable Equation*, 243.

54. Sun Ra, "Of Coordinate Vibrations," in *The Immeasurable Equation*, 262.

55. Ibid.

56. Sun Ra, "New Horizons," in *The Immeasurable Equation*, 255.

57. Ibid.

58. Sun Ra, "The Skilled Way," in *The Immeasurable Equation*, 341.

59. Sun Ra, "The Equal And The Opposite," in *The Immeasurable Equation*, 157.

60. Sun Ra, "The Neglected Plane of Wisdom," in *The Immeasurable Equation*, 250–251. As the editors point out, this poem appears on early catalogs for Sun Ra's record company, Saturn, accompanied by the phrase "Registered 1955." While no evidence exists that Sun Ra copyrighted the poem, if that date refers to its composition, "The Neglected Plane of Wisdom" constitutes one of his earliest works.

61. Sun Ra, "The Stage of Man," in *The Immeasurable Equation*, 363.

62. See *Sun Ra Research* 5 (1995), inside front cover.

63. Qtd. in Szwed, *Space Is the Place*, 247.

CHAPTER 9: EL SATURN

1. Szwed, *Space Is the Place*, 123.

2. Sites, "Radical Culture in Black Necropolis," 702.

3. AAC, box 13, folder 13.

4. Sites, "Radical Culture in Black Necropolis," 703.

5. Szwed, *Space Is the Place*, 34. Sadly, these recordings no longer exist.

6. P. Hinds, conversation with Tommy Hunter, April 9 and 13, 1998, 76.

7. Campbell, Trent, and Pruter, "From Sonny Blount to Sun Ra." The recording also appears on Anderson, *Sun Ra: The Eternal Myth Revealed*, disc 3.

8. Sun Ra, *Spaceship Lullaby (1954–1960)*, Atavistic UMS/ALP243, 2003, CD. Sun Ra's early work with vocal groups also appears on several recordings issued by Norton Records: Sun Ra, *Interplanetary Melodies: Sun Ra and His Arkestra*, Norton CED 352, 2009, CD; ED-352, 2009, LP. Sun Ra, *The Second Stop is Jupiter: Sun Ra and His Arkestra*, Norton CED 353, 2009, CD; ED-353, 2009, LP. Sun Ra, *Rocket Ship Rock: Sun Ra and His Arkestra*, Norton CED 354, 2009, CD; ED-354, 2009, LP. Recordings that were released as singles (with the exception of four sides by the Metros) can be heard on Sun Ra, *The Singles*, two discs, Evidence 22164-2, 1996, CD. See Campbell, Trent, and Pruter, "From Sonny Blount to Sun Ra," for a scrupulous account of the vocal-group recordings.

9. John Corbett claims as much in his liner notes to *Spaceship Lullaby*, but Sites finds no evidence of such a contest beyond a 1955 bill proposed in the Illinois legislature for a new state song. See Sites, "Radical Culture in Black Necropolis," 717n80.

10. Qtd. in Szwed, *Space Is the Place*, 92.

11. Sites, "Radical Culture in Black Necropolis," 706.

12. Charles Mingus and Max Roach, notable exceptions, founded Debut Records in 1952 and recorded a number of top musicians (Kenny Dorham, Thad Jones, Hank Mobley, and Paul Bley) before closing shop in 1957. See the entries on Mingus and Roach in Barry Kernfeld, ed., *The New Grove Dictionary of Jazz* (New York: St. Martin's, 1984).

13. Rycenga, "Interview with Sun Ra" [1988].

14. Robert Campbell, "Sun Ra: Supersonic Sounds from Saturn," *Goldmine*, January 22, 1993. Copy archived at AAC, box 1, folder 50.

15. Szwed, *Space Is the Place*, 152.

16. Sites, "Radical Culture in Black Necropolis," 701.

17. Royalties statement dated 7/2/64, AAC, box 17, folder 3.

18. Edward W. Whitman, *The Book of Saturn* (London: Whitman Publishing, n.d.), n.p. A copy is archived at AAC, box 43, folder 5. The quotation appears on an unnumbered page.

19. George King, ed., *Cosmic Voice: Aetherius Speaks to Earth*, 2 vols. (London: n.p., 1957–1961), 1:26. Archived at AAC, box 44, folder 3.

20. Notebook, AAC, box 13, folder 12. Images appear in Corbett, Elms, and Kapsalis, *Pathways to Unknown Worlds*, 88–93. In an even more ambitious graphic fantasy, Abraham decorated a Panasonic electronics catalog with a pencil drawing of a "Treasure Map for El Saturn," depicting the land masses of Europe, Africa, South America, and India (and an equally large "parking Lot") overflown by huge quarter notes bearing the words "Sun Ra," the whole tableau watched over by a single Egyptian eye and including gold foil swatches signifying "Money to Fight Ignorance" and "Food for the Hungry." Construction paper cutouts demarcate "El Saturn's Fully Equipped Recording Studio" and "Record Pressing Plant." Abraham clearly had big ambitions for El Saturn. See AAC, box 134, folder 4.

21. Campbell, Trent, and Pruter, "From Sonny Blount to Sun Ra." The single was recorded at Balkan Studios on March 22, 1956, and released later that year. It bears the serial number Z1111. Campbell notes that a 78 rpm disc must have been in the works, although none has ever surfaced: a printed 78 label dated May 31, 1956, on the back can be found at AAC, box 17, folder 7.

22. Campbell, Trent, and Pruter, "From Sonny Blount to Sun Ra."

23. Columbia Records introduced the 33⅓ long-playing vinyl record in 1948. It originally held about twenty-two minutes of music per side.

24. Szwed, *Space Is the Place*, 154.

25. Corbett, "Obscure Past, Bright Futures: Saturn Records in Silhouette," in Corbett, Elms, and Kapsalis, *Traveling the Spaceways*, 41. Producing records by sponsorship more closely resembles book publishing by subscription than a pyramid scam as that term is understood today.

26. AAC, box 17, folder 7.

27. Ibid.

28. Szwed, *Space Is the* Place, 154.

29. Campbell, Trent, and Pruter, "From Sonny Blount to Sun Ra."

30. Szwed, *Space Is the Place*, 169. *Jazz by Sun Ra, Vol. 1* was released as Transition TRLP J-10 in early 1957. The material recorded for the second Transition LP would not be issued until 1968, when Delmark released it under the title *Sound of Joy: Sun Ra and the Arkestra* (Delmark DS-414; later release, Delmark DD-414, 2012, CD).

31. AAC, box 16, folder 8. The ad appears here as a proof from the magazine. Its bold declaration would appear frequently in later promotional material for the Arkestra. "Concert FI" probably signifies fidelity to live performance as a measure of the music's quality. Record companies in the fifties advanced a host of such terms, most familiar among them "Hi-Fi" for "high-fidelity."

32. *Jazz by Sun Ra, Vol. 1* (Transition TRLP J-10, 1957, LP) was rereleased in 1967 by Delmark under the title *Sun Song* as an LP (DL-411 and DS-411) and again in 1991 as a CD (DD-411). The full pamphlet serves as the liner notes to the compact disc, which is cited here. Typography from the original has been partly retained.

33. Liner notes, *Sun Song.*

34. Ibid.

35. Ibid.

36. Ibid.

37. Harriet Choice, "Rah, rah, . . . sunny Mr. Ra," *Chicago Tribune*, September 10, 1972. Archived at AAC, box 1, folder 8.

38. Assorted business cards. AAC, box 17, folder 7.

39. Business card "Copyright 1973," AAC, box 89, folder 6.

40. "From the world of . . . Saturn Records." AAC, box 18, folder 10.

41. AAC, box 17, folder 7.

42. Sun Ra, "the end," in Corbett, *The Wisdom of Sun Ra*, 141.

43. The flyer promotes the Arkestra's LP *Jazz in Silhouette*. AAC, box 15, folder 6 (1 of 2).

44. A gifted graphic artist, Dangerfield designed much of El Saturn's early printed matter, but little is known of his later activities. His work appears beautifully reproduced in Corbett, Elms, and Kapsalis, *Traveling the Spaceways*. For a discussion of black graphic designers contemporary with Dangerfield, see Victor Margolin, "El Saturn Records and Black Designers in Chicago," in Corbett, Elms, and Kapsalis, *Traveling the Spaceways*, 45–52.

45. Liner notes, Sun Ra, *Super-Sonic Jazz.*

46. Ibid.

47. AAC, box 16, folder 3.

48. Szwed, *Space Is the Place*, 273.

49. Ibid.

50. Sites, "Radical Culture in Black Necropolis," 703.

51. "You never knew what you'd get paid," said Vertamae Grosvenor, one of the "ethnic voices" in the later Arkestra. "$5, $15. But you always got something." Qtd. in Szwed, *Space Is the Place*, 118.

52. AAC, box 18, folder 18.

53. AAC, box 19, folder 9.

54. AAC, box 18, folder 18.

55. Ibid.

56. AAC, box 19, folder 3.

57. AAC, box 23, folder 6.

58. AAC, box 18, folder 7.

59. Corbett, "Obscure Past, Bright Future: Saturn Records in Silhouette," in Corbett, Elms, and Kapsalis, *Traveling the Spaceways*, 42.

60. Transcribed from a draft of the letter in Abraham's hand, AAC, box 17, folder 7. A facsimile of the typed letter appears in Corbett, Elms, and Kapsalis, *Pathways to Unknown Worlds*, 127.

61. Ibid.

62. Reproductions of these tickets appear in this book as well as Corbett, Elms, and Kapsalis, *Pathways to Unknown Worlds*, 82.

63. Small promotional poster, AAC, box 25, folder 5.

64. Liner notes, Sun Ra, *Super-Sonic Jazz*.

65. Corbett relates this tale of healing in Corbett, Elms, and Kapsalis, *Traveling the Spaceways*, 41.

CHAPTER 10: ISOTOPE TELEPORTATION

1. Bilandic blamed the formidable blizzard—or perhaps the inability to get the streets quickly plowed—for his loss to Jane Byrne in the 1979 Democratic mayoral primary.

2. Internet sources provide the readiest information about the history of the Chicago "L." See in particular Pacyga, *Chicago: A Biography*, 219, 237; "Histories and Chronologies," Chicago-l.org, www.chicago-l.org; and Ronald Dale Karr, "Rapid Transit System," in *Encyclopedia of Chicago*, ed. Janice L. Reiff, Ann Durkin Keating, and James R. Grossman (Chicago: Chicago Historical Society, 2005), www.encyclopedia.chicagohistory.org/pages/1042.html. For a gorgeous gallery of early images, see "Early Years of Chicago's 'L,'" *Chicago Tribune*, December 6, 2013, http://galleries.apps.chicagotribune.com/chi-131205 -early-years-chicago-elevated-train-pictures/.

3. Qtd. in "Original 'L' Companies," Chicago-l.org, www.chicago-l.org/ history/4line.html.

4. "The CTA Takes Over: Resurrection through Modernization (1947– 1970)," Chicago-l.org, www.chicago-l.org/history/CTA2.html.

5. Kevin Whitehead, "Sun Ra's Chicago Music: El is a Sound of Joy," in Corbett, Elms, and Kapsalis, *Traveling the Spaceways*, 24.

6. On the slave ship as technology of terror, see Marcus Rediker, *The Slave Ship: A Human History* (New York: Viking, 2007).

7. Ibid., 311.

8. Rick Theis, "Fallen Angel," interview with Sun Ra, *Semiotext(e)* 12 (1984), http://semiotexte.com/?p=680.

9. Sun Ra and His Myth Science Arkestra, *Interstellar Low Ways*, Evidence 22039, 1993, CD; original release (titled *Rocket Number Nine Take Off for the Planet Venus*), Saturn SR 9945-2-M/N, 1966, LP.

10. I owe this insight to conversation with my dear friend C. S. Giscombe.

CHAPTER 11: CRY OF JAZZ

1. Campbell, Trent, and Pruter describe many of these clubs in detail in "From Sonny Blount to Sun Ra."

2. Wilbur Green played electric bass with the Arkestra until May 1956, helping to create what Campbell, Trent, and Pruter describe as a "highly distinctive ensemble sound." Sproles joined the band in the fall of 1956, as did Cochran. See Campbell, Trent, and Pruter, "From Sonny Blount to Sun Ra."

3. This material would not appear until 1967, when it was released on the Delmark label.

4. Campbell, Trent, and Pruter, "From Sonny Blount to Sun Ra."

5. Shot in black and white and thirty-four minutes long, *The Cry of Jazz* would take several years to complete. It was released on April 3, 1959, although a note appeared in the *Chicago Defender* announcing an October 1958 date; see Campbell, Trent, and Pruter, "From Sonny Blount to Sun Ra."

6. The tunes Bland used, all previously recorded, were "Call for All Demons," "Urnack," "Super Blonde," "Blues at Midnight," and "Demon's Lullaby" (Campbell, Trent, and Pruter, "From Sonny Blount to Sun Ra"). For a draft copy of a permission agreement, see AAC, box 16, folder 8 (1 of 2).

7. Campbell, Trent, and Pruter, "From Sonny Blount to Sun Ra." Interestingly, the draft contract between KHTB Productions and Enterplan Publishing Company, to have been signed by Alton Abraham, Herman S. Blount, and Edward O. Bland, stipulates that KHTB Productions was "to give credits [. . .] to the writers and only the particular writers, Le Sun Ra and Julian Priester, of the said musical compositions," namely "Blues at Midnight," "Demon's Lullaby," "Urnack," "Super Blonde," and "Call for all Demons." The contract was never signed; see AAC, box 16, folder 8 (1 of 2).

8. Bland's film provides the sole glimpse of the early Arkestra in action, as Campbell, Trent, and Pruter note: "*The Cry of Jazz* contains the only film footage of the band from the Chicago period: scenes of the Arkestra filmed at 5 or 6 club gigs between 1956 and 1958" ("From Sonny Blount to Sun Ra"). Because the recordings were made *before* the film, musicians in the footage do not sync with the music they appear to play. The effect is a luscious montage of the Arkestra's

members and sounds. Music composed and played by Paul Severson and Eddie Higgins also appears in the film. See Campbell, Trent, and Pruter, "From Sonny Blount to Sun Ra," for a scrupulous accounting of soundtrack and credits.

9. The musician and composer Paul Severson appears on a number of Chicago recordings from the mid-1950s, some with Eddie Higgins. Severson played trumpet, trombone, and keyboards (Campbell, Trent, and Pruter, "From Sonny Blount to Sun Ra").

10. For jazz musicians, a "chorus" signifies one complete set of a song's chords (as "verse" does for sung music), barring intros or endings. A chorus provides the basic unit for improvising over a song form.

11. *The Cry of Jazz*, dir. Edward Bland (Chicago: KHTB Productions, 1959). All quotations transcribed directly from the film.

12. See *Sun Ra Research* 25 (October 1999), back cover.

13. Miles Davis, *Kind of Blue*, Columbia CK 40579, 1986, CD; original release, Columbia CS 8136, 1959, LP. Ornette Coleman, *The Shape of Jazz to Come*, Atlantic 1317-2, 1990, CD; original release, Atlantic SD 1317, 1959, LP. John Coltrane, *Giant Steps*, Atlantic 1311-2, 1987, CD; original release, Atlantic 1311, 1959, LP. Sun Ra, *Jazz in Silhouette*, Evidence 22012-2, 1991, CD; original release, Saturn K70P3590/K70P3591 (quoted phrase from liner notes).

14. John Corbett, "Obscure Past, Bright Future," in Corbett, Elms, and Kapsalis, *Traveling the Spaceways*, 42. A more mundane explication of the name appears on several copies of an American Federation of Musicians contract for a job at the Sutherland Lounge signed on June 13, 1959, about the time Sun Ra was working on *Jazz in Silhouette*. Tantalizingly, the lines for "Employer" read "Gay Silhouettes" followed by "Clarice Pollard." Could the LP's evocative title contain a biographical reference? See AAC, box 16, folder 8 (2 of 2).

15. Jacket copy, Sun Ra, *Jazz in Silhouette*.

16. Ibid.

17. Ibid.

CHAPTER 12: SPUTNIK

1. Campbell, Trent, and Pruter, "From Sonny Blount to Sun Ra."

2. Recordings of the Cosmic Rays appear on Sun Ra, *Spaceship Lullaby*. The rehearsal recording of the Crystals singing "Little Sally Walker" is included on *The Second Stop is Jupiter*. This group should not be confused with the much more successful all-female New York quartet of the same name famous in the sixties.

3. Qtd. in Szwed, *Space Is the Place*, 179.

4. See George Adamski and Desmond Lee, *Flying Saucers Have Landed* (London: Werner Laurie, 1953). A letter in the Alton Abraham Collection, signed by

one Charlotte Blob (the publisher, apparently, of *The Cosmic Newsletter*), indicates that Abraham was in the audience when Adamski spoke in Chicago in September 1964 (AAC, box 18, folder 12).

5. AAC, box 14, folder 4. Bryant writes in cursive on blank paper and illustrates his sighting with a formation of five dots. The two lights from the south seem to propagate waves.

6. AAC, box 44, folder 3.

7. Campbell, Trent, and Pruter ("From Sonny Blount to Sun Ra") suggest that "Adventur in Space" might originally have been titled "Journey in Discland," a possibility that shows Sun Ra turning his music willfully toward themes of space. This track can be heard on Sun Ra, *The Singles*; the others, on Anderson, *Sun Ra: The Eternal Myth Revealed*, disc 12.

8. Harry Harper, *Dawn of the Space Age* (London: Sampson Low, 1946). The phrase first appeared as the title of an article written by Harper and featured on the cover of the British magazine *Everybody's Weekly* (January 19, 1946). Harper predicted that in the future, humans would "penetrate the stratosphere and conquer outer space" (8–9).

9. Qtd. in Szwed, *Space Is the Place*, 173.

10. Back cover liner notes (LP), Sun Ra, *Super-Sonic Jazz*, AAC, box 81.

11. Ibid. The Evidence compact disc of *Super-Sonic Jazz* reprints both poems on its liner, as well as images of both covers, but not the listening instructions. See liner notes, Sun Ra, *Super-Sonic Jazz*.

12. Ibid.

13. Ibid. In an interview, Marshall Allen reports that Sun Ra had fully arrived at his understanding of space music by the time the Arkestra made its first recording for the Transition label, "but he had to develop the musicians. To the concept of something different." See "It Makes You Booomph! Marshall Allen Interviewed by Edwin Pouncy," *Sun Ra Arkive* 1 (December 2002), 8, www.the-temple.net/astroblack/sunraarkive/issue1/sra1p_8.html.

14. Liner notes, Sun Ra, *Super-Sonic Jazz*.

15. Ibid. Recall the following from "what must negroes do to be saved": "REALITY CAN BECOME REAL ONLY IF APPROACHED FROM THE POINT OF CULTURE AND ART," in Corbett, *The Wisdom of Sun Ra*, 128.

16. Liner notes, Sun Ra, *Super-Sonic Jazz*.

17. Ibid.

18. Bruce Cameron Reed, *The History and Science of the Manhattan Project* (New York: Springer, 2013), 179.

19. J. G. Ballard, "Introduction to the French Edition," *Crash* (1973; repr., New York: Vintage, 1985), 3.

20. The best history of these issues remains Walter A. McDougall, *The Heavens and the Earth: A Political History of the Space Age* (New York: Basic Books, 1985). See also William E. Burrows, *This New Ocean: The Story of the First Space Age* (New York: Random House, 1998); Everett C. Dolman, *Astropolitik: Classical Geopolitics in the Space Age* (New York: Routledge, 2001); and Howard E. McCurdy, *Space and the American Imagination* (Baltimore, MD: Johns Hopkins University Press, 2011).

21. On the problem of creating a space free for technological exploitation, see McDougall, *The Heavens and the Earth*, especially chapter 4, "While Waiting for Technocracy: The ICBM and the First American Space Program," 97–111.

22. For a brief description of the aims and outcomes of the International Geophysical Year (IGY), see ibid., 59–62. The IGY occurred over a span of months during which the Arkestra was refining its sound toward making its first El Saturn LP.

23. See ibid., 132–140.

24. President's Science Advisory Committee, *Introduction to Outer Space* (Washington, DC: GPO, 1958), n.p., www.fas.org/spp/guide/usa/intro1958.html.

25. Ibid., 1. *Star Trek* garbles Ike's sloganeering with its masculinized "where no man has gone before."

26. National Security Council Planning Board, "Preliminary U.S. Policy on Outer Space," (NSC 5814/1), June 20, 1958, 4, http://marshall.wpengine.com/wp-content/uploads/2013/09/NSC-5814-Preliminary-U.S.-Policy-on-Outer-Space-18-Aug-1958.pdf.

27. McDougall, *The Heavens and the Earth*, 186.

28. Ibid., 180.

29. Qtd. in ibid., 172.

30. Qtd. in National Aeronautics and Space Council, "Draft Statement of U.S. Policy on Outer Space," (NSC 5918/1), December 17, 1959, 8, http://marshall.wpengine.com/wp-content/uploads/2013/09/NSC-5918-1-U.S.-Policy-on-Outer-Space-26-Jan-1960.pdf.

31. McDougall, *The Heavens and the Earth*, 157.

32. Szwed, *Space Is the Place*, 236.

33. These figures appear at "United States Federal, State, and Local Government Spending Fiscal Year 1957," usgovernmentspending.com, www.usgovernmentspending.com/year_spending_1957USbf_15bs2n#usgs302.

34. Hinds and Hinds, conversation with Sun Ra and Charles Blass, 1.

35. Szwed, *Space Is the Place*, 140.

36. Qtd. in ibid., 382.

CHAPTER 13: ROCKETRY

1. Campbell, Trent, and Pruter, "From Sonny Blount to Sun Ra."

2. Szwed, *Space Is the Place*, 179.

3. Ibid., 180.

4. Campbell, Trent, and Pruter, "From Sonny Blount to Sun Ra."

5. The release of "recently discovered" live Arkestra recordings is something of an industry unto itself and seems unlikely ever to run out of material. Early examples include Sun Ra, *Music From Tomorrow's World*; material released on Anderson, *Sun Ra: The Eternal Myth Revealed*; the additional tunes included on ESP's two-disc rerelease of Sun Ra, *Nothing Is*, ESP-Disk' 4060, 2010, CD (original release, ESP-Disk' 1045, 1969, LP, from a college tour recorded in 1964); and the "Lost Reels" series of recordings issued by Transparency, largely if illegally culled from later performances.

6. Tunes from the Elks hall session with space-type titles include "Space Mates," "Lights on a Satellite," "Space Loneliness," "Somewhere in Space," "Interplanetary Music," and "Rocket Number Nine Take Off for the Planet Venus." The batch of compositions copyrighted together as "Space Loneliness: A Sound Concerto" include "Space Loneliness," "Lights on a Satellite," "Fate in a Pleasant Mood," and "State Street" (Campbell, Trent, and Pruter, "From Sonny Blount to Sun Ra").

7. Corbett, Elms, and Kapsalis, *Traveling the Spaceways*, 41.

8. Qtd. in McDougall, *The Heavens and the Earth*, 303.

9. Ibid., 202.

10. Qtd. in ibid., 303.

11. Ibid., 381.

12. For a thorough and incisive discussion of systems engineering and the emergence of technocracy during the Space Age, see Nicholas de Monchaux, *Spacesuit: Fashioning Apollo* (Cambridge, MA: MIT Press, 2012), esp. 45–50.

13. McDougall, *The Heavens and the Earth*, 382.

14. Ibid., 383, 382.

15. *The Magic Sun*, dir. Phill Niblock (Experimental Intermedia, 1966; rerelease, Atavistic DJ-861, 2005, DVD).

16. Qtd. in Szwed, *Space Is the Place*, 173.

17. See de Monchaux, *Spacesuit*, 327–342.

18. Qtd. in Szwed, *Space Is the Place*, 174.

19. Ibid.

CHAPTER 14: TOMORROWLAND

1. For a mesmerizing tour through those images and icons, see Steve Holland and Alex Summersby, *Sci-Fi Art: A Graphic History* (New York: HarperCollins, 2009); and Forrest J. Ackerman and Brad Linaweaver, *Worlds of Tomorrow: The Amazing Universe of Science Fiction Art* (Portland, OR: Collectors, 2004).

2. Megan Prelinger, *Another Science Fiction: Advertising the Space Race 1957–1962* (New York: Blast Books, 2010), 15.

3. For an exhaustive reckoning, see Bill Warren, *Keep Watching the Skies! American Science Fiction Movies of the Fifties, the 21st Century Edition* (Jefferson, NC: McFarland, 2010). Examples of the visual images that promotional material for such movies circulated can be seen at Cinemacom.com: "80 Great Posters of Not So Great and Even Worse Sci-Fi Movies 1950–1965," www.cinema com.com/50s-sci-fi-REST.html. Adilifu Nama approaches science fiction film from a black perspective in "R Is for Race, Not Rocket: Black Representation in American Science Fiction Cinema," *Quarterly Review of Film and Video* 26, no. 2 (2009): 155–166.

4. Information about fifties and sixties science fiction television abounds on the Internet, for instance, at the IMDb site; see "Sci-Fi Television in the 1950s," www.imdb.com/list/ls000097346/. The definitive bibliographic reference (an exhaustive work of fan scholarship) remains Alan Morton's *The Complete Directory to Science Fiction, Fantasy and Horror Television Series: A Comprehensive Guide to the First 50 Years, 1946–1996* (Peoria, IL: Other Worlds, 1997).

5. McDougall, *The Heavens and the Earth*, 100.

6. For a joyous romp through the nostalgic world of early science fiction toys and games, see S. Mark Young, Steve Duin, and Mike Richardson, *Blast Off! Rockets, Robots, Ray Guns and Rarities from the Golden Age of Space Toys* (New York: Dark Horse Comics, 2001).

7. Mike was less a conventional bomb than an apparatus containing the material that produced the first successful thermonuclear explosion. For a compilation of strangely beautiful and chilling images of atomic and thermonuclear explosions, see Michael Light, *100 Suns, 1945–1962* (New York: Knopf, 2003).

8. The *Collier's* series, edited by Cornelius Ryan, ran from 1952 to 1954 and included articles by a pantheon of rocket scientists including Willy Ley, Fred Lawrence Whipple, Joseph Kaplan, and Heinz Haber. The first three articles were visionary advertisements for an American space program: "Man Will Conquer Space Soon," "Man on the Moon," and "More about Man on the Moon." The *Collier's* articles became the basis for Walt Disney's series of *Disneyland* television episodes entitled "Man in Space," "Man in the Moon," and "Mars and Beyond."

9. Cornelius Ryan, ed., "Man Will Conquer Space Soon: What Are We Waiting For?," *Collier's*, March 22, 1952, 23.

10. Ibid.

11. Ibid.

12. *Spaceways*, dir. Terence Fisher (Hammer Film Productions, 1953; rerelease, Image Entertainment, 2012, DVD).

13. Ibid. This and the following quotations are transcribed from the film.

14. "Man in Space," *Disneyland* television program, March 9, 1955. Portions are available on YouTube. This and the following quotations are transcribed from the program.

15. Such "facts" include a questionable account of the first military use of rockets, which may have occurred at a battle at the Chinese city of "Kai Fun Foo" (Kai-fung-fu).

16. *The Day the Earth Stood Still*, directed by Robert Wise (20th Century Fox, 1951; rerelease, 20th Century Fox, 2003, DVD). This and the following quotation are transcribed from the film.

17. H. L. Gold, "For Adults Only," *Galaxy Science Fiction*, October 1950, 3.

CHAPTER 15: INTERPLANETARY EXOTICA

1. *Forbidden Planet*, directed by Fred M. Wilcox (Metro-Goldwyn-Mayer, 1956; rerelease, Warner Home Video, 2010, DVD.).

2. Harry Revel, Leslie Baxter, and Dr. Samuel J. Hoffman, *Music out of the Moon: Music Unusual Featuring the Theremin*, Request Records RR 231-1, 1995, CD; original release, Capitol H2000, 1950, LP.

3. Qtd. in Szwed, *Space Is the Place*, 98.

4. Les Baxter, *Ritual of the Savage (Le Sacre du Sauvage)*, Rev-Ola CR REV 171, 2006, CD; original release, Capitol T-228, 1951, ten-inch LP. The original recording appeared under the French title with the English in parentheses.

5. As can be heard on Martin Denny, *Exotica*, Rev-Ola CR REV 101, 2005, CD; original release, Liberty LRP 3034, 1957, LP.

6. Francesco Adinolfi, *Mondo Exotica: Sounds, Visions, Obsessions of the Cocktail Generation* (Durham, NC: Duke University Press, 2008), 123.

7. Attilio Mineo, *Man in Space with Sounds*, Subliminal Sounds SUBCD 4, 2011, CD; original release, World's Fair Records, LP-55555, 1962, LP.

8. Liner notes, Arthur Ferrante and Louis Teicher, *Soundproof: The Sound of Tomorrow Today!*, El Records ACMEM 124CD, 2012, CD; original release, Westminster WP 6014, 1956, LP.

9. Ferrante and Teicher recorded *Soundproof* before the advent of echo machines and digital reverb effects. The record's title refers to their need to soundproof the studio in which it was made in order to maximize the sonic profile of the technologies and materials used in the process. According to their personal manager, Scott W. Smith, Ferrante and Teicher created the thick reverb that suffuses their pianos by "sending the sound by wire to the floor below's tile bathroom . . . to speakers inside. Then mics were placed outside the bathroom door . . . [and] looped to a delay and sent back upstairs to the mix room!! Echo 'chambers' were not yet invented!" See M. Schott, "The Album Cover Art Gallery," Tralfaz Archives, www.tralfaz-archives.com/coverart/F/Ferrante/ferrante_soundproof.html.

10. Adinolfi, *Mondo Exotica*, 156.

11. Liner notes, Pete Rugolo, *Music from Out of Space*, Mercury SR 60118, 1959, LP.

12. Ibid.

13. Martin Denny, *Primitiva*, Rev-Ola CR REV 103, 2005, CD; original release, Liberty LRP 3087, 1958, LP.

14. Esquivel and His Orchestra, *Other Worlds, Other Sounds*, RCA Victor 74321 35747 2, 1996, CD; original release, RCA Victor LSP-1753, 1958, LP.

15. Qtd. in Adinolfi, *Mondo Exotica*, 152.

16. Esquivel and His Orchestra, *Exploring New Sounds in Hi-Fi Stereo*, RCA Victor 74321 47871 2, 1997, CD; original release, RCA Victor, LPM-1978, 1958, LP. The Ondioline was an electronic keyboard instrument designed and manufactured in France by Georges Jenny. Capable of a rich palette of sounds, it was a vacuum-tube precursor to the synthesizer.

17. Les Baxter, *Space Escapade*, El Records ACMEM 171CD, 2009, CD; original release, Capitol T-968, 1958, LP.

18. Ibid., liner notes.

19. Russ Garcia, *Fantastica*, Liberty T-7005, 1958, LP.

20. Ibid.

21. Richard Marino, *Out of this World*, Liberty LMM 13007, 1961, LP, cover copy.

22. Marty Manning, *The Twilight Zone*, Columbia CL 1586, 1961, LP, cover copy.

23. Frank Comstock, *Project Comstock: Music from Outer Space*, Warner Brothers WS 1463, 1962, LP, cover copy.

24. Adinolfi, *Mondo Exotica*, 146.

25. Betty Carter, *Out There with Betty Carter*, Blue Moon BMCD 1622, 2005, CD; original release, Peacock PLP 90, 1958, LP.

26. Duke Ellington, "The Race for Space," in *The Duke Ellington Reader*, ed. Mark Tucker (Oxford: Oxford University Press, 1996), 296.

27. Sam Lazar, *Space Flight*, Universal Victor MVCJ-19120, 1998, CD; original Argo LP-4002, 1960, LP.

28. Grant Green, *Born to Be Blue*, Blue Note CPD 7 84432 2, 1989, CD; original release, Blue Note BST 84432, 1985 (recorded 1962), LP. Lou Donaldson, *The Natural Soul*, Blue Note CDP 7 84108 2, 1989, CD; original release, Blue Note BLP 4108, 1962, LP.

29. John Coltrane, *Sun Ship*, Impulse! AS 9211, 1995, CD; original release, Impulse! AS-9211, 1971, LP.

30. George Russell, *Jazz in the Space Age*, American Jazz Classics 99024, 2011, CD; original release, Decca DL 9219, 1960, LP.

31. Corbett, "Obscure Past, Bright Future," in Corbett, Elms, and Kapsalis, *Traveling the Spaceways*, 38. The description of those flying nymphets comes from the record jacket.

32. Sun Ra, "[I always called myself Sun Ra]," In *The Immeasurable Equation*, 457.

33. Sun Ra, "In This Age," in *The Immeasurable Equation*, 465.

CHAPTER 16: SPACE MUSIC

1. Sun Ra, *Interstellar Low Ways*, cover copy.

2. Tom Buchler, "The Making of Lanquidity," *Sun Ra Arkive* 2 (2003): 34, www.the-temple.net/astroblack/sunraarkive/issue2/sra2p_34.html.

3. Rycenga, interview with Sun Ra, November 2, 1988, part one, 5.

4. "A Treatise on Rebirth and the Law of Consequence," 8, AAC, box 15, folder 9.

5. Ibid. I have made light editorial emendations.

6. Szwed, *Space Is the Place*, 111.

7. Qtd. in ibid., 258–259.

8. Qtd. in ibid., 298.

9. Qtd. from a note in Abraham's hand describing the musicians with Sun Ra "from the beginning," AAC, box 14, folder 1.

10. "Interview with Sun Ra Pt. 2," AAC, box 13, folder 9.

11. Sun Ra, "[I always called myself Sun Ra]," in *The Immeasurable Equation*, 457.

12. Ibid.

13. Sun Ra, *Sun Song*, liner notes.

14. Sun Ra, "[I am not of this planet]," in *The Immeasurable Equation*, 460.

15. See Szwed, *Space Is the Place*, 183–195.

16. Ibid., 194.

17. Ibid.

18. For a discussion of the relationship between free jazz and the Black Arts Movement, see Lorenzo Thomas, "Ascension: Music and the Black Arts Movement," in *Jazz among the Discourses*, ed. Krin Gabbard (Durham, NC: Duke University Press, 1995), 256–273.

19. Szwed, *Space Is the Place*, 190.

20. Ibid., 191.

21. Ibid., 187.

22. Ibid.

23. Sun Ra, *Sun Ra Visits Planet Earth*, Evidence 22039, 1992, CD; original release, Saturn 9956-11-A/B, 1966 LP.

24. Sun Ra, *Sound Sun Pleasure!!*, Evidence 22014, 1992, CD; original release, Saturn 512, 1966 LP.

25. Sun Ra, *Nubians of Plutonia*, Evidence 22066, 1993, CD; originally released as Sun Ra, *Lady with the Golden Stockings*, Saturn SR 9956-11E/F, 1966, LP.

26. Sun Ra, *We Travel the Space Ways*, Evidence 22038, 1992, CD; original release, Saturn HK 5445, 1966, LP. Sun Ra, *Fate in a Pleasant Mood*, Evidence 22068, 1993, CD; original release, Saturn 9956-2-A/B, 1965, LP. Readers curious about chronology should consult Robert L. Campbell and Christopher Trent's meticulous discography, *The Earthly Recordings of Sun Ra*.

27. Qtd. in Szwed, *Space Is the Place*, 338.

28. Writing in the *Chicago Daily News* on February 20, 1962, Tony Weitzel memorably describes the Arkestra's New York landing: "Chicago's Le Sun Ra took his Cosmic Space Jazz Group to New York and spooked the critics into a tizzy. (His stuff sounds like a Chinese opera in an earthquake)." AAC, box 132, folder 2.

29. Sun Ra, *The Futuristic Sounds of Sun Ra*, Savoy Jazz SVY 17259, 2003, CD; original release, Savoy MG12169, 1961, LP. Sun Ra, *Bad and Beautiful*, Evidence 22038, 1992, CD; original release, Saturn 532, 1972, LP.

30. This draft appears in a notebook that also contains many equations, poems, doodles, drawings, phone numbers, and other miscellanea, all in Sun Ra's hand; see AAC, box 13, folder 9.

31. R. Cargill Hall, *Lunar Impact: The NASA History of Project Ranger* (1977; repr., Mineola, NY: Dover, 2010), 256–270.

32. Sun Ra, *Secrets of the Sun*, Atavistic ALP266CD, 2008, CD; original Saturn GH 9954 E/F, 1965, LP. Sun Ra, *Art Forms of Dimensions Tomorrow*, Evidence 22036, 1992, CD; original release, Saturn 9956, 1965, LP.

33. Sun Ra, *When Sun Comes Out*, Evidence 22068, 1993, CD; original release, Saturn 2066, 1963, LP. Sun Ra, *The Invisible Shield*, Black Lion CD 877640-2 (titled *Janus*), 2000, CD; original Saturn 529, 1974, LP.

34. Sun Ra, *When Angels Speak of Love*, Evidence 22216-2, 2000, CD; original release, Saturn 1966, 1966, LP. Sun Ra, *Cosmic Tones for Mental Therapy*, Evidence 22036, 1992, CD; original release, Saturn 408, 1967 LP.

35. Sun Ra, *Sun Ra Featuring Pharoah Sanders and Black Harold*, ESP-Disk' 4054, 2009, CD; original release, ESP-Disk' 4054, 1974, LP.

36. Sun Ra, *Heliocentric Worlds of Sun Ra, Volume 1*, ESP-Disk' 1014-2, 1992, CD; original release, ESP-Disk' 1014, 1965, LP. Sun Ra, *Heliocentric Worlds of Sun Ra, Volume 2*, ESP Disk' 1017-2, 1993, CD; original release, ESP-Disk' 1017, 1966, LP. Sun Ra, *The Magic City*, Evidence 22069, 1993, CD; original release, Saturn LPB 711, 1966, LP.

37. Sun Ra, *Strange Strings*, Atavistic ALP263CD, 2007, CD; original release, Thoth Intergalactic KH-5472, 1967, LP. Sun Ra, *Outer Spaceways Incorporated*, 3 discs, Freedom CD 740147 (titled *Spaceways*), 1998, CDs; original release, Saturn 143000A/B, 1974, LP. Sun Ra, *Nothing Is*.

38. This accounting of Sun Ra's 1960s output is by no means complete. See Campbell and Trent, *The Earthly Recordings of Sun Ra*, for full details.

39. Qtd. in Tam Fiofori, "Sun Ra's Space Odyssey," *Down Beat* 37, May 1970, 14.

40. Bill Mathieu, "*Other Planes of There* & *Sun Ra and his Solar Arkestra Visit Planet Earth*," *Down Beat*, June 1966, 32. Archived at AAC, box 4, folder 9.

41. Sun Ra, "[I always called myself Sun Ra]," 457.

42. Qtd. in Fiofori, "Sun Ra's Space Odyssey," 14.

43. John L. Wasserman, "Sun Ra—A Man for the Space Age," *Sun Ra Research* 2 (July 1995): 9.

44. Sun Ra, *Angels and Demons at Play*, Evidence 22066, 1993, CD; original release, Saturn SR 9956-2-O/P, 1965, LP.

45. I'm describing "Reflects Motion" as originally released on Saturn and reissued by Atavistic. The original take was longer on both ends, making for a variety of available versions.

46. Fred Moten, *In the Break: The Aesthetics of the Black Radical Tradition* (Minneapolis: University of Minnesota Press, 2003), 89.

47. The quote is Sun Ra's response to the drunken question, "What's happenin'?" in the film *Space Is the Place*, directed by John Coney (North American Star Systems, 1974; rerelease, Plexifilms, 2003, DVD).

48. Sun Ra, "[I always called myself Sun Ra]," 458.

49. Qtd. in Szwed, *Space Is the Place*, 216.

50. Hinds and Hinds, conversation with Sun Ra, October 13, 1984, 4.

51. Szwed describes the "space chord" as "a collectively improvised tone cluster at high volume" that creates "a new mood, opening up fresh tonal areas" (*Space Is the Place*, 214).

52. Carnegie Hall Concert Program, AAC, box 22, folder 5.

53. *The Forbidden Playground*, directed by Maxine Haleff, 1968. Szwed describes the Carnegie Hall performances in *Space Is the Place*, 253–254.

54. Carnegie Hall Concert Program, AAC, box 22, folder 5.

CHAPTER 17: MYTH-SCIENCE

1. Sun Ra modified the Arkestra's name at whim, apparently to suit circumstances, mood, and agenda. Szwed (*Space Is the Place*, 95) counts over fifty different versions. Among my favorite are a few he doesn't mention: Sun Ra and the Intergalactic Jet Set Bible Belt Smasher Omniverse Infinity Arkestra, Sun Ra and his American Destiny-Changing Arkestra, and Sun Ra and his Outer Space Love Adventure Jet Set Arkestra. See Campbell and Trent, *The Earthly Recordings of Sun Ra*, for the full panoply.

2. Sun Ra, *Secrets of the Sun*; Sun Ra, *Art Forms of Dimensions Tomorrow*; Sun Ra, *Strange Strings*.

3. Sun Ra, *Cosmic Tones for Mental Therapy*. This title refers to an incident, corroborated by an entry in one of Abraham's notebooks, that took place during an Arkestra gig at a mental hospital. Here's Szwed: "While [the band was] playing, a woman who it was said had not moved or spoken for years got up from the floor, walked directly to [Sun Ra's] piano, and cried out, 'Do you call that *music*?' Sonny was delighted with her response, and told the story for years afterwards as evidence of the healing powers of music" (*Space Is the Place*, 92).

4. A few of the El Saturn LPs that bear this blurb on the back cover include the following: Sun Ra, *Atlantis*, Evidence 22067, 1993, CD; original release, Saturn ESR 507, 1969, LP. Sun Ra, *Continuation*, Corbett vs. Dempsey CvsD CD009, 2013, CD; original release, Saturn 520, 1970, LP. Sun Ra, *My Brother the Wind*, Saturn 521, 1970, LP. Sun Ra, *Discipline 27-II*, Saturn 538, 1973, quadraphonic LP. Sun Ra, *Soul Vibrations of Man*.

5. Sun Ra, "The Air Spiritual Man," in *The Immeasurable Equation*, 451.

6. Sun Ra, "Of Notness," in *The Immeasurable Equation*, 268.

7. Sun Ra, "Music of the Spheres," in *The Immeasurable Equation*, 243.

8. Ibid.

9. Sun Ra, "Black Prince Charming," in *The Immeasurable Equation*, 82.

10. Sun Ra, "The Air Spiritual Man," 451.

11. Ibid., 450.

12. Ibid, 451.

13. "Afrofuturism" is a lively contemporary cultural movement that crosses blackness with visions of the future, especially as imagined through new technologies and new media. The cultural critic Mark Dery coined the term in *Flame Wars* (Durham, NC: Duke University Press, 1993), 180. The term appears there in "Black to the Future," an interview that he conducted with Samuel Delaney, Greg Tate, and Tricia Rose. Alondra Nelson established a website devoted to Afrofuturism and gave the term academic credibility in "Afrofuturism," ed. Nelson, special issue, *Social Text* 20, no. 2 (2002), which was devoted to the subject. See also Kodwo Eshun, "Further Considerations on Afrofuturism," *New Centennial Review* 3, no. 2 (2003): 287–302. Signaling the movement's currency, Ytasha L. Womack published a book entitled *Afrofuturism: The World of Black Sci-Fi and Fantasy Culture* (Chicago: Chicago Review Press, 2013). The gamut of musical Afrofuturism runs from the space funk of Parliament/Funkadelic and the hip-hop futurism of Deltron 3030 to the deep house of Hieroglyphic Being or the electronica of Ras G to the more recent pop outings of Janelle Monáe. See chapter 21 of this book, "Continuation."

14. Sun Ra, "The Visitation," in *The Immeasurable Equation*, 414.

15. Qtd. in Szwed, *Space Is the Place*, 332.

16. Sun Ra, "The Outer Darkness (1972, version 1)," in *The Immeasurable Equation*, 294.

17. Sun Ra, "The Outer Darkness (1972, version 2)," in *The Immeasurable Equation*, 295.

18. Ibid.

19. Ibid.

20. Sun Ra, "Astro Black," in *The Immeasurable Equation*, 74. The poem is sung on Sun Ra, *Astro Black*, Impulse! AS-9255, 1973, quadraphonic LP.

21. Sun Ra, "Message to Black Youth" (1971), in *The Immeasurable Equation*, 240.

22. Ibid.

23. Ibid.

24. Ibid., 241.

25. Sun Ra, "The Black Rays Race," in *The Immeasurable Equation*, 83.

26. Sun Ra, "[I always called myself Sun Ra]," in *The Immeasurable Equation*, 458.

27. Sun Ra, "My Music is Words," in *The Immeasurable Equation*, 467.

28. Ibid., 468.

29. Deborah Ray, interview with Sun Ra, *American Black Journal*, Detroit Public Television, 1981, available online at http://abj.matrix.msu.edu/video full.php?id=29-DF-13.

30. Peter Hinds, conversation with Sun Ra, December 11, 1989, *Sun Ra Research* 32 (February 2001): 19.

31. Qtd. in Szwed, *Space Is the Place*, 298.

32. Ibid., 256.

33. Brent Hayes Edwards, "The Race for Space: Sun Ra's Poetry," in *The Immeasurable Equation*, 32.

34. Qtd. in Szwed, *Space Is the Place*, 316.

35. Draft for articles of incorporation, Saturn "II" Research, AAC, box 17, folder 7. A facsimile of this draft appears in Corbett, Elms, and Kapsakis, *Pathways to Unknown Worlds*, 98.

36. Sun Ra, *My Brother the Wind, Volume II*, Evidence 22040, 1992, CD; original release, Saturn 523, 1971, LP.

37. Sun Ra, "The Air Spiritual Man," 328.

38. Qtd. in Szwed, *Space Is the Place*, 315.

39. Sun Ra, "Happy Space Age To You," *Esquire: The Magazine for Men*, July 1969, 5.

CHAPTER 18: BLACK MAN IN THE COSMOS

1. Szwed, *Space Is the Place*, 266. Receipts from a rent book covering the years 1969 through 1972 show "Mr. Sun Ra" paying ninety dollars a month in rent to Mrs. Henrietta Allen (AAC, box 15, folder 6). Sun Ra's Philadelphia years deserve much fuller treatment than this or most other studies provide. One happy exception is chapter 14 ("Sun Ra: Composer from Saturn") in Randall Grass, *Great Spirits: Portraits of Life-Changing World Music Artists* (Jackson: University Press of Mississippi, 2009), 31–60.

2. Peter Hinds, conversation with Tommy Hunter, April 13, 1998, *Sun Ra Research* 33 (April 2001): 44–45.

3. The success of Jimi Hendrix helped Miles see the possibilities in performing for large venues. See Miles Davis with Quincy Trope, *Miles: The Autobiography* (New York: Touchstone, 1989), 291–310.

4. John Sinclair, "Self-Determination Music," *Jazz and Pop*, August 1970, 49.

5. Sun Ra graced the cover of *Rolling Stone*'s April 19, 1969, issue.

6. See notebooks and financial records, AAC, boxes 20 and 22; and Campbell and Trent, *The Earthly Recordings of Sun Ra*.

7. Szwed, *Space Is the Place*, 249.

8. Ibid., 250.

9. Ibid., 257. Grass (*Great Spirits*, 50) characterizes such performances as "a strange mix of improvisation, orchestration, spirituality, solemn ritual,

apparent nonsense, humor, showbiz spectacle, and astonishing musicianship."

10. Invented by Bob Sebastian and used extensively by Sun Ra, the Outer Space Visual Communicator (OVC) consisted of a huge bank of switches and seven foot pedals that allowed an artist to make "visual music" in constantly shifting colors and patterns. See "Visual Music Systems, Inc.," visualmusicsystems.com, www.visualmusicsystems.com/ovc.htm.

11. Qtd. in Szwed, *Space Is the Place*, 364.

12. Sun Ra, "My Music is Words," in *The Immeasurable Equation*, 460.

13. Peter Hinds, conversation with Sun Ra, June 17, 1988, *Sun Ra Research* 24 (August 1999): 2.

14. Rycenga, "Interview with Sun Ra" [1988].

15. Szwed, *Space Is the Place*, 310. Consult, for instance, the radio-broadcast recording released as Sun Ra, *The Antique Blacks*, Art Yard, ARTYARD CD 010, 2009, CD; original release, Saturn 81774, 1974, LP.

16. Qtd. in Szwed, *Space Is the Place*, 312.

17. Program for concert for the Pan Africa Study Tour Committee, University of California at Berkeley, AAC, box 3, folder 53.

18. Ray, interview with Sun Ra.

19. John Hinds and Peter Hinds, "December 4, 1985, Oakland, CA," *Sun Ra Research* 1 (May 1995): 5.

20. A copy of the recorded lecture, as well as Sun Ra's syllabus for "The Black Man and the Cosmos," appears at the Open Culture website, www.openculture.com/2014/07/full-lecture-and-reading-list-from-sun-ras-1971-uc-berkeley-course.html. The lecture also appears on Sun Ra, *The Creator of the Universe*, two discs, Transparency 0301, n.d., CD.

21. Yosef A. A. Ben-Yochannan, *Black Man of the Nile and His Family* (New York: Black Classics, 1972); Henry Dumas, *Ark of Bones and Other Stories*, ed. Eugene B. Redman (New York: Random House, 1974); LeRoi Jones and Larry Neal, eds., *Black Fire: An Anthology of Afro-American Writing* (New York: William Morrow, 1968). Szwed provides a fuller account of Sun Ra's syllabus in *Space Is the Place*, 294.

22. See Szwed, *Space Is the Place*, 329–330. For an illuminating discussion of the relationship between Sun Ra's politics and the Panthers, see Kreiss, "Appropriating the Master's Tools," 57–81.

23. Szwed, *Space Is the Place*, 329–330.

24. "Sun Ra Talks On 'The Possibility of Altered Destiny,'" Sun Ra (The Sun Ra Arkestra), *Live from Soundscape*, two discs, DIW 388, 1979, CD, disc 2.

CHAPTER 19: SPACE IS THE PLACE

1. "Synopsis," *Space Is the Place*, AAC, box 3, folder 6.

2. All quotations come from the rereleased version of the movie with restored footage, *Space Is the Place: Sun Ra and His Intergalactic Solar Arkestra*, dir. John Coney (Plexifilm, 2003), DVD. See also the more recent rerelease by Harte Recordings, *Space Is the Place*, limited edition (Harte Recordings, 2015), which contains commentary by the producer Jim Newman and essays by the director John Coney and the screenwriter Seth Hill.

3. The word "utopia" originates with Sir Thomas More's book of the same name, published in 1516. It is a pun Sun Ra would have liked: "eu-topia" sounds the same but means "happy place."

4. Sun Ra, "My Music is Words," in *The Immeasurable Equation*, 467.

5. Ibid.

6. Ibid., 468.

7. Ibid., 471.

8. Hinds and Hinds, "December 4, 1985, Oakland, CA," 5.

9. Ibid., 1.

10. Closing chant, *Atlantis*.

11. Sun Ra's first recorded encounter with the Moog synthesizer (a modular model, according to Campbell and Trent) is found on *My Brother the Wind*, recorded in 1969.

12. Peter Hinds, conversation with Robert Moog, September 9, 1991, *Sun Ra Research* 30 (October 2000): 42.

13. Ibid.

14. Qtd. in Trevor Pinch and Frank Tracco, *Analog Days: The Invention and Impact of the Moog Synthesizer* (Cambridge, MA: Harvard University Press, 2004), 72.

15. Ibid., 234.

16. Qtd. in ibid., 235.

17. Henry Dumas, "An Interview with Sun Ra: Excerpts from a Longer Article (In Progress)," *Hiram Poetry Review* 3 (1967): 32. Archived at AAC, box 1, folder 4.

18. Qtd. in Pinch and Tracco, *Analog Days*, 223.

19. Ibid., 233.

20. Nat Hentoff, "The New Jazz," *Newsweek*, December 12, 1966, 101. Archived at AAC, box 1, folder 3.

21. These lines, frequently repeated in performance, also appear in Sun Ra, *The Immeasurable Equation*, 331.

22. Jim Newman, producer of *Space Is the Place*, confirms Johnnie Keyes's role in the movie (personal communication).

23. Sun Ra's remark about the NAACP appears in Szwed, *Space Is the Place*, 332.

24. These lines also acquire recitative force and appear in two slightly different versions in Sun Ra, *The Immeasurable Equation*, 164, 392.

25. Sun Ra, *Space is the Place*, Impulse! IMPD 249, 1998, CD; original release, Blue Thumb BTS 41, 1973, LP. Sun Ra, *Astro Black*. Sun Ra, *Discipline 27-II*.

26. "Intergalactic Correspondence," 3, AAC, box 3, folder 8.

27. Ibid., 6.

28. Ibid., 9.

29. Ibid., 5.

30. Ibid., 7.

31. Ibid., 10.

32. AAC, box 13, folder 7. All following quotations in this chapter come from this source.

CHAPTER 20: TOKENS OF HAPPINESS

1. Sun Ra, *Space is the Place*. Campbell and Trent (*The Earthly Recordings of Sun Ra*, 191) note that "a second Blue Thumb LP from these sessions was planned but never issued. The master seems to have been lost."

2. Ed Michel, "Ed Michel's Complete Liner Notes for Impulse's *Space is the Place* Re-issue," *Sun Ra Arkive* 2 (2003): 24, www.the-temple.net/astroblack/sunraarkive/issue2/sra2p_24.html.

3. Ed Michel, "Ed Michel's Complete Liner Notes for Evidence's 'The Great Lost Sun Ra Albums,'" *Sun Ra Arkive* 2 (Jan. 2003): 29, www.the-temple.net/astroblack/sunraarkive/issue2/sra2p_29.html.

4. Ibid.

5. Ibid.

6. Sun Ra, *Pathways to Unknown Worlds*, Evidence 22218, 2000, CD; original release, Impulse! ASD-9298, 1975, quadraphonic LP. The latter two recordings (Impulse! AS-9296 and AS-9297, respectively) saw release as a two-disc boxed set under the title *The Great Lost Sun Ra Albums: Cymbals and Crystal Spears*, Evidence ECD 22217-2, 2000, CD.

7. Szwed, *Space Is the Place*, 333.

8. Qtd. in ibid.

9. Ibid., 334.

10. For those interested in getting a feel for the Arkestra's stage show, video of these performances is a good place to start. Sun Ra and an abbreviated Arkestra appeared on *Saturday Night Live* on May 20th, 1978. A clip from the performance can be downloaded for free from WFMU's "Beware of the Blog," http://blog.wfmu.org/freeform/2005/11/sun_ra_vs_satur.html. The video is grainy, but the playing, chanting, and dancing is gorgeous, especially on "Space is the Place" and "Sound Mirror." Sun Ra and another avatar of the Arkestra played *Michelob Presents Night Music*, hosted by the saxophonist David Sanborn, on December 10, 1989. It's a rollicking performance, particularly of "You Got to Face the Music," and can be found on YouTube, www.youtube.com/watch?v=1qjiQwD7VCI.

11. The National Endowment for the Arts first bestowed the Jazz Master distinction in 1982. Other recipients that year were the trumpet players Roy Eldridge and Dizzy Gillespie.

12. Szwed, *Space Is the Place*, 358.

13. "Sun Ra," Wikipedia, https://en.wikipedia.org/wiki/Sun_Ra.

14. Jack Lloyd, "Sun Ra and His Airs So Rare," *Philadelphia Inquirer*, December 23, 1988, http://articles.philly.com/1988-12-23/entertainment/26225363_1_arkestra-sun-ra-outer-space.

15. Howard Reich, "Sun Ra Dazzles New Fans with His Arkestra," *Chicago Tribune*, October 1, 1990, http://articles.chicagotribune.com/1990-10-01/news/9003210842_1_arkestra-sun-ra-marshall-allen.

16. Rich Theis, "Sun Ra," *Option*, September–October 1983, 50.

17. Sun Ra, *Holiday for Soul Dance*, Evidence 22011, 1992; original release, Saturn ESR 508, 1970, LP.

18. Campbell and Trent, *The Earthly Recordings of Sun Ra*.

19. Szwed (*Space Is the Place*, 225) describes the chagrin of the saxophonist Russell Procope (who played for Fletcher Henderson early in his career) "when he heard John Gilmore reproduce the same mistake he had made on an original 1933 recording with the Henderson band."

20. See Dan and Dale (as "The Sensational Guitars of Dan & Dale"), *Batman and Robin*, Universe UV 016, 2001, CD; original release, Tifton S-78002, 1966, LP. The Dan and Dale group was an avatar of the Blues Project, which included Al Kooper and Steve Katz. "I'm Gonna Unmask the Batman" was written by Alton Abraham and the Saturn recording artist Lacy Gibson.

21. Campbell and Trent, *The Earthly Recordings of Sun Ra*, 599–603.

22. John Gilmore, liner notes, Sun Ra, *Super-Sonic Jazz*, CD.

23. Performance flyer, AAC, box 3, folder 54.

24. The other tracks on the recording are "Spontaneous Simplicity," "Lights on a Satellite," "Ombre Monde #2" (Shadow World), "A Salutation from the

Universe," and "Calling Planet Earth"—a typical set of space music. The actual show was of course much longer than six tunes. See Campbell and Trent, *The Earthly Recordings of Sun Ra*; and Sun Ra, *Live in Paris at the "Gibus,"* Universe, UV 079, 2003, CD (original release, Atlantic 40540, 1975, LP). It is worth remembering that the title for an early LP containing mostly standards was *Sound Sun Pleasure!!* (recorded 1958 and released 1970).

25. Reich, "Sun Ra Dazzles New Fans."

26. Sun Ra, *St. Louis Blues: Solo Piano*, Improvising Artists Inc. 123858-2, 1992, CD; original release, Improvising Artists Inc. IAI 37.38.58, 1978, LP.

27. Sun Ra (The Sun Ra Arkestra), *Live at Praxis, 1984*, Golden Years of New Jazz GY5/6, 2000, CD; also released as a two-disc set, Vinyl Lovers 901110, 2010, LP; originally released as three discs: 1, Praxis CM 108, 1984, LP; 2, Praxis CM 109, 1985, LP; 3, Praxis CM 110, 1986, LP. Other recordings that capture the Arkestra's joyous celebration of swing include Sun Ra (Sun Ra Arkestra), *Sunrise in Different Dimensions*, hatOLOGY 698, 2011, CD (original release, two discs, Hat Hut Records 2R17, 1981, LP); and Sun Ra, *Unity*, two discs, Horo HDP 19-20, 1978, LP.

28. John Litweiler, "Mood Swings Fire Sun Ra's Jazz Orbit," *Chicago Tribune*, September 9, 1988, http://articles.chicagotribune.com/1988-09-09/features/8801290107_1_arkestra-sun-ra-jazz-band.

29. Sun Ra (The Sun Ra Arkestra), *Reflections in Blue*, Black Saint BSR 0101 CD, 1987, CD; original release, Black Saint BSR 0101, 1987, LP.

30. Sun Ra (The Sun Ra Arkestra), *Hours After*, Black Saint, 120 111-2, 1989, CD; original release, Black Saint 120 111-1, 1989, LP.

31. Sun Ra, *Blue Delight*, A&M SP 5260, 1989, CD; SP5630, 1989, LP.

32. Ibid., liner notes.

33. Sun Ra, *Purple Night*, A&M 75021 5324 2, 1990, CD.

34. Peter Hinds, conversation with Sun Ra, December 25, 1987, *Sun Ra Research* 35 (October 2001): 36.

CHAPTER 21: CONTINUATION

1. Lady Gaga, "Venus," *Artpop*, Streamline/Interscope, 2013, CD.

2. RocketNumberNine [Ben Page and Tom Page], *You Reflect Me*, Trace DIG003, 2009, MP3. Zombie Zombie, *Rocket Number 9 EP*, Versatile VER079, 2012, LP. Yo La Tengo, *Nuclear War*, Matador, OLE 568-2, 2002, CD. Sun Ra, *Nuclear War*, Atavistic USM/ALP222CD, 2001, CD; original release, Y Records RA 2, 1984, LP.

3. John Coltrane, *Interstellar Space*, Impulse! 314 543 415-2, 2000, CD; original release, Impulse! ASD 9277, 1974, LP.

4. Qtd. in Szwed, *Space Is the Place*, 77–78. A list, written in Abraham's hand, identifying "the many musicians Sun Ra has helped thru the years" includes the following: "John Coltrane; Tenor. Spiritual Advice" (AAC, box 13, folder 13).

5. Szwed, *Space Is the Place*, 210.

6. Amiri Baraka [LeRoi Jones] and Sun Ra and the Myth-Science Arkestra, *A Black Mass*, Son Boy Records 1, 1999, CD; original release, Jihad Productions 1968, 1968, LP.

7. Qtd. in Szwed, *Space Is the Place*, 210. The remark originally appeared in *Black World* 20 (1971): 206. The typographical high jinks belong to Baraka. He also emphasized the connection between Sun Ra and the New Thing in his "Apple Cores" columns for *Down Beat*. See Baraka, *Black Music*, 126–139. On free jazz as a social practice, see Iain Anderson, *This Is Our Music: Free Jazz, the Sixties, and American Culture* (Philadelphia: University of Pennsylvania Press, 2007); Daniel Fischlin, Ajay Heble, and George Lipsitz, *The Fierce Urgency of Now: Improvisation, Rights, and the Ethics of Cocreation* (Durham, NC: Duke University Press, 2013). On the musical conventions of free jazz, see Ekkehard Jost, *Free Jazz* (New York: Da Capo, 1994).

8. Gilmore left the Arkestra for a stretch in 1964 to tour Japan and Europe with Art Blakey's Jazz Messengers.

9. Sun Ra, "My Music is Words," in *The Immeasurable Equation*, 469–470.

10. Amiri Baraka [LeRoi Jones], "Apple Cores #3," in *Black Music*, 129.

11. Albert Ayler, *Spiritual Unity*, ESP Disk' 1002, 2005, CD; original release, ESP Disk' 1002, 1965, LP. Ornette Coleman, *Free Jazz: A Collective Improvisation*, Rhino R275208, 1998, CD; original release, Atlantic SD 1364, 1961, LP. Archie Shepp, *Four for Trane*, Impulse! IMPD 218, 1997, CD; original release, Impulse! A-71, 1964, LP. John Coltrane, *Ascension*, Impulse! B0012401-02, 2009, CD; original release, Impulse! AS-95, 1965, LP.

12. Qtd. in liner notes to Sun Ra, *Interstellar Low Ways*.

13. Terry Moran, review of *The Heliocentric Worlds of Sun Ra*, *Sounds and Fury*, April 1966, n.p. Archived at AAC, box 4, folder 7.

14. Ibid.

15. Mathieu, *"Other Planes of There."*

16. Qtd. in Peter Shapiro, "Blues and the Abstract Truth," philcohran.com, www.philcohran.com/pc_wr_fr.htm.

17. George Lewis, *A Power Stronger Than Itself: The Association for the Advancement of Creative Musicians* (Chicago: University of Chicago Press, 2008), 116.

18. Phil Cohran and the Artistic Heritage Ensemble, *On the Beach*, Zulu Records 0004, 1968, LP. Phil Cohran and the Artistic Heritage Ensemble, *Malcolm X Memorial*, Zulu Records MR-016, 1968, LP.

19. Shapiro, "Blues and the Abstract Truth."

20. Art Ensemble of Chicago, *People in Sorrow*, Odeon CJ32-5013, 1988, CD; original release, Nessa Records N-3, 1968, LP. Art Ensemble of Chicago, *Les Stances á Sophie*, Soul Jazz Records CD191, 2008, CD; original release, Pathé 2C 062-11365, 1970, LP.

21. iCrates, "Interview with Idris Ackamoor of 'The Pyramids,'" http://blog .culturalodyssey.org/wp-content/uploads/2012/02/2.-iCrates-master.pdf.

22. Robert Hurwitt, "Idris Ackamoor, Cultural Odyssey Evolving," SFGate .com, www.sfgate.com/performance/article/Idris-Ackamoor-Cultural-Odyssey-evolving-5371505.php.

23. The Pyramids, *Lalibela*, Pyramid Records 3093, 1973, LP. The Pyramids, *King of Kings*, Pyramid Records 3093-4, 1974, LP. The Pyramids, *Birth/Speed/Merging*, Pyramid Records 30935, 1976, LP.

24. This phrase appears in a description accompanying a YouTube clip (still image only) of the Pyramids' "Aomawa," www.youtube.com/watch?v=n6 wJJUKN-uQ.

25. Idris Ackamoor, *The Music of Idris Ackamoor, 1971–2004*, two discs, EM Records EM1062DCD, 2006, CD.

26. The Pyramids, *Otherworldly*, Cultural Odyssey CO-183-5, 2011, CD.

27. iCrates, "Interview with Idris Ackamoor."

28. Sean Kitching, "Playing the Cosmo Song: Thurston Moore and John Sinclair on Sun Ra," *The Quietus*, http://thequietus.com/articles/15387-john-sin clair-thurston-moore-interview.

29. Szwed, *Space Is the Place*, 243.

30. White Panther News Service, "For Immediate Release," *Sun Ra Research* 5 (February 1996): 12.

31. Szwed, *Space Is the Place*, 245.

32. Kitching, "Playing the Cosmo Song." Moore must be referring to "Rocket Reducer No. 62 (Rama Lama Fa Fa Fa)" or more likely the last track on *Kick Out the Jams*, entitled "Starship."

33. Ibid.

34. Ibid. Sun Ra, *Out There A Minute*, Blast First BFFP 42, 1989, CD.

35. Kitching, "Playing the Cosmo Song."

36. See, for instance, the following: Marc Ribot (Marc Ribot y Los Cubanos Postizos), *The Prosthetic Cubans*, Atlantic 83116-2, 1998, CD. Marc Ribot (Marc Ribot's Ceramic Dog), *Party Intellectuals*, PI Recordings PI 27, 2008, CD. Marc Ribot (Marc Ribot's Ceramic Dog), *Your Turn*, Northern Spy NSCD 038, 2013, CD. Marc Ribot (The Marc Ribot Trio), *Live at the Village Vanguard*, PI Recordings PI 153, 2014, CD.

37. Here's a sampling: Need New Body, *Need New Body*, File 13 Records FT41, CD. The Thing and Neneh Cherry, *The Cherry Thing*, Smalltown Supersound

STS229, 2012, CD. Shibusashirazu Orchestra, *Lost Direction*, Moers Music 03016CD, 2005, CD. Shibusashirazu Orchestra, *Paris Shibu Bokyoku: Live at Maison de la Culture du Japon à Paris*, two discs, Chitei Records BF41/42F, 2008, CD. Amayo's Fu-Arkist-Ra, *Afrobeat Disciples (1st Kung Fu Lesson of Life)*, Amenawon, 2001, CD.

38. Alondra Nelson, "Introduction: Future Texts," in Nelson, *Afrofuturism*, 9.

39. In a 1974 interview with *The News* (Mexico City), Sun Ra described his music as a sort of "auto-futurism" that "represents part of the life of people who never lived" (AAC, box 133, folder 9).

40. The song appears on George Clinton and Parliament's *The Clones of Dr. Funkenstein*, Casablanca 842 620-2, 1990, CD; original release, Casablanca NBLP 7034, 1976, LP.

41. Qtd. in George Lipsitz, *Footsteps in the Dark: The Hidden Histories of Popular Music* (Minneapolis: University of Minnesota Press, 2007), 104.

42. George Clinton and Parliament, *Chocolate City*, Casablanca 836 700-2, 1990, CD; original release, Casablanca NBLP 7014, 1975, LP. George Clinton and Parliament, *The Mothership Connection*, Casablanca 824 502-2, 1990, CD; original release, Casablanca NBLP 7022, 1975, LP. George Clinton and Parliament, *Funkentelechy vs. The Placebo Syndrome*, Casablanca 824 501-2, 1990, CD; original release, Casablanca NBLP 7084, 1977, LP.

43. "P. Funk (Wants to Get Funked Up)," *The Mothership Connection*.

44. Ibid.

45. George Clinton and Parliament, "Prelude," *Clones of Dr. Funkenstein*.

46. *George Clinton: The Mothership Connection*, prod. George Clinton, Pioneer Artists, 1998, DVD. The film documents the early days of the P-Funk Earth Tour, which would last almost two years, and contains footage of a concert at Hofheinz Pavilion in Houston, Texas.

47. Sun Ra, "UFO," *On Jupiter*, Art Yard, ARTYARD CD 204, 2005, CD; original release, Saturn 101679, 1979, LP.

48. Listen, too, to Sun Ra, *Lanquidity*, Evidence 22220-2, 2000, CD; original release, Philly Jazz PJ 666, 1978, LP. Funk gets lyrical and groove turns interstellar transport.

49. Kitching, "Playing the Cosmo Song."

50. Afrika Bambaataa and the SoulSonic Force, *Planet Rock*, Tommy Boy TB 823, 1982, LP single.

51. "Afrika Bambaataa," Wikipedia, http://en.wikipedia.org/wiki/Afrika_Bambaataa.

52. Kool Keith's breakthrough came with Ultramagnetic MCs on *Critical Beatdown*, Next Plateau Records PLCD 1013, 1988, CD.

53. "Dr. Octagon," Wikipedia, http://en.wikipedia.org/wiki/Dr._Octagon.

54. Kool Keith, "3000," *Dr. Octagonecologyst*, Bulk Recordings CD902, 1996, CD.

55. Deltron 3030 [Dan the Automator, Del the Funky Homosapien, and Kid Koala], *Deltron 3030*, 75 Ark 75033, 2000, CD.

56. Madvillain [Daniel Dumile and Otis Jackson Jr.], *Madvillainy*, Stones Throw Records STH2065, 2004, CD.

57. Paul D. Miller, *Viral Sonata*, Asphodel ASP0976, 1997, CD. DJ Spooky [Paul D. Miller], *Celestial Mechanix*, two discs, Thirsty Ear THI57148.1, 2004, CD. Azaelia Banks, *Fantasea*, self-release, 2012, MP3.

58. Janelle Monáe, *ArchAndroid*, two discs, Badboy Entertainment 512256-1, 2010, LP. Janelle Monáe, *The Electric Lady*, Badboy Entertainment 536102-2, 2013, CD.

59. Szwed, *Space Is the Place*, 376.

60. Sun Ra, *New Steps*, Atomic Records 76812, 2009, CD; original release, two discs, Horo HPD 25-26, 1978, LP. Sun Ra, *Unity*.

61. Sun Ra, *Disco 3000*, Art Yard ARTYARD CD 101, 2009, CD; original release, Saturn CMIJ 78, 1978, LP. Sun Ra, *Media Dream*, Art Yard ARTYARD CD 002, 2008, CD; original release, Saturn 1978, 1978, LP.

62. Charles Cohen, *Music for Dance and Theater*, two discs, Morphine 021LP, 2013, LP.

63. Frédéric Galliano, *Nangadef Maafric*, What's Up Records 9608, 1996, LP. The Avalanches, *Electricity*, XL Recordings 7243 5461680 4, 2001, CD; original release, Modular Recordings MODVL002, 1999, LP single. Sun Ra, *Strange Celestial Road*, Rounder 3035, 1988, CD; original release, Rounder 3035, 1980, LP.

64. Spaceboys, *Sonic Fiction*, Nylon Discographics NYLONCD007, 2003, CD. RocketNumberNine [Ben Page and Tom Page], *MeYouWeYou*, Smalltown Supersound STS241LP, 2013, LP.

65. The Dining Rooms, *Tre*, Schema SCCD 355, 2003, CD.

66. Freedom Satellite, "Astro Black (The Big Wow Mix)," *Vienna Scientists V: The 10th Anniversary*, Vienna Scientists Recordings VIE0 020 CD, 2009, CD.

67. Mono/Poly [Charles E. Dickerson], *Golden Skies*, Brainfeeder BFCD 046, 2014, CD.

68. Sun Araw [Cameron Stallones], *Beach Head*, Not for Fun Records NFF 140, 2008, LP. Consider, too, the synthesizer on Sun Araw's collaboration *Sun Araw and M. Geddes Gengras Meet the Congos: Icon Give Thank*, FRKWYS vol. 9, RVNG International FRKWYS09, 2012, CD, DVD. Sun Rise Above (Sun R.A.), *Every Day I Wake Up on the Wrong Side of Capitalism*, self-release, 2001, CD.

69. Eshun, *More Brilliant Than the Sun*, 00(-002) [sic].

70. Ibid., 00(-005).

71. See "Sun Ra Changed My Life: 13 Artists Reflect on the Influence and Legacy of Sun Ra," *The Vinyl Factory*, www.thevinylfactory.com/vinyl-factory-releases/sun-ra-changed-my-life-13-artists-reflect-on-the-legacy-and-influence-of-sun-ra/.

72. Osunlade, *A Man with No Past Originating the Future*, two discs, Yoruba Records YSD48, 2013, LP.

73. "Sun Ra Changed My Life."

74. "Mike Huckaby Takes on Sun Ra for *Reel-to-Reel Edits*," *FACT*, www.factmag .com/2011/03/08/mike-huckaby-takes-on-sun-ra-for-reel-to-reel-edits-vol-1/.

75. "UFO" and "Antique Blacks" appear on Mike Huckaby, *Sun Ra: The Mike Huckaby Reel-to-Reel Edits, Volume 1*, Kindred Spirits/Art Yard KSAY-MH01, 2011, twelve-inch LP. "To Nature's God," "Friendly Galaxy," and "Space Is the Place" appear on Mike Huckaby, *Sun Ra: The Mike Huckaby Reel-to-Reel Edits, Volume 2*, Kindred Spirits/Art Yard KSAY MH02, 2011, twelve-inch LP.

76. Africa Hitech [Mark Pritchard and Steve Spacek], *93 Million Miles*, Warp Records WARPCD 199, 2011, CD.

77. Flying Lotus [Steven Ellison], *Cosmogramma*, Warp Records WARPCD 195, 2010, CD.

78. Patrick Sisson, "Flying Lotus," *Pitchfork*, http://pitchfork.com/features/interviews/7793-flying-lotus/.

79. *Space Is the Place*, dir. Coney.

80. Ras G [Gregory Shorter Jr.], "Back on the Planet," *Back on the Planet*, two discs, Brainfeeder BF039, 2013, LP.

81. Ras G, "Natural Melanin Being," *Back on the Planet*.

82. Hear it all at Ras G, "Cosmic Tones 4 Mental Therapy!!!!!!," *Soundcloud*, https://soundcloud.com/ras_g/cosmic-tones-4-mental-therapy.

83. Ibid.

84. John Hinds, conversation with Sun Ra, October 31, 1991, *Sun Ra Research* 30 (October 2000): 28.

85. Von Freeman, *The Improvisor*, Premonition Records, 90757, 2002, CD. Matana Roberts, *Coin Coin Chapter One: Gens de Couleur Libres*, two discs, Constellation CST079-1, 2011, LP.

86. Tortoise, *TNT*, Thrill Jockey THRILL 050, 1998, CD.

87. Chicago Underground, *Boca Negra*, Thrill Jockey THRILL 228, 2010, CD. Chicago Underground, *Locus*, Northern Spy NSCD 052, 2014, CD. Chad Taylor also plays drums with the Marc Ribot Trio.

88. Exploding Star Orchestra, *We Are All From Somewhere Else*, Thrill Jockey THRILL 181, 2007, CD.

89. Exploding Star Orchestra, *Stars Have Shapes*, Delmark DMK 595, 2010, CD.

90. Ken Vandermark, *Free Jazz Classics, Vols. 1 and 2*, two discs, Atavistic ALP137CD, 2001, CD.

91. Ken Vandermark (Spaceways Incorporated), *Thirteen Cosmic Standards by Sun Ra & Funkadelic*. Atavistic ALP120CD, 2000, CD.

92. The Vandermark 5, *Single Piece Flow*, Atavistic ALP47CD, 1997, CD. The Vandermark 5, *Annular Gift*, Not Two Records MW 825-2, 2009, CD.

93. Tiger Hatchery, *Sun Worship*, ESP Disk' ESP 5003, 2013, CD.

94. Rory Gibb, "Time for Harmony in This World: An Interview with Hieroglyphic Being," *The Quietus*, http://thequietus.com/articles/10213-hieroglyphic-being-jamal-moss-interview.

95. Hieroglyphic Being (Jamal Moss), *ANKH*, Music From Mathematics MFM CD-010, 2010, CD. Hieroglyphic Being, *The Sun Man Speaks*, Music From Mathematics MFM CD-009, 2010, CD. Hieroglyphic Being, *Cosmo Rhythmatic*, Music From Mathematics MFM CD-018, 2011, CD. Hieroglyphic Being, *Strange Strings*, Music From Mathematics MFM CD-016, 2011, CD. Hieroglyphic Being, *Seer of Cosmic Visions*, two discs, Planet Mu ZIQ 349, 2014, LP.

96. Gibb, "Time for Harmony."

97. Hieroglyphic Being, *A Synthetic Love Life*, two-discs, +++-+++ 10, 2013, LP.

98. Lauren Martin, "Ra's House: An Interview with Fhloston Paradigm," *thump*, http://thump.vice.com/en_uk/words/fhloston-paradigm-interview.

OUTRO: EXTENSIONS OUT

1. The following scenario of Sun Ra on his deathbed weaves together his words from a variety of sources. He passed from this planet in a hospital in Birmingham, Alabama, having traveled by train in the company of one of his musicians, the trumpeter Jothan Callins, from Philadelphia to his childhood home in bad health the previous January. Sun Ra's sister, Mary Jenkins, cared for him until he required hospitalization. His earthly remains lie buried at Elmwood Cemetery in Birmingham. A sentence from Szwed's biography inspires this closing meditation: "He had reached the seventy-ninth anniversary of his arrival on earth, but he had stopped trying to speak and now only grabbed the hands of those who reached out to him, gripping them so hard that it sometimes took two people to pry his fingers loose" (379).

BIBLIOGRAPHY

ARCHIVES

Alton Abraham Collection of Sun Ra, 1822–2008 (AAC). Special Collections Research Center, University of Chicago Library, University of Chicago, Illinois.

PRINT, FILM, AND ELECTRONIC SOURCES

Ackerman, Forrest J., and Brad Linaweaver. *Worlds of Tomorrow: The Amazing Universe of Science Fiction Art*. Portland, OR: Collectors, 2004.

Adamski, George, and Desmond Lee. *Flying Saucers Have Landed*. London: Werner Laurie, 1953.

Adinolfi, Francesco. *Mondo Exotica: Sounds, Visions, Obsessions of the Cocktail Generation*. Durham, NC: Duke University Press, 2008.

Adoff, Arnold, ed. *The Poetry of Black America: Anthology of the 20th Century*. New York: Harper and Row, 1973.

"Afrika Bambaataa." Wikipedia. https://en.wikipedia.org/wiki/Afrika_Bambaataa.

Anderson, Iain. *This Is Our Music: Free Jazz, the Sixties, and American Culture*. Philadelphia: University of Pennsylvania Press, 2007.

Andrews, Bruce, and Charles Bernstein, eds. *The L=A=N=G=U=A=G=E Book*. Carbondale: Southern Illinois University Press, 1984.

Ballard, J. G. "Introduction to the French Edition." *Crash*. 1973. Reprint, New York: Viking, 1985.

Baraka, Amiri Imamu [LeRoi Jones]. *Black Music*. 1968. Reprint, New York: Da Capo, 1998.

Ben-Yochannan, Yosef A. A. *Black Man of the Nile and His Family*. New York: Black Classics, 1972.

Blake, William. *The Complete Poetry and Prose of William Blake*. Rev. ed., edited by David V. Erdman. Berkeley: University of California Press, 1982.

Bone, Robert. "Richard Wright and the Chicago Renaissance." *Callaloo* 9 (Summer 1986): 446–468.

Bone, Robert, and Richard A. Courage. *The Muse in Bronzeville: African American Creative Expression in Chicago, 1932–1950*. New Brunswick, NJ: Rutgers University Press, 2011.

Brooks, Gwendolyn. "kitchenette building." In *Selected Poems*, 3. New York: Harper and Row, 1963.

Buchler, Tom. "The Making of Lanquidity," *Sun Ra Arkive* 2 (2003): 34, http://www.the-temple.net/astroblack/sunraarkive/issue2/sra2p_34.html.

Burroughs, William S. *The Job: Interviews with William S. Burroughs*. New York: Penguin, 1989.

———. *Nova Express*. 1964. Reprint, New York: Grove, 1992.

Burrows, William E. *This New Ocean: The Story of the First Space Age*. New York: Random House, 1998.

Campbell, Robert. "Sun Ra: Supersonic Sounds from Saturn." *Goldmine*, January 22, 1993.

Campbell, Robert L., and Christopher Trent. *The Earthly Recordings of Sun Ra*. 2nd edition. Redwood, NY: Jazz Cadence Books, n.d.

Campbell, Robert L., Christopher Trent, and Robert Pruter. "From Sonny Blount to Sun Ra: The Chicago Years." Revised October 13, 2013. http://myweb.clemson.edu/~campber/sunra.html.

Corbett, John. *Extended Play: Sounding Off from John Cage to Dr. Funkenstein*. Durham, NC: Duke University Press, 1994.

———. "From the Windy City to the Omniverse: Sun Ra's Chicago Life as Street Priest and Father of D.I.Y. Jazz." *Down Beat*, December 2006, 34–39.

———, ed. *The Wisdom of Sun Ra: Sun Ra's Polemical Broadsheets and Streetcorner Leaflets*. Chicago: WhiteWalls, 2006.

Corbett, John, and Aye Aton. *Sun Ra and Aye Aton: Space, Interiors and Exteriors, 1972*. New York: PictureBox, 2013.

Corbett, John, Anthony Elms, and Terry Kapsalis, eds. *Pathways to Unknown Worlds: Sun Ra, El Saturn and Chicago's Afro-Futurist Underground 1954–68.* Chicago: WhiteWalls, 2006.

———. *Traveling the Spaceways: Sun Ra, the Astro Black and Other Solar Myths.* Chicago: WhiteWalls, 2010.

Crandell, Evan, and Lisa Lorenzino. "Nurturing a Joyful Noise: Examining Sun Ra's Philosophies as a Model for Music Education." *Canadian Music Educator* 54, no. 3 (2013): 25–29.

"The CTA Takes Over: Resurrection through Modernization (1947–1970)." Chicago-l.org. http://www.chicago-l.org/history/CTA2.html.

Cutler, Chris. "In the Realm of Lightning." In *Omniverse Sun Ra*, edited by Hartmut Geerken and Bernhard Hefele, 67–84. Wartaweil, Germany: Waitawhile, 1994.

Davis, Miles, with Quincy Troupe. *Miles: The Autobiography.* New York: Touchstone, 1989.

The Day the Earth Stood Still. Film. Directed by Robert Wise. 20th Century Fox, 1951; rerelease, 20th Century Fox, 2003, DVD.

Deleuze, Gilles. *Kant's Critical Philosophy.* Translated by Hugh Tomlinson and Barbara Habberjam. Minneapolis: University of Minnesota Press, 1985.

Dery, Mark. *Flame Wars.* Durham, NC: Duke University Press, 1993.

Dolman, Everett C. *Astropolitik: Classical Geopolitics in the Space Age.* New York: Routledge, 2001.

Drake, St. Clair, and Horace R. Cayton. *Black Metropolis: A Study of Negro Life in a Northern City.* Rev. and enlarged ed. New York: Harcourt, Brace and World, 1970.

"Dr. Octagon." Wikipedia. https://en.wikipedia.org/wiki/Dr._Octagon.

Dumas, Henry. *Ark of Bones and Other Stories.* Edited by Eugene B. Redman. New York: Random House, 1974.

———. "An Interview with Sun Ra: Excerpts from a Longer Article (In Progress)." *Hiram Poetry Review* 3 (1967): 31–32.

Dyja, Thomas. *The Third Coast: When Chicago Built the American Dream.* New York: Penguin, 2013.

"Early Years of Chicago's 'L.'" *Chicago Tribune.* December 6, 2013. http://galleries.apps.chicagotribune.com/chi-131205-early-years-chicago-elevated-train-pictures/.

Ehrenhalt, Alan. *The Lost City: Discovering the Forgotten Virtues of Community in the Chicago of the 1950s.* New York: Basic Books, 1995.

"80 Great Posters of Not So Great and Even Worse Sci-Fi Movies 1950–1965." Cinemacom. http://www.cinemacom.com/50s-sci-fi-REST.html.

Ellington, Duke. "The Race for Space." In *The Duke Ellington Reader*, edited by Mark Tucker, 293–296. Oxford: Oxford University Press, 1996.

Eshun, Kodwo. "Further Considerations on Afrofuturism." *New Centennial Review* 3, no. 2 (2003): 287–302.

———. *More Brilliant Than the Sun: Adventures in Sonic Fiction*. London: Quartet Books, 1998.

Fiofori, Tam. "Sun Ra's Space Odyssey." *Down Beat*, May 1970, 14–17.

Fischlin, Daniel, Ajay Heble, and George Lipsitz. *The Fierce Urgency of Now: Improvisation, Rights, and the Ethics of Cocreation*. Durham, NC: Duke University Press, 2013.

Forbidden Planet. Film. Directed by Fred M. Wilcox. Metro-Goldwyn-Mayer, 1956; rerelease, Warner Home Video, 2010, DVD.

Ford, Theodore P. *God Wills the Negro*. Chicago: Geographical Institute Press, 1939.

Gabbard, Krin, ed. *Jazz among the Discourses*. Durham, NC: Duke University Press, 1995.

Geerken, Hartmut, and Bernhard Hefele, eds. *Omniverse Sun Ra*. Wartaweil, Germany: Waitawhile, 1994.

George Clinton: The Mothership Connection. Film. Prod. George Clinton. Pioneer Artists, 1998, DVD.

Gibb, Rory. "Time for Harmony in This World: An Interview with Hieroglyphic Being." *The Quietus*. http://thequietus.com/articles/10213-hieroglyphic-being-jamal-moss-interview.

Gold, H. L. "For Adults Only." *Galaxy Science Fiction*, October 1950, 3.

Grass, Randall. *Great Spirits: Portraits of Life-Changing World Music Artists*. Jackson: University Press of Mississippi, 2009.

Hall, R. Cargill. *Lunar Impact: The NASA History of Project Ranger*. 1977. Reprint, Mineola, NY: Dover, 2010.

Harper, Harry. *Dawn of the Space Age*. London: Sampson Low, 1946.

Hentoff, Nat. "The New Jazz." *Newsweek*, December 12, 1966, 101.

Hinds, John. Conversation with Sun Ra, October 31, 1991. *Sun Ra Research* 30 (October 2000): 24–35.

Hinds, John, and Peter Hinds, eds. *Sun Ra Research*. Fanzine. San Francisco: Omni. http://www.comunalsocieties.hamilton.edu/islandora/object/ham LibCom%3A456.

———. Conversation with Sun Ra, October 13, 1984. *Sun Ra Research* 19 (October 1998): 1–9.

———. Conversation with Sun Ra and Charles Bass, November 15, 1991. *Sun Ra Research* 1 (May 1995): 1–5.

———. Conversation with Sun Ra and Carl LeBlanc, October 31, 1988. *Sun Ra Research* 15 (February 1998): 1–9.

———. "December 4, 1985, Oakland, CA." *Sun Ra Research* 1 (May 1995): 4–6.

Hinds, Peter. Conversation with Robert Moog, September 9, 1991. *Sun Ra Research* 30 (October 2000): 42–43.

———. Conversation with Sun Ra, June 17, 1988. *Sun Ra Research* 24 (August 1999): 1–5.

———. Conversation with Sun Ra, December 25, 1987. *Sun Ra Research* 35 (October 2001): 25–31.

———. Conversation with Sun Ra, December 11, 1989. *Sun Ra Research* 32 (February 2001): 1–47.

———. Conversation with Tommy Hunter, April 9 and 13, 1998. *Sun Ra Research* 32 (February 2001): 48–76.

———. Conversation with Tommy Hunter, April 13, 1998. *Sun Ra Research* 33 (April 2001): 1–49.

Hirsch, Arnold R. *Making the Second Ghetto: Race and Housing in Chicago, 1940–1960.* Chicago: University of Chicago Press, 1998.

"Histories and Chronologies." Chicago-l.org. http://www.chicago-l.org.

Holland, Steve, and Alex Summersby. *Sci-Fi Art: A Graphic History.* New York: HarperCollins, 2009.

Hurwitt, Robert. "Idris Ackamoor, Cultural Odyssey Evolving." SFGate.com. http://www.sfgate.com/performance/article/Idris-Ackamoor-Cultural-Odyssey-evolving-5371505.php.

iCrates. "Interview with Idris Ackamoor of 'The Pyramids.'" http://blog.cultural odyssey.org/wp-content/uploads/2012/02/2.-ICrates-master.pdf.

"It Makes You Booomph! Marshall Allen Interviewed by Edwin Pouncy." *Sun Ra Arkive* 1 (Dec. 2002), 7–9. http://www.the-temple.net/astroblack/sunra arkive/issue1/sra1p_7.html.

James, George G. M. *Stolen Legacy: The Greeks Were Not the Authors of Greek Philosophy, but the People of North Africa, Commonly Called the Egyptians.* New York: Philosophical Library, 1954.

Jones, LeRoi [Amiri Baraka], and Larry Neal, eds. *Black Fire: An Anthology of Afro-American Writing.* New York: William Morrow, 1968.

Jost, Ekkehard. *Free Jazz.* New York: Da Capo, 1994.

Kant, Immanuel. *Critique of the Power of Judgment.* Translated by Paul Guyer and Eric Matthews. Rev. ed. Cambridge: University of Cambridge Press, 2001.

Karr, Ronald Dale. "Rapid Transit System." In *Encyclopedia of Chicago,* edited by Janice L. Reiff, Ann Durkin Keating, and James R. Grossman. Chicago:

Chicago Historical Society, 2005. http://www.encyclopedia.chicagohistory
.org/pages/1042.html.

Keeling, Kara, and Josh Kun, eds. *Sound Clash: Listening to American Studies.* Baltimore, MD: Johns Hopkins University Press, 2012.

Kernfeld, Barry, ed. *The New Grove Dictionary of Jazz.* New York: St. Martin's, 1984.

King, George, ed. *Cosmic Voice: Aetherius Speaks to Earth.* 2 vols. London: n.p., 1957–1961.

Kitching, Sean. "Playing the Cosmo Song: Thurston Moore and John Sinclair on Sun Ra." *The Quietus.* http://thequietus.com/articles/15387-john-sinclair-thurston-moore-interview.

Kreiss, Daniel. "Appropriating the Master's Tools: Sun Ra, the Black Panthers, and Black Consciousness, 1952–1973." *Black Music Research Journal* 28, no. 1 (2008): 57–81.

———. "Performing the Past to Claim the Future: Sun Ra and the Afro-Future Underground, 1954–1968." *African American Review* 45, nos. 1–2 (2012): 197–203.

Lewis, George E. "Forward: After Afrofuturism." *Journal of the Society for American Music* 2, no. 2 (2008): 139–153.

———. *A Power Stronger Than Itself: The Association for the Advancement of Creative Musicians.* Chicago: University of Chicago Press, 2008.

Light, Michael. *100 Suns, 1945–1962.* New York: Knopf, 2003.

Lipsitz, George. *Footsteps in the Dark: The Hidden Histories of Popular Music.* Minneapolis: University of Minnesota Press, 2007.

Litweiler, John. "Mood Swings Fire Sun Ra's Jazz Orbit." *Chicago Tribune,* September 9, 1988. http://articles.chicagotribune.com/1988-09-09/features/8801290107_1_arkestra-sun-ra-jazz-band.

Lloyd, Jack. "Sun Ra and His Airs So Rare." *Philadelphia Inquirer,* December 23, 1988. http://articles.philly.com/1988-12-23/entertainment/26225363_1_arkestra-sun-ra-outer-space.

Lock, Graham. *Blutopia: Visions of the Future and Visions of the Past in the Work of Sun Ra, Duke Ellington, and Anthony Braxton.* Durham, NC: Duke University Press, 1999.

Mackey, Nathaniel. *Discrepant Engagement: Dissonance, Cross-Culturality, and Experimental Writing.* Cambridge: Cambridge University Press, 1993.

The Magic Sun. Film. Directed by Phill Niblock. Experimental Intermedia, 1966; rerelease, Atavistic DJ-861, 2005, DVD.

Majer, Gerald. *The Velvet Lounge: On Late Chicago Jazz.* New York: Columbia University Press, 2005.

Martin, Lauren. "Ra's House: An Interview with Fhloston Paradigm." *thump*. http://thump.vice.com/en_uk/words/fhloston-paradigm-interview.

Mathieu, Bill. *"Other Planes of There & Sun Ra and His Solar Arkestra Visit Planet Earth."* *Down Beat*, June 1966, 32–33.

McCurdy, Howard E. *Space and the American Imagination*. Baltimore, MD: Johns Hopkins University Press, 2011.

McDougall, Walter A. *The Heavens and the Earth: A Political History of the Space Age*. New York: Basic Books, 1985.

McRae, Barry. "Sun Ra." *Jazz Journal* 19, no. 8 (1966): 15–16.

Michel, Ed. "Ed Michel's Complete Liner Notes for Evidence's "The Great Lost Sun Ra Albums." *Sun Ra Arkive* 2 (Jan. 2003): 27–30. http://www.the-temple.net/astroblack/sunraarkive/issue2/sra2p_27.html.

———. "Ed Michel's Complete Liner Notes for Impulse's *Space is the Place* Reissue." *Sun Ra Arkive* 2 (Jan. 2003): 24–26. www.the-temple.net/astroblack/sunraarkive/issue2/sra2p_24.html.

Michelob Presents Night Music. Hosted by David Sanborn. Television broadcast. December 10, 1989. https://www.youtube.com/watch?v=1qjiQwD7VCI.

"Mike Huckaby Takes on Sun Ra for *Reel-to-Reel Edits*." *FACT*. www.factmag.com/2011/03/08/mike-huckaby-takes-on-sun-ra-for-reel-to-reel-edits-vol-1/.

Miller, Paul D. [DJ Spooky]. *Rhythm Science*. Cambridge, MA: MIT Press, 2004.

Monchaux, Nicholas de. *Spacesuit: Fashioning Apollo*. Cambridge, MA: MIT Press, 2011.

Moran, Terry. Review of *The Heliocentric Worlds of Sun Ra*. *Sounds and Fury*, April 1966, n.p.

Morton, Alan. *The Complete Directory to Science Fiction, Fantasy and Horror Television Series: A Comprehensive Guide to the First 50 Years, 1946–1966*. Peoria, IL: Other Worlds, 1997.

Moten, Fred. *In the Break: The Aesthetics of the Black Radical Tradition*. Minneapolis: University of Minnesota Press, 2003.

Nama, Adilifu. "R Is for Race, Not Rocket: Black Representation in American Science Fiction Cinema." *Quarterly Review of Film and Video* 26, no. 2 (2009): 155–166.

National Aeronautics and Space Council. "Draft Statement of U.S. Policy on Outer Space." NSC 5918/1. December 17, 1959. http://marshall.wpengine.com/wp-content/uploads/2013/09/NSC-5918-1-U.S.-Policy-on-Outer-Space-26-Jan-1960.pdf.

National Security Council Planning Board. "Preliminary U.S. Policy on Outer Space." NSC 5814/1. June 20, 1958. http://marshall.wpengine.com/wp-content/uploads/2013/09/NSC-5814-Preliminary-U.S.-Policy-on-Outer-Space-18-Aug-1958.pdf.

Nelson, Alondra, ed. "Afrofuturism." Special issue. *Social Text* 20, no. 2 (2002).

Nielson, Aldon Lynn. *Black Chant: Languages of African-American Postmodernism.* Cambridge: Cambridge University Press, 1997.

Nietzsche, Friedrich. *The Birth of Tragedy.* Translated by Douglas Smith. Oxford: Oxford University Press, 2008.

Office of the Comptroller General. *Decisions of the Comptroller General of the United States.* Vol. 24, July 1, 1944, to June 30, 1945. Washington, DC: GPO, 1946.

O'Keeffe, Tadhg. "Street Ballets in Magic Cities: Cultural Imaginings of the Modern American Metropolis." *Popular Music History* 4, no. 2 (2009): 111–125.

"Original 'L' Companies." Chicago-l.org. http://www.chicago-l.org/history/4line.html.

Pacyga, Dominic A. *Chicago: A Biography.* Chicago: University of Chicago Press, 2009.

Parker, George Wells. *The Children of the Sun.* 1918. Reprint, Baltimore, MD: Black Classics, 1981.

Pinch, Trevor, and Frank Tracco. *Analog Days: The Invention and Impact of the Moog Synthesizer.* Cambridge, MA: Harvard University Press, 2004.

Prelinger, Megan. *Another Science Fiction: Advertising the Space Race 1957–1962.* New York: Blast Books, 2010.

President's Science Advisory Committee. *Introduction to Outer Space.* Washington, DC: GPO, 1958. www.fas.org/spp/guide/usa/intro1958.html.

Primack, Bret. "Captain Angelic: Sun Ra." *Down Beat,* May 4, 1978, 14–16, 40–41.

Ragain, Nathan. "A 'Reconcepted Am': Language, Nature, and Collectivity in Sun Ra and Henry Dumas." *Criticism* 54, no. 4 (2012): 539–565.

Ray, Deborah, producer. "Sun Ra." *American Black Journal.* Television broadcast. Detroit Public Television, 1981. http://abj.matrix.msu.edu/videofull.php?id=29-DF-13.

Rediker, Marcus. *The Slave Ship: A Human History.* New York: Viking, 2007.

Reed, Bruce Cameron. *The History and Science of the Manhattan Project.* New York: Springer, 2013.

Reich, Howard. "Sun Ra Dazzles New Fans with His Arkestra." *Chicago Tribune,* October 1, 1990. http://articles.chicagotribune.com/1990-10-01/news/900 3210842_1_arkestra-sun-ra-marshall-allen.

Rollefson, T. Griffith. "The 'Robot Voodoo Power Thesis': Afrofuturism and Anti-Anti-Essentialism from Sun Ra to Kool Keith." *Black Music Research Journal* 28, no. 1 (2008): 197–215.

Ryan, Cornelius, ed. "Man Will Conquer Space Soon: What Are We Waiting For?" *Collier's*, March 22, 1952.

Rycenga, Jennifer. "Interview with Sun Ra." Transcribed and edited by Dan Plonsey. [1988]. http://www.plonsey.com/beanbenders/SUNRA-interview .html.

———. Interview with Sun Ra, November 2, 1988, part one. *Sun Ra Research* 2 (July 1995): 1–7.

———. Interview with Sun Ra, November 2, 1988, part five. *Sun Ra Research* 26 (December 1999): 1–15.

Saturday Night Live. Hosted by Buck Henry. Television broadcast. May 20, 1978. http://blog.wfmu.org/freeform/2005/11/sun_ra_vs_satur.html.

Schmitt, Carl. *Political Theology: Four Chapters on the Concept of Sovereignty*. Translated by George Schwab. Cambridge, MA: MIT Press, 1985.

Schott, M. "The Album Cover Art Gallery." Tralfaz Archives. http://tralfaz-archives.com/coverart/F/Ferrante/ferrante_soundproof.html.

"Sci-Fi Television in the 1950s." IMDb.com. http://www.imdb.com/list/ls0000 97346/.

Shapiro, Peter. "Blues and the Abstract Truth." philcohran.com. http://www .philcohran.com/pc_wr_fr.htm.

Shattuck, Gardiner H. "Wallace Fard." American National Biography Online. http://www.anb.org/articles/08/08-00457.html.

Shelley, Percy Bysshe. *Shelley's Poetry and Prose*. Edited by Donald H. Reiman and Sharon B. Powers. New York: Norton, 1977.

Shukaitis, Stevphen. "Space Is the (Non)Place: Martians, Marxists, and the Outer Space of the Radical Imagination." *Sociological Review* 57, no. 1 (2009): 98–113.

Sinclair, John. "Self-Determination Music." *Jazz and Pop*, August 1970, 48–50.

———, ed. *Sun Ra: Interviews and Essays*. London: Headpress, 2009.

Sisson, Patrick. "Flying Lotus." *Pitchfork*. http://pitchfork.com/features/inter views/7793-flying-lotus/.

Sites, William. "Radical Culture in Black Necropolis: Sun Ra, Alton Abraham, and Postwar Chicago." *Journal of Urban History* 38, no. 4 (2012): 687–719.

———. "'We Travel the Spaceways': Urban Utopianism and the Imagined Spaces of Black Experimental Music." *Urban Geography* 33, no. 4 (2012): 566–592.

Smith, Grafton Elliot. *The Ancient Egyptians and the Origins of Civilization*. Rev. ed. 1923. Reprint, Freeport, NY: Books for Libraries, 1971.

Space Is the Place: Sun Ra and His Intergalactic Solar Arkestra. Film. Directed by John Coney. North American Star Systems, 1974; rerelease, Plexifilms, 2003, DVD.

Space Is the Place (Limited Edition). Multiple formats. Harte Recordings, 2015, DVD, CD, and text.

Spaceways. Film. Directed by Terence Fisher. Hammer Film Productions, 1953; rerelease, Image Entertainment, 2012, DVD.

Sun Ra. "The Black Man and the Cosmos." Lecture 3. Berkeley Department of Afro-American Studies, 1971. http://www.openculture.com/2014/07/full-lecture-and-reading-list-from-sun-ras-1971-uc-berkeley-course.html. Also available on *Sun Ra: The Creator of the Universe*. Transparency 0301, n.d, CD.

————. "Happy Space Age To You." *Esquire: The Magazine for Men*, July 1969, 46.

————. *The Immeasurable Equation: The Collected Poetry and Prose*. Compiled and edited by James Wolf and Hartmut Geerken. Norderstedt, Germany: Waitawhile, 2005.

————. *Prophetika*. Edited by Miriam Linna. New York: Kicks Books, 2014.

————. "Sun Ra Interview (Helsinki 1971)." Video. http://nuvoid.blogspot.com/2012/04/sun-ra-sunday_22.html.

————. *This Planet Is Doomed: The Science Fiction Poetry of Sun Ra*. Edited by Miriam Linna. New York: Kicks Books, 2011.

"Sun Ra." Wikipedia. https://en.wikipedia.org/wiki/Sun_Ra.

"Sun Ra Changed My Life: 13 Artists Reflect on the Influence and Legacy of Sun Ra." *The Vinyl Factory*. http://www.thevinylfactory.com/vinyl-factory-releases/sun-ra-changed-my-life-13-artists-reflect-on-the-legacy-and-influence-of-sun-ra/.

Swenson, John. "Images of Tomorrow Disguised as Jazz." *Rolling Stone*, March 4, 1993, 63.

Swiboda, Marcel. "Re Interpretations: Sun Ra's Egyptian Inscriptions." *Parallax* 13, no. 2 (2007): 93–106.

Szwed, John F. *Space Is the Place: The Lives and Times of Sun Ra*. New York: Da Capo, 1998.

Tchiemessom, Aurelien. *Sun Ra: Un noir dans le cosmos*. Paris: Harmattan, 2004.

Theis, Rick. "Fallen Angel." Interview with Sun Ra. *Semiotext(e)* 12 (1984). http://semiotexte.com/?p=680.

————. "Sun Ra." *Option*, September–October 1983, 48–51.

Thomas, Lorenzo. "Ascension: Music and the Black Arts Movement." In *Jazz among the Discourses*, ed. Krin Gabbard, 256–273. Durham, NC: Duke University Press, 1995.

————. "'Classical Jazz' and the Black Arts Movement." *African American Review* 29, no. 2 (1995): 237–240.

————. "The Mathemagic of Sun Ra." *Ann Arbor Sun*, April 5–19, 1974, 16–17.

Travis, Dempsey J. "Bronzeville." In *Encyclopedia of Chicago*, edited by Janice L. Reiff, Ann Durkin Keating, and James R. Grossman. Chicago: Chicago Historical Society, 2005. http://www.encyclopedia.chicagohistory.org/pages/171.html.

"United States Federal, State, and Local Government Spending Fiscal Year 1957." usgovernmentspending.com. http://www.usgovernmentspending.com/year_spending_1957USbf_15bs2n#usgs302.

Van der Bliek, Rob, ed. *The Thelonious Monk Reader*. Oxford: Oxford University Press, 2001.

"Visual Music Systems, Inc." visualmusicsystems.com. http://www.visualmusicsystems.com/ovc.htm.

Volney, Constantin-François. *The Ruins; or, Meditations on the Revolutions of Empires; and the Law of Nature*. Baltimore, MD: Black Classics, 1991.

Wald, Gayle. "Soul Vibrations: Black Music and Black Freedom in Sound and Space." *American Quarterly* 63, no. 3 (2011): 673–696.

Warren, Bill. *Keep Watching the Skies! American Science Fiction Movies of the Fifties, the 21st Century Edition*. Jefferson, NC: McFarland, 2010.

Wasserman, John L. "Sun Ra—A Man for the Space Age." *Sun Ra Research* 2 (July 1995): 9–10.

Weheliye, Alexander. *Phonographies: Grooves in Sonic Afro-Modernity*. Durham, NC: Duke University Press, 2005.

White Panther News Service. "For Immediate Release." *Sun Ra Research* 5 (February 1996): 12.

Whitman, Edward W. *The Book of Saturn*. London: Whitman Publishing, n.d.

Wilkinson, Sir Gardner. *The Manners and Customs of the Ancient Egyptians*. 3rd ed. 5 vol. London: John Murray, 1847.

Womack, Ytasha L. *Afrofuturism: The World of Black Sci-Fi and Fantasy Culture*. Chicago: Chicago Review Press, 2013.

Wright, Richard. *Native Son*. 1940. Reprint, New York: Harper Perennial, 1992.

Young, S. Mark, Steve Duin, and Mike Richardson. *Blast Off! Rockets, Robots, Ray Guns, and Rarities from the Golden Age of Space Toys*. New York: Dark Horse Comics, 2001.

DISCOGRAPHY

Ackamoor, Idris. *The Music of Idris Ackamoor, 1971 2004*. Two discs. EM Records EM1062DCD, 2006, CD.

Africa Hitech [Mark Pritchard and Steve Spacek]. *93 Million Miles*. Warp Records WARPCD 199, 2011, CD.

Amayo's Fu-Arkist-Ra. *Afrobeat Disciples (1st Kung Fu Lesson of Life)*. Amena-won, 2001, CD.

Anderson, Michael. *Sun Ra: The Eternal Myth Revealed, Vol. 1*. Fourteen discs. Transparency 0316, 2011, CD.

Art Ensemble of Chicago. *Les Stances à Sophie*. Soul Jazz Records, CD191, 2008, CD. Original release, Pathé 2C 062-11365, 1970, LP.

———. *People in Sorrow*. Odeon CJ32-5013, 1988, CD. Original release, Nessa Records N-3, 1969, LP.

The Avalanches, *Electricity*. XL Recordings 7243 5461680 4, 2001, CD. Original release, Modular Recordings MODVL002, 1999, LP single.

Ayler, Albert. *Spiritual Unity*. ESP Disk' 1002, 2005, CD. Original release, ESP Disk' 1002, 1965, LP.

Bambaataa, Afrika, and the SoulSonic Force. *Planet Rock*. Tommy Boy TB 823, 1982, LP single.

Banks, Azaelia. *Fantasea*. Self-release, 2012, MP3.

Baraka, Amiri [LeRoi Jones], and Sun Ra and the Myth-Science Arkestra. *A Black Mass*. Son Boy Records 1, 1999, CD. Original release, Jihad Productions 1968, 1968, LP.

Bass, Sid. *From Another World*. RCA 74321781712, 2000, CD. Original release, Vik LX-1053, 1956, LP.

Baxter, Les. *African Jazz*. Blue Moon BMCD 860, 2015, CD. Original release, Capitol T-1117, 1959, LP.

———. *Caribbean Moonlight*. Capitol T-733, 1956, LP.

———. *The Passions*. Oriental Pacific OP-1920-2, 1995, CD. Original release, Capitol LAL-486, 1954, ten-inch LP.

———. *Ports of Pleasure*. Capitol T-868, 1957, LP.

———. *Ritual of the Savage (Le Sacre du Sauvage)*. Rev-Ola CR REV 171, 2006, CD. Original release, Capitol T-228, 1951, ten-inch LP.

———. *Space Escapade*. El Records ACMEM 171CD, 2009, CD. Original release, Capitol T-968, 1958, LP.

———. *Tamboo!* Universe UV 161, 2006, CD. Original release, Capitol T-655, 1955, LP.

Carter, Betty. *Out There with Betty Carter*. Blue Moon BMCD 1622, 2005, CD. Original release, Peacock PLP 90, 1958, LP.

Chicago Underground. *Boca Negra*. Thrill Jockey THRILL 228, 2010, CD.

———. *Locus*. Northern Spy NSCD 052, 2014, CD.

Clinton, George, and Parliament. *Chocolate City*. Casablanca 836 700-2, 1990, CD. Original release, Casablanca NBLP 7014, 1975, LP.

———. *The Clones of Dr. Funkenstein*. Casablanca 842 620-2, 1990, CD. Original release, Casablanca NBLP 7034, 1976, LP.

———. *Funkentelechy vs. The Placebo Syndrome*. Casablanca 824 501-2, 1990, CD. Original release, Casablanca NBLP 7084, 1977, LP.

———. *The Mothership Connection*. Casablanca 824 502-2, 1990, CD. Original release, Casablanca NBLP 7022, 1975, LP.

Cohen, Charles. *Music for Dance and Theater*. Two discs. Morphine 021LP, 2013, LP.

Cohran, Phil, and the Artistic Heritage Ensemble. *On the Beach*. Zulu Records 0004, 1968, LP.

———. *Malcolm X Memorial*. Zulu Records MR-016, 1968, LP.

Coleman, Ornette. *Free Jazz: A Collective Improvisation*. Rhino R275208, 1998, CD. Original release, Atlantic SD 1364, 1961, LP.

———. *The Shape of Jazz to Come*. Atlantic 1317-2, 1990, CD. Original release, Atlantic SD 1317, 1959, LP.

Coltrane, John. *Ascension*. Impulse! B0012401-02, 2009, CD. Original release, Impulse! AS-95, 1965, LP.

———. *Giant Steps*. Atlantic 1311-2, 1987, CD. Original release, Atlantic 1311, 1959, LP.

———. *Interstellar Space*. Impulse! 314 543 415-2, 2000, CD. Original release, Impulse! ASD 9277, 1974, LP.

———. *Sun Ship*. Impulse! AS 9211, 1995, CD. Original release, Impulse! AS-9211, 1971, LP.

Comstock, Frank. *Project Comstock: Music from Outer Space*. Warner Brothers, WS 1463, 1962, LP.

Dan and Dale (as "The Sensational Guitars of Dan & Dale"). *Batman and Robin*. Universe UV 016, 2001, CD. Original release, Tifton S-78002, 1966, LP.

Davis, Miles. *Kind of Blue*. Columbia CK 40579, 1986, CD. Original release, Columbia CS 8136, 1959, LP.

Deltron 3030 [Dan the Automator, Del the Funky Homosapien, and Kid Koala]. *Deltron 3030*. 75 Ark 75033, 2000, CD.

Denny, Martin. *Exotica*. Rev-Ola CR REV 101, 2005, CD. Original release, Liberty LRP 3034, 1957, LP.

———. *Primitiva*. Rev-Ola CR REV 103, 2005, CD. Original release, Liberty LRP 3087, 1958, LP.

The Dining Rooms. *Tre*. Schema SCCD 355, 2003, CD.

DJ Spooky [Paul D. Miller]. *Celestial Mechanix*. Two discs. Thirsty Ear THI57148.1, 2004, CD.

Donaldson, Lou. *The Natural Soul*. Blue Note CDP 7 84108 2, 1989, CD. Original release, Blue Note BLP 4108, 1962, LP.

Ellington, Duke. Duke Ellington's Spacemen. *The Cosmic Scene*. Mosaic MCD-1001, 2007, CD. Original release, Columbia CL1198, 1958, LP.

Esquivel and His Orchestra. *Exploring New Sounds in Hi-Fi Stereo*. RCA Victor 74321 47871 2, 1997, CD. Original release, RCA Victor, LPM-1978, 1959, LP.

———. *Other Worlds Other Sounds*. RCA Victor 74321 35747 2, 1996, CD. Original release, RCA Victor LSP 1753, 1958, LP.

Exploding Star Orchestra. *Stars Have Shapes*. Delmark DMK 595, 2010, CD.

———. *We Are All from Somewhere Else*. Thrill Jockey THRILL 181, 2007, CD.

Ferrante, Arthur, and Louis Teicher. *Soundproof: The Sound of Tomorrow Today!* El Records ACMEM 124CD, 2012, CD. Original release, Westminster WP 6014, 1959, LP.

Flying Lotus [Steven Ellison]. *Cosmogramma*. Warp Records WARPCD 195, 2010, CD.

Freedom Satellite. "Astro Black (The Big Wow Mix)." *Vienna Scientists V: The 10th Anniversary*. Vienna Scientists Recordings VIE0 020 CD, 2009, CD.

Freeman, Von. *The Improvisor*. Premonition Records, 90757, 2002, CD.

Galliano, Frédéric. *Nangadef Maafric*. What's Up Records 9608, 1996, LP.

Garcia, Russ. *Fantastica*. Liberty 7005, 1958, LP.

Green, Grant. *Born to Be Blue*. Blue Note CPD 7 84432 2, 1989, CD. Original release, Blue Note BST 84432, 1985 (recorded 1962), LP.

Hieroglyphic Being [Jamal Moss]. *ANKH*. Music From Mathematics MFM CD-010, 2010, CD.

———. *Cosmo Rhythmatic*. Music From Mathematics MFM CD-018, 2011, CD.

———. *Seer of Cosmic Visions*. Two discs. Planet Mu ZIQ 349, 2014, LP.

———. *Strange Strings*. Music From Mathematics MFM CD-016, 2011, CD.

———. *The Sun Man Speaks*. Music From Mathematics MFM CD-009, 2010, CD.

———. *A Synthetic Lovelife*. Two discs. +++-+++ 10, 2013, LP.

Huckaby, Mike. *Sun Ra: The Mike Huckaby Reel-to-Reel Edits, Volume 1*. Kindred Spirits/Art Yard KSAY-MH01, 2011, twelve-inch LP.

———. *Sun Ra: The Mike Huckaby Reel-to-Reel Edits, Volume 2*. Kindred Spirits/Art Yard KSAY MH02, 2011, twelve-inch LP.

Kool Keith [Keith Thornton]. *Dr. Octagonecologyst*. Bulk Recordings CD902, 1996, CD.

Lady Gaga. "Venus." *Artpop*. Streamline/Interscope, 2013, CD.

Lazar, Sam. *Space Flight*. Universal Victor MVCJ-19120, 1998, CD. Original release, Argo LP-4002, 1960, LP.

Madvillain [Daniel Dumile and Otis Jackson Jr.]. *Madvillainy*. Stones Throw Records STH2065, 2004, CD.

Manning, Marty. *The Twilight Zone*. Columbia CL 1586, 1961, LP.

Marino, Richard. *Out of this World*. Liberty LMM 13007, 1961, LP.

MC5. *Kick Out the Jams*. Elektra 9 6894-2, 1991, CD. Original release, Elektra EKS 74042, 1969, LP.

Miller, Paul D. *Viral Sonata*. Asphodel ASP0976, 1997, CD.

Mineo, Attilio. *Man in Space with Sounds*. Subliminal Sounds SUBCD 4, 2011, CD. Original release, World's Fair Records LP-55555, 1962, LP.

Mitchell, Roscoe. *Roscoe Mitchell Sextet: Sound*. Delmark DE-408, 1996, CD. Original release, Delmark DL-408, 1966, LP.

Monáe, Janelle. *ArchAndroid*. Two discs. Badboy Entertainment 512256-1, 2010, LP.

———. *The Electric Lady*. Badboy Entertainment 536102-2, 2013, CD.

Mono/Poly [Charles E. Dickerson]. *Golden Skies*. Brainfeeder BFCD 046, 2014, CD.

Need New Body. *Need New Body*. File 13 Records FT41, CD.

Osunlade. *A Man with No Past Originating the Future*. Two discs. Yoruba Records YSD48, 2013, LP.

The Pyramids. *Birth/Speed/Merging*. Pyramid Records 30935, 1976, LP.

———. *King of Kings*. Pyramid Records 3093-4, 1974, LP.

———. *Lalibela*. Pyramid Records 3093, 1973, LP.

———. *Otherworldly*. Cultural Odyssey CO-183-5, 2011, CD.

Ras G [Gregory Shorter Jr.]. *Back on the Planet*. Two discs. Brainfeeder BF039, 2013, LP.

———. "Cosmic Tones 4 Mental Therapy!!!!!!" *Soundcloud*. https://soundcloud.com/ras_g/cosmic-tones-4-mental-therapy.

Revel, Harry, Leslie Baxter, and Dr. Samuel J. Hoffman. *Music Out of the Moon: Music Unusual Featuring the Theremin*. Request Records RR 231-1, 1995, CD. Original release, Capitol H2000, 1950, LP.

Reuell, Harry, and the Stuart Phillips Orchestra. Music from Out of Space. MGM E3287, LP.

Ribot, Marc (Marc Ribot's Ceramic Dog). *Party Intellectuals*. PI Recordings PI 27, 2008, CD.

———. (Marc Ribot's Ceramic Dog). *Your Turn*. Northern Spy NSCD 038, 2013, CD.

———. (The Marc Ribot Trio). *Live at the Village Vanguard*. PI Recordings PI 153, 2014, CD.

———. (Marc Ribot y Los Cubanos Postizos). *The Prosthetic Cubans*. Atlantic 83116-2, 1998, CD.

———. (Marc Ribot and Spiritual Unity). *Spiritual Unity*. PI Recordings PI 15, 2005, CD.

Roberts, Matana. *Coin Coin Chapter One: Gens de Couleur Libres*. Two discs. Constellation CST079-1, 2011, LP.

RocketNumberNine [Ben Page and Tom Page]. *MeYouWeYou*. Smalltown Supersound STS241LP, 2013, LP.

———. *You Reflect Me*. Trace DIG003, 2009, MP3.

Rugolo, Pete. *Music from Out of Space*. Mercury SR 60118, 1959, LP.

Russell, George. *Jazz in the Space Age*. American Jazz Classics 99024, 2011, CD. Original release, Decca DL 9219, 1960, LP.

Shepp, Archie. *Four for Trane*. Impulse! IMPD 218, 1997, CD. Original release, Impulse! A-71, 1964, LP.

Shibusashirazu Orchestra. *Lost Direction*. Moers Music 03016CD, 2005, CD.

———. *Paris Shibu Bokyoku: Live at Maison de la Culture du Japon à Paris*. Two discs. Chitei Records BF41/42F, 2008, CD.

Spaceboys. *Sonic Fiction*. Nylon Discographics NYLONCD007, 2003, CD.

Sun Araw (Cameron Stallones). *Beach Head*. Not for Fun Records NFF 140, 2008, LP.

———. *Sun Araw and M. Geddes Gengras Meet the Congos: Icon Give Thanks*. FRK-WYS, vol. 9. RVNG Intnl. FRKWYS09, 2012, CD/DVD.

Sun Ra. *Angels and Demons at Play*. Evidence 22066, 1993, CD. Original release, Saturn SR 9956-2-O/P, 1965, LP.

———. *The Antique Blacks*. Art Yard, ARTYARD CD 010, 2009, CD. Original release, Saturn 81774, 1974, LP.

———. *Art Forms of Dimensions Tomorrow*. Evidence 22036, 1992, CD. Original release, Saturn 9956, 1965, LP.

———. *Astro Black*. Impulse! AS-9255, 1973, quadraphonic LP.

———. *Atlantis*. Evidence 22067, 1993, CD. Original release, Saturn ESR 507, 1969, LP.

———. *Bad and Beautiful*. Evidence 22038, 1992, CD. Original release, Saturn 532, 1972, LP.

———. *Blue Delight*. A&M CD 5260, 1989, CD; SP 5630, 1989, LP.

———. *Concert for the Comet Kohoutek*. ESP Disk' 3033, 1993, CD.

———. *Continuation*. Corbett vs. Dempsey CvsD CD009, 2013, CD. Original release, Saturn 520, 1970, LP.

———. *Cosmic Tones for Mental Therapy*. Evidence 22036, 1992, CD. Original release, Saturn 408, 1967, LP.

———. *The Creator of the Universe*. Two discs. Transparency 0301, n.d., CD.

———. *Crystal Spears*. Evidence 22217-2, 2000, CD. Original release, Impulse! AS-9297, unissued, LP.

———. *Cymbals*. Evidence 22217-2, 2000, CD. Original release, Impulse! AS-9296, unissued, LP.

———. *Discipline 27-II*. Saturn 538, 1973, quadraphonic LP.

———. *Disco 3000*. Art Yard ARTYARD CD 101, 2009, CD. Original release, Saturn CMIJ 78, 1978, LP.

———. *Fate in a Pleasant Mood*. Evidence 22068, 1993, CD. Original release, Saturn 9956-2-A/B, 1965, LP.

———. *The Futuristic Sounds of Sun Ra*. Savoy Jazz SVY 17259, 2003, CD. Original release, Savoy MG12169, 1961, LP.

———. *The Great Lost Sun Ra Albums: Cymbals and Crystal Spears*. Two discs. Evidence ECD 22217-2, 2000, CD.

———. *Heliocentric Worlds of Sun Ra, Volume 1*. ESP-Disk' 1014-2, 1992, CD. Original release, ESP-Disk' 1014, 1965, LP.

———. *Heliocentric Worlds of Sun Ra, Volume 2*. ESP Disk' 1017-2, 1993, CD. Original release, ESP-Disk' 1017, 1966, LP.

————. *Holiday for Soul Dance*. Evidence 22011, 1992. Original release, Saturn ESR 508, 1970, LP.

————. *Interplanetary Melodies: Sun Ra and His Arkestra*. Norton CED 352, 2009, CD; ED-352, 2009, LP.

————. *Interstellar Low Ways*. Evidence 22039, 1993, CD. Original release (titled *Rocket Number Nine Take Off for the Planet Venus*), Saturn SR 9945-2-M/N, 1966, LP.

————. *The Invisible Shield*. Black Lion CD 877640-2 (titled *Janus*), 2000, CD. Original release, Saturn 529, 1974, LP.

————. *Jazz by Sun Ra, Vol. 1*. Transition TRLP J-10, 1957, LP.

————. *Jazz in Silhouette*. Evidence 22012-2, 1991, CD. Original release, Saturn K70P3590/K70P3591, 1959, LP.

————. *Lanquidity*. Evidence 22220-2, 2000, CD. Original release, Philly Jazz PJ 666, 1978, LP.

————. *Live in Paris at the "Gibus."* Universe UV 079, 2003, CD. Original release, Atlantic 40540, 1975, LP.

————. *The Magic City*. Evidence 22069, 1993, CD. Original release, Saturn LPB 711, 1966, LP.

————. *Media Dream*. Art Yard ARTYARD CD 002, 2008, CD. Original release, Saturn 1978, 1978, LP.

————. *Music from Tomorrow's World: Sun Ra and His Arkestra, Chicago 1960*. Atavistic ALP 237, 2002, CD.

————. *My Brother the Wind*. Saturn 521, 1970, LP.

————. *My Brother the Wind, Volume II*. Evidence 22040, 1992, CD. Original release, Saturn 523, 1971, LP.

————. *My Way is the Spaceways: Sun Ra and His Arkestra*. Norton CED-391, 2014, CD; ED-391, 2014, LP.

————. *New Steps*. Atomic Records 76812, 2009, CD. Original release, two discs, Horo HPD 25-26, 1978, LP.

————. *Nothing Is*. Two discs. ESP-Disk' 4060, 2010, CD. Original release, ESP-Disk' 1045, 1969, LP.

————. *Nubians of Plutonia*. Evidence 22066, 1993, CD. Original release (titled *Lady with the Golden Stockings*), Saturn SR 9956-11E/F, 1966, LP.

————. *Nuclear War*. Atavistic USM/ALP222CD, 2001, CD. Original release, Y Records RA 2, 1984, LP.

————. *On Jupiter*. Art Yard, ARTYARD CD 204, 2005, CD. Original release, Saturn 101679, 1979, LP.

————. *The Outer Darkness: Sun Ra and His Arkestra*. Norton CED 367, 2010, CD; ED 367, 2010, LP.

———. *Outer Spaceways Incorporated*. Three discs (titled *Spaceways*). Freedom CD 740147, 1998, CD. Original release, 1974, Saturn 143000A/B, 1974, LP.

———. *Out There a Minute*. Blast First BFFP 42, 1989, CD.

———. *Pathways to Unknown Worlds*. Evidence 22218, 2000, CD. Original release, Impulse! ASD-9298, 1975, LP.

———. *Purple Night*. A&M 75021 5324 2, 1990, CD.

———. *Rocket Ship Rock: Sun Ra and His Arkestra*. Norton CED 354, 2009, CD; ED-354, 2009, LP.

———. *The Second Stop is Jupiter: Sun Ra and His Arkestra*. Norton CED 353, 2009, CD; ED-353, 2009, LP.

———. *Secrets of the Sun*. Atavistic ALP266CD, 2008, CD. Original release, Saturn GH 9954 E/F, 1965, LP.

———. *The Singles*. Two discs. Evidence 22164-2, 1996, CD.

———. *The Solar Myth Approach, Volume I*. Affinity AFF 760, 1991, CD. Original release, BYG Actuel 529.320, 1972, LP.

———. *The Solar Myth Approach, Volume II*. Affinity AFF 760, 1991, CD. Original release, BYG Actuel 529.321, 1972, LP.

———. *The Soul Vibrations of Man*. Saturn 771, 1977, LP.

———. *Sound of Joy: Sun Ra and the Arkestra*. Delmark DD-414, 2012, CD. Original release, Delmark DS-414, 1968, LP.

———. *Sound Sun Pleasure!!* Evidence 22014, 1992, CD. Original release, Saturn 512, 1970, LP.

———. *Space is the Place*. Impulse! IMPD 249, 1998, CD. Original release, Blue Thumb BTS 41, 1973, LP.

———. *Spaceship Lullaby (1954–1960)*. Atavistic UMS/ALP243, 2003, CD.

———. *St. Louis Blues: Solo Piano*. Improvising Artists Inc. IAI 123858-2, 1992, CD. Original release, Improvising Artists Inc. IAI 37.38.58, 1978, LP.

———. *Strange Celestial Road*. Rounder 3035, 1988, CD. Original release, Rounder 3035, 1980, LP.

———. *Strange Strings*. Atavistic ALP263CD, 2007, CD. Original release, Thoth Intergalactic KH-5472, 1967, LP.

———. *Strange Worlds in My Mind: Sun Ra and His Arkestra*. Norton CED 365, 2010, CD; ED-365, 2010, LP.

———. *The Sub-Dwellers: Sun Ra and His Arkestra*. Norton CED 366, 2010, CD; ED-366, 2010, LP.

———. *Sun Ra Featuring Pharoah Sanders and Black Harold*. ESP Disk' 4054, 2009, CD. Original release, ESP-Disk' 4054, 1974, LP.

———. *Sun Ra Visits Planet Earth*. Evidence 22039, 1992, CD. Original release, Saturn 9956-11-A/B, 1966, LP.

————. *Sun Song*. Delmark DD-411, 1990, CD. Original release, 1967, Delmark DL-411, 1967, LP.

————. *Super-Sonic Jazz*. Evidence 22015, 1991, CD. Original release, Saturn H7OPo216, 1957, LP.

————. *Unity*. Two discs. Horo HDP 19-20, 1978, LP.

————. *We Travel the Space Ways*. Evidence 22038, 1992, CD. Original release, Saturn HK 5445, 1966, LP.

————. *When Angels Speak of Love*. Evidence 22216-2, 2000, CD. Original release, Saturn 1966, 1966, LP.

————. *When Sun Comes Out*. Evidence 22068, 1993, CD. Original release, Saturn 2066, 1963, LP.

————. (The Sun Ra Arkestra). *Hours After*. Black Saint 120 111-2, 1989, CD; Black Saint 120 111-1, 1989, LP.

————. (The Sun Ra Arkestra). *Live at Praxis, 1984*. Golden Years of New Jazz GY5/6, 2000, CD. Also released as two discs, Vinyl Lovers 901110, 2010, LP. Original release, three discs: 1, Praxis CM 108, 1984, LP; 2, Praxis CM 109, 1985, LP; 3, Praxis CM 110, 1986, LP.

————. (The Sun Ra Arkestra). *Live from Soundscape*. Two discs. DIW 388, 1994, CD.

————. (The Sun Ra Arkestra) *Reflections in Blue*. Black Saint BSR 0101 CD, 1987, CD; Black Saint BSR 0101, 1987, LP.

————. (The Sun Ra Arkestra). *Sunrise in Different Dimensions*. hatOLOGY 698, 2011, CD. Original release, two discs, Hat Hut Records 2R17, 1981, LP.

Sun Rise Above (Sun R.A.). *Every Day I Wake Up on the Wrong Side of Capitalism*. Self-release, 2001, CD.

The Thing and Neneh Cherry. *The Cherry Thing*. Smalltown Supersound STS229, 2012, CD.

Tiger Hatchery. *Sun Worship*. ESP Disk' ESP 5003, 2013, CD.

Tortoise. *TNT*. Thrill Jockey THRILL 050, 1998, CD.

Ultramagnetic MCs. *Critical Beatdown*. Next Plateau Records PLCD 1013, 1988, CD.

The Vandermark 5. *Annular Gift*. Not Two Records MW 825-2, 2009, CD.

————. *Single Piece Flow*. Atavistic ALP47CD, 1997, CD.

Vandermark, Ken. *Free Jazz Classics Vols. 1 & 2*. Two discs. Atavistic ALP137CD, 2001, CD.

———— (Spaceways Incorporated). *Spaceways Incorporated: Thirteen Cosmic Standards by Sun Ra & Funkadelic*. Atavistic ALP120CD, 2000, CD.

Yo La Tengo. *Nuclear War*. Matador, OLE 568-2, 2002, CD.

Zombie Zombie. *Rocket Number 9 EP*. Versatile VER079, 2012, LP.

CREDITS

AND PERMISSIONS

TEXT

Sun Ra Quotations Throughout

The author is grateful to the Sun Ra Estate LLC and Irwin Chusid for extending nonexclusive permission to quote from the many works Sun Ra created during his lifetime. All works are copyright © Enterplanetary Koncepts/Sun Ra LLC.

Epigraph

Quotation from Amiri Baraka on Sun Ra, permission by Chris Calhoun Agency, © Amiri Baraka.

Chapter 3: Bronzeville

Gwendolyn Brooks, "kitchenette building," in *Selected Poems* (New York: Harper and Row, 1963), 3. Reprinted by consent of Brooks Permissions.

Chapter 8: Immeasurable Equation

Sun Ra, "The Neglected Plane of Wisdom," in *The Immeasurable Equation*, 250–251. Courtesy of Hartmut Geerken, Waitawhile.

Chapter 17: Myth-Science

Sun Ra, "Astro Black," in *The Immeasurable Equation*, 74. The poem is sung on Sun Ra, *Astro Black*, Impulse! AS-9255, 1973, quadraphonic LP. Courtesy of Hartmut Geerken, Waitawhile.

PHOTOS

The author is grateful to John Corbett and Terri Kapsalis for assistance with obtaining rights to reprint images held in the Alton Abraham Collection of Sun Ra, Special Collections Research Center, the University of Chicago Library.

Sonny Blount, early 1950s (above), and Sun Ra, late 1980s (below). Courtesy of the University of Chicago Library's Special Collections Research Center.

Sun Ra and the Arkestra performing in Chicago, late 1950s. Courtesy of the University of Chicago Library's Special Collections Research Center.

Claude Dangerfield, unused design for record jacket. Courtesy of the University of Chicago Library's Special Collections Research Center.

Thmei Research cover stock and Saturn Research letterhead. Courtesy of the University of Chicago Library's Special Collections Research Center.

Sun Ra broadsheet, mid-1950s. Courtesy of the University of Chicago Library's Special Collections Research Center.

Tickets to performances of Sun Ra and his Arkestra sponsored by the Atonites and the Campaign Committee for the Mayor of Bronzeville. Courtesy of the University of Chicago Library's Special Collections Research Center.

Promotional flyer for Sun Ra and his Arkestra. Courtesy of the University of Chicago Library's Special Collections Research Center.

Record jackets for *Super-Sonic Jazz* (the "void" cover) and *Jazz in Silhouette*. Courtesy of the University of Chicago Library's Special Collections Research Center.

Saturn Records catalog of singles and a "Handy Katalog," mid- to late-1960s. Courtesy of the University of Chicago Library's Special Collections Research Center.

The cover to Sun Ra, *The Immeasurable Equation*. Courtesy of the University of Chicago Library's Special Collections Research Center.

A page from a Sun Ra notebook, mid-1960s. Courtesy of the University of Chicago's Special Collections Research Center.

Sun Ra, mid-1960s. Courtesy of the University of Chicago's Special Collections Research Center.

Sun Ra and Arkestra (and friends) parading in New York, 1966. Courtesy of the University of Chicago's Special Collections Research Center.

Record jacket, *Interstellar Low Ways*, 1969; first released as *Rocket Number Nine Take Off for the Planet Venus*, 1966. Courtesy of the University of Chicago's Special Collections Research Center.

Promotional poster, Carnegie Hall performance, 1968. Courtesy of the University of Chicago's Special Collections Research Center.

Promotional poster for the film *Space Is the Place*. Design by Curtis Schreier, © North American Star System.

Members of the Sun Ra Arkestra, early 1970s. Courtesy of the University of Chicago's Special Collections Research Center.

Sun Ra in Birmingham, Alabama, at the first *City Stages* weekend, 1989. Courtesy of Rowland Scherman.

Program for a Sun Ra Health Benefit Concert. Courtesy of the University of Chicago's Special Collections Research Center.

INDEX